"By centering a disability justice framework and the various intersections of disability and sexuality, *Exploring Sexuality and Disability: A Guide for Human Service Professionals* challenges readers to reflect and unlearn existing biases and to expand their worldview to not only consider but prioritize the sexual rights of disabled communities. This comes at a pivotal time as the world still grapples with the realities of an ongoing pandemic yet continues to marginalize the needs and priorities of disabled people. This is an essential, practical resource that will serve as a catalyst for meaningful and necessary conversations for human service professionals and will undoubtedly lead to increased best practices in the field, as well as amplify the voices and demands of disabled people."
—**Jayleen Galarza Patterson**, *PhD, LCSW, CST, Associate Professor of Social Work and Gerontology, Shippensburg University*

"This book does a phenomenal job of providing a much-needed, intersectionally aware resource for professionals in the fields of sex and disability. It is also a necessary read for anyone working or training in the fields of health, wellness, communication, relationships, and more. The topics explored here are of vital importance to so many clients and patients, and the editor and authors have done an exceptional job of providing accessible, compassionate, and authentic perspectives."
—**Ruth Neustifter**, *PhD, RP, RMFT, Associate Professor, University of Guelph, ON, Canada*

"Discussing sexuality and disability with nuance, dissecting privilege, acknowledging neurodivergence, and not shying away from the fact that all people need to have access to sexuality education is refreshing. The abuse of disabled people has been living in the dark for far too long and this book not only brings to light the fact that it happens, but also gives ways to interrupt abusive cycles through concrete examples backed by research methodologies. I can't wait to use this text in my classroom and teachings."
—**Lexx Brown-James**, *PhD, LMFT, CSE, CSES, Founder @ The Institute, Swarthmore, PA*

"This book is an impressive and fresh knowledge-share on disability and sexuality, providing an invaluable personal and professional resource with its research, lived experience, and observations. It covers an inclusive breadth of topics discussing how social, physical, and mental processes intersect and impact the sexual expression of disabled people. With Disability Justice rooted in every article's framing, readers can experience a unique educational opportunity by exploring modern-day sexual issues and best practices in a well-researched and comprehensive text."
—**Robin Wilson-Beattie**, *Disability Sexual and Reproductive Health Educator*

# EXPLORING SEXUALITY AND DISABILITY

Offering a current, comprehensive, and intersectional guide for students, practitioners, and researchers, this book synthesizes existing scholarship on culturally responsive practices that assist in exploring, understanding, and affirming the sexuality(ies) of disabled, chronically ill, neurodivergent, and Mad individuals.

Drawing on an intersectional framework, it integrates insights drawn from an interdisciplinary body of scholarship including psychology, social work, sociology, history, political science, women and gender studies, cultural studies, and education along with perspectives from the practitioners who are actively defining the next generation of best practices.

By highlighting the incredible resilience and resistance of disabled individuals' and communities' sexuality and sexual well-being, this book challenges narratives that rely primarily on a one-dimensional view derived from the medical model and the view of disability as something to be "fixed" – or at least tolerated – rather than celebrated. In a world that pathologizes and devalues the sexual existence of disabled individuals, it illustrates how to create thriving communities and relationships, and how they can organize to find their voice, providing a counter-narrative of empowerment that fosters hopefulness, power, and health.

It will be of interest to all scholars, students, and professionals across a variety of professions, including social work, psychology, counseling, policy, healthcare, education, community organizing, and multiple social service settings.

**Shanna Katz Kattari**, PhD, MEd, CSE, is a certified sexuality educator, an associate professor at the University of Michigan School of Social Work and Department of Women's and Gender Studies, and the director of the [Sexuality | Relationships | Gender] Research Collective. Their work focuses on disability and ableism; sexuality and sexual health; and queer- and trans-affirming care. Find out more about their work at ShannaKattari.com.

# EXPLORING SEXUALITY AND DISABILITY

A Guide for Human Service Professionals

Edited by Shanna Katz Kattari

LONDON AND NEW YORK

Designed cover image: © Getty Images

First published 2024
by Routledge
4 Park Square, Milton Park, Abingdon, Oxon OX14 4RN

and by Routledge
605 Third Avenue, New York, NY 10158

*Routledge is an imprint of the Taylor & Francis Group, an informa business*

© 2024 selection and editorial matter, **Shanna Katz Kattari**; individual chapters, the contributors

The right of Shanna Katz Kattari to be identified as the author of the editorial material, and of the authors for their individual chapters, has been asserted in accordance with sections 77 and 78 of the Copyright, Designs and Patents Act 1988.

All rights reserved. No part of this book may be reprinted or reproduced or utilised in any form or by any electronic, mechanical, or other means, now known or hereafter invented, including photocopying and recording, or in any information storage or retrieval system, without permission in writing from the publishers.

*Trademark notice*: Product or corporate names may be trademarks or registered trademarks, and are used only for identification and explanation without intent to infringe.

*British Library Cataloguing-in-Publication Data*
A catalogue record for this book is available from the British Library

*Library of Congress Cataloging-in-Publication Data*
Names: Kattari, Shanna K., editor.
Title: Exploring sexuality and disability : a guide for human service professionals / edited by Shanna Katz Kattari.
Description: Abingdon, Oxon ; New York, NY : Routledge, 2024. | Includes bibliographical references and index.
Identifiers: LCCN 2023014251 (print) | LCCN 2023014252 (ebook) | ISBN 9781032311548 (hardback) | ISBN 9781032311517 (paperback) | ISBN 9781003308331 (ebook)
Subjects: LCSH: People with disabilities—Sexual behavior. | Sexual health. | People with disabilities—Services for.
Classification: LCC HQ30.5 .E97 2024  (print) | LCC HQ30.5 (ebook) | DDC 306.7087—dc23/eng/20230421
LC record available at https://lccn.loc.gov/2023014251
LC ebook record available at https://lccn.loc.gov/2023014252

ISBN: 978-1-032-31154-8 (hbk)
ISBN: 978-1-032-31151-7 (pbk)
ISBN: 978-1-003-30833-1 (ebk)

DOI: 10.4324/9781003308331

Typeset in Sabon
by Apex CoVantage, LLC

*To all of the hot, sexy, sultry, loving, fucking, and slutty crip, ill, Mad, and disabled folks whose authentic selves deserve to shine so brightly in this world.*

*To my loves, who unreservedly support me when I am a still day and also when I am a hurricane.*

*To Dominique Courts, whose commitment to mental health and social justice touched so many. Dominique's calm smile and soothing energy fills our heart, even though they are no longer earthside. Rest easy.*

*And to those of us who fight so hard to be seen, heard, and validated while living in a world that often tries to erase us.*

# CONTENTS

*List of Contributors*   *xiii*
*Acknowledgments*   *xix*

    Introduction   1
    *Shanna Katz Kattari*

**PART ONE**
**History and Community Work**   **11**

1  A (Very Brief) History of Disability and Sexuality Policy   13
    *Ari S. Gzesh, Shanna Katz Kattari, Nicolás Juárez, and Madelyne J. Mayer*

2  Able-Bodied Women Killing Disabled Babies: How Modern Narratives on Disability and Abortion Erase Disabled People From the Reproductive Justice Movement   28
    *Elena Gormley*

3  For Us, By Us: Mutual Aid Efforts in Disabled Queer and Trans Communities   47
    *Brendon T. Holloway, Jax Kynn, and Hannah Boyke*

## PART TWO
## Exploring the Specifics — 63

4 Infinity and Rainbows: Supporting the Sexuality of
Neurodivergent People — 65
*Shanna Katz Kattari, E. B. Gross, Kari L. Sherwood,
and C. Riley Hostetter*

5 Access Isn't Optional: Sexuality and Intellectual/
Developmental Disabilities — 81
*Shanna Katz Kattari and Kari L. Sherwood*

6 Sexuality, Hearing Loss, and d/Deaf Individuals — 96
*Kari L. Sherwood, Shanna Katz Kattari, and Alison Wetmur*

7 "Love Is Merely a Madness": Sexuality and Madness
in a Cisheteropatriarchal Culture — 108
*Laura Yakas*

8 Blindness and Sexuality — 124
*Robin Mandell and Hillary K. Hecht*

9 No Spoons for Spooning: Navigating Sexuality,
Chronic Illness, and Chronic Pain — 139
*Shanna Katz Kattari*

## PART THREE
## Diverse Types of Practice — 153

10 Disability-Affirming Sex Therapy — 155
*Erin Martinez and Emma Hertzel*

11 Exploring a Methodology of Care: Creating Research
With Disabled Queer Individuals and Community — 170
*Bri Noonan and Elisabeth Z. Lacey*

12 Ready, Willing, and Able: Sexuality Education for
Disabled Individuals — 187
*Autumn Dae Miller and Tiffini (Tiff) Lanza*

| | |
|---|---|
| 13 Disabled and/or Chronically Ill Survivors of Sexual Violence and Intimate Partner Violence<br>*L. B. Klein, Rose C. B. Singh, Jax Kynn, and Kiley J. McLean* | 201 |
| 14 Exploring the Intersections of Sex Work and Disability: What Helping Professionals Should Consider<br>*Kimberly Fuentes, Adrienne Graf, and Meg Panichelli* | 214 |
| 15 Resisting "Too Young": Anti-Adultism in Disability and Sexual Health Justice Advocacy<br>*syd lio riley* | 230 |

**PART FOUR**
**Across Intersecting Identities** — **247**

| | |
|---|---|
| 16 Racialization of Disability and Sexuality: A Historical and Contemporary Perspective Within the United States<br>*Natasha M. Lee-Johnson and Nahime G. Aguirre Mtanous* | 249 |
| 17 Navigating Disability and Sexuality in Old Age<br>*Jess Francis and Hillary K. Hecht* | 267 |
| 18 Trans Enough, Queer Enough, and Disabled Enough: Exploring Issues of Gatekeeping and Legitimacy of Trans, Queer, and Disabled Identities Through Sexuality<br>*Al Wauldron, Flyn Alexander, and Shanna Katz Kattari* | 283 |
| 19 We'll Make Our Own Space: Making LGBTQ+ Spaces Accessible<br>*Jax Kynn, Hannah Boyke, and Brendon T. Holloway* | 299 |
| 20 Sexual Well-Being Among Young Disabled People<br>*Ami Goulden* | 318 |
| 21 Compulsory Monogamy Is Disabling: Connecting Disability Justice and Critical Non-Monogamy<br>*Laura Yakas and Nicole Ariel Lopez* | 335 |

22 Caring for Disabled Kinksters: Context and Practical
   Guidance for Providers                                        351
   *Maria L. Morrero, Nicole Ariel Lopez,*
   *Hillary K. Hecht, Erin E. Dobbins, and*
   *Grace Argo*

23 Weight Stigma, Desirability, and Disability                    366
   *Hillary K. Hecht, Erin N. Harrop, and Ben Lemanski*

*Index*                                                           *382*

# CONTRIBUTORS

**Flyn Alexander** (they/he) is a white, transmasculine, neurodivergent queer therapist, activist, facilitator, writer, researcher, and social worker committed to lifelong healing, unlearning, and dismantling systems of oppression through their various actions and practices. Flyn works from an intersectional, queer, feminist, person-centered perspective, unpacking the ways the medical model has influenced and harmed his clients, our collective community, and society with its various intrenched institutions; through uncovering this harm, Flyn aspires to aid their clients in shaping their own healing, shifting and growing their perspectives, and empowering them on their own path of healing and unlearning.

**Nahime G. Aguirre Mtanous**, AM, LSW, (she/her/hers) has received her bachelor's and master's degrees from the University of Chicago, where she specializes in affirming therapeutic applications for neurodivergent folk. Her therapeutic work and research have received various awards and commendations, including the University of Chicago's Diversity Award for neurodiversity advocacy, the National Heumann-Armstrong Award in 2021 for advocacy against discrimination for people with mental illnesses, and a LEND fellowship to support her research for social and mental health supports for neurodivergent people with disabilities.

**Grace Argo** (she/her) is a PhD candidate in Women's and Gender Studies and History at the University of Michigan, Ann Arbor.

**Hannah Boyke** (they/them/theirs) is a queer nonbinary social work doctoral student at Michigan State University. Hannah's research examines systemic inequities that emerge at the intersection of the criminal legal and immigration enforcement systems.

**Erin E. Dobbins** (she/her) is a doctoral student in Health Policy and Management with a background in state and federal healthcare policy implementation and evaluation. Her current work focuses on how chronically ill and disabled people access and navigate healthcare.

**Jess Francis**, PhD, (she/her) is a research investigator at the Institute for Social Research. Her research is primarily situated at the intersection of aging, technology use, and well-being.

**Kimberly Fuentes**, MSW, (she/her/hers) is a PhD student in social welfare at the UCLA Luskin School of Public Affairs. She is a participatory action research scholar-activist and Director of Services and Outreach for the Sex Worker Outreach Project Los Angeles (SWOP LA).

**Elena Gormley**, MSW, (she/ella) is a social worker and independent scholar in Chicago, whose work and practice areas encompass workforce development, behavioral health crisis intervention policy, family policing system abolition, and being called a simultaneous threat to the integrity of the profession while having no knowledge or understanding of what social work is supposed to be about. Her work is taught at social work programs across the United States.

**Ami Goulden** (she/her/hers) is a registered social worker and Assistant Professor in the School of Social Work at Memorial University in St. John's, Newfoundland, Canada.

**Adrienne Graf**, MSW, LCSW, is Professor of Practice at The School of Social Work at Portland State University.

**E. B. Gross** (she/they) is a doctoral student at University of Michigan in Social Work and Developmental Psychology, researching gender identity development and factors that impact how families come to understand and accept TGD members, as well as LGBTQIA+ health and mental health. Prior to their doctoral studies, she obtained an MSW from Simmons University and provided individual, family and group therapy to homeless, low-income, and LGBTQIA+ people of all ages in New York City and Rhode Island.

**Ari S. Gzesh**, MSW, is pursuing a PhD degree in social welfare at University of Pennsylvania's School of Social Policy & Practice and serves as Fellow in Leadership Education and Adolescent Health (LEAH) at Children's Hospital of Philadelphia.

**Erin N. Harrop** (they/them/theirs) is Assistant Professor at the University of Denver. Their research focuses on weight stigma, eating disorders, and weight-inclusive healthcare practices.

**Hillary K. Hecht**, MSW, (they/them/theirs) is a doctoral candidate in health policy and management. Their research focuses on organizational policies, increasing equitable access to care, and anti-fat bias in healthcare.

**Emma Hertzel** (she/her) is a psychotherapist based in Tempe, Arizona, specializing in many modalities including individual and couple's sex therapy.

**Brendon T. Holloway**, MSW, (he/him) is a PhD candidate and adjunct faculty in the Graduate School of Social Work at the University of Denver. Brendon's research centers trans and nonbinary communities with focuses on healthcare access, mutual aid, and trans joy.

**C. Riley Hostetter**'s (they/them) work centers critical approaches to social work and systemic inequities, prioritizing queer and trans communities. They strive to engage in this work from transformative and abolitionist lenses.

**Nicolás Juárez** (he/him/his) is a doctoral student in the Joint Program for Social Work & Anthropology at the University of Michigan. His research is concerned with environmental injustice, cause advocacy, and sociopolitical theory.

**Shanna Katz Kattari**, PhD, MEd, CSE, (they/them/theirs) is a certified sexuality educator, an associate professor at the University of Michigan School of Social Work and Department of Women's and Gender Studies, and the director of the [Sexuality | Relationships | Gender] Research Collective. Their work focuses on disability and ableism; sexuality and sexual health; and queer- and trans-affirming care. Find out more about their work at ShannaKattari.com.

**L. B. Klein**, PhD, MSW, MPA, (they/she) is an assistant professor in the Sandra Rosenbaum School of Social Work and core faculty in the Sexual Violence Research Initiative at the University of Wisconsin-Madison.

**Jax Kynn** (they/them/theirs) is a queer, nonbinary feminist scholar and doctoral student at Michigan State University's School of Social Work. Jax's research focuses on queer and trans youth and the role of involvement in the juvenile justice and child welfare systems as sites of institutional betrayal.

**Elisabeth Z. Lacey** ("Zee", they/them) is a white, queer, disabled, gender fluid doctoral candidate in gender studies at Arizona State University (ASU). They are currently writing their dissertation which explores the impact of gender roles on formations of "acceptable" grief and grieving in the United States.

**Tiffini (Tiff) Lanza**, PhD, (they/them) is Executive Director at Maverique Therapeutic Services, a nonprofit private practice that provides services to the disabled, neurodiverse, LGBTQIA+, and BIPOC communities, as well as survivors of trauma. Dr. Lanza is passionate about providing quality therapy, education, and training around sexuality topics for marginalized communities.

**Natasha M. Lee-Johnson**, MSW, M.Ed., (she/her) is Robert Wood Johnson Foundation Health Policy Research Scholar at Louisiana State University, where she focuses her doctoral research on the acquisition of sexual health and gender expression knowledge among Black AFAB people.

**Ben Lemanski** (he/him/his) is a fat, queer therapist who works with queer folks, trans individuals, and the fat community to provide a safe space for unlearning the "-isms" that unfortunately plague our society. As a fat person, he believes it's important to disrupt the typical narrative of fatness as it is much more nuanced than most believe; fat bodies are valid bodies!

**Nicole Ariel Lopez** (they/them/theirs) received their MSW from the University of Michigan after earning a BA degree in Japanese language and literature, psychology, and minor in human sexuality from the University of Kansas. They currently work as a therapist with individuals and couples from a diverse range of backgrounds, including folks who are identified as LGBTQIA2S+, kinky/on the BDSM spectrum, and consensually non-monogamous.

**Robin Mandell**, BA, RYT-200, (she/her/hers) is a writer, yoga teacher, and disabled advocate/activist living in Seattle.

**Erin Martinez** (she/her/hers) is a clinical social worker and certified sex therapist who specializes in trauma-informed treatment that yields healing, well-being, and pleasure. She is also a lecturer at the University of Michigan School of Social Work.

**Madelyne J. Mayer** (they/them/theirs) is a white, Jewish, nonbinary femme from Sarasota, Florida. They are currently pursuing a master's degree in social work at the University of Michigan.

**Kiley J. McLean**, MSW, MSEd, (she/her/hers) is a doctoral candidate in the Sandra Rosenbaum School of Social Work and a research assistant at the Waisman Center at the University of Wisconsin-Madison.

**Autumn Dae Miller** (she/her/hers) is Director of the Clinical Department at KenCrest and believes deeply in creating a space to nurture professionals to find the skills and comfort in working with disabled and neurodivergent folks. In 2000, Autumn was invited to become a peer tutor in a learning support classroom; it was in that tiny room full of laughter, love, and true understanding that she found her purpose and her people.

**Maria L. Morrero**, Clinical LLMSW, (she/her/hers) is a disabled Philadelphian with a background in anthropology and gender studies. Her current interests include BDSM, disability studies, and biraciality and colorism in the United States.

**Bri Noonan** (they/them/theirs) is a white, queer, nonbinary artist-scholar located in Phoenix, AZ, whose work explores chronic illness and queerness in conversation with disability studies and queer theory often utilizing artistic narrative to investigate intersectional identities. They graduated with a BFA degree in photography in May 2013 and an MA degree in social and cultural pedagogy with a Certificate in Disability Studies in May 2021 from ASU.

**Meg Panichelli**, PhD, MSW, (she/her/hers) is Assistant Professor in the Department of Undergraduate Social Work at West Chester University of PA.

**syd lio riley** (he/they/ze) is a white, disabled, genderqueer young person whose advocacy and research primarily revolves around transformative justice, specifically as it relates to queerness, transness, youth, disability, and carceral ideologies. Currently, lio is earning hir MSW at the University of Michigan with an interest in exploring alternative approaches to neuronormative therapeutic modalities to provide affirming care to autistic and attention-deficit/hyperactivity disorder (ADHD) children and youth.

**Kari L. Sherwood**, MS, MEd, MSW, LLMSW, (she/her) is a PhD candidate in social work and developmental psychology at the University of Michigan. She develops and evaluates technology-based interventions to improve employment outcomes for autistic young adults.

**Rose C. B. Singh**, MSW, (she/they) is a practicing social worker, a sessional lecturer at Dalhousie University, and a doctoral student at Memorial University of Newfoundland and Labrador.

**Al Wauldron** (they/them/theirs) is a psychotherapist and clinical social worker, whose work with others attempts to synthesize personal experiences and systemic frameworks to create understanding, meaning, and transformation in people's lives. Al works from multiple therapeutic approaches based on clients' needs, including attachment theory, emotionally focused therapy (EFT), internal family systems (IFS), cognitive behavioral therapy (CBT), dialectical behavioral therapy (DBT), trauma-informed practice, and mindfulness. Al graduated with a master's degree in social work from the UM in 2022, specializing in LGBTQIA2S+ and neurodivergent experiences, including ADHD and autism spectrum.

**Alison Wetmur**, PhD, (she/her) was born deaf to hearing parents and became a member of the Deaf Community after college. Currently, Dr. Wetmur teaches and provides mental health services in CT.

**Laura Yakas**, PhD, (she/her/hers) is Mad Queer Slut, an Indigenous (Māori) woman, and an anthropologist who studies oppression and anti-oppression. She is passionate about disability/Mad Justice and enjoys sharing this passion with social work students at the University of Michigan and with audiences who come to see her radical musical stand-up comedy!

# ACKNOWLEDGMENTS

After I edited my first book, I told my partners, Leo Kattari and Allie DeMars, to never let me agree to do so again. Editing is even more laborious when you want to do it from a critical, community grounded approach, ensuring often excluded voices, people, and experiences are centered. It means more time-connecting folks, more mentoring, and more copyediting. As much joy as the final book was, it was exhausting.

Therefore, you can imagine their surprise when only a year after my previous book was published, I was proposing another one (after this one, I think I am done for a bit! Even my students are reminding me to say no more often). However, their support is unwavering, whether it is staying up until 5 am "just to get the chapter draft finished!" or helping me copyedit my own chapters. I love them both so very dearly and feel incredibly lucky to have them behind, next to, under, and all around me. Every new ice pack delivered and medication refill picked up on my behalf gave me just enough extra spoons to see this through.

This book would not have happened without the support of two PhD students in the Joint Social Work PhD Program at the University of Michigan School of Social Work. Kari L. Sherwood and E. B. Gross were incredible rockstars, from taking on support roles in extra chapters to doing leg work on images, and even just listening to me kvetch about why I opted to do another book. Sexuality and disability are not quite either of their areas, yet they opted to engage in this work with open hearts, and for that, I am so thankful.

All of the authors of each chapter bring such life to this work. Academics, yes, and educators, therapists, researchers, artists, and community members are coming together to share their vision for what it means to support disabled people in having affirming sexual experiences in this world. They dealt with my own struggles with long COVID as I tried to keep this book moving forward while simultaneously taking care of myself as my own body mind's capacity kept shifting. They are who created this beautiful work.

Writing this book during the COVID pandemic (which is still ongoing) was a wild experience. It was written almost completely from my bedroom in my home. Almost three years of fairly intensive isolation, having to delay needed medical care, watching the world move by while leaving disabled and chronically ill people, including people like me, in the dust, sentencing us to rot in our homes while they pretended like COVID was just a mild cold. My online community held me and inspired me. We laughed together, cried together, and raged together. Never let anyone say that virtual connections are not as valid as those face to face; my crip friends on Twitter, Facebook, Instagram, TikTok, and elsewhere on the interwebs are what have allowed me to survive this dystopian world that seems to have no qualms with letting people like me/like us waste away.

To the Sparkle Unicorns, who cheered me through this, and so much more; thank you. I know I would not have made to where I am without you. Similarly, to Meg and Ginny, with whom I felt so connected as we all were incredibly isolated during COVID, you heard and validated me when I needed it the most. To Alex, my best femme locally, who I have only seen in person a handful of times due to both of us following strict protocols (and who dropped off many a gluten-free vegetarian snack on my porch), thank you for keeping me grounded, for helping me channeling my feelings, and for feeding me – heart, soul, and stomach.

To my crip ancestors, those are no longer with us, and to our disability justice leaders, including those who are still here and have paved the road before me/us. To Leah Lakshmi Piepzna-Samarasinha, Mia Mingus, Patty Berne, Stacey Milbern, Sami Schalk, Eli Clare, Stella Young, Lydia X. Z. Brown, Jina Kim, Patrick Califia, Lorraine Hutchins, Ellen Samuels, Mitchell Tepper, Bethany Stevens, Miriyam Netzorg, Judy Heumann, Amanda Arkansassy Harris, and the many others, whose work and lives have led me here. To the disabled people no longer with us due to ableism – interpersonal and systemic; I am sorry the world didn't care for you more; we are trying to change it.

Finally, my animal companions were beyond crucial in the creation of this book. Kinsey, my 18-year-old black cat who first joined me back in 2005, was in my arms every moment writing the proposal. He transitioned back to stardust in May 2022, and I didn't know how to go on without him. Luckily, Vlad and Artemis ("the Young Bucks," two very energetic, massive, three-year-old rescue cats), Sir Catrick Stewart (our gumpy old orange cat), Captain Sadie (our newest tiny addition of a feline), and Marla Pooch (a rescued five-year-old blue nose pitbull) held me, pushed me, snuggled me, helped with meltdowns and sensory overwhelm, and made me laugh when I needed it most. These animals helped me literally to survive, without which, this book would never have been finished.

# INTRODUCTION

*Shanna Katz Kattari*

The first time I considered writing a book about sexuality and disability was in November 2008 – I was sitting awake in a hotel room with my mother and sister, who were both sleeping. Painsomnia, the experience of pain which makes it hard to sleep, and the inability to sleep resulting in increased pain, was keeping me up. When you can't sleep, and you can't read or watch TV, you get to thinking.

At the time, I was a well-known sex blogger and emerging sex educator. Despite sexuality and disability not really being my main wheelhouse, I was one of the only people in the arena of sex blogging, sex toy sales, sexuality education, and ethical porn circles who was talking about these topics at all (alongside Mitchell Tepper, whose work was critical). People had started asking me to speak about, write on, and generally engage around the topics "sex and disability." Back home from the hotel, late the next night, I tossed together a free WordPress website, emailed a bunch of people in my sexuality network, and tried to curate a collection of people's stories, poems, and other written experiences about sex and disability. I wanted to be to sexuality and disability what sex educator Tristan Taormino is to anal sex, what sexual health advocate Heather Corinna is to affirming sex education for young people, what adult performer Nina Hartley is to educational adult films, and what sex educator Semona Baston (Dirty Lola) is to sex toys.

I received a few initial submissions to my new project and started shopping around my idea, thrilled at the prospect of bringing more attention to the subject. Unfortunately, many popular press publishers just were not interested at the time; they pointed out Miriam Kaufman, Cory Silverberg, and Fran Odette's amazing book, *The Ultimate Guide to Sex and Disability* (2003), which had been published five years prior. In their minds, one book

DOI: 10.4324/9781003308331-1

was all that was needed on this topic, and it had already been written. I was encouraged to consider approaching academic presses, as there might be possible interest there. However, at the time, I wasn't an academic, so I let my dream of leading the way in sexuality and disability go.

A few years later, Robert McRuer and Anna Mollow's edited collection *Sex and Disability* was published (2012), filling this gap with an excellent set of essays. I felt at ease having given up on my idea, happy that at least others were doing the work – but the idea for an updated version of the Ultimate Guide, or something a little different, perhaps targeting people with disabilities specifically, continued swirling in my brain. Luckily for the world, A. Andrews produced *A Quick and Easy Guide to Sex & Disability* in 2020, an adorable, inclusive, and illustrated short guide for disabled people and those who love them. Even as I have edited and written chapters for this book, *the Routledge Handbook of Disability and Sexuality* was published in 2022, exploring these topics from more academic and theoretical perspectives. As more conversations on disability and sexuality continue to fill both the sexuality community and the disability community, I am delighted to not be seen as "the" person anymore, but rather, part of a pool of folks with lived experience of disability who want to educate academics, individuals, and community members about the joys and challenges of sex and disability.

Over 14 years after I first had the 2:00 am idea to write a book on sexuality and disability, I am finally writing and editing this book. It is a completely different concept than the one I had back then; instead of sharing writings of disabled folks, this book is a guide for educators, therapists, counselors, case managers, community organizers, caregivers, guardians, healthcare professionals, and of course, disabled people themselves. Each chapter is designed to offer some background on a specific facet of sexuality and disability, take the reader through some best practices, offer a case study or activity for reflection on how this might connect to their practice, and share some resources for people to dive in more deeply. The book is designed to be used however is best for you – to be read cover to cover or a chapter at a time as needed, to be a textbook, a resource guide, and/or just some fun and interesting reading for those who want to learn more. This book, hopefully, is for you.

Another important piece I considered with this book was the absolute necessity of having people with lived experience of disability, meaning actually disabled people, writing it. Often, especially in more academic books, people outside of a marginalized community or experience writing about them. Books on practice with trans and gender-diverse people are often written by cisgender people, and those on racism have often been written by white authors. In creating this book, I wanted to ensure that the voices of disabled people, whether providers or community members, were centered throughout. The vast majority of the authors in this collection are disabled, chronically ill, Mad, neurodivergent, Deaf, etc. I've found that this changes the feel of the chapters for me, making it feel more connective, authentic, and meaningful I hope that it feels this way to you.

As a book written mostly by disabled individuals, this has been a different process than how many nondisabled folks write. We have written these chapters during a global pandemic – a mass disabling event in which disabled people, and especially chronically ill individuals, have been even more left behind and isolated than usual. The ableism that comes from all sides surrounding COVID, including from supposed "progressive" folks, is so oppressive and makes it challenging to do work of any type when we have been told it is positive that since most of those dying ARE disabled, so it is ok to go back to "normal." Plus, as disabled authors, our bodyminds, disabled lives, and access needs are constantly shifting. This meant that I intentionally built extra time into our timeline so that deadlines could be flexible, and that people who originally committed could graciously shift off their chapters to take care of themselves. These chapters have been written not only from office desks, certainly, but also from beds, couches, and hospitals, while lying on heating pads and snuggling ice packs, while heavily medicated and/or while navigating high amounts of emotional and physical pain, while fighting for accommodations and having our basic needs met, while seeking diagnoses or reeling from new ones, while in and out of mental health crises, while stimming or in sensory overwhelm, while organizing and advocating, while reeling from the death of one of our co-authors, and while sobbing at the state of our world.

In reading this far, you may have already encountered language that is new to you. Folks are sometimes confused about what the words disability or disabilities cover. Some people define disability as very specific experiences that are enumerated in policies. Others have favorite definitions they carry close to their heart. In this book, the experience of disability means having a ***bodymind***, a term popularized by Eli Clare that operates in a different way than societal expectations and norms (2017). While people commonly define disability as needing a wheelchair, being blind, being d/Deaf or hard of hearing, having post-traumatic stress disorder (PTSD), etc., we are casting a wider net here to be as inclusive as possible.

Disability includes ***neurodivergence***, which in someone's brain operates in a different way than what is defined as typical, and can include autism, attention-deficit/hyperactivity disorder, anxiety, depression, PTSD, obsessive compulsive disorder, Tourette's, traumatic brain injury, Down syndrome, and more (Gregory, 2022). Disability includes ***Mad*** folks, a term reclaimed by those with Mad Pride (Curtis et al., 2011), encompassing individuals with mental illness/mental health diagnoses that include (but are not limited to!) bipolar disorder, schizophrenia, borderline personality disorder, suicidal ideation, and more. Disability includes ***chronic illness***, those who are ***chronically ill***, and those navigating ***chronic pain***, such as those with endometriosis, fibromyalgia, "long COVID," irritable bowel syndrome, postural orthostatic tachycardia syndrome, mast cell activation syndrome, various types of cancer, and migraine headaches. In the Deaf community and culture, some *Deaf/hard-of-hearing* individuals do not consider themselves to be disabled but rather feel that society is just not caught up with speaking their language and understanding their culture; others find affirmation in holding a disabled identity (Lane, 2002). We include this community here as well.

Disability can be a large tent with room for so many, offering solidarity and connection, rather than gatekeeping access to community. Disability crosses every other group: there are people who are racialized and disabled, disabled queer and trans people, disabled young people, and people who become disabled as they age. While much of the media's portrayal of disability and disabled people is of white, cisgender, heterosexual, English speaking (or nonverbal) individuals, that is, not what the "average" disabled person looks like. Our community spans every other identity as well; there is no "norm" of disability.

Disabled people have and continue to experience extreme rates of harm in our society, in every country around the world. From high rates of under and unemployment to high rates of interpersonal violence to societal eugenics and lack of access to basic necessities such as housing, healthcare, education, and supplies, our society has consistently marginalized and oppressed individuals of this community in every aspect from the institutional to the interpersonal (Breiding & Armour, 2015; Chirwa et al., 2020; Hästbacka et al., 2016; McDonald et al., 2015; Naami et al., 2012; Saugeres, 2011; Savage, 2021). These challenges, a response to societal devaluing of disability and the natural diversity of bodyminds, are not limited to these realms, and such oppression is evident in how disabled sexuality is treated.

When it comes to sexuality, disabled people are frequently infantalized and viewed as nonsexual entities, and/or seen as hypersexual simply for having any sexuality at all. Policies and laws have been enacted to forcibly sterilize disabled people, prohibit them from having loving romantic and/or sexual partnerships, and prevent them from accessing affirming sexuality education (Aderemi, 2014; Bathje et al., 2021; Serrato Calero et al., 2021; Wade, 2002; World Health Organization, 2014; Wos et al., 2021). While many of these things will be touched on in this book, as they are an important part of understanding disabled people's experiences, they will not be centered. Rather, this is a book of unbridled ***disabled joy*** and passion, where the authors and I celebrate disabled people as sexual beings, offer suggestions on how to best support disabled people in exploring and affirming their sexuality, and look toward our communal knowledge as disabled individuals, disability and sexuality scholars, sex educators, sex therapists, and other practitioners within both the disability and sexuality communities.

I am often asked to speak on disability, and almost as often, I am asked why I refer to myself as disabled, chronically ill, neurodivergent, autistic, etc., as compared to having disabilities, having chronic illnesses, being neurodivergent, having autism/being on the spectrum. The language I use for myself is *identity-first language*, where we put the identity or descriptor first, as we do with most other identities and experiences, such as a wheelchair user, disabled people, a fat person, a gay man, a Latina woman, or a young nonbinary person. This pushes back against the idea that disability is so horrible or problematic that it must be separate from the person, and centers it as part of our identities, like all of our other identity experiences. Others may prefer using *person-first language*, in which we would say a person in a wheelchair, people with disabilities, etc. Note: do not use with other identities; saying a man with gay tendencies just does not land the same way! In practice, mirror the language your clients use, of course, and also consider how language that separates someone from their experience can impact them.

There is no right or wrong answer as far as language use beyond trying to mirror the language of the person and/or communities with whom you work (Dunn & Andrews, 2015). There are divided preferences about the use of each, with a recent international study of disabled people finding that 49% preferred identity-first language, 33% preferred person-first language, and 18% had no preference (Sharif et al., 2022). For the purposes of this book, authors have chosen the language that best fits their individual style and preferences, and while many of us have chosen to center identity-first language throughout our writing, you will note some instances of person-first language in quotes from existing research, to honor and affirming the experiences of certain people in our case studies, etc.

Another key point to understanding working with the disabled community is the difference between the medical model of disability and the social model of disability. In the *medical model of disability*, almost all impairments and medical conditions are viewed as something aberrant from the "norm," as something to be fixed (Marks, 1997). The medical model generally pushes for walking over rolling, speaking over signing or typing, privileging certain types of communication styles, processing styles, and physical experiences over others. Often, those following the model will push disabled people toward a certain end goal, regardless of the cost (financial, physical, social, etc.) to the person themself. Several British disability scholars created (and later updated) the *social model of disability* (Oliver, 1990, 2013; Shakespeare, 2006), which essentially states that it is our society itself that is disabling people. This model suggests that if we had a society that did not have prejudice and stereotypes against people with diverse bodyminds, and if we had flexible work schedules, accepted different communication styles, and made everything accessible from the start, the people with impairments and medical conditions would no longer be disabled, but instead just be seen as part of normal human diversity (Barnes, 2019).

As with the identity-first versus person-first language, there is no one right answer here. The medical model has caused a lot of harm and has much to answer for, and at the same time, many people living with chronic pain and chronic illness (myself included!) do wish to have their pain and illness managed and/or treated medically. The social model is incredibly useful to look at and understand *ableism*, which is the word for the devolution of disability and discrimination/prejudice against disabled people (Hehir, 2002), yet for those who are having active suicidal ideation or are currently in physical pain, the model offers little in the way of tangible support. Some people who do disability work/work with the disability community have been discussing the need for some sort of *interactional model* that takes both the medical model and social model into account in order to meet the needs of all disabled people in a variety of ways (Chan et al., 2009; Smart, 2009; Tate & Pledger, 2003). I invite you to think about how these different models may play out in your work, and how this might shift in the world you strive for.

Another set of definitions which are important is the distinction between disability rights and disability justice. The concept of *disability rights* refers to the fact that all people, including those with disabilities, are deserving of basic human rights. Activists in the *disability rights movements* in various countries have advocated and fought for access in healthcare, accessible housing, public accommodations, educational accommodations, deinstitutionalization, protection from communicable diseases (such as COVID-19), etc. (Antova, 2020; Bagenstos, 2009; Cooper, 1999; Hayashi & Okuhira, 2001; Jolley et al., 2018; Khudorenko, 2011; Köbsell, 2006; Mladenov & Brennan, 2021; Sabatello, 2014). Much of the historic disability rights movement has been led by cisgender, heterosexual, and white individuals. On the other hand, the **disability justice** movement was created and is currently led predominantly by queer and trans disabled people of color. Disability justice builds forward from where the disability rights movement left off and operates on ten basic principles:

- *Intersectionality*, as we recognize that each person has multiple identities, both privileged and oppressed, and disability can also be understood by how it has been shaped by other identities;
- *Leadership of Those Most Impacted*, which recognizes that when we examine ableism in the context of other historical systems of oppression, we must be led by those who have the most experience with those systems;
- *An Anti-Capitalist Politic*, as a critique of productivity politic, and a rejection of the idea that a person is only as valuable as the labor they can provide society;

- **Commitment to Cross Movement Organizing**, in which Disability Justice change how other social justice movements (including racial justice, trans justice, abolitionist) conceptualize disability and understand ableism, to create a unified front;
- **Recognizing Wholeness**, to accept and value people for their whole and authentic selves, and not expecting them to make themselves more palatable or into bite size pieces;
- **Sustainability**, which means we must pace ourselves, both individually and collectively, in order for our movement to be sustainable over time;
- **A Commitment to Cross Disability Solidarity**, which is an explicit valuing and honoring of the shared knowledge and engagement of all of our community members, with an understanding that separation and isolation functions to undo our work toward collective liberation;
- **Interdependence**, wherein we can see the liberation of all living being and living systems, as well as the land, as being key to the overall liberation of our own communities;
- **Collective Access**, through which access needs can be shared, without shame, in a communal space, and then be met based upon an individual's needs, desires, and a group or organization's capacity;
- **Collective Liberation**, to ask the question "How do we move together?" across abilities, ages, race, class, national origin, and more, and where no bodymind is left behind (Berne et al., 2018; Sins Invalid, 2015).

Similar to the fact that disability can be defined in many different ways and examines for a variety of lenses, so too can the concept of sexuality. Even in putting together this book, I was challenged as to how wide or narrow to make it. I would include sex education, sexual and reproductive health, sure, but what about kink? Non-monogamy? Sexuality research? What about sexual and intimate partner violence? Parenting? Politics? Spirituality? Sexuality as a fundamental human right? All of these topics are part of human sexuality, and all of them intersect with disability and disability politics. On the other hand, I could only include so many chapters, and I had a strict final word count.

I turned to our new ancestor Dennis Dailey's model of the **Circles of Sexuality**, which indicates that concepts of sexuality should include sensuality, intimacy, sexual health and reproduction, and sexualization, along with how these circles intersect with our own values, and those of the clients we serve (Dailey, 1981). Thus, I've included as much as I can, knowing that this book is still just the tip of the iceberg and that the concepts of sexuality and disability can cover so many other areas that are not explored. My hope is that you, the reader, whether you are a student, professor, or practitioner, use this book and the resources within as a jumping off point, a place to start your journey, rather than to end it. Perhaps one day it will be sitting on a shelf so full of sexuality and disability books that it simply fades into the background, but for now, I offer it as an introduction to many of the various facets that make up the wide range of what is covered by sexuality and disability.

# References

Aderemi, T. J. (2014). Teachers' perspectives on sexuality and sexuality education of learners with intellectual disabilities in Nigeria. *Sexuality and Disability, 32*(3), 247–258.

Andrews, A. (2020). *A quick & easy guide to sex & disability*. Limerence Press.

Antova, I. (2020). Disability rights during Covid-19: Emergency law and guidelines in England. *Medical Law Review, 28*(4), 804–816.

Bagenstos, S. R. (2009). Law and the contradictions of the disability rights movement. In *Law and the contradictions of the disability rights movement*. Yale University Press.

Barnes, C. (2019). Understanding the social model of disability: Past, present and future. In *Routledge handbook of disability studies* (pp. 14–31). Routledge.

Bathje, M., Schrier, M., Williams, K., & Olson, L. (2021). The lived experience of sexuality among adults with intellectual and developmental disabilities: A scoping review. *The American Journal of Occupational Therapy, 75*(4).

Berne, P., Morales, A. L., Langstaff, D., & Invalid, S. (2018). Ten principles of disability justice. *WSQ: Women's Studies Quarterly, 46*(1), 227–230.

Breiding, M. J., & Armour, B. S. (2015). The association between disability and intimate partner violence in the United States. *Annals of Epidemiology, 25*(6), 455–457.

Chan, F., Gelman, J. S., Ditchman, N., Kim, J.-H., & Chiu, C.-Y. (2009). The World Health Organization ICF model as a conceptual framework of disability. In F. Chan, E. Da Silva Cardoso, & J. A. Chronister (Eds.), *Understanding psychosocial adjustment to chronic illness and disability: A handbook for evidence-based practitioners in rehabilitation* (pp. 23–50). Springer Publishing Co.

Chirwa, E., Jewkes, R., Van Der Heijden, I., & Dunkle, K. (2020). Intimate partner violence among women with and without disabilities: A pooled analysis of baseline data from seven violence-prevention programmes. *BMJ Global Health, 5*(11), e002156.

Clare, E. (2017). *Brilliant imperfection: Grappling with cure*. Duke University Press.

Cooper, M. (1999). The Australian disability rights movement lives. *Disability & Society, 14*(2), 217–226.

Curtis, T., Curtis, T., Dellar, R., & Esther, L. (Eds.). (2011). *Mad pride*. Chipmunk Publishing Ltd.

Dailey, D. (1981). Sexual expression and ageing. In D. Berghorn & D. Schafer (Eds.), *The dynamics of ageing: Original essays on the processes and experiences of growing old* (pp. 311–330). Westview Press.

Dunn, D. S., & Andrews, E. E. (2015). Person-first and identity-first language: Developing psychologists' cultural competence using disability language. *American Psychologist, 70*(3), 255.

Gregory, E. (2022, October 4). What does it mean to be neurodivergent? *Forbes*. www.forbes.com/health/mind/what-is-neurodivergent/

Hästbacka, E., Nygård, M., & Nyqvist, F. (2016). Barriers and facilitators to societal participation of people with disabilities: A scoping review of studies concerning European countries. *Alter*, *10*(3), 201–220.

Hayashi, R., & Okuhira, M. (2001). The disability rights movement in Japan: Past, present and future. *Disability & Society*, *16*(6), 855–869.

Hehir, T. (2002). Eliminating ableism in education. *Harvard Educational Review*, *72*(1), 1–33.

Jolley, E., Lynch, P., Virendrakumar, B., Rowe, S., & Schmidt, E. (2018). Education and social inclusion of people with disabilities in five countries in West Africa: A literature review. *Disability and Rehabilitation*, *40*(22), 2704–2712.

Kaufman, M., Silverberg, C., & Odette, F. (2003). *The ultimate guide to sex and disability: For all of us who live with disabilities, chronic pain, and illness*. Cleis Press.

Khudorenko, E. A. (2011). Problems of the education and inclusion of people with disabilities. *Russian Education & Society*, *53*(12), 82–91.

Köbsell, S. (2006). Towards self-determination and equalization: A short history of the German disability rights movement. *Disability Studies Quarterly*, *26*(2).

Lane, H. (2002). Do deaf people have a disability? *Sign Language Studies*, *2*(4), 356–379.

Marks, D. (1997). Models of disability. *Disability and Rehabilitation*, *19*(3), 85–91.

McDonald, K. E., Williamson, P., Weiss, S., Adya, M., Blanck, P., & DBTAC: Southeast ADA Center PAR Research Consortium. (2015). The march goes on: Community access for people with disabilities. *Journal of Community Psychology*, *43*(3), 348–363.

McRuer, R., & Mollow, A. (Eds.). (2012). *Sex and disability*. Duke University Press.

Mladenov, T., & Brennan, C. S. (2021). The global COVID-19 disability rights monitor: Implementation, findings, disability studies response. *Disability & Society*, *36*(8), 1356–1361.

Naami, A., Hayashi, R., & Liese, H. (2012). The unemployment of women with physical disabilities in Ghana: Issues and recommendations. *Disability & Society*, *27*(2), 191–204.

Oliver, M. (1990). *The politics of disablement*. Palgrave Macmillan.

Oliver, M. (2013). The social model of disability: Thirty years on. *Disability & Society*, *28*(7), 1024–1026.

Sabatello, M. (2014). A short history of the international disability rights movement. In M. Sabatello & M. Schulz (Eds.), *Human rights and disability advocacy* (pp. 13–24). University of Pennsylvania Press.

Saugeres, L. (2011). (Un) accommodating disabilities: Housing, marginalization and dependency in Australia. *Journal of Housing and the Built Environment*, *26*(1), 1–15.

Savage, L. (2021). *Intimate partner violence: Experiences of women with disabilities in Canada, 2018* (pp. 1–23). Juristat, Canadian Centre for Justice Statistics.

Serrato Calero, M., Delgado-Vázquez, Á. M., & Díaz Jiménez, R. M. (2021). Systematized review and meta-synthesis of the sterilization of women with disabilities in the field of social science: From Macroeugenics to Microeugenics. *Sexuality Research and Social Policy*, *18*(3), 653–671.

Shakespeare, T. (2006). The social model of disability. *The Disability Studies Reader*, *2*, 197–204.

Sharif, A., Aedan, L. M., & Kianna, R. B. (2022). *Should I say "disabled people" or "people with disabilities"? Language preferences of disabled people between identity-and person-first language.* The 23rd International ACM SIGACCESS Conference on Computers and Accessibility (Athens, Greece) (ASSETS'22), Association for Computing Machinery, New York, NY, USA, To Appear.

Sins Invalid. (2015, June 10). *Disability justice: A working draft by Patty Berne.* www.sinsinvalid.org/blog/disability-justice-a-working-draft-by-patty-berne

Smart, J. F. (2009). The power of models of disability. *Journal of Rehabilitation*, 75(2), 3.

Tate, D. G., & Pledger, C. (2003). An integrative conceptual framework of disability: New directions for research. *American Psychologist*, 58(4), 289–295. https://doi.org/10.1037/0003-066X.58.4.289

Wade, H. (2002). Discrimination, sexuality and people with significant disabilities: Issues of access and the right to sexual expression in the United States. *Disability Studies Quarterly*, 22(4).

World Health Organization. (2014). *Eliminating forced, coercive and otherwise involuntary sterilization: An interagency statement.* OHCHR, UN Women, UNAIDS, UNDP, UNFPA, UNICEF and WHO. https://apps.who.int/iris/bitstream/handle/10665/112848/9789241507325_eng.pdf?sequence=1&isAllowed=y

Wos, K., Kamecka-Antczak, C., & Szafrański, M. (2021). In search of solutions regarding the sex education of people with intellectual disabilities in Poland-participatory action research. *European Journal of Special Needs Education*, 36(4), 517–530.

# PART ONE
# History and Community Work

# 1
# A (VERY BRIEF) HISTORY OF DISABILITY AND SEXUALITY POLICY

*Ari S. Gzesh, Shanna Katz Kattari, Nicolás Juárez, and Madelyne J. Mayer*

Though disabled people have existed in all cultures, and in every shape and size, the extent to which they are accorded agency of their own bodies has been based on myriad factors. This chapter examines several common threads that interweave through the studies of disability and sexuality, such as access, education, autonomy, and care, many of which have also been codified in policy.

We begin by examining the conceptualization of disability from a societal and historical lens, offering a brief overview of scholars who have critiqued the seemingly dichotomized construction of sexuality and disability. We then explore historical underpinnings for how and why disability policies have emerged, both in the United States (U.S.) and across the world. In each setting, we ask how these policies have been used to either support or control the sexuality of disabled folks. We conclude with an activity that explores the impact of policies on sexual agency of disabled people, and the implications for sexuality education.

## Conceptualizing Disability

A common thread through the history of both disability and sexuality is the juxtaposition of "normal" and "abnormal," as imposed by societal norms (Rubin, 1984). Through the functional or medical model of disability, the distinction of normal versus abnormal is found in an individual's (in)ability to perform certain functional activities. Moreover, when it comes to sexuality, disabled individuals are often sorted into a binary with two challenging outcomes; they are either seen as naive, innocent, unable to consent, and therefore are viewed as nonsexual members of society, or conversely, simply by being sexual AND disabled, they are labeled as hypersexual, as promiscuous, even as freaks (Kijak, 2011; Wilkinson et al., 2015). As Shuttleworth states:

> The transgression of normative notions of embodiment and function – normative in the sense of being able to walk, talk verbally, perceive visually, hear audibly, cognize, or behave in a so-called rational way – affects not only how disabled people are viewed as persons in society but also how they are constructed as sexual subjects, which is often as asexual or hypersexual. The barriers to sexual expression, sexual well-being, and sexual relationships that many disabled people confront can often be traced to the symbolic meanings and values that are called up from the cultural imaginary by these transgressions of normative embodiment.
>
> *(2007, p. 4)*

Major foundational texts in disability studies rarely address sex in detail, while the larger field of sexuality studies (even in feminist and queer theory) is also lacking. "A polarization, in the cultural imagination, between sex and disability means that each of these terms potentially disables recognition of the other" (McRuer & Mollow, 2012, p. 23). The authors posit that ableist logic precludes sex in the presence of disability and vice versa.

### Public Charge: The Body Politics and the Politics of Bodies

Regulation of bodies as vectors of sexuality only became codified into law when anxieties regarding race were pervasive: In the United States, the Page Act of 1875 was followed in short order by the Chinese Exclusion Act (1882; Soennichsen, 2011), the Scott Act (1888; Soennichsen, 2011), and subsequently the Immigration Act (Ward, 1907). These acts sought to exclude potential citizens predicated on race. However, in tandem, the Immigration Act of 1882 introduced the idea of "public charge," which allowed immigration officials to bar "any convict, lunatic, idiot, or any person unable to take care of him or herself without becoming a public charge" from immigrating to the United States (quoted in Rosales, 2020, p. 1618). This frame of public charge, of someone who would have to rely on the state or social services to take care of themselves, became a way to exclude people who were either physically and/or mentally disabled from entering into the country.

These legislative means of controlling freedom and autonomy were predicated on categories of exclusion delineated by race, gender, and disability, co-producing the architecture of coercion and harm that is still in practice today. Ableism, racism, sexism, and other forms of oppression are all tied together, and as Fannie Lou Hamer once noted in a speech at the 1971 National Women's Political Caucus "nobody is free until everybody's free"; this is a concrete example of how oppression and discrimination of various types has laid its foundations in our laws, interweaving with one another to strengthen policies, actions, and even beliefs that create tiers of individuals based on their identities. Often, people do not even realize that these laws existed, that some such laws are still on the books, and that they were building blocks of the institutionalized oppression that we face in today's world. Moreover, such laws were not unique to the United States; Canada passed the Immigration Act of 1869 which, similarly, excluded any "lunatic, idiotic, deaf and dumb, blind or infirm person" from entering into the country (Thibault et al., 2017, p. 5). These ableist frames directly targeted disabled people as undesirable and unable to become citizens and residents of the United States and Canada. To this day, these acts remain in effect and continue to disproportionately bar disabled people from immigration and continue to perpetuate the violent idea that only able-bodied people deserve to be part of these countries (Bagenstos, 2021; Wong, 2012).

One of the primary drivers for the creation of disability as an identity category can be traced to the transition from agrarian society to industrial capitalism. The shift to an urban workforce in a wage economy reduced families' capacity to care for partly productive members. Capitalism demanded intact, interchangeable bodies as grist for the mill of industrialization. As Sarah Rose explores in her 2017 book *No Right to Be Idle: The Invention of Disability, 1840s–1930s*:

> [T]he problem of disability lay not in their actual impairments of the work they did, but rather in the meanings attributed to those impairments by policy makers and employers, as well as how those meanings intersected with a rapidly shifting workplace, changing family capacities, policies aimed at preventing dependency, and the complexity of disability itself.
>
> *(p. 3)*

By the end of World War I, disability became synonymous with reliance on public dependency, poor citizenship, and inability to care for oneself or work productively, which therefore conflated disability with burden and further setting the stage for coercive corporeal control due to capitalist values of productivity as worth.

## Intersections of Disability and Sexuality

The intersections of disability and policy have not been merely about the administration of services or access to certain rights but have often become proxies for coercive forms of controlling bodies, including exclusion of disabled bodies marked undesirable or even dangerous. While the full extent of these legal maneuvers is far greater than any overview can cursorily cover, the following case studies should highlight the long legal history of such policies in modern day nation-states, and the ways in which they continue to inform and curtail services for disabled populations.

*Eugenics*

Coined by Sir Francis Galton in the late 19th century, the eugenics movement sought to eliminate populations deemed inferior or disabled through control of reproduction. Based on misguided and ableist understandings of genetics, eugenicists believed that if they prevented disabled people from reproducing, they could prevent disability from appearing in the population.

Informed by this misbelief, several bills came to pass. In 1907, Indiana passed the first sterilization eugenics bill which made it mandatory for "imbeciles" and "idiots" in state custody to be sterilized (Stern, 2007). This was followed by the Virginia Sterilization Act of 1924, resulting in numerous Virginians being sterilized, and ultimately leading to the infamous 1927 *Buck v. Bell* case, wherein the Supreme Court reaffirmed Virginia's right to sterilize women against their will, to prevent "mentally disabled" people from being born (Nourse, 2011). In the Court's ableist logic, "three generations of imbeciles are enough" (Nourse, 2011, p. 114).

Such policies were not contained to the United States. In England, where the eugenics movement was born, the Mental Deficiency Act of 1913 legalized the forced institutionalization of "idiots" and "imbeciles" and segregated them from other people to deter them from having children with others (Jarrett & Walmsley, 2019). Similarly, the Canadian states of Alberta and British Columbia passed sterilization laws, which allowed forced sterilization of those marked mentally deficient (Dack, 2020). Even today, eugenics continues to be propagated in the ways that disabled fetuses are regularly aborted (see more about this in Chapter 2). Ultimately, eugenics is not only based on pseudoscience, but it also presumes, in the most violent way, that disabled life is equivalent to a life not worth living (Roll-Hansen, 2010; Wilson, 2021).

Eugenics continues to be practiced, though perhaps in less explicit ways. For example, take the case of Ashely X, a disabled six-year-old girl in the United States, in 2006 – less than 20 years ago. As she began to grow and there was a potential for early puberty, her parents expressed on concerns about taking care of her when she was bigger, as well as fear of sexual abuse if she developed secondary sex characteristics (Kirschner et al., 2007). The solution decided upon by Ashley's physicians and her parents, which they referred to casually as "The Ashley Treatment," was to put her on high-dose estrogen to slow her growth, and then perform a hysterectomy and breast bud removal (essentially a preemptive mastectomy) on Ashely (Kirschner et al., 2007).

This happened despite the December 2006 Convention on the Rights of Persons with Disabilities, adopted by the United Nations General Assembly, noting that "every person with disabilities has a right to respect for his or her physical and mental integrity on an equal basis with others" (p. 11). Washington state, where Ashley and her family lived, and where this "treatment" took place, also had policies on the books preventing such things from happening without a court order; in fact, later investigations into "the Ashely Treatment," initiated by the Washington Protection & Advocacy System, the Disability Law Center (DLC), and the National Disability Rights Network, found that Children's Hospital and Regional Medical Center violated state law in allowing this treatment. It should be noted as well that the American College of Obstetrics and Gynecology had recently stated that hysterectomy shouldn't be adopted as a primary or initial treatment for navigating menstruation and puberty, nor should it be used for involuntary sterilization for disabled girls and women, and has continued to uphold this position. Their position paper states

> in disabled women with limited functional capability, indications for major surgical procedures remain the same as in other patients. In all cases, indications for surgery must meet standard criteria, and the benefits of the procedure must exceed known procedural risks.
>
> *(2016, p. e24)*

The case of Ashley X is one where policies should have protected the rights of this disabled child, and yet our society's ideological beliefs about disability and eugenics, informed by decades of ableism, still allowed for this young person to have much of her agency around her sexual and reproductive health taken from her.

Today, policy related to disability continues to be informed by ableist assumptions which strip disabled people of their autonomy (Belt & Dorfman, 2019). These policies often relegate disabled people into guardianships or necessitate forced abortions in order to prevent them from reproducing (Andrews et al., 2022; Belt & Dorfman, 2019). As in the case of Ashley X, there are also many challenges with the wants and needs of the partners and/or guardians of disabled people clashing with the rights of disabled people themselves. More disability-affirming policy, ideally led by actually disabled people and their chosen accomplices, is needed to chip away at the policies that have served to harm us, and instead, created policies that support the freedom, rights, and agency of disabled people in all facets of life, including our sexual and reproductive choices.

### *Sexuality Education Policy and Disabled People*

In 1994, the International Conference on Population and Development's Programme of Action, which is now commonly known as the "Cairo Agenda," made an explicit call to governments around the world to provide sexuality education to promote the well-being of adolescents (Haberland & Rogow, 2015). In response, there have been many strides made in policies affirming sexuality education and access to information on sexuality and reproductive health for young people and adults alike. However, despite these shifts, many countries have still not created clear policies around sexuality education, and even among those who have, disability often continues to be left out of this policy (Haberland & Rogow, 2015). The following are some examples how sexuality and sexuality education policies in different areas internationally meet, or do not meet, the needs of their disabled community members.

### United States

During the 20th century, private, nonprofit, and governmental bodies became more involved in public health screenings and recordkeeping, and sex education in public schools slowly became more widely practiced. During the 1940s, Stanford Blish, who is considered by some to be the "Father of Sex Education for Deaf Youth," published three comprehensive articles in the *Volta Review* encouraging residential schools for deaf youth to add sex education to their curriculum, one of the first calls for disability specific sexuality education (Fitz-Gerald & Fitz-Gerald, 1998). It took several decades for the spark of Blish's articles to catch on, but in the late 1950s, instructors from the Illinois and New Jersey Schools for the Deaf began developing sex education curricula. By 1975, about 66% of deaf residential schools had sex education programs, but most of them were short-term and/or crisis-oriented, and professionals in the field were often poorly trained (Fitz-Gerald & Fitz-Gerald, 1998).

In the 1970s, human rights movements across the nation began to alter American culture. Professional publications on human sexuality began emphasizing sex education for all, including those with disabilities, aging persons, unmarried persons, and bisexual and "homosexual" people (Fitz-Gerald & Fitz-Gerald, 1998). This decade saw an expansive cultural shift in favor of students' rights. In a huge win for minors, on June 9, 1977, the U.S. Supreme Court extended the right of privacy to minors to access information and services related to nonprescription contraceptives (*Carey v. Population Services Int'l*, 1977). Additionally, Title IX of the Education Amendments of 1972 student pregnancy could no longer be used as a legitimate means for dismissal from residential schools (The Pregnant Scholar, 2022).

Now, in the 2020s, there continues to be debates around the country on whether sex education should focus on abstinence-only or comprehensive, medically accurate information. There continues to be little included in sex education policies around content that explores sexual pleasure, healthy relationships, and communications skills in sexuality policies, and these policies which vary across states, counties, and even school districts (Sexuality Information and Education Council of the United States [SIECUS], 2022). Unfortunately, even less policy specifically engages disability and access to sexuality education, meaning disabled individuals, and especially disabled young people often have no access to formal sexuality education. In fact, the latest report by SIECUS, the largest sexuality education policy advocacy organization in the country, does not even mention disability while assessing sexuality education policies across states, indicating how little disability is included in these conversations (2022).

*Africa*

Like most continents, Africa contains a multitude of countries, each with their own histories and cultures. Given many of the increasing rates of unplanned pregnancies and STIs, including HIV/AIDS, in multiple countries within Africa, in 2003, the lack of sexual education was declared to be public health issue in multiple African countries, given the evidence that sex education can help support behaviors that reduce risk of transmission of these diseases (Ministry of Basic Education, Sport and Culture, & Ministry of Higher Education, Training and Employment Creation, 2003). Unfortunately, while this, and subsequent policies have been enacted to support sexuality education around the sexual and reproductive health and rights of all African people, little to none have been focused on sexuality and disability, and the existent support for disabled Africans has been based in more of a "pity" model, rather than empowerment model (Hanass-Hancock et al., 2021).

Access to and policies regarding sexuality education vary country to country. While several countries might be considered "behind" the times of Western sexuality education, due to the spread-out nature of these countries and populations, high rates of poverty, cultural differences/needs, and more (Eustace et al., 2015), we cannot measure efficacy of sexuality education solely through a white, Western lens. This is one of the challenges of Western-centric research, with most published sexuality/disability research and policy having emerged from North America, Europe, and Australia (Hanass-Hancock et al., 2021). A curriculum review conducted in Southern and Eastern African countries noted concerns about approximately 70% of the content within their sexuality education curricula, in that they did not feel it met extant standards (UNESCO & UNFPA, 2012). However, this review centered many sexuality assumptions grounded in cultures outside of Africa, and therefore did not consider the cultural factors that are key in sexuality education programs in these countries. In fact, many African societies still use their own traditional practices to meet sexuality education needs of their young people (Eustace et al., 2015).

### Ghana

One example is that many culture groups practice family- and/or clan-centered initiation ceremonies that include content around sex and sexuality, and support socializing individuals into a community, or through a coming-of-age process (Munthali & Zulu, 2007). Among the Krobo people in Ghana, their puberty initiation rites for girls and young women aim to socialize them into the traditionally expected roles of womanhood, marriage, and parenting (Eustace et al., 2015). Another recent study out of Ghana notes that "sexual ableism manifests in both policy and practice-based impediments to access. When sexuality education is provided, it is often inaccessible, devoid of disability-specific considerations, and communicates desexualizing messages for people with disabilities" (Shamrock & Ginn, 2021, p. 629). Clearly, more policies need to be grounded in the cultural beliefs of African communities while also meeting the sexual health needs of disabled individuals around consent, safety, health, and pleasure.

### Europe

Despite the fact that a large portion of the research on disability and sexuality has been conducted in Europe, the fact remains that there continue to be challenges, as discussed later. A recent scoping review of the literature on sexuality education for children and young people with disabilities in Europe noted many issues for this population (Michielsen & Brockschmidt, 2021). While all European countries have ratified the United Nations Convention on the Rights of Persons with Disabilities (CRPD) that states that disabled people have a right "to decide freely and responsibly on the number and spacing of their children and to have access to age-appropriate information, reproductive and family planning education" (United Nations, 2006), the implementation of this policy has not yet made its way into practice.

Many European countries have some of the most progressive, in-depth, and integrated sexuality education policies in the world (Haberland & Rogow, 2015), yet the needs of disabled individuals regarding sexuality education continue to go unmet. The scholars conducting this review found that there continues to be infantilization of disabled young people through sexuality education, including perpetuation of the belief that disabled people are not/will not be sexual or sexually active. Additionally, due to the high rates of victimization of this population, the sexuality education young disabled people receive tends to focus solely on protection and safety, rather than pleasure, communication, and positive sexual experience (Michielsen & Brockschmidt, 2021). They also found that those providing sexuality education to disabled young people had little training and even less institutional support regarding the guidelines and policies. There continues to be a lot of shame and taboo about providing such education, and also a lot of confusion around whose responsibility it is to provide disabled youths with sexuality education; teachers, parents, support workers, caregivers, or others. Finally, there were issues of both how to provide quality sexuality education when groups of disabled people had such varied support needs and ability to process information, as well as the fact that when this population has so many other needs, sexuality education appears to fall by the wayside. A lack of clear policies surrounding sexuality education and disabled individuals in the European region has clearly resulted in a huge gap for disabled young people in accessing comprehensive and affirming sexuality education (Michielsen & Brockschmidt, 2021).

## Mainland China

In mainland China, their government began to include discussions of birth control in middle school curriculum in the late 1950s, and through the 1960s, some basic sex education was considered to be a crucial part of physiology (Aresu, 2009). Similarly, in 1963, the Chinese government decided that promoting medically accurate sexual knowledge among their students was of importance, and until the 1970s, sex education was focused on as an important part of the healthy upwards growth of the population (Aresu, 2009). During the Cultural Revolution in the 1960s, topics containing sex and sexuality were banned from all pieces of the curriculum, and following this, China's One Child Policy emerged, which then brought back topics related to contraceptives, birth control, sex education, and even eugenics to the national political conversation (Leung et al., 2019). In 1992, the first school-based health education policy guidelines were shared, and these were operationalized by the Chinese Government into both primary and secondary schools in 1992 (Aresu, 2009). These guidelines were then revised in 2003 and 2009 by China's Ministry of Education; not surprisingly, in line with most countries discussed here, these guidelines do not name disability rights or the importance of disability-inclusive sexuality education.

## Hong Kong

In the 1960s, the Family Planning Association of Hong Kong began the process of promoting sexuality education across Hong Kong with a focus on contraceptive knowledge and family planning (Lee, 2005). Then in 1986, Hong Kong's Education Department put forth further detailed guidelines on sexuality education taking place in secondary schools including recommendations on topics, resources, and references, with this set of the guidelines being updated in 1997 (Leung et al., 2019). However, disability has not been named in any part of these guidelines, and they have not been revised since.

A shift occurred in 2000 when the Education Department opted to integrate sexuality education into the curriculum of *Moral and Civic Education*, and then later revised this further in 2008, with a goal of supporting schools to implement sexuality education more systematically, rather than piecemeal (Leung et al., 2019). However, a problem with this new version of the curriculum does not have a framework entailing what sexuality education means. Disability remains absent in all Hong Kong governmental policies surrounding sexuality education.

### Australia

The *National Disability Strategy* 2010–2020, based in Australia, offers a framework for disability rights within the country. While it did not mention sexual rights in relation to disability rights, it at least noted this as an area for change in the future, specifically the importance of accessible sexual healthcare (Bahner, 2019; Commonwealth of Australia, 2011). However, in 2021, *Australia's Disability Strategy 2021–2031* was released (Commonwealth of Australia, 2021) and while this contains explicit calls to include and affirm disabled people across all identities (including gender and sexuality), and quotes the National Women's Health Strategy 2018 regarding the need to "increase access to information, diagnosis, treatment and services for sexual and reproductive health; enhance and support health promotion and service delivery for preconception, perinatal and maternal health" of all women (2021, p. 27), there is nothing naming sexuality rights as part of disability rights.

Interestingly enough, the *Disability Inclusion Act [DIA]* of New South Wales explicitly names sexual rights to be among the core components of disability rights; "People with disability have the right to realize their physical, social, sexual, reproductive, emotional and intellectual capacities" (New South Wales Government, 2014, General Principles #4). This means that while there are no policies specifically mandating disabled people have access to sexuality education and support, in NSW, many disability support organizations include sexuality education and related supports as part of their services (Bahner, 2019). However, while this policy allows for providing sexuality education, providers (including personal attendants) are not allowed to support their disabled clients in things related to actual sexual activity needs, such as preparation and positioning, leaving a gap in meeting the sexuality access needs of disabled people, even with this more inclusive policy. This policy also makes for an interesting discussion, as sex work is legal in NSW, but the Australian National Disability Insurance Scheme, which covers a large portion of disabled individuals, will not cover sex therapy or sex workers (Bahner, 2019). For more information on the intersections of sex work and disability, including experiences of disabled sex workers, please see Chapter 13.

## Classroom Activity

Take a moment to reflect on your location (geographically, institutionally, socio-politically, etc.). Then take about 20–30 minutes to do some research and reflect on the following questions. Jot down some of your thoughts, either digitally or on paper, and then return to the larger group, synchronously or asynchronously, to share your reflections.

- What policies exist surrounding disability and disabled people at the national level? What about in your province, state, or territory? What about in your county, city, town, village? What about at your organization or institution?
- What policies exist surrounding sexuality and sex at the national level? What about in your province, state, or territory? What about in your county, city, town, and village? What about at your organization or institution?
- How do these policies interact, if at all, at the intersection of sexuality and disability? Is sexuality education mandated, and if so, how inclusive (or not) is it of disabled individuals?
- Do these policies, or others, serve to affirm the rights surrounding and access to sexuality and sexual/reproductive health of disabled people, or limit these rights and/or constrain disabled people?
- How might you, both personally and professionally, engage these policies? How will you advocate for more inclusive and affirming policies? How might your practice need to shift in order to work within these policies and/or meet the needs of disabled people outside of these policies?

## Exploring More Impact of Policy on Sexuality, Sexuality Education, and Disability

Despite all these shifts toward access over the past few decades, sexuality education for disabled people, especially disabled young people, continues to be particularly fraught. For more information about this, please see Chapter 4 for information on sexuality and neurodivergence, Chapter 5 for more on sexuality and intellectual/developmental disabilities, Chapter 11 on sexuality education for disabled people more generally, and Chapter 19 about sexual well-being among young disabled individuals. Though most human service professionals may think about their work being interpersonal only, or focused on the "micro" level, this chapter indicates the need for all individuals who work with disabled communities and in sexuality spaces to better understand how sexuality and disabilities policies have been and continue to be used to control of minds of disabled people worldwide. There is a need for more systemic and "macro"-level intervention by people who care, and the role of such advocacy falls on all of us.

## Resources

### Websites

ADA.gov
adatd.org
decolonizingfitness.com
disabilityjustice.org
dredf.org – Disability Rights Education & Defense Fund
them.us
transsexzine.com

### Podcasts

"ACCESS: A Podcast About Abortion"
"The Access Aisle" by Able South Carolina
"The Balut Kiki Project: Uniquely Pinoy. Unapologetically Queer"
"Day in Washington: The Disability Policy Podcast"
"Disability After Dark" with Andrew Gurza
"Disability Visibility" with Alice Wong
"Included: The Disability Equity Podcast" by Johns Hopkins University Disability Health Research Center
"Sex Ed with DB"
"Virgin Territory" by SHIP

### YouTube

"(Sex)abled: Disability Uncensored" short documentary (www.youtube.com/watch?v=qA02OShNQr8)
Sexuality and Disability: Forging Identity in a World that Leaves You Out (www.youtube.com/watch?v=akGYugciSVw)

### Other

Leah Lakshmi Piepzna-Samarasinha's blog (https://brownstargirl.org/blog/)
Sins Invalid – disability justice-based performance project
'Undressing Disability' Campaign by Enhance the UK

## References

American College of Obstetricians and Gynecologists. (2016). Committee opinion no. 668: Menstrual manipulation for adolescents with physical and developmental disabilities. *Obstetrics and Gynecology, 128*(2), e20–e25.

Andrews, E. E., Ayers, K. B., Stramondo, J. A., & Powell, R. M. (2022). Rethinking systemic ableism: A response to Zagouras, Ellick, and Aulisio. *Clinical Ethics*. https://doi.org/10.1177/14777509221094472

Aresu, A. (2009). Sex education in modern and contemporary China: Interrupted debates across the last century. *International Journal of Educational Development*, 29(5), 532–541.

Bagenstos, S. R. (2021). The new eugenics. *Syracuse Law Review, 71*, 751–765.

Bahner, J. (2019). Mapping the terrain of disability and sexuality: From policy to practice. *Ars Vivendi Journal, 11*, 27–47. https://eprints.whiterose.ac.uk/145194/

Belt, R., & Dorfman, D. (2019). Disability, law, and the humanities. In S. Stern (Ed.), *The Oxford handbook of law and humanities* (pp. 145–162). Oxford University Press.

Carey v. Population Services Int'l, 431 U.S. 678. (1977). https://supreme.justia.com/cases/federal/us/431/678/

Commonwealth of Australia. (2011). *National disability strategy 2010–2020*. www.dss.gov.au/sites/default/files/documents/05_2012/national_disability_strategy_2010_2020.pdf

Commonwealth of Australia. (2021). *Australia's disability strategy 2021–2031*. www.disabilitygateway.gov.au/sites/default/files/documents/2021-11/1786-australias-disability.pdf

Dack, M. (2020). The Alberta eugenics movement and the 1937 amendment to the sexual sterilization act. In F. W. Stahnisch & E. Kurbegović (Eds.), *Psychiatry and the legacies of eugenics: Historical studies of Alberta and beyond* (pp. 103–118). AU Press.

Eustace, R. W., Asiedu, G. B., & Mkanta, W. N. (2015). Sexuality education in Africa. In *Evidence-based approaches to sexuality education* (pp. 356–369). Routledge.

Fitz-Gerald, D. R., & Fitz-Gerald, M. (1998). A historical review of sexuality education and deafness: Where have we been this century? *Sexuality and Disability, 16*(4), 249–268.

Haberland, N., & Rogow, D. (2015). Sexuality education: Emerging trends in evidence and practice. *Journal of Adolescent Health, 56*(1), S15–S21.

Hamer, F. L. (1971). *Nobody's free until everybody's free* (pp. 10–11). National Women's Political Caucus. https://doi.org/10.14325/mississippi/9781604738223.003.0017

Hanass-Hancock, J., Mthethwa, N., Bean, T., de Lora, P., Mnguni, M. A., & Bakaroudis, M. (2021). *Sexual and reproductive health and rights and disability policy analysis*. www.samrc.ac.za/sites/default/files/files/2021-11-22/BtS%20Policy%20Report%20-%20Sexual%20and%20Reproductive%20Health%20Disability%20Policy%20Analysis.pdf

Jarrett, S., & Walmsley, J. (2019). Intellectual disability policy and practice in twentieth-century United Kingdom. In J. Walmsley & S. Jarrett (Eds.), *Intellectual disability in the twentieth century* (pp. 177–194). Policy Press.

Kijak, R. J. (2011). A desire for love: Considerations on sexuality and sexual education of people with intellectual disability in Poland. *Sexuality and Disability, 29*, 65–74.

Kirschner, K. L., Brashler, R., & Savage, T. A. (2007). Ashley X. *American Journal of Physical Medicine & Rehabilitation, 86*(12), 1023–1029. https://doi.org/10.1097/PHM.0b013e31815b77b2

Lee, M. Y. G. (2005). Strategies in school sexuality education in Hong Kong. *Journal of Youth Studies, 8*, 105–113.

Leung, H., Shek, D. T., Leung, E., & Shek, E. Y. (2019). Development of contextually-relevant sexuality education: Lessons from a comprehensive review of adolescent sexuality education across cultures. *International Journal of Environmental Research and Public Health*, 16(4), 621. https://doi.org/10.3390/ijerph16040621

McRuer, R., & Mollow, A. (2012). *Sex and disability*. Duke University Press.

Michielsen, K., & Brockschmidt, L. (2021). Barriers to sexuality education for children and young people with disabilities in the WHO European region: A scoping review. *Sex Education*, 21(6), 674–692.

Ministry of Basic Education, Sport and Culture, & Ministry of Higher Education, Training and Employment Creation. (2003). *National policy on HIV/AIDS for the education sector*. Solitaire Press. http://web.archive.org/web/20131108060907/www.youth-policy.com//Policies/NBANatl_Pol_HIV_AIDS_Education_Sector.pdf

Munthali, A., & Zulu, E. (2007). The timing and role of initiation rites in preparing young people for adolescence and responsible sexual and reproductive behaviour in Malawi. *African Journal of Reproductive Health*, 11(3), 150–167.

New South Wales Government. (2014). *Disability Inclusion Act*. https://legislation.nsw.gov.au/~/view/act/2014/41/full

Nourse, V. (2011). *Buck v. Bell*: A constitutional tragedy from a lost world. *Pepperdine Law Review*, 39, 101–118.

The Pregnant Scholar. (2022). *Title IX basics*. The Pregnant Scholar. https://thepregnantscholar.org/title-ix-basics/

Roll-Hansen, N. (2010). Eugenics and the science of genetics. In A. Bashford & P. Levine (Eds.), *Oxford handbook of the history of eugenics* (pp. 80–97). Oxford University Press.

Rosales, A. N. (2020). Excluding "undesirable" immigrants: Public charge as disability discrimination. *Michigan Law Review*, 119, 1613–1638.

Rose, S. F. (2017). *No right to be idle: The invention of disability, 1840s-1930s*. The University of North Carolina Press.

Rubin, G. (1984). Thinking sex: Notes for a radical theory of the politics of sexuality. In R. Parker & P. Aggleton (Eds.), *Culture, society and sexuality: A reader* (pp. 150–187). Routledge.

Sexuality Information and Education Council of the United States. (2022). *Sex Ed state law and policy chart SIECUS state profiles: July 2022*. https://siecus.org/wp-content/uploads/2021/09/2022-Sex-Ed-State-Law-and-Policy-Chart.pdf

Shamrock, O. W., & Ginn, H. G. (2021). Disability and sexuality: Toward a focus on sexuality education in Ghana. *Sexuality and Disability*, 39(4), 629–645.

Shuttleworth, R. (2007). Critical research and policy debates in disability and sexuality studies. *Sexuality Research & Social Policy*, 4(1), 1–14.

Soennichsen, J. (2011). *The Chinese Exclusion Act of 1882*. ABC-CLIO.

Stern, A. M. (2007). We cannot make a silk purse out a sow's ear: Eugenics in the Hoosier heartland. *Indiana Magazine of History*, 103, 3–38.

Thibault, A., Bonenfant, C., Djerroud, S., Guerry, L., Lebedeva, A., Ricardo, R., & Bruneau, V. A. R. (2017). *Spouse and partner immigration to Canada: History and current issues in Canadian immigration policy*. Social Sciences and Humanities Research Council of Canada. https://cridaq.uqam.ca/wp-content/uploads/2021/09/DAoust-Anne-Marie_No-40-Rapport-Canada_english_VF.pdf

UNESCO and UNFPA. (2012). *Sexuality education: A ten-country review of school curricula in East and Southern Africa*. UNESCO/UNFPA. https://esaro.unfpa.org/sites/default/files/pub-pdf/ESA%20Sexuality%20Education%20Curriculum%20Scan%20Report_FINAL.pdf

United Nations. (2006). *Convention on the rights of persons with disabilities (CRPD)*. United Nations. www.un.org/en/development/desa/population/migration/general assembly/docs/globalcompact/A_RES_61_106.pdf

Ward, R. D. (1907). The New Immigration Act. *The North American Review*, 185(619), 587–593.

Wilkinson, V. J., Theodore, K., & Raczka, R. (2015). "As normal as possible": Sexual identity development in people with intellectual disabilities transitioning to adulthood. *Sexuality and Disability*, 33(1), 93–105.

Wilson, R. A. (2021). Dehumanization, disability, and eugenics. In M. Kronfeldner (Ed.), *The Routledge handbook of dehumanization* (pp. 173–186). Taylor & Francis Group.

Wong, E. (2012). Not welcome: A critical analysis of ableism in Canadian immigration policy from 1869 to 2011. *Critical Disability Discourse*, 4. https://cdd.journals.yorku.ca/index.php/cdd/article/view/34877

# 2

# ABLE-BODIED WOMEN KILLING DISABLED BABIES

How Modern Narratives on Disability and Abortion Erase Disabled People From the Reproductive Justice Movement

*Elena Gormley*

### Disability, Pregnancy, and the Tyranny of Vulnerability

When Alaska Governor Sarah Palin was announced as John McCain's running mate, her public mentions of the challenges of raising a child with Down syndrome became part of public discourse and were even mentioned in her speech at the 2008 Republican National Convention (Steinhauer & Harmon, 2008). While Palin's convention comments were explicitly about having a disability advocate in the McCain Administration, Palin's celebration of Trig Palin was also implicitly announcing an adherence to a specific anti-abortion framework found in many conservative Christian communities: that disabled children are a divine gift and that abortion is a rejection of this divine gift from God (Meyer, 2015). In many Christian communities, "burdens" and challenges, including family tragedies and healthcare challenges, are seen as signs of divine attention that should be taken on without complaint; however, a body of personal insights from parents of disabled children and other contemporary research on disabilities within Christian communities demonstrate that Christian parents face spiritual and material challenges when raising disabled children and require support from their church communities. (Lipiec, 2019; Tautges, 2020; Whitt, 2016). Naturally, many contemporary disability activists reject the language of "burden" as being ableist and placing blame on disabled people for their disabilities (Rajkumar, 2022). The pandemic and public health rhetoric regarding COVID-19 spurred "My Disabled Life Is Worthy" – a grassroots online movement from disabled activists fearing that austerity policies would kill disabled people during the pandemic (Alperstein, 2022; Barbarin, 2022; Pagano, 2022). The standardization of testing amniotic fluid during pregnancy to detect fetal abnormalities was already fraught prior to the overturning of *Roe v. Wade*, with some disabled people criticizing the practice out of concerns that doing so is equivalent to eugenics, particularly within disability community social media networks (Doki Doki Waku Waku, 2020; genrericdubstep.tumblr.com, 2018; withasmoothroundstone.tumblr.com, 2014). The mainstreaming of the argument that people seeking abortions due so for eugenic purposes erases the fact that disabled people get pregnant and frequently seek out abortion care, and that ableism in reproductive healthcare creates barriers to accessing adequate pregnancy care, maternity care, and abortion care.

In her book *Down Girl: The Logic of Misogyny* and on her social media, Kate Manne uses the terms "caremongering" and "tyranny of vulnerability" (2018) to describe a specific set of expectations that women face in how they perform everyday tasks or exert autonomy, particulary bodily autonomy (2017). Anyone politicized as a woman under the patriarchy face the *tyranny of vulnerability* when they do anything (read: literally everything) that could possibly cause harm to another vulnerable person or group. In the context of pregnancy, assuming that every pregnant person will want to have an abortion if their child would be disabled, and further assuming that pregnant people who do have abortions due to reported indications of disability in fetal tests do so out of cruelty or eugenics, is a clear demonstration of Manne's framework. It is also important to note, particularly in the context of pregnancy and abortion, that this misogynistic "tyranny of vulnerability" is also weaponized against transgender pregnant people. One of the most harmful aspects of patriarchy is the default assumption that all pregnant people are women and mothers to be.

The argument that some people must be systematically denied their fundamental human rights out of the need to "protect the vulnerable" has already garnered significant legislative and court victories by American Christofascists. While Christofascism was originally coined in the 1970s, Christian fascist movements have sought to gain power in South America and the United States more recently (Bowers, 2021). In order to effectively counter the harmful impacts of the criminalization of abortion, the reproductive justice and disability justice movements must center the experiences of disabled pregnant people and acknowledge that "abortion on demand without apology" is not simply an empty slogan, but the *bare minimum demand* because pregnancy and childbirth can cause both temporary and permanent disabilities.

## Eugenics, Pregnancy, Disability, and Junk Science: How We Got Into This Mess to Begin With

The eugenics movement is traced back to the late 19th century, and the work of Sir Francis Galton, a cousin of Charles Darwin who saw the possibility of using Darwin's theory of natural selection to perfect society by "breeding out" undesirable people and groups (National Human Genome Research Institute, n.d.). British and American advocates for eugenics saw the opportunity to use this pseudoscience to create a utopian society by eliminating any number of people, at a time when the Industrial Revolution and rampant capitalist exploitation were causing significant and visible public health crises (Pernick, 1997). While the work of noted social reformers, including Margaret Sanger (Gandy, 2015), Mary Richmond (Kennedy, 2008), and Jane Addams (Chapman & Withers, 2018; Kennedy, 2008), frequently included comments that promoted the legalization and expansion of birth control as a method to reduce the number of physically and cognitively disabled people (Hall, 2022), the eugenics movement also sought to control and eliminate people using false science that links religious and political beliefs, ethnicity, and race to heritable genetics (Kennedy, 2008). Sanger's and Addams' comments were extremely foul, are roundly criticized today by many social justice advocates, and were also criticized in their time. One important thing to note is that Margaret Sanger's and Jane Addams' political views on eugenics were extremely mainstream; if your great-great-great grandparents were middle-class White Anglo Saxon Protestants in the late 19th century, they likely had the exact same (or even more harmful) beliefs regarding eugenics. The eugenics movement cannot be discussed without also addressing the parallel development of racialized antisemitism in Europe, which created a racial categorization for Jewish people in stark contrast to Jewish law and communal practice (Goldstein, 2020; Jews for Racial and Economic Justice, 2017; MacMaster, 2007), which became the political and philosophical framework for the Final Solution and the Shoah/Holocaust (Goldstein, 2020).

Contemporary leaders in reproductive justice and social work have criticized some leaders affiliated with the eugenics movement or sought to contextualize some figures statements that supported eugenics (Gandy, 2015). However, the eugenics movement's contemporary impact can be seen in current policies that seek to eliminate people's right to self-determination in having and raising children, the unfathomable number of people seeking relief and reparations for having been sterilized by the state, and poor public health messaging regarding the role of genetic testing to detect certain health conditions and disorders.

Some health conditions and hereditary cancers can now be screened by genetic testing, which allows prospective parents to then assess healthcare options with full informed consent. One of the most well-known examples is the now widespread practice of screening for diseases and hereditary cancers known to disproportionately impact Ashkenazi and Sephardic Jewish communities (Sarnoff Center for Jewish Genetics, n.d.). This example demonstrates why a default assumption that any prospective parent wanting to screen for possible health conditions with all available tools is doing so out of a desire to perform eugenics is, to put it quite mildly, *profoundly* inappropriate. However, even with advances in genetic testing, the possibility of using genetic testing to outright eliminate common health conditions is dramatically oversold. For example, a widespread criticism of Autism Speaks involves the organization's work on genetic testing, and repeated statements by the co-founder expressing a wish for autism to be "cured" and using catastrophizing language to describe autism (Shire, 2017). Currently, genetic testing can possibly indicate the risk factors for other conditions or identify possible treatments. The term "treatment" isn't clearly defined in many of these contexts, so it is unclear if the goal is interventions that can alleviate some aspects of being autistic in a world hostile to neurodiversity, or if "treatment" is the pursuit of "making autistic people as neurotypical as possible" – which can naturally exacerbate distrust of mainstream autism advocacy organizations. Additionally, *there is no current genetic test for autism, let alone a prenatal test for autism* (Wright, 2019; Zaraska, 2019), because autism is also impacted by environmental factors alongside some genetic markers, such a test faces significant barriers to being developed, approved, and implemented (Zaraska, 2019).

However, an unfortunate combination of poor messaging from Autism Speaks about genetic testing for autism, the limitations regarding prenatal testing, a pattern of inappropriate statements from leadership and a failure to archive deleted statements, and other criticisms have fostered considerable distrust and an environment where misinformation can flourish – especially online. Autism Speaks emphasized the importance of early detection and identifying the possible causes of autism despite the fact that it is not possible to use genetic testing in this way (Autism Speaks, n.d.a). Making matters worse is a history of leaders within the organization making inappropriate comments (Shire, 2017), and the organization's continued promotion of Applied Behavioral Analysis (ABA) therapy (Autism Speaks, n.d.b) while autistic adults have grown more critical of ABA therapy (Millman, 2019). Additionally, Autism Speaks was roundly criticized for a partnership with Sesame Street to market an "Early Detection" program (Bever, 2019). Add all of this together, plus a decades-long game of "Internet Telephone," where this tangled history gets repeated and flourished on forums and social media, and you get an environment where many people are convinced that prenatal testing for autism is imminent and that able-bodied and neurotypical parents would selectively abort autistic children. In fact, in researching the historic context for these claims, I could only find fact sheets that made this specific accusation with no citation, and op-eds corrected due to a lack of evidence that Autism Speaks or other organizations have made any explicit call to implement prenatal screening for autism. To be clear – what Autism Speaks has done is plenty terrible – particularly in the elevation of ABA therapy to the public and to other mental health practitioners. We do not need to cause greater stress and anxiety to people already facing mistreatment by exaggerating or falsifying information. When we create an archetype and scapegoat of able-bodied pregnant people aborting disabled children due to their ableist and eugenicist beliefs, we conveniently allow large and powerful organizations off the hook for their pattern of poor policies that stigmatize and harm disabled people.

The concern over prenatal testing for autism and selective abortion is also rooted in the established practice of screening for Down syndrome during pregnancy. The fact that a sensitive prenatal test for Down syndrome exists and has an influence on the decision-making of pregnant people – pregnant women in particular – is a source of ire for some political conservatives (Hentoff, 2011), who view pregnant people having bodily autonomy in ways they disagree with as comparable to genocide (Will, 2018). George F. Will and other conservative commentators view having as much medical information as possible during pregnancy as an existential danger to a vulnerable group of disabled people (Will, 2018), at the hands of (presumably) cruel and selfish able-bodied women. A great deal of American right-wing rhetoric about Down syndrome and selective abortion is not found in countries with higher rates of abortion and prenatal testing for Down syndrome. Rather, the focus is on educating parents about all their options and resources for supporting children with Down syndrome (Zhang, 2020). Breakthroughs in medical treatment and services mean that people with Down syndrome live longer; however, the specific symptoms of Down syndrome vary widely and include serious cardiac and respiratory health conditions (Bull et al., 2022), and the impact of Down syndrome cannot be detected in a prenatal screening. During the same timeframe that antichoice activists condemned Scandinavian countries for enacting genocide and eugenics due to widespread access of healthcare, and policies that enshrine basic bodily autonomy and human rights, these countries have engaged in forcing children of immigrants in "ghettoes" to adhere to Danish Christian practices or risk losing public assistance (Barry & Sorensen, 2018) and placing elderly Swedes in congregate facilities on end-of-life care during the pandemic (Brusselaers et al., 2022), both of which have not garnered a similar degree of public outrage among right-wing political groups.

### Whose Pregnancy Is It Anyway?

Debates around the right to have an abortion due to prenatal testing that indicates physical, cognitive, or neurological disability hinges on a series of profoundly false assumptions: that only women get pregnant and give birth, that only able-bodied women get pregnant and give birth, and that disabled children do not grow up and become disabled adults who have sex and need access to the full spectrum of reproductive healthcare. In popular news coverage around Down syndrome, even nuanced depictions emphasize people with Down syndrome in their relationship as the children of able-bodied and neurotypical adults, and not adults who will one day have families of their own (Zhang, 2020). In fact, some researchers have historically relied on completely fictitious case scenarios regarding parents seeking sterilization of disabled adults to discuss questions of medical ethics (Pham & Lerner, 2001) instead of basing research on real-life cases of disabled adults being sterilized by the state due to disability in the decades after the *Buck v. Bell* Supreme Court ruling (Harris, 2020; Morain, 1986; Stern, 2011; Villarosa, 2022), or the real-life disabled couples who face restrictions from family members on building a home, getting married, and having children (Pullen, 2016).

The problematic erasure of disabled people from reproductive justice activism has been elevated by disabled activists themselves, and contemporary online disability activism seeks to challenge the infantilization of disabled people and openly address disability, sexuality, and sexual health (Stevenson et al., 2011; Enujioke et al., 2021; Hole et al., 2022). *Any* discussion of the supposed tensions between disability rights and reproductive justice must start with naming the fact that disabled people deserve full bodily autonomy and the right to have abortions and have and raise children, and both have children and abortions without facing oppression by the state.

We must also avoid the pitfall of considering the state oppression of disabled people for having children as some relic of the past. In 2018 in Florida, Alysha Princess Cesaire had her newborn child seized by the state after being reported by a hospital worker for her disability. In the ensuing investigation and lawsuit, emails from Kim Gorsuch, a social worker employed by the Broward, included criticisms of Cesaire's ability to parent her child, and admonished her family for creating a plan to assist Cesaire in caring for her son instead of "get[ting] (sic) her on some kind of birth control???" (Miller, 2022). Ms. Gorsuch's comments are shocking in their callousness and ignorance of social work's stated values and ethics, and even more shocking that they were emailed from a government employee account in a state known for its robust sunshine laws. If experienced social workers are making such bold assertions that disabled people must have their reproductive decisions governed by family members in our current environment, social work is not as politically progressive as we would like to assume. A recent body of literature and advocacy within the social work profession, produced by both researchers and directly impacted parents, demonstrates that ableism against disabled parents is a serious issue in the contemporary family policing (better known as the "child welfare") system requiring significant policy changes to better protect the free association rights of disabled parents to raise their children (Albert & Powell, 2020; Frunel & Lorr, 2022; Powell, 2022; Shriver Center on Poverty Law, 2020; Jmac For Families, n.d.; Staver, 2022).

The continued state oppression of disabled parents for caring for and raising their children is happening at the same time that states are criminalizing people for having abortions and this two-pronged attack is not by accident. For all of the claims that conservatives want disabled people to be raised in loving and supportive homes instead of being aborted, in reality, the right wing does not want disabled people to exist, let alone have children or exercise their First Amendment rights to free association. In fact, many of the Evangelical Christians who were encouraged to adopt children in a wave of Christian adoption advocacy are now reporting a lack of support from their church communities, and outright shunning of children with complex behavioral health needs, resulting the need for creation support networks for Evangelical Christian women to receive support and resources, including respite care (Duin, 2022).

### Who Does the Work of Raising Children in a Society With No Safety Net?

Anne Helen Peterson's 2020 interview with sociologist Jessica Calacro ran in her newsletter under the provocative title *Other Countries Have Social Safety Nets: The U.S. Has Women* (Petersen, 2020). The conversation between Peterson and Calacro centered on how American women shouldered unequal parenting burdens during the COVID-19 pandemic due to a lack of supports and services for working parents who could no longer send their children to school in-person. While childcare remains "a fucking mess" in the United States (Kiesling, 2022), the severity of the pandemic also stretched women thin in countries with a less-precarious social safety net (Linden et al., 2022; Jang & Kwon, 2023; Kobayashi et al., 2021; Petersson & Hansson, 2021). This unequal parenting burden existed long before the pandemic; the pandemic simply amplified the unfair division of parenting labor as the superficial supports of an inadequate education system disappeared for many. Perhaps an appropriate addendum to Jessica Calacro's interview would be "Other Countries Have Women and a Social Safety Net. The U.S. Only Has Women." Ensuring that children are cared for around the clock is intensive and exhausting. Disabled people have criticized assumptions that caring for disabled children is burdensome, most notably pushing back on the narrative that nondisabled parents should mourn all of their lost opportunities due to having to care for disabled children (Sinclair, 1993) and have created the National Disability Day of Mourning in part to demonstrate the deadly cost of harmful narratives about parenting disabled children (Disability Day of Mourning, 2023).

It is important to highlight the intensive and unequal parenting labor in a society that does not adequately provide supports and services to disabled people without blaming disabled people for such inequities. The work to ensure that schools understand that the requirements of the IDEA act are federal law, and not suggestions, largely falls on parents advocating on behalf of their children, and that other countries report different approaches to support for disabled children, their families, and prenatal testing (Raz, 2004) while also recognizing that parenting stress is an experience that transcends borders (Lee & Chiang, 2017; You et al., 2018; Mendoza et al., 2015). Writer Nicole Chung has written extensively on the difficult balance of preparing for IEP meetings and advocating for her autistic daughter without coming off as too adversarial for a national audience, and yet even has the benefit of a national audience, a flexible schedule, and a spouse who partners in advocacy – many things that many other parents do not have (Brooks & Chung, 2017; Chung, 2017, 2020). During the 2021–2022 school year, Chicago Public Schools could not meet its legal obligations to transport disabled students well into February 2022, and the district has been under a Corrective Action plan due to a systematic denial of legally required supports and services during the 2016–2017 and 2017–2018 school years (Chicago Public Schools, n.d., Pena, 2022). Having to relentlessly advocate that a disabled child receives legally required supports and services in a system where it is by design extremely difficult if not impossible to receive these services is difficult, and even more difficult for disabled parents advocating on behalf of their disabled children (Crawford, 2003).

## A World Free of Ableism Will Require Free Abortion on Demand and Without Apology

In a better world without ableism, where disabled people have easy access to universal supports and services and accommodations, there will still be a need for universal abortion access and care. Similarly, a world without ableism would be a world without the grinding demands for productivity under capitalism, where all people would be guaranteed all the resources needed to ensure a dignified life, and where abortion would need to exist as a universal public good. One popular argument regarding abortion and healthcare resources hinges on the serious issue that abortions occur due to a lack of resources, and that the high costs associated with childbirth and parenting can dissuade people from "choosing life," in the hopes of highlighting the hypocrisy of anti-abortion activists who are not interested in ensuring that these resources freely exist (Bruenig, 2022). This is a false argument. People get abortions because they do not want to be pregnant and give birth, and "I do not want to be pregnant right now" is a completely valid reason to not endure pregnancy and birth, regardless of the person's access to resources. Limiting abortion access by demanding people provides a "good" reason, and not "bad" reasons for wanting abortions hinges on the same frameworks that effectively push disabled people out of needed supports and resources. Neither is socially just.

## Pregnancy and Childbirth Are Disabling

Pregnancy, even at the best of times, often involves losing mobility, temporary and permanent joint pain, temporary and permanent urinary and fecal incontinence, temporary and permanent nausea and acid reflux, temporary and permanent changes in sensory processing, gestational diabetes, and temporary and permanent changes in thought, mood, and behavior. We inherently recognize that pregnancy dramatically changes physical ability in the courtesy signs that reserve parking spaces closer to store entrances for pregnant people, and even the ability to receive temporary permits to park in disabled parking lot spaces.

Sarah Palin has not been in the public eye to the same degree as when she was Sen. McCain's running mate, and Trig Palin is now an adolescent. She received public attention and criticism after her son was featured in a meme due to rightwing backlash at Brett Kavanaugh during his Supreme Court confirmation hearings, including from disability advocates and parents of disabled children (Perry, 2019). While a great deal of Ms. Palin's public persona is wrapped in being the mother of a disabled child, Ms. Palin has herself experienced pregnancy and childbirth five times, and presumably some of the temporary and permanently disabling conditions associated with pregnancy and childbirth. Ergo, we cannot think about her experience only as the mother of a disabled child but also as someone who has lived experience with at least temporary disability and impairment. Notably, Ms. Palin's 26-year career in politics and political commentary ended when her friend and former legislative colleague Mary Peltola beat Palin and Nick Begich in the special and general election for Alaska's lone seat in Congress (Ruskin, 2022). Peltola campaigned as the "Pro-Fish, Pro-Family, Pro-Choice, Pro-Worker, Pro-Alaska" candidate (Peltola, 2022).

Right now, in our post-Roe world, groups of medical ethicists now must determine when pregnancy complications are so life-threatening to the point where doctors can perform abortions without fearing criminalization by the state – thus endangering the lives of pregnant people (Oxner & Mendez, 2022; Klibanoff, 2022; Keller, 2022). The Internet "blew up" after a ten-year-old child had to travel from Ohio to Indiana in order to receive an abortion (Rudavsky & Fradette, 2022; McCammon & Sullivan, 2022). Amidst the foul clamor about "fact checking," the veracity of a child being sexually abused, impregnated, and given healthcare (Schladen, 2022; Cook et al., 2022), there was little attention given to the fact that a ten-year-old victim of child sexual abuse was enduring significant psychological trauma and would have risked severe disability and potentially death, if forced to give birth. Disability justice movements have long recognized that the coalition of people impacted by disability is very broad, because any number of life events, including the natural aging process, will cause disability. Much of Hellen Keller's socialist politics was rooted in the recognition that exploited factory workers were regularly blinded and deafened by unsafe machinery and a lack of workplace safety policies (Rosenthal, 2023, n.d.). How would our discourse around abortion and disability change when we recognize pregnant people and people who have given birth as part of the disability community? Would recognizing that "disability moms" and "curebies," an in-group term for a subset of neurotypical parents devoted to "curing" their children of autism (Harmon, 2004), have also experienced disability create points of solidarity and understanding, or are these bridges too far to cross?

**Best Practices**

Social service workers, educators, therapists, community organizers, and advocates working at the intersections of abortion rights, reproductive justice, and disability justice should be aware of all of these nuances when addressing abortion, reproductive healthcare, pregnancy, birth, and parenting, with clients, patients, and all relevant stakeholders. Best practices for working in reproductive and disability justice include:

1. **Knowledge of the local legal and political landscape.** As many states are actively criminalizing people seeking abortions, and there is already a long history of involving the family policing (a.k.a. child welfare system) system against disabled parents and caregivers, practitioners should be knowledgeable of all local and state laws, and prepare safeguards to prevent the criminalization of clients or community members for seeking abortions.
2. **Knowledge of local resources:** Know the location, hours, and intake information for the nearest abortion provider and abortion fund. Reach out to organizations directly or other workers/clients to get feedback on how they assist and advocate for disabled clients.
3. **Advocate for Accessibility:** If you notice or receive information about access barriers to abortions, prenatal care, and postnatal care, advocate for the removal of these access barriers.
4. **Avoiding assumptions and judgments:** People's reasons for getting an abortion are very personal – don't make assumptions about these reasons. Likewise, someone's reason for getting an abortion might conflict with your individual beliefs regarding abortion. Remember our primary ethical obligation to support the right to self-determination.
5. **Design for Accessibility:** When developing education materials, advocacy materials, fact sheets, resource lists, or other materials regarding abortion and reproductive justice, use key components of universal design and accessibility, including plain language, alt text, and appropriate language, photos, and graphic illustrations. Recruit and appropriately compensate any consultants and editors to review and make accessibility recommendations on education and advocacy materials.

6. **Use accurate information:** Ensure that information you share about abortion, and any connected disability concerns, such as information about prenatal testing, and resources for disabled parents and caregivers is accurate and based on reliable resources. As mentioned in the chapter, there is a long history of sharing inaccurate information, or rightwing groups seeking to control specific narratives by amplifying their resources. Check dates, check for dead links, and check organizations and their funders.

**Case Study/Activity**

Use the following guiding questions for class discussion, whether as a class or in small groups to explore these topics further:

1. What assumptions about disability and abortion are prevalent in your program, at your internship sites, or among other systems you interact with (such as family, community groups, and religious groups)? As a social worker, how would you work to address assumptions about disability and abortion that are harmful?
2. What historical or current practices within social work align with reproductive justice and disability justice? What historical or current practices within social work conflict with reproductive justice and disability justice frameworks and movements?
3. Examine the case of Alysha Princess Cesaire and the inappropriate comments made about Cesaire's parenting ability by Florida social worker Kim Gorsuch.

   As a social worker, how would you address a situation where another social worker was emailing inappropriate comments about a disabled person's parenting ability and choices. What risks would you need to consider? What resources would you need to be supported in confronting institutional ableism in your workplace?

**Conclusion**

Countering the connected extremist movements that seek to force people to be pregnant against their will, and seek to eliminate the rights of disabled people to have children, will require a recognition that abortion rights and disability rights are not in opposition with each other. We must recognize that the threat to disabled people lies not with a cartoonish strawman of an able-bodied woman aborting a disabled baby, but in the many rightwing reactionaries, many of them people who have experienced the disabling conditions of pregnancy and childbirth, who want the state to dictate the terms of disabled people's reproductive rights. Social workers and healthcare professionals *must* challenge this rhetoric wherever it manifests and place themselves between clients seeking life-saving healthcare and any state entity that would deny that care, regardless of the professional legal risks. Social work has often prioritized temporary discomfort over justice liberation, and it is up to us to re-frame the profession's priorities.

**Acknowledgments:** I want to acknowledge my mother Patricia Johns, who did not tell anyone besides my father and her dentist that she was pregnant until she had her results from prenatal pregnancy screening.

## Resources

*While many of these resources aren't explicitly about the combined intersection of disability justice and reproductive justice, they are important resources for any social worker advocating for disabled people's right to self-determination in creating the families they choose, and provide frameworks on how to challenge false binaries between ability and disability, and clients and providers.*

**Pregnancy Justice** (Formerly National Advocates of Pregnant Women): Legal advocacy group that defends people criminalized for their pregnancy outcomes. Pregnancyjusticeus.org

**Alliance for Community Services:** Chicago-based group of service providers and service recipients. www.allianceforcommunityservices.org/

**Movement for Family Power:** National Organization dedicated to supporting families rights to raise their children without interference from the family policing system. Movementforfamilypower.org

**Jmac For Families:** New York City-based organization centered in abolishing the family policing system, with ample resources on educating families about their rights during a child welfare investigation, and resources for mandated reporters on centering a "mandated supporting" model in their work. https://jmacforfamilies.org/

**Moms United Against Violence and Incarceration:** Chicago-based grassroots organization centered in supporting incarcerated criminalized survivors and advocating for their release from Illinois jails and prisons. www.facebook.com/MomsUnitedChi/

**Love + Protect:** Originally the Chicago Committee to Free Melissa Alexander. Love and Protect provides support to incarcerated survivors and advocates for their release. https://loveprotect.org/

**If/When/How:** National legal advocacy group that provides legal support and representation for people criminalized for having self-managed abortions. www.ifwhenhow.org/

**Ascend Justice:** Chicago- and Illinois-based organization providing holistic legal representation for domestic violence survivors, including family defense support for survivors involved in the Illinois family policing system. www.ascendjustice.org/

**Illinois Prison Project**: Illinois-based legal advocacy organization that assists with Illinois clemency petitions, including programs devoted to clemency for criminalized survivors and incarcerated people with chronic health conditions. Illinoisprisonproject.org

**Access Living**: Illinois-based disability justice policy organization. www.accessliving.org/

**Collaborative for Community Wellness**: Chicago-based collaborative of current and former CDPH mental health clinic patients, service providers, and advocates fighting to re-build public mental healthcare infrastructure in Chicago without police. www.collaborativeforcommunitywellness.org/

**upEND Movement**: National organization based out of the University of Houston Graduate College of Social Work, rooted in abolishing the family policing system. https://upendmovement.org/

**Policing by Another Name: Mandated Reporting as State Surveillance**: Shriver Center on Poverty Law webinar about issues with mandated reporting and the family policing system. Features the chapter author alongside advocates from across the United States. www.youtube.com/watch?v=EetnqS0csKM

**Your Family or Its Health**: Intersections Between the Foster Care and Healthcare Systems: Shriver Center on Poverty Law webinar about the challenges that families face attempting to receive healthcare without being ensnared in the family policing system: www.youtube.com/watch?v=EetnqS0csKM

## References

Albert, S. M., & Powell, R. M. (2020). Supporting disabled parents and their families: Perspectives and recommendations from parents, attorneys, and child welfare professionals. *Journal of Public Child Welfare*, 15(5), 529–529. https://doi.org/10.1080/15548732.2020.1751771

Alperstein, O. (2022, January 19). *My disabled life is worthy*. Institute for Policy Studies. Retrieved December 2, 2022, from https://ips-dc.org/my-disabled-life-is-worthy/

As small as a world and as large as alone. (2014). *Different view on (at least) one point . . .* [Tumblr post]. https://withasmoothroundstone.tumblr.com/post/92899607585/what-do-you-think-about-the-assertion-that-abortion

Autism Speaks. (n.d.a). Retrieved July 31, 2022, from www.autismspeaks.org/expert-opinion/should-i-or-we-have-genetic-testing-autism

Autism Speaks. (n.d.b). Retrieved May 14, 2022, from https://www.autismspeaks.org/applied-behavior-analysis

Barbarin, I. (2022, March 16). *The pandemic tried to break me, but I know my black disabled life is worthy*. Cosmopolitan. Retrieved December 2, 2022, from www.cosmopolitan.com/entertainment/a39355245/imani-barbarin-black-disabled-activist-self-love/

Barry, E., & Sorensen, M. S. (2018, July 2). In Denmark, harsh new laws for immigrant "ghettos". *The New York Times*. Retrieved July 31, 2022, from www.nytimes.com/2018/07/01/world/europe/denmark-immigrant-ghettos.html

Bever, L. (2019, September 19). How a 'Sesame Street" Muppet became embroiled in a controversy about autism. *The Washington Post*. Retrieved May 14, 2023, from https://www.washingtonpost.com/health/2019/09/19/how-sesame-street-muppet-became-embroiled-controversy-over-autism/

Bowers, P. (2021, January 21). *A field guide to Christofascism – by Paul Bowers*. Retrieved December 1, 2022, from https://brutalsouth.substack.com/p/a-field-guide-to-christofascism

Brooks, E., & Chung, C. (2017, March 22). A conversation about disability rights in education. *Catapult*. Retrieved May 14, 2023, from https://catapult.co/stories/a-conversation-about-disability-rights-in-education

Bruenig, E. (2022, November 10). Make birth free. *The Atlantic*. Retrieved December 2, 2022, from www.theatlantic.com/ideas/archive/2022/07/post-roe-pro-life-parental-support/661473/

Brusselaers, N., Steadson, D., Bjorklund, K., Breland, S., Stilhoff Sörensen, J., Ewing, A., Bergmann, S. & Steineck, G. (2022). Evaluation of science advice during the COVID-19 pandemic in Sweden. *Humanities and Social Sciences Communications*, 9, 91. https://doi.org/10.1057/s41599-022-01097-5

Bull, M. J., Trotter, T., Santoro, S. L., Christensen, C., Grout, R. W., & Council on Genetics. (2022, May). Health supervision for children and adolescents with down syndrome. *Pediatrics*, 149(5), e2022057010. doi:10.1542/peds.2022-057010

Chapman, C., & Withers, A. J. (2018). *A violent history of benevolence: Interlocking oppression in the moral economies of social working*. University of Toronto Press.

Chicago Public Schools. (n.d.). *ISBE student specific corrective action*. Retrieved July 31, 2022, from www.cps.edu/services-and-supports/special-education/ISBE-student-specific-corrective-action/

Chung, N. (2017, March 9). The worry I no longer remember living without. *Hazlitt*. Retrieved March 14, 2023 from https://hazlitt.net/feature/worry-i-no-longer-remember-living-without

Chung, N. (2020, September 15). My child has a disability. What will her education be like this year? *The New York Times*. Retrieved May 14, 2023, from https://www.nytimes.com/interactive/2020/09/10/magazine/special-education-covid.html

Cook, T., Bruner, B., Trombly, M., & Eom, D. (2022, July 26). Ohio man charged in rape of 10-year-old that led to Indiana abortion. *The Indianapolis Star*. Retrieved December 2, 2022, from www.indystar.com/story/news/2022/07/13/ohio-man-charged-rape-10-year-old-led-indiana-abortion/10048529002/

Crawford, N. (2003). Parenting with a disability: The last frontier. *The American Psychological Association Monitor on Psychology*. Retrieved May 14, 2023, from https://www.apa.org/monitor/may03/challenges

Disability Day of Mourning. (2023). *Memorial lists 2023*. Retrieved May 14, 2023 from https://disability-memorial.org/memorial-lists-2023

Doki Doki Waku Waku. (2020, February 26). *People will accept eugenics so long as it proves them valid in some way . . .* [Tumblr post]. https://trans-mom.tumblr.com/post/611067356630908928/people-will-accept-eugenics-so-long-as-it-proves

Duin, J. (2022, June 13). Evangelical adoptions: Churches are AWOL in helping parents of special needs kids. *Newsweek*. Retrieved July 31, 2022, from www.newsweek.com/2022/06/24/evangelical-christian-adoption-movement-hit-tsunami-mentally-ill-children-1712533.html

Enujioke, S. C., Leland, B., Munson, E., & Ott, M. A. (2021). Sexuality among adolescents with intellectual disability: Balancing Autonomy and protection. *Pediatrics*, 148(5). https://doi.org/10.1542/peds.2021-050220

Frunel, L., & Lorr, S. (2022). Lived experience and disability justice in the Family Regulation System. *Columbia Journal of Race and Law, 12*(1). https://doi.org/10.52214/cjrl.v12i1.9924

Gandy, I. (2015, August 20). How false narratives of Margaret Sanger are being used to shame black women. *Rewire News Group*. Retrieved May 14, 2023, from https://rewirenewsgroup.com/2015/08/20/false-narratives-margaret-sanger-used-shame-black-women/

genericdubstep.tumblr.com. (2018, August 16). *Getting an abortion because you don't want children? Cool getting an abortion because you don't want a disabled child? That's eugenics and you're a fucking Nazi* [Tumblr post]. https://at.tumblr.com/genericdubstep/getting-an-abortion-because-you-dont-want/4yktx8zkr2ko Genetic testing for autism.

Goldstein, W. S. (2020). The racialization of the Jewish question. *Religion and Theology, 27*(3–4), 179–201. doi: https://doi.org/10.1163/15743012-02703001

Hall, R. E. (2022). Social work's feminist façade: Descriptive manifestations of white supremacy. *The British Journal of Social Work, 52*(2), 1055–1069. https://doi.org/10.1093/bjsw/bcab093

Harmon, A. (2004, December 20). How about not 'curing' us, some autistics are pleading. *The New York Times*. Retrieved December 1, 2022, from www.nytimes.com/2004/12/20/health/how-about-not-curing-us-some-autistics-are-pleading.html

Harris, J. (2020, October 14). *Why Buck v. Bell Still Matters. Harvard Law Bill of Health*. Retrieved May 14, 2023, from https://blog.petrieflom.law.harvard.edu/2020/10/14/why-buck-v-bell-still-matters/

Hentoff, N. (2011, November 29). *Down syndrome genocide*. The Cato Institute. https://www.cato.org/commentary/down-syndrome-genocide#

Hole, R., Schnellert, L., & Cantle, G. (2022). Sex: What is the big deal? Exploring individuals' with intellectual disabilities experiences with sex education. *Qualitative Health Research, 32*(3), 453–464. https://doi.org/10.1177/10497323211057090

Jang, H., & Kwon, S.-H. (2023). Understanding women's empowerment in post-Covid Korea: A historical analysis. *The Economic and Labour Relations Review, 33*(2), 351–376. https://doi.org/10.1177/10353046221078880

Jews for Racial and Economic Justice. (2017). *Understanding antisemitism: An offering to our movements*. Jews for Racial and Economic Justice. Retrieved May 14, 2023, from https://www.jfrej.org/news/2017/11/understanding-antisemitism-an-offering-to-our-movement

Jmac For Families. (n.d.). *Mandated supporting*. Jmac for Families. Retrieved May 14, 2023, from https://jmacforfamilies.org/mandated-supporting

Keller, R. (2022, November 2). *A Missouri Hospital is the first under federal investigation for denying an emergency abortion*. KCUR 89.3 – NPR in Kansas City. Retrieved December 2, 2022, from www.kcur.org/news/2022-11-02/missouri-hospital-emergency-abortion-federal-investigation-reproductive-health-politics

Kennedy, A. C. (2008). Eugenics, "Degenerate Girls," and social workers during the progressive era. *Affilia, 23*(1), 22–37. https://doi.org/10.1177/0886109907310473

Kiesling, L. (2022, November 30). *What is it this time? What is it this time?* Retrieved December 2, 2022, from www.thecut.com/2022/11/essay-rsv-covid-flu-surge.html

Klibanoff, E. (2022, June 23). Doctors report compromising care out of fear of Texas abortion law. *The Texas Tribune*. Retrieved December 2, 2022, from www.texastribune.org/2022/06/23/texas-abortion-law-doctors-delay-care/

Kobayashi, T., Maeda, M., Takebayashi, Y., & Sato, H. (2021). Traditional gender differences create gaps in the effect of covid-19 on psychological distress of Japanese workers. *International Journal of Environmental Research and Public Health*, 18(16), 8656. https://doi.org/10.3390/ijerph18168656

Lee, J. K., & Chiang, H.-M. (2017). Parenting stress in South Korean mothers of adolescent children with autism spectrum disorder. *International Journal of Developmental Disabilities*, 64(2), 120–127. https://doi.org/10.1080/20473869.2017.1279843

Linden, K., Domgren, N., Zaigham, M., Sengpiel, V., Andersson, M. E., & Wessberg, A. (2022). Being in the shadow of the unknown – Swedish women's lived experiences of pregnancy during the Covid-19 pandemic, a phenomenological study. *Women and Birth*, 35(5), 440–446. https://doi.org/10.1016/j.wombi.2021.09.007

Lipiec, D. (2019). People with disabilities as a gift and a challenge for the Church. *HTS Teologiese Studies/Theological Studies*, 75(4). https://doi.org/10.4102/hts.v75i4.5449

MacMaster, N. (2007). "Black Jew - white Negro" Anti-Semitism and the construction of cross-racial stereotypes. *Nationalism and Ethnic Politics*, 6(4), 65–82. https://doi.org/10.1080/13537110008428612

Manne, K. (2017). *Down girl: The logic of misogyny*. Oxford University Press.

Manne, K. [@Kate_Manne] (2018, January 28). "Caremongering" is not a typo btw. It is a term from my misogyny book, complementary to the "tyranny of vulnerability" which threatens to condemn any woman who has any causal connection that isn't maximally conducive to maximum net utility for any vulnerable person or creature. [Tweet]. *Twitter*. https://twitter.com/kate_manne/status/957720123577683968?s=20

McCammon, S., & Sullivan, B. (2022, July 26). *Indiana doctor says she has been harassed for giving an abortion to a 10-year-old*. NPR. Retrieved December 2, 2022, from www.npr.org/2022/07/26/1113577718/indiana-doctor-abortion-ohio-10-year-old

Mendoza, P., Noriega, J. A. V., & Hurtado, M. (2015). Family satisfaction profiles of Mexican parent with a child with intellectual disabilities. *Revista De Humanidades Y Sciencia Sociales*, 2(3), 61–75.

Meyer, J. (2015, December 30). *JBMW, fall 2015: Children are a divine gift not a human right*. The Council on Biblical Manhood and Womanhood. Retrieved December 1, 2022, from https://cbmw.org/2015/11/30/children-are-a-divine-gift-not-a-human-right-biblical-clarity-and-gospel-comfort-for-those-contemplating-in-vitro-fertilization-ivf/

Miller, C. M. (2022). *Florida seized a 4-day old from a mother with a disability*. US News and World Report. Retrieved July 31, 2022, from www.usnews.com/news/best-states/florida/articles/2022-02-20/florida-seized-a-4-day-old-from-a-mother-with-a-disability

Millman, C. (2019, March 17). *Is Aba really "Dog training for children"? A professional dog trainer weighs in*. NeuroClastic. Retrieved May 14, 2023, from https://neuroclastic.com/is-aba-really-dog-training-for-children-a-professional-dog-trainer-weighs-in/

Morain, D. (1986, August 23). Woman with Down's syndrome is sterilized after court approves. *Los Angeles Times*. Retrieved July 31, 2022, from www.latimes.com/archives/la-xpm-1986-08-23-mn-15812-story.html

National Human Genome Research Institute. (n.d.). Eugenics: Its origin and development (1883–present). *genome.gov*. Retrieved May 14, 2023, from https://www.genome.gov/about-genomics/educational-resources/timelines/eugenics

Oxner, R., & Mendez, M. (2022, July 16). Texas hospitals are putting pregnant patients at risk by denying care out of fear of abortion laws. *KERA News*. Retrieved May 14, 2022, from https://www.keranews.org/health-wellness/2022-07-16/texas-hospitals-are-putting-pregnant-patients-at-risk-by-denying-care-out-of-fear-of-abortion-laws

Pagano, J. (2022, January 23). #mydisabledlifeisworthy highlights disability community's pandemic frustrations: "we are seen as collateral damage". *Yahoo!* Retrieved December 2, 2022, from www.yahoo.com/lifestyle/my-disabled-life-is-worthy-hashtag-covid-19-175110018.html

Pernick, M. S. (1997). Eugenics and public health in American history. *American Journal of Public Health*, 87(11), 1767–1772. https://doi.org/10.2105/ajph.87.11.1767

Perry, D. (2019, July 25). Your disabled child is not a prop. *Pacific Standard*. Retrieved May 14, 2023, from https://psmag.com/social-justice/your-disabled-child-is-not-a-prop

Peltola, M. [@MaryPeltola]. (2022, November 17). Pro-fish pro-family pro-choice pro-worker pro-Alaska that's how I campaigned. That's how I'm going to legislate [Tweet]. *Twitter*. https://twitter.com/marypeltola/status/1593332952590606340

Pena, M. (2022, February 23). Chicago comes closer to solving school bus woes six months into school year. *Chalkbeat Chicago*. Retrieved July 31, 2022, from https://chicago.chalkbeat.org/2022/2/23/22948193/chicago-public-schools-covid-bus-transportation-students-with-disabilities

Petersen, A. H. (2020, November 11). *Other countries have social safety nets. The U.S. has women*. Culture Study. https://annehelen.substack.com/p/other-countries-have-social-safety

Petersson, C. C., & Hansson, K. (2021). Social work responses to domestic violence during the Covid-19 pandemic: Experiences and perspectives of professionals at women's shelters in Sweden. *Clinical Social Work Journal*, 50(2), 135–146. https://doi.org/10.1007/s10615-022-00833-3

Pham, H. H., & Lerner, B. (2001). In the patient's best interest? Revisiting sexual autonomy and sterilization of the developmentally disabled. *Western Journal of Medicine*, 175(4), 280–283. https://doi.org/10.1136/ewjm.175.4.280

Powell, R. (2022). Achieving justice for disabled parents and their children: An abolitionist approach. *Yale Journal of Law and Feminism*, 33(2). https://doi.org/10.2139/ssrn.3916265

Pullen, C. (2016, October 6). Couples with Down syndrome don't need to be sterilised, they need support. *The Sydney Morning Herald*. Retrieved July 31, 2022, from www.smh.com.au/lifestyle/couples-with-down-syndrome-dont-need-to-be-sterilised-they-need-support-20161005-grv6no.html

Rajkumar, S. (2022, August 8). How to talk about disability sensitively and avoid ableist tropes. *NPR*. Retrieved December 2, 2022, from www.npr.org/2022/08/08/1115682836/how-to-talk-about-disability-sensitively-and-avoid-ableist-tropes

Raz, A. (2004). "Important to test, important to support": Attitudes toward disability rights and prenatal diagnosis among leaders of support groups for genetic disorders in Israel. *Social Science & Medicine*, 59(9), 1857–1866. https://doi.org/10.1016/j.socscimed.2004.02.016

Rosenthal, K. (2023, April 1). Helen Keller was one of the great American socialists. *Jacobin Magazine*. Retrieved May 14, 2023, from https://jacobin.com/2023/04/helen-keller-socialism-disability-socialist-party

Rosenthal, K. (n.d). The politics of Helen Keller. *International Socialist Review*. Retrieved May 14, 2023, from https://isreview.org/issue/96/politics-helen-keller/index.html

Rudavsky, S., & Fradette, R. (2022, July 8). Patients head to Indiana for abortion services as other states restrict care. *The Indianapolis Star*. Retrieved December 2, 2022, from www.indystar.com/story/news/health/2022/07/01/indiana-abortion-law-roe-v-wade-overturned-travel/7779936001

Ruskin, L. (2022, September 5). Mary Peltola, the first Alaska Native heading to Congress, journeys home to the river. *NPR*. Retrieved May 14, 2023, from https://www.npr.org/2022/09/05/1120805820/mary-peltola-the-first-alaska-native-heading-to-congress-journeys-home-to-the-ri

Sarnoff Center on Jewish Genetics. (n.d.). Jewish genetics FAQs. *jewishgenetics.org*. Retrieved May 14, 2023, from https://www.jewishgenetics.org/genetic-disorders/jewish-genetic-disorder-faqs/

Schladen, M. (2022, July 14). Arrest confirms Indiana abortion for Ohio 10-year-old. *Ohio Capital Journal*. Retrieved December 2, 2022, from https://ohiocapitaljournal.com/2022/07/13/arrest-confirms-indiana-abortion-for-ohio-10-year-old/

Shire, E. (2017, April 14). "Autism speaks"– but should everyone listen? *The Daily Beast*. Retrieved July 31, 2022, from www.thedailybeast.com/autism-speaks-but-should-everyone-listen

Shriver Center on Poverty Law. (2020, December 10). *Before you call DCFS*. Shriver Center on Poverty Law. https://www.povertylaw.org/article/before-you-call-dcfs/

Sinclair, J. (1993). *Don't mourn for us*. Retrieved July 31, 2022, from www.autreat.com/dont_mourn.html

Staver, A. (2022, March 28). Disabled parents say their differences are being used against them in Ohio family courts. *The Columbus Dispatch*. Retrieved July 31, 2022, from www.dispatch.com/story/news/2022/03/28/disabled-parents-ohio-family-courts-treat-them-unfairly-ableism/7139758001/

Steinhauer, J., & Harmon, A. (2008, September 6). Parents of special-needs children divided over Palin's promise to help. *The New York Times*. Retrieved July 30, 2022, from www.nytimes.com/2008/09/07/us/politics/07needs.html

Stern, A. M. (2011). Sterilized in the name of public health. *American Journal of Public Health*, 95(7), 1128–1138. https://doi.org/10.2105/ajph.2004.041608

Stevenson, J. L., Harp, B., & Gernsbacher, M. A. (2011). Infantilizing autism. *Disability Studies Quarterly*, 31(3). https://doi.org/10.18061/dsq.v31i3.1675

Tautges, P. (2021, May 25). *Children with disabilities are a gift from the lord*. Counseling One Another. Retrieved December 1, 2022, from https://counselingoneanother.com/2020/11/23/children-with-disabilities-are-a-gift-from-the-lord/

Villarosa, L. (2022, June 8). The long shadow of Eugenics in America. *The New York Times*. Retrieved July 31, 2022, from www.nytimes.com/2022/06/08/magazine/eugenics-movement-america.html

Whitt, J. D. (2016). In the image of God: Receiving children with special needs. *Review & Expositor*, 113(2), 205–216. https://doi.org/10.1177/0034637316638244

Will, G. F. (2018, March 17). Questioning the "final solution" for Down syndrome people. *New York Post*. Retrieved July 31, 2022, from https://nypost.com/2018/03/16/questioning-the-final-solution-for-down-syndrome-people/

Wright, J. (2019, April 10). Genetic testing for autism, explained. *Spectrum News*. Retrieved May 14, 2023, from https://www.spectrumnews.org/news/genetic-testing-autism-explained/

You, S., Lee, Y., & Kwon, M. (2018). Effect of parenting stress in Korean mothers of children with disabilities on life satisfaction: Moderating effect of intrinsic religious orientation. *Journal of Applied Research in Intellectual Disabilities, 32*(3), 591–599. https://doi.org/10.1111/jar.12553

Zaraska, M. (2019, August 14). The problems with prenatal testing for autism. *Spectrum News*. Retrieved May 14, 2023, from https://www.spectrumnews.org/features/deep-dive/the-problems-with-prenatal-testing-for-autism/

Zhang, S. (2020, December). The last children of Down syndrome. *The Atlantic*. Retrieved July 31, 2022, from www.theatlantic.com/magazine/archive/2020/12/the-last-children-of-down-syndrome/616928/

# 3

# FOR US, BY US

## Mutual Aid Efforts in Disabled Queer and Trans Communities

*Brendon T. Holloway, Jax Kynn, and Hannah Boyke*

### Introduction

Mutual aid has existed since humans have existed. However, the concept of mutual aid did not gain mainstream traction until the COVID-19 pandemic began impacting communities from all parts of the world. Proliferated by the COVID-19 pandemic, mutual aid efforts were exacerbated by the racial justice uprisings in the United States (U.S.) in 2020, a result of the violent murder of George Floyd at the hands of the police in Minnesota, the invasion of Ukraine in 2022, the protests in Iran in 2022, and multiple climate crises, such as wildfires and rising temperatures, which have impacted communities across the world. Now more than ever before, communities are turning to mutual aid with an awareness that formal systems will not meet our needs. There is a shared understanding that we are all we have, and the systems in place will not protect us, care for us, or provide for us (Spade, 2021). This understanding is especially prominent among marginalized communities, including disabled and chronically ill communities, and queer and trans communities.

Before proceeding, we want to acknowledge how we are defining queer and trans people in this chapter. We use the term queer to encompass those who are lesbian, gay, bisexual, queer, pansexual, asexual, demisexual, questioning, and more. We acknowledge that not all LGBQ+ individuals are identified as queer, yet given the political underpinnings of mutual aid and queerness, we have chosen to use queer. We use the term trans to represent not only anyone who is a binary transgender identity – such as trans women and trans men – but also those who are nonbinary, such as genderqueer, genderfluid, and agender individuals. Often, we will reference the "queer and

DOI: 10.4324/9781003308331-5

trans community" to represent mutual aid efforts that are specific to both communities.

## What Is Mutual Aid?

Mutual aid, coined by Peter Kropotkin (1902), was initially described as century-long practices of collective care. While this was mutual aid's first debut in the literature, mutual aid efforts have existed as long as people have existed. Humans have made it this far due to collaborating with one another and coordinating in ways that help one another survive. However, systemic forces, such as capitalism and colonization, have deeply impacted how individuals connect with one another. We live in a world today, specifically the Western world, where we are put in competition with one another for survival and forced to rely on hostile systems (Spade, 2021). Because of these hostile systems and the forced nature of independence over collaboration, mutual aid is a radical act (Spade, 2021).

### *Defining Mutual Aid*

Since mutual aid was documented in the academic literature, it has been redefined and re-conceptualized across time. Nelson et al. (1998) define mutual aid as settings where individuals with a common experience come together to share their knowledge and resources and to provide and receive social support. More recently, Dean Spade (2021) defines mutual aid as the radical act of caring for one another while working together to transform the world. This includes viewing mutual aid as the collective coordination to meet each other's needs with an awareness that the systems in place will not meet those needs. Spade (2021) also identifies three key components of mutual aid:

1. Mutual aid efforts work to meet survival needs and build a shared understanding about why individuals or groups do not have what they need.

    This means that people work together to understand what mutual aid is, why certain individuals or groups are not getting what they need, and how mutual aid can meet those needs. Most often, the individuals or groups not getting their needs met hold multiple marginalized identities and endure significant societal oppression.
2. Mutual aid efforts mobilize people, expand solidarity, and build movements.

    Once there is a shared understanding of what mutual aid is and how mutual aid can meet survival needs, the next goal is for a mutual aid group to bring together a group of people who are working toward the same goal. By doing so, mutual aid groups can join in solidarity with one another, building a movement rooted in collective care.

3. Mutual aid efforts are participatory, solving problems through collective action versus waiting for saviors.

    Mutual aid is participatory in nature, bringing together many people who have a shared interest in collaboration as a means toward collective action. Instead of depending on the government, nonprofits, or any other "saviors" to meet community needs, mutual aid groups solve problems and address inequities as a group, creating an interdependence between one another rather than a dependence on systems.

*Ongoing Versus Acute Mutual Aid*

Mutual aid is a form of political participation where people come together to change political conditions. Changing political conditions takes time. Mutual aid efforts most often gain popularity in the mainstream media during acute crises (e.g., natural disasters), but mutual aid should be viewed as ongoing given the context of the violent systems we are forced to navigate daily (e.g., capitalism). For mutual aid to be sustainable, there needs to be a collective recognition and commitment from those involved in mutual aid groups that mutual aid is ongoing. While committing to long-term mutual aid may sound daunting and time intensive, there are many ways to get involved and support mutual aid efforts over time.

Examples of ongoing mutual aid efforts include prison letter writing projects, such as Black & Pink, where people get connected to LGBTQ+ pen pals in prisons to build relationships, participate in harm reduction, and help build a movement against policing and prisons. Another example of mutual aid is The Oakland Power Projects, which strengthen the skills of individuals to respond to emergencies, minimizing police contact. Community members are trained to respond to mental health crises, chronic health problems, and acute health emergencies to prevent police contact with communities that have been historically harmed, violated, and killed by the police. Other types of mutual aid include offering temporary housing to unhoused young people, providing transportation to disabled people to medical appointments, and participating in meals trains for people who are recovering from surgery.

## Mutual Aid in Disabled, Queer, and Trans Communities

Mutual aid groups welcome all who want to get involved. However, mutual aid has historically existed and been utilized among communities who experience marginalization, such as communities of color, chronically ill and disabled communities, and queer and trans communities. For the purposes of this chapter, we will center the experiences of disabled, queer, and trans communities, but want to acknowledge that mutual aid is often interconnected and intersectional in terms of identities.

## *Mutual Aid in Disabled Communities: The System Will Not Protect Us*

Disabled mutual aid resists the ableist social structure that defines disabled people as void of self-determination, disposable, and excludable. Capitalist norms of productivity and profitability justify the payment of subminimum wages to disabled employees, and the strict definitions of disability and employment requirements of Social Security Disability Insurance (SSDI) leave many in precarious economic spaces. In an interview on Bri M's *Power Not Pity* podcast, Ade Raphael – a Black disabled musician – discussed her experiences as a "stage 4c nasopharyngeal carcinoma cancer survivor," of mistreatment by medical professionals, and being in the "liminal space that is coverage under Medicaid" (2019). After receiving cancer treatment, Ade found that working a 30-hour week meant getting ill (Raphael, 2019). While Ade navigates daily life with her disability, she receives no support from the government. Ade makes too much money to qualify for Medicaid but not enough money to meet her needs, and she has been denied access to disability insurance because she did not meet the employment-length requirements (Raphael, 2019). Ade's story demonstrates the unwillingness of the system to protect disabled people. Importantly, however, the government is not the sole perpetrator of such violence; corporatized nonprofits operating on charity models of aid similarly silence and ignore the disabled communities that they purport to help. In nonprofits, the hierarchical control of resources normalizes a situation in which an organization "spends big money on research but won't buy respirators for those who need them; big money on the next genetic breakthrough, but not on lift bars to make bathrooms accessible" (Clare, 2009, p. 123). Within this context of structural and institutionalized ableism, it is apparent that "the whole organism is poisoned" (Anzaldúa, 1981, p. 208). Disabled mutual aid – survival without the system, and survival in spite of the system – comprises radical acts of resistance.

### *Interdependence: Solidarity Not Charity*

Since mutual aid provides disabled communities with control of what they get, how they get it, what they give, and how they give it, mutual aid counters traditional charity-based forms of aid. The concept and value of interdependence is integral to disabled mutual aid's resistance to charity models of aid. Interdependence honors the ways in which everyone depends on each other, and it challenges the assumption that independence is both possible and a worthwhile goal (Sins Invalid, 2019). Mia Mingus – a queer, disabled, Korean writer and educator – demonstrates the transformative role of interdependence as a framework for disabled mutual aid:

> Interdependence moves us away from the myth of independence, and towards relationships where we are all valued and have things to offer.

It moves us away from knowing disability only through "dependence," which paints disabled bodies as being a burden to others, at the mercy of able-bodied people's benevolence. We become charity cases, a way for able bodied people to feel better about themselves and we in turn, internalize our sense of being as burden, sad, and tragic. All of this sets up a dynamic where disabled people feel like we have to be "liked" in order to receive basic daily access to live and where able-bodied people feel entitled to receive praise and recognition for providing access . . . this dynamic of disabled people being "dependent" on able bodied people shapes so many disabled people's lives and is the foundation upon which so much domination, control, violence and abuse happens.

*(Mingus, 2017, para. 36)*

Interdependence thus expands the concept of aid to capture a more holistic, community driven understanding of well-being, security, survival, and need (Mingus, 2017).

*What Does Disabled Mutual Aid Look Like?*

Mutual aid emerges through a range of activities, services, and relationships that support disabled community members' economic, emotional, physical, and social well-being. Mutual aid ranges from setting up meal trains to establishing communal housing to allow disabled community members to care for each other. Leah Lakshmi Piepzna-Samarasinha discusses the "small" and often informal acts of mutual aid through the concept of "care webs" (2018, p. 32). Per Piepzna-Samarasinha, care webs "break from the model of paid attendant care as the only way to access disability support. Resisting the model of charity and gratitude, they are controlled by the needs and desires of the disabled people running them" (2018, p. 41). Because care webs center disabled individuals as controllers of care, they disrupt the ableist understandings of disabled folks solely as the receivers of care (Sins Invalid, 2019). Piepzna-Samarasinha offers examples of how care webs look in daily life:

> *Hey B. needs more care shifters, can you repost this Facebook note? Can we share the access van ride over to the city? . . . If I take your manual wheelchair and load it up with takeout, we'll all have food. Can you go with me to the clinic and take notes while I talk to my doctor?* [emphasis original].
>
> *(2018, p. 32)*

Care webs develop through community connections and are sustained through community relationships. Furthermore, care webs counter the traditional hierarchical and bureaucratic forms of care promoted by the state and corporatized nonprofits.

Disabled communities have used online organizing to develop mutual aid for transportation, access, and personal care needs when traveling. Asian Pacific Islander American disability activists and scholars Mia Mingus, Stacey Milburn, and Leah Lakshmi Piepzna-Samarasinha developed *Creating Collective Access* in Detroit, a mutual aid project that connected disabled conference attendees, drawing on collective resources to meet access needs and promote community (Creating Collective Access, 2010; Mingus, 2010). Another example of online organizing for mutual aid is the Radical Access Mapping Project (RAMP) developed by a queer disabled activist based in Vancouver, Canada, which began in 2009. RAMP has focused primarily on spreading information on ableism and accessibility, conducting accessibility audits and video captioning (RAMP, n.d.). Accessibility audits were collective projects that provided "useful, accurate, broad-based and up-to-date accessibility information about the physical environment" to allow disabled folks to "make informed choices about what events and spaces [they] participate in and support" (RAMP, n.d.). Critical Design Lab offers a similar form of mutual aid, using "digital media and social practice to craft replicable protocols that treat accessibility as research-creation, an aesthetic world-building practice, and an invitation to assemble community" (Critical Design Lab, n.d.). Critical Design Lab is guided by Dr. Aimi Hamraie, a queer disabled Iranian and Southwest Asian and Northern African scholar (Critical Design Lab, n.d.).

*Disabled Mutual Aid and COVID-19*

In the context of the COVID-19 pandemic, mutual aid within disabled communities has remained indispensable for reinforcing self-determination, honoring and (re)generating interdependence, and fostering survival. Neighborhood pods have allowed communities to remain connected and share resources (Mutual Aid Medford and Summerville, 2020). Community groups, such as the Disability Justice Culture Club and the Cross Bay Mutual Aid Project in California, have brought community members together to offer grocery drop offs, homecare, community-based resources, transportation, and connect community members for phone and online conversations (Disability Justice Culture Club, n.d.-a, n.d.-b; Cross Bay Mutual Aid Project, n.d.). Additional forms of mutual aid include knowledge sharing about safety protocols on social media, giving face masks to disabled community members, organizing group chats with loved ones, checking in, scheduling "Zoom crip dance parties and craft nights," and no questions asked cash donations from organizations such as Crip Fund (Piepzna-Samarasinha, 2021).

The rise of mainstream mutual aid efforts since the start of the COVID-19 pandemic can be understood as a form of emergency, reactionary aid. Piepzna-Samarasinha (2018) discussed such forms of mutual aid, called "emergency-response care webs," which arise "when someone able-bodied becomes temporarily or permanently disabled and their able-bodied network of friends springs into action" (p. 52). In these situations, mutual aid efforts are typically short-lived. Piepzna-Samarasinha responds to emergency care webs stating "*Wow, when it's your mountain-climbing friend who gets hit riding their bike, you care, huh? For me and the other folks who are always disabled, not so much, huh?* [emphasis original]" (2018, p. 52). Here, the ableism that often underlies emergency, reactionary mutual aid efforts is wholly apparent. Arani introduces a similar situation when discussing the experiences of Vicky, an activist who is a Black queer cisgender woman:

> [W]hile the racial justice projects blossoming around the city align with those Vicky has organized, she feels further marginalized by this outpouring of care for Black communities because few people have reached out to her seeking collaboration or offering support for her existing projects.
> *(2020, pp. 655–656)*

Such efforts mobilize on the basis of exclusion and ignorance of long-standing community developed projects, foreclosing the possibility of interdependence between groups and communities.

Ableist understandings of care have shaped many of the new mainstream mutual aid projects that arose in response to COVID-19. Piepzna-Samarasinha (2021) reflected on their experience interacting with a mutual aid project that only offered aid in the form of grocery deliveries. When they offered to provide services or resources that supported their safety and accessibility as a disabled person, Piepzna-Samarasinha notes that the project ignored their message. They assert that "there were many other mutual aid groups I have heard of that seemed to not think about disabled people or ableism at all – as people who wanted to organize, as people other than faceless recipients of care" (Piepzna-Samarasinha, 2021, para 13). In this context, projects conceptualize and carry out mutual aid in ways that deny disabled folks' participation as givers of aid. As a result, these mutual aid efforts run counter to the development of interdependence.

Even with the rise in mutual aid since the beginning of the COVID-19 pandemic, many disabled communities experience an "absence" of mutual aid opportunities (Arani, 2020). Alexia Arani illustrates a tension between the rise of mutual aid and its apparent absence: "my friend Chito, a disabled trans and queer Latinx person, continued to struggle to find rides to the grocery store, medical appointments, and recovery meetings – a problem they've been navigating long before the onset of COVID-19" (2020, p. 655). Per

Arani, Chito's experience is also made difficult by concerns of their safety, for they "do not feel safe accepting rides from strangers, especially given the multiple points of precarity they inhabit as a disabled TQPoC" (p. 655). Such examples highlight the exclusion that arises when mutual aid lacks a foundation in community and solidarity. Without a horizontal distribution of decision-making power and clear involvement of disabled and trans or queer community members, many mainstream projects come closer to charity than mutual aid.

## Mutual Aid in Queer and Trans Communities

Mutual aid has a long history within queer and trans communities, and mutual aid has been used to challenge heterosexist and cissexist structures that oppress queer and trans individuals. Even a short history of queer and trans mutual aid requires recognition of the work of Marsha P. Johnson and Sylvia Rivera. Johnson and Rivera were at the forefront of the events leading to the Stonewall Riots of 1969 (Shepard, 2013). However, as two poor trans people of color, they were largely excluded by cisgender, White gay men, and lesbian women in mainstream LGBTQ+ rights groups. Johnson and Rivera's activism fought against homonormative assimilation and centered the needs and experiences of LGBTQ+ people of color, especially sex workers and trans and queer youth – individuals whom conventional gay advocacy groups largely ignored (Shepard, 2013).

Excluded and ignored by mainstream gay activism, Rivera founded Street Transvestite Action Revolutionaries (STAR) along with Johnson and Bubbles Rose Marie. Rivera utilized STAR to bring attention to the unique oppression that trans people of color and sex workers – who were often poor trans people of color – experienced (Shepard, 2013). STAR protested police brutality of sex workers and LGBTQ+ community members. In an interview with Leslie Fienberg, Rivera described STAR as an organization "for the street gay people, the street homeless people, and anybody that needed help at that time" (Morancy, 2022, para. 10). STAR members penned a manifesto that outlined their ideology and goals; STAR was a means to pursue equal rights for the LGBTQ+ community and keep queer and trans sex workers out of jail.

STAR offered instrumental support to LGBTQ+ individuals who were left behind by affluent and assimilative gay organizations. Rivera and Johnson provided housing, clothing, and money to anyone who needed it. Maximizing their limited financial resources, STAR used creative means for providing temporary housing: sneaking people into hotel rooms (as Rivera once recalled, "you can sneak 50 people into two hotel rooms" (Morancy, 2022, para. 10) and housing dozens in a tractor trailer parked in a Manhattan lot in NYC. After losing their temporary housing, Rivera sought out a more permanent place, and STAR eventually found a home at 213 East Second Street in Manhattan. This long term location allowed STAR to be a safe place for unhoused queer and trans youth and sex workers to sleep, eat, and get clothing (Feinberg, 2006).

The STAR founders funded the community space through sex work and wanted to keep the youth from hustling on the streets themselves. When a STAR member was arrested, the other members would plan fundraising events to pay for legal representation for the individual in jail. Rivera and Johnson become surrogate mothers to the youth that stayed at STAR house. STAR provided necessities to their community during a time when queer and trans people of color, especially those who engaged in sex work, were ignored and othered by both mainstream society and gay men and lesbian organizations.

STAR's legacy has shaped queer and trans communities, which have carried on the tradition of utilizing their platforms for mutual aid. Now, mutual aid is often carried out through social media, as it connects queer and trans individuals internationally. For example, Rio (he/they; @thebrooklynbruja), an autistic trans advocate, uses Instagram to publicize calls for mutual aid. To his audience of 10,000+ followers, Rio posts mutual aid requests from community members on their Instagram account. Rio describes their work as "a form of suicide prevention and harm reduction." When describing their motivations, Rio illustrates the role of mutual aid in collective healing:

> Collective healing is vital to singular individual healing. I do what I do because I have a deep love for community and I know that I can only heal fully when I also am able to help and watch my community heal too. And unfortunately in a capitalist world, money speaks and it's a necessity for survival.
>
> *(2022)*

Rio's work channels the key elements of mutual aid – survival, reciprocity, interdependence, and solidarity.

### *The Intersections of Mutual Aid in Queer, Trans, and Disabled Communities*

The HIV/AIDS epidemic in the United States can be understood as a mass disabling event that significantly impacted queer and trans communities. In 1981, five gay men were diagnosed with a rare form of pneumonia that only occurred in people with very compromised immune systems (Benjamin, 1989). Shortly after that, 41 gay men were diagnosed with a rare form of cancer, Kaposi's Sarcoma. These men were among the first recorded cases of acquired immunodeficiency syndrome (AIDS) in the United States

(Altman, 1982; Kher, 1982). Between 1981 and 1984, many gay men, intravenous drugs users, and hemophiliacs contracted rare opportunistic diseases and died. As Larry Kramer, a gay AIDS activist, said in a 2004 speech: "in those four years, almost every gay man who had fucked in America had been exposed to the virus" (Kramer, 2004, para. 66). There was little knowledge about how the virus spread, and it could take 5–15 weeks for symptoms to present after contracting HIV. As a result, there was a significant period of time in which AIDS was spreading silently until 1982 when the CDC officially recognized the virus as a public health issue (Gallo, 2006).

Media representations of individuals living with HIV/AIDS were stigmatizing and heterosexist. HIV/AIDS was framed as a consequence of immoral homosexual encounters (Altman, 1982). The lack of scientific knowledge, even among medical professionals, along with the stigma around HIV/AIDS led to a slow development of resources, services, funding, government subsidies, and treatment options (Gallo, 2006). This inadequate societal response to the "gay cancer" epidemic meant that there was no formal acknowledgment of the large numbers of people dying of AIDS (Gallo, 2006). Many queer and trans people during this time watched their loved ones slowly wither away from rare infections, while the American government merely observed. Larry Kramer recalled, "I have recently gone through my diaries of the worst of the plague years. I saw day after day a notation of another friend's death" (Kramer, 2004, para. 49).

Without support from the government, the LGBTQ+ community was left to care for their own. This mass disabling event inspired transformational grassroots activism and gave rise to many queer networks of mutual aid (Finkelstein, 2020). People with HIV/AIDS were not generally isolated from their communities; they relied on their relatives, chosen family, and friends to help shoulder the continuous grief and loss and mental and physical health issues that accompanied an AIDS diagnosis (McHugh, 2021). Social networks became caregiver and advocate networks (Turner & Catania, 1997). There were many people who became informal caregivers to their dying friends and partners who could not afford inpatient hospital costs (Muraco & Fredriksen-Goldsen, 2011). These networks also helped to connect people with HIV/AIDS to the small number of doctors willing to treat them. This culture of care within the LGBTQ+ community grew as treatments for HIV/AIDS became available and HIV/AIDS shifted from an immediate death sentence to a chronic illness.

Additionally, queer activists with the Coalition for Women Prisoners and Coalition to Support Women Prisoners at Chowchilla challenged the medical neglect and mistreatment experienced by women prisoners living with HIV/AIDS, most of whom were people of color (Piepzna-Samarasinha, 2018). These networks shared safer sex supplies and medications for HIV/AIDS, held protests at prisons, collected and shared information about the women who died while incarcerated, and established an HIV/AIDS counselor certification process for the women who were incarcerated (Metanoia, n.d.). Even more, these coalitions engaged in legal activism for the compassionate release of women inmates living with HIV/AIDS, including Joann Walker who was a Black AIDS activist and inmate at the Chowchilla prison until she received compassionate release two months before her death in 1994 (Metanoia, n.d.).

## What Does Mutual Aid Look Like Today?

Today, mutual aid is more well known than ever before. Mutual aid efforts are happening across the globe in response to ongoing crises ranging from disaster relief to abortion rights in the U.S. to the Russian government's invasion of Ukraine. Mutual aid is happening in many different forms, allowing people to get involved at different levels based on their capacity. Mutual aid today looks like the following: helping pregnant people cross state lines in the U.S. to access a safe abortion; providing housing for people who are forced to leave Ukraine due to the Russia-Ukraine war; crowdfunding efforts to access needed healthcare or to pay bills; meal trains for trans individuals who are recovering from a gender-affirming surgery and disabled people who need their updated homes and/or equipment for accessibility, and so much more. Mutual aid is happening in all areas of the world, and the more people who get involved, the more sustainable mutual aid will become.

## Effective Practices for Supporting Mutual Aid Efforts

After reading this chapter, you may ask yourself: *What can I do to support mutual aid efforts?* We know that it may be difficult to know where to start. As such, we wanted to provide you with effective practices for supporting mutual aid efforts and building your own mutual aid toolkit as you embark on this journey.

### Key Things to Know as You Get Started

- Mutual aid is about solidarity, not charity. The charity model is about giving back (a top-down approach) whereas mutual aid is about sharing resources and building solidarity with one another.
- Mutual aid is nonhierarchical. Mutual aid has a horizontal decision-making structure where decisions are made based on the group's consensus.
- Mutual aid is ongoing and not just a response to acute crises. We should be working together before, during, and after crises. If you view mutual aid as temporary, you may be using a charity model versus being in solidarity with your community.
- Mutual aid is about collaboration, not competition.

*Connecting Clients to Mutual Aid*

- Research mutual aid efforts and projects in your area. For example, you can google, "mutual aid Denver" and find several mutual aid groups in Denver, Colorado.
- If you're having trouble finding mutual aid groups, don't hesitate to turn to Reddit or Facebook groups.
- Think about the clients you support and reflect on the systems you may refer them to. Are these systems harmful? Is one system in particular harmful? Would a mutual aid group better meet this person's needs?
- Add mutual aid groups to your list of referrals! Mutual aid can be just as, or even more, valuable than the formal systems in place.

*Case-Study Example*

Jesse (they/them) is a 21-year-old multiracial trans person with chronic pain who receives low-cost health services at the community health clinic where you work. Jesse is currently working as a barista at a coffee shop, making enough money to pay for necessities but not enough to save money. Jesse has been trying to work 40 hours each week but has been struggling with chronic pain. Because of the community clinic's low-cost services, Jesse was able to begin hormone therapy one year ago. Before starting hormones, Jesse came out to their mom and dad. Coming out to their parents strained their relationship, and their parents have not spoken with them since. Fortunately, Jesse still has the support of their friends even though most of them are away at college or working all the time.

Jesse is now seeking gender-affirming top surgery. The community health clinic that Jesse has been going to does not offer surgeries, but Jesse's previous case worker at the clinic recommended a few surgeons within driving distance for Jesse to check out. After doing some research, none of the surgeons within 500 miles accept Jesse's insurance or offer a sliding scale. As Jesse's new case worker, you meet with them to assess their situation. Jesse expresses that they experience significant gender dysphoria due to their chest, which has severely impacted their mental health. Jesse shares that they have recently quit their favorite hobby – Zumba at the local community center – because of their gender dysphoria, worsening mental health, and chronic pain. It becomes clear that Jesse is in dire need of surgery.

*Guiding Questions*

- What are the intersecting issues impacting Jesse in this case?
- Considering that Jesse has no excess income and has exhausted all surgery options within 500 miles, how might you support Jesse in pursuing surgery?

- What are some resources that may help Jesse access surgery sooner? What role may mutual aid play in this?

## Conclusion

Sometimes the systems we were taught about and forced to navigate are unable to meet our needs. When these systems fail, many turn to mutual aid. As discussed in this chapter, mutual aid is the radical act of caring for one another while working together to transform the world. Mutual aid is directly linked to the liberation of disabled people, queer and trans people, Black and Indigenous people, people of color, women, poor and working-class people, displaced people, fat people, and all life on this planet. We are all we have, and now more than ever, we need to take care of each other and the planet we inhabit. Going forward, we hope that this chapter encourages you to think outside the systems of oppression and connect those you support with communities who will care for them.

## Resources

Introduction to Mutual Aid. www.youtube.com/watch?v=uJaeblrlW_Q&t=1769s; https://files.libcom.org/files/Mutual+Aid-An+Introduction.pdf

Learn more about mutual aid: What is Mutual Aid? https://bigdoorbrigade.com/what-is-mutual-aid/

Mutual Aid: A Factor of Evolution by Peter Kropotkin. https://theanarchistlibrary.org/library/petr-kropotkin-mutual-aid-a-factor-of-evolution

Mutual Aid, Trauma, and Resiliency. https://theanarchistlibrary.org/library/the-jane-addams-collective-mutual-aid-trauma-and-resiliency

## References

Altman, L. K. (1982, May 11). New homosexual disorder worries health officials. *The New York Times*.

Anzaldúa, G. (1981). La Prieta. In C. Moraga & G. Anzaldúa (Eds.), *This bridge called my back: Writings by radical women of color* (pp. 198–209). Third Woman Press.

Arani, A. (2020). Mutual aid and its ambivalence: Lessons from sick and disabled trans and queer people of color. *Feminist Studies*, 46(2), 653–662. https://doi.org/10.1353/fem.2020.0033

Benjamin, A. E. (1989). Perspectives on a continuum of care for persons with HIV illness. *Medical Care Review*, 46(4), 411–437.

Clare, E. (2009). *Exile and pride: Disability, queerness, and liberation*. Duke University Press.

Creating Collective Access. (2010, June 10). *Pod people!* https://creatingcollectiveaccess.wordpress.com/2010/06/10/pod-people/

Critical Design Lab. (n.d.). *Critical design lab*. https://www.mapping-access.com/

Cross Bay Mutual Aid Project. (n.d.). *Cross-bay mutual aid project*. https://airtable.com/shrijh8BPzR1gWN0T

Disability Justice Culture Club. (n.d.-a). *East bay disabled folks COVID19 support request form*. https://docs.google.com/forms/d/e/1FAIpQLSc7LLhYN243k6xFlmQH26lAN9EoRXgEQGrghbqL8Ttc1K8YNA/viewform

Disability Justice Culture Club. (n.d.-b). *Disability justice culture club*. www.facebook.com/disabilityjusticecultureclub/?ref=page_internal

Feinberg, L. (2006, September 24). Street transvestite action revolutionaries. *Workers World*. www.workers.org/2006/us/lavender-red-73

Finkelstein, R. (2020, May 7). Opinion: A lesson learned from the AIDS crisis for dealing with COVID-19. *City Limits*. https://citylimits.org/2020/05/07/opinion-a-lesson-from-the-aids-crisis-for-dealing-with-covid-19/

Gallo, R. C. (2006). A reflection on HIV/AIDS research after 25 years. *Retrovirology*, 3, 72. https://doi.org/10.1186/1742-4690-3-72

Kher, U. (1982, July 27). A name for the Plague. *Time*.

Kramer, L. (2004). *Larry Kramer speech at Cooper Union*. www.towleroad.com/2004/11/larry_kramer_sp/

Kropotkin, P. A. (1902). *Mutual aid: A factor or evolution*. McClure Phillips and Company.

McHugh, B. (2021, January 20). Community care in the AIDS crisis. *JSTOR Daily*. https://daily.jstor.org/community-care-in-the-aids-crisis/

Metanoia. (n.d.). *Metanoia: Transformation through AIDS archives and activism. HIV/AIDS activism at the Central California women's facility in the early 1990s*. ONE Archives Foundation. https://metanoia.onearchives.org/exhibit/activism-in-central-california

Mingus, M. (2010, August 23). Reflections from Detroit: Reflections on an opening: Disability justice and creating collective access in Detroit. *Incite National*. https://incite-national.org/2010/08/23/reflections-from-detroit-reflections-on-an-opening-disability-justice-and-creating-collective-access-in-detroit/

Mingus, M. (2017, April 12). Access intimacy, interdependence and disability justice. *Leaving Evidence*. https://leavingevidence.wordpress.com/2017/04/12/access-intimacy-interdependence-and-disability-justice/

Morancy, J. (2022, January 19). *Marsha P. Johnson*. The University of Chicago. https://womanisrational.uchicago.edu/2022/01/19/marsha-p-johnson/

Muraco, A., & Fredriksen-Goldsen, K. (2011). "That's what friends do": Informal caregiving for chronically ill midlife and older lesbian, gay, and bisexual adults. *Journal of Social & Personal Relationships*, 28, 1073–1092. http://dx.doi.org/10.1177/0265407511402419

Mutual Aid Medford and Somerville. (2020, March 11). *Neighborhood pods how to*. https://docs.google.com/document/d/1j8ADhLEuKNDZ1a_opmzudywJPKMXcNKu01V1xY2MiIA/edit#

Nelson, G., Ochocka, J., Griffin, K., & Lord, J. (1998). "Nothing about me, without me": Participatory action research with self-help/mutual aid organizations for psychiatric consumers/survivors. *American Journal of Community Psychology*, 26(6), 881–912. https://doi.org/10.1023/A:1022298129812

Piepzna-Samarasinha, L. L. (2018). *Care work: Dreaming disability justice*. Arsenal Pulp Press.

Piepzna-Samarasinha, L. L. (2021, October 3). *How disabled mutual aid is different than abled mutual aid*. Disability Visibility Project. https://disabilityvisibilityproject.com/2021/10/03/how-disabled-mutual-aid-is-different-than-abled-mutual-aid/

Radical Access Mapping Project. (n.d.). *About RAMP.* https://radicalaccessiblecommunities.wordpress.com/about-ramp/

Raphael, A. (2019, March 5). *Awakening our powers feat* [Ade Raphael (Episode 6)]. Power Not Pity. www.powernotpity.com/episode6.html

Shepard, B. (2013). From community organization to direct services: The street trans action revolutionaries to Sylvia Rivera law project. *Journal of Social Service Research, 39*(1), 95–114. https://doi.org/10.1080/01488376.2012.727669

Sins Invalid, S. (2019). *Skin, tooth, and bone: The basis of movement is our people* (2nd ed.). Sins Invalid.

Spade, D. (2021). *Mutual aid: Building solidarity during this crisis (and the next).* Verso.

Turner, H. A., & Catania, J. A. (1997). Informal caregiving to persons with AIDS in the United States: Caregiver burden among central cities residents eighteen to forty-nine years old. *American Journal of Community Psychology, 25*(1), 35–59.

**PART TWO**
# Exploring the Specifics

# 4

# INFINITY AND RAINBOWS

Supporting the Sexuality of Neurodivergent People

*Shanna Katz Kattari, E. B. Gross, Kari L. Sherwood, and C. Riley Hostetter*

### Introduction

"Neurodivergent" refers to a specific subset of the population that identifies as having neurological differences considered divergent to those of the rest of the population, who are referred to as "neurotypical." Various disabilities fall under the neurodivergent umbrella, including autism spectrum disorder, attention-deficit/hyperactivity disorder (ADHD), epilepsy, dyslexia, dyscalculia, dysgraphia, dyspraxia, traumatic brain injury, Tourette's syndrome, intellectual disability, obsessive compulsive disorder, specific learning disorders, fetal alcohol spectrum disorder, and post-traumatic stress disorder (PTSD) (Neff, 2021; Sapiets, 2021). Some also consider mental health conditions including anxiety and depression to be neurodivergent (Armstrong, 2015). Many of these conditions are covered in more depth elsewhere in this book. To learn more about working with clients around sexuality and mental health, madness, and other such issues, see Chapter 7; to learn about sexuality and intellectual or developmental disability, see Chapter 5.

The term "neurodiversity" was coined by Australian sociologist Judy Singer in 1998 and refers to cognitive variations in the human brain around how people socialize, learn, and think. Neurodiversity advocates view neurodivergence from a strength-based perspective. For example, Blume (1998) said, "Neurodiversity may be every bit as crucial for the human race as biodiversity is for life in general." In her book, *Neuroqueer Heresies*, Walker (2021) differentiates between a neurodiversity paradigm and a pathology paradigm. Walker calls for a shift in perspective, particularly from the medical community, away from deficit-centered language and toward language which more accurately represents the neurodivergent experience (e.g., using identity-first language, discontinuation of the word "normal").

Neurodivergent prevalence has been estimated between 15% and 20% of the global population. These estimates are rough due to the under-diagnosis and late diagnosis of people assigned female at birth and people of color for most of these conditions, and the substantial overlap between neurodivergent conditions (Doyle, 2020). In contrast to a medicalized, deficit-based approach, neurodiversity advocacy efforts have pushed for neurodivergent individuals being more widely embraced in society, schools, and the workplace (Colombo-Dougovito et al., 2020). Additionally, oftentimes a rainbow spectrum is used by neurodivergent activists to represent neurodiversity, and the diversity within the neurodivergent population itself. These efforts and activism around self-determination, empowerment, and advocacy also extend to holding space for neurodivergent folks around sexuality.

**What Do We Know?**

When it comes to sexuality, as elsewhere, not all neurodivergent conditions are the same. Each may have a variety of different impacts on how people engage with sexuality and sex education. Some neurodivergent folks, like many disabled groups, have long been labeled as asexual. However, also like many other disabled groups, neurodivergent folks, particularly autistics, have spoken up and debunked this myth (Bennett et al., 2018). Like neurotypical people, neurodivergent folks are diverse, and their interest, desires, and needs relating to sex and sexuality will differ based on condition, personal history, and preference. Later, we briefly review the literature on some of the conditions under the neurodivergent label, beginning with autism.

*Autism*

Autism is a neurological condition which affects how autistic people experience the world around them (Autistic Self Advocacy Network [ASAN], 2022). Autism can impact cognitive, emotional, social, and sensory systems within the brain and body. The ways in which autism presents and manifests are heterogeneous, meaning they vary greatly from person to person. It should be noted that the vast majority of autistic adults have moved away from using the puzzle piece (a logo that was created by allistic/not autistic individuals) and toward the infinity sign to represent that vast variety of experiences underneath the autism umbrella.

Sexuality within autistic communities has often been viewed from a deficit and problem-based perspective (Gougeon, 2010). Having particular sexual interests and needs can be seen as outside of the norm, even when the particularities themselves are viewed as socially acceptable. Framing sexuality in terms of problematic preferences leads to these sexual acts being broadly pathologized (Bertilsdotter Rosqvist & Jackson-Perry, 2020). Exploring self-reported enablers and barriers to intimacy for autistic individuals, Sala et al. (2020) found that autistic individuals and non-autistic individuals alike shared similar themes across both categories. There was an expressed need for communication, respect, and safety, among others, as well as barriers through interpersonal conflicts. Autistic individuals highlighted uncertainty in relationships and communication as additional barriers to intimacy (Sala et al., 2020).

Despite this, other reports have noted that over half of autistic individuals have been in committed relationships, have positive attitudes toward sexuality, and found no correlation between lack of relationship experience and a lack in social skills (Byers et al., 2013). However, many autistic adolescents have reported little interest in sexual relationships (Joyal et al., 2021). The contrast in reports emphasizes the importance in acknowledging the heterogeneity among autistic individuals. Some autistic individuals may also experience certain types of intimacy or sexual stimulation as overwhelming and may prefer engaging in more solo sexual acts – but this preference was not attributed to autism-specific behavioral traits or sexual knowledge, further emphasizing the range of sexuality among autistic people (Byers et al., 2013). Among autistic folks who engage in romantic relationships, Barnett and Maticka-Tyndale (2015) found that practicing explicit communication, referred to as "literal declaration," was helpful in maintaining intimate relationships. More broadly, opportunities for self-determination among autistic individuals are important in developing positive identities and personal growth across various facets of life, including sexuality (Kim, 2019).

Research suggests that autistic individuals report increased rates of "homosexuality," with some studies finding that up to 70% of autistic people have been identified as non-heterosexual (Weir et al., 2021; George & Stokes, 2018a, 2018b). Autistic individuals were also more likely to report higher rates of gender diversity and gender dysphoria than their neurotypical peers, as well as a greater level of indifference about the gender identity of a sexual or romantic partner (Dewinter et al., 2015).

Autistic people, particularly youths, lack access to sexual and relationship education (Hannah & Stagg, 2016). One study found that nearly 40% of autistic youth in junior high and high school did not receive sexual education in school or in their communities (Holmes et al., 2020). Often autistic youth turn to the internet for education, but this information can be difficult to sort through, incorrect, and/or misleading (Crehan et al., 2022). Many neurotypical youths will engage in sexual and relationship education with their peers; however, this is less common among autistic youths (Crehan et al., 2022). The lack of adequate and appropriate sexual education for autistic youth may also manifest in a lower sexual consciousness, and an increase in inappropriate sexual behavior (Pecora et al., 2020; Brown-Lavoie et al., 2014). Risk of sexual victimization also increases when sexual knowledge decreases, with Brown-Lavoie et al. (2014) noting that increasing sexual knowledge may serve to partially mediate this risk of sexual victimization. This risk may be exacerbated by a gap in abilities to interpret the intentions of neurotypicals, as well as difficulty with generalizing sexual education from a classroom setting to a real-life scenario (Hannah & Stagg, 2016). These difficulties can lead to problems including boundary crossings for both the individual and their sexual partner(s), as well as difficulty in determining and expressing one's own preferences in sexual situations (Hannah & Stagg, 2016).

### Epilepsy

Epilepsy is a neurological condition characterized by recurrent seizures. Epilepsy may have more consistent sexual effects across people than some other disabilities, because it is reliably correlated with differences in the functions of gonads (e.g., testes or ovaries), which can, among other impacts, contribute to diminished sexual drive or libido, called hyposexuality (Luef, 2008). Hyposexuality is common among people with epilepsy, and may be more common among women (Harden, 2005; Luef, 2008; Karan et al., 2015). There is some evidence that medication can help reduce symptoms of low sexual desire if it is causing distress to an individual, but these symptoms may worsen the longer a person has epilepsy. A study of sexuality in adolescent girls with epilepsy found no differences from the general population (Karan et al., 2015; de Vincentiis et al., 2008). Rarely, there are sexual aspects to epileptic seizures or post-seizure recovery, including involuntary touching of one's genitals or seeing sexual aura-images (Luef, 2008).

### Attention-Deficit/Hyperactivity Disorder

The impact of attention-deficit/hyperactivity disorder (ADHD) on sexuality may be less consistent. ADHD is a neurodevelopmental condition associated with difficulties with inhibitory control in different areas including attention, cognition, mood, and movement. There are different subtypes of ADHD, including predominantly inattentive, predominantly hyperactive, and combined types (CHADD, 2022; WHO, 2019). As with autism, some of the research has taken a deficit-based view. Numerous studies have explored potential links between ADHD and hypersexuality, pornography use, or paraphilias (e.g., Bőthe et al., 2019). Two meta-analyses examining this relationship found that while there is not consistent evidence that hypersexuality or paraphilia are more common among ADHD, the reverse does seem to be true – that is, ADHD does seem to be more common among people with hypersexuality or paraphilias (Korchia et al., 2022; Soldati et al., 2021).

There has been limited research focused specifically on sexual function or challenges in people with ADHD; in a systematic review, Soldati et al. (2020) found just seven articles focused on sexual function and six on sexual dysfunction. Their synthesis of the findings indicates that many people with ADHD report higher levels of sexual desire than the general population, but this may vary by ADHD subtype. People with ADHD may also report lower levels of sexual satisfaction, due to experiencing distracting thoughts or difficulty processing sensory stimuli during sexual encounters, difficulties with finding partners or maintaining relationships, or difficulty holding attention long enough to build sufficient emotional safety to engage in sex (Soldati et al., 2020). Impulsivity and inattention can also complicate partners' ability to focus on and meet one another's sexual needs, which along with negative impacts on self-esteem-related ADHD may contribute toward a tendency to sexual aversion or negative emotions after sex (Soldati et al., 2020).

### *Impacts of Trauma: TBI and PTSD*

While some neurodiverse conditions, like epilepsy and ADHD, are congenital (although not always identified until adulthood), others, like traumatic brain injury (TBI) or post-traumatic stress disorder (PTSD), come about as the result of a traumatic experience. The impact of these events is not uniform over time or between people. TBI, for instance, can cause increase or decrease in sexual desire, and can impact arousal and ability to reach orgasm (Sander & Maestas, 2014). The experience of a traumatic brain injury in a partner can also impact someone's sexuality. Traumatic injuries take a physical and emotional toll on loved ones as well, and changes to a partner's mood, cognition, or self-esteem can be misinterpreted as a loss of sexual interest (Downing & Ponsford, 2018; Fraser et al., 2020). In addition to changes in mood, cognition, and behavior, traumatic brain injuries can cause physical changes that impact sexuality, including ongoing pain, mobility changes, and fatigue (Sander & Maestas, 2014).

Other traumatic events may cause fewer physical changes but have long lasting effects on mood, thoughts, attention, and how information processing; a constellation of changes known as PTSD, which may significantly impact how people feel about their bodies and sexual relationships (Weaver, 2009). PTSD symptoms are a result of changes to the brain that can occur when a person feels extremely threatened. They may include hyperarousal (feeling constantly on guard), depression and intrusive thoughts, issues with attention and focus, dissociation (uncontrolled "zoning out" or feeling separate from oneself or one's environment) or intense memories or flashbacks (WHO, 2019). PTSD can be caused by a wide variety of experiences, and affects all people differently. Negative impacts on mood, thinking, and self-esteem, especially avoidance or "numbing" symptoms, can lead to a reduced sexual desire or pleasure (Richardson et al., 2020). These issues can occur regardless of the traumatic events experienced, but survivors of sexual violence may have particular issues when resuming sexual relationships. Sexual intimacy may include stimuli that trigger intrusive memories or flash backs, leading to distress or lashing out in defense (Martinson et al., 2013).

### The Bigger Picture

It must be noted that this review does not cover all of the literature, or even all of the conditions that fall under the neurodivergent umbrella – to do so would be a book in itself! What we have covered so far is rather meant to be an overview of some of what is known about a few particular conditions (as noted, others are covered elsewhere in this book), and the types of issues that may arise when working with neurodivergent people around sexuality.

It is clear neurodivergence can impact people's approach to sexuality and sexual intimacy in a variety of ways. Many of these relate to sensory preferences – that is, how much and what type of sensory input people enjoy. Across conditions, neurodivergent people may be hypersensitive – much more reactive to stimuli, and needing a gentler touch or other sensory input, or hyposensitive – less reactive and potentially needing more or firmer touch or other sensory input, or being more generally sensory seeking. There are eight sensory systems: olfactory (smell), visual (sight), gustatory (taste), auditory (sound), tactile (touch), vestibular (balance), interoception (internal body signals), and proprioception (motor control/planning) (STAR Institute, 2022). Neurodivergent folks' unique sensory processing tendencies may include being hypersensitive to noises or touch, which can be related to volume, pressure, or specific types of stimuli (e.g., dislike certain sounds or words, prefer certain fabrics/materials). Others may prefer deep or slow touch, or have strong preferences about smells (including potentially the detergents used on sheets). Some people may engage in "stimming," behaviors that help them regulate their level of stimulation. Importantly, while strong sensory preference is common among many neurodivergent people, the preferences themselves differ broadly; partners and providers should work to discuss these needs openly to help build safe, enjoyable sexual relationships for each individual.

### What Does This Mean for Our Clients and Communities?

Neurodivergent clients face a number of challenges related to their sexuality. They may experience frustration, confusion, or loneliness related to navigating a world that views sexuality and intimacy in neurotypical ways. All humans have a right to engage in healthy sexuality if desired, and neurodivergent people can build trusting, enjoyable, enthusiastic sexual relationships with others who share their conditions, have other conditions, or with neurotypical partners who can communicate openly and effectively about their and their partners' needs and desires.

There are a number of ways in which mental health professionals, and society more broadly, can help reduce the barriers neurodivergent people face to fulfilling sexual lives. First and foremost is self-education, and examination of assumptions and biases. Many people have unconscious beliefs about who is or is not interested in or capable of a healthy sexual relationship, and these should be brought forward and challenged. Providers should be aware of all people's sexual rights, and advocate for their ability to engage in safe and consensual sexual relationships.

Provision of sex education is also extremely important. Autistic people report significantly less access to sex education than others (Joyal et al., 2021; Brown-Lavoie et al., 2014), and sex education is typically focused on neurotypical learners. This can impact people across the broad spectrum of neurodivergent conditions, including those such as dyslexia and dyscalculia that can affect how people are able to access statistics and other printed educational materials. In addition to therapists and sex therapists who are educated and specialized in work with neurodivergent folks, there is also a need for more inclusive sex education curricula, including both more broadly accessible curricula and those that are tailored specifically to different neurodivergent groups. For instance, many autistic people report interest in learning more about sexuality and gaining sexual knowledge, particularly around the social components of intimacy, communication, and consent.

Furthermore, research about autistic individuals, particularly youths, often relies on reports from family members, as opposed to individuals themselves, often leading to discrepancies (Hong et al., 2016). Inquiries around gender and sexuality are often presented in a binarized fashion, but as noted, autistic people report a range of gender and sexual identities, which does not align with limited categorizations. Therapists, researchers, and teachers alike should speak to neurodivergent individuals themselves, and use terminology that is broad enough to capture their experiences and perspectives.

## Best Practices

There are a multitude of ways to support neurodivergent individuals when it comes to helping them have happy, healthy, and sexually affirming lives. For the purposes of this chapter, we are going to divide these practices into offering education and therapy in affirming and inclusive ways, and then tips to offer your clients that may help them in their own sex lives to explore and affirm their authentic selves.

## *Offering Neurodivergent-Inclusive Education and/or Therapy*

First, ensuring that the spaces in which you offer education and/or therapy are inclusive to this community is paramount. Some of this includes the built environment; are your spaces designed for people who might experience sensory overload or sensory sensitivity? Think about forgoing overhead fluorescent lights in lieu of having several smaller lights or lamps (Wi-Fi-enabled bulbs where you can change brightness and color easily are fairly cheap and great for customizing spaces quickly), or if you have no control over this, consider dimming or turning off a significant portion of the overhead lighting. Make sure you are not somewhere particularly loud (like right next to a crowded hallway or a classroom with high ceilings that echo), and if you are near noises, consider offering soft ear plugs, noise defender headphones, or other noise reducing options to those joining you in that space. Avoid using scents, such as fragrance plug ins, scented candles, incense, perfumes, or fresh paint in these spaces.

Having neurodivergent-friendly furniture, such as softer materials, various sitting options that include sitting on comfy items on the floor and standing as choices, different height chairs, places where someone can curl up, etc., having weight blankets, can be very helpful. Offering stims and fidget toys, such as pops-its, puzzles, stuffed animals, crystals, silly putty, fidget spinners/cubes, and pillows with reversible sequins, will allow people attending your educational or therapeutic space not only the option to stim, but they express consent that such behavior is welcome in that space.

As many neurodivergent individuals may find connection using nonverbal communication more comfortable and effective than speaking out loud, having virtual options for them to connect to education or therapy is ideal, especially if they are able to use the chat box to communicate. However, for sessions or trainings in-person, you can also have options for people to anonymously text in questions, write questions on a piece of paper that can be handed in, and even have non-word-based communication options, such as red/yellow/green signs that could be shown based on their comfort level with the conversation or discussion, sliders to indicate level of comfort or overwhelm, nonverbal based discussion boards where words can be pointed at or selected, or other alternative communication methods. Even asking them to share some of their favorite memes, TikToks, or content creators can be a great way to connect and communicate outside of verbal/spoken communication styles.

## *Tips for Exploring and Practicing Sexuality*

When it comes to supporting neurodivergent people in their sexuality practices, there are a lot of suggestions that can make their experiences much more affirming. One of the most important is that of communication. Whether someone is autistic, has OCD, or is navigating PTSD, etc., the importance of clear communication between all parties cannot be overstated. This should not be only framed around consent (although also incredibly necessary), but around all aspects of sexuality, from what language someone would like used about themselves and their body parts to how they might need to communicate if they are overwhelmed sensorily, are triggered, or even need to be nonverbal due to high levels of delight and enjoyment.

Suggesting various communication styles for before, during, and after sex or other intimacy time, such as texting, written notes, signing (e.g., either an official signed language or other agreed-upon signs), asking "curiosity"-based questions (e.g., "I'm curious as to what you mean when you say you want to 'get at me'?" or "You said you'd like me to communicate more during sex; can you tell me what that looks like to you?"), head nods or shakes, thumbs up, thumbs sideways, thumbs down, etc. can provide a useful jumping off point. Similarly, doing some role play about what a potential interaction with a partner(s) might look like could help to alleviate anxiety leading up to these experiences. This practice should include setting boundaries (e.g., "Please don't approach me from behind") as well as establishing things that an individual would like to happen, such as having a debrief conversation after play time. Remind people you are working with that it is absolutely okay to have a shift in needs during sex, that they can ask for a pause to figure out what is going on for them, or that it is of course acceptable for them to end any sexual interaction at any point can be helpful reminders.

Other things to think about include sensory needs. Some individuals may be uncomfortable with certain components of sexual intimacy, such as the feeling of lube. Offering suggestions such as wearing gloves, or trying out a thicker or thinner lube, could allow them to still use this important component without activating too much of their sensory sensitivity. Encouraging people to take a shower or bath before or after sex can help contain some worries about sensations as well as intrusive thoughts about cleanliness that some people might experience.

In some cases, individuals might need extra stimulation to stay present, so suggesting they bring a less intrusive stim or fidget device to the bedroom, add music or lights to increase sensory input, etc., could allow them to focus more on themselves or their partners while participating in sexual activity. Conversely, others may feel overwhelmed by sexual stimulation as is, so offering ideas like using ear plugs/ear defenders and blindfolds could be useful in supporting them in controlling their external sensory stimuli.

It's also nice to support neurodivergent clients in knowing that there is no one "right" way to have sex; some may enjoy kissing, while others might prefer intimate interactions that don't involve kissing. Others might choose not to participate in a certain act because it brings up painful memories, or initiates intrusive thoughts – reminding them that they get to decide exactly what they do (and don't!) want to do could be useful. Similarly, reinforcing the idea that there are many ways to be close and intimate with partners that do not involve being sexual is a good reminder, especially as there are asexual, demisexual, and nonsexually active neurodivergent people as well.

## Case Study

Rachel is a 26-year-old Black, cisgender, heterosexual woman who uses she/her pronouns. For three years, beginning when she was 11 years old, she was repeatedly sexually assaulted by her mother's boyfriend, who entered her room at night and touched her on her breasts, as well as inserted his fingers into her vagina. Although it took a long time, Rachel was eventually able to tell her mother about the abuse. Her mother broke up with the boyfriend and kicked him out of the home. They decided together to press charges and her mother was supportive during the court case, which they won.

Rachel reports feeling few lingering effects of this experience; she works as a registered nurse and is in a happy relationship of about one year with her boyfriend, Victor. Victor is a 24-year-old, Latino, cisgender, heterosexual man who uses he/him pronouns and works in advertising. The two recently moved in together and enjoy many of the same things, and Rachel generally enjoys her sex life with Victor, but feels worried because she is uncomfortable with certain types of stimulation, particularly any digital-genital stimulation or touching of her breasts, due to her trauma.

Rachel presented to therapy alone to discuss these concerns, as well as her fears that her discomfort with breast stimulation might impact her ability to breastfeed a child, which is very important to her for the future. She noted that she has not told Victor about what happened to her and would prefer not to. So far, he has respected her boundaries about particular sexual activities, but Rachel reported wanting to put her assault completely behind her and no longer have it affect her life. She noted that, especially with breast touching, Victor at times forgets her preferences. Rachel has been able to tolerate this and does not experience flashbacks, but it reduces her enjoyment of the sexual encounter and she described "zoning out" because of it.

Rachel's therapist talked with her about the ways that traumatic experiences can affect our brains and how we relate to different stimuli, both those related and unrelated to the experience, and discussed the possibility that her "zoning out" might be a form of dissociation. Rachel noted comfort and enjoyment with most other sexual activities, and initially indicated that the stimulation she described was her only trigger to trauma. With exploration, Rachel realized that she also tends to wake up afraid if Victor comes to bed after she has fallen asleep, and that situations that make her feel trapped may be triggering even if they are unrelated to her trauma (for instance, she recalled feeling very panicky when she heard a fight happening outside while she was under a hair dryer at a salon).

Rachel and her therapist collaborated on a plan to begin to safely expose her to stimulation which had been triggering. She began experimenting with touching her own breasts while in the shower, paying close attention to her breath and emotions. She was able to slowly move past discomfort to feeling more neutral about this type of touch. During this process, Rachel and her therapist discussed how she had made sense of her trauma and its impact on other areas of her life, including her relationship with her mother and her thoughts about becoming a parent herself. Eventually, Rachel reported wanting to experiment with breast stimulation with Victor, and shared that this was no longer a trigger to dissociation or discomfort, although she still did not find it particularly arousing.

Rachel concluded that she was not interested in engaging in digital penetration, and after discussing it with her therapist, she chose to bring Victor into a session to talk about her needs. She still preferred not to share the details of her trauma but was able to tell him that the boundaries she had set around sexual touching had to do with some things that had happened in her past. Victor shared he had thought this might be the case, and affirmed he loved her and did not need her to tell him more for him to respect her needs. The pair processed Victor's occasional "forgetting" relating to touching her breasts, and Victor apologized, noting that he could have been more thoughtful in those moments.

This allowed for an atmosphere of trust and openness in the space, in which Rachel was able to share that she could be startled awake when he came to bed after her. The pair engaged in creative collaboration around this, and decided that Victor should turn on the lights when he came to bed and Rachel was already asleep. Victor noted not wanting to wake her, but they decided that it would be better for her to wake up fully and then go back to sleep together than be startled awake.

## Case Study Questions

After reviewing the case, take some time to contemplate the following questions, which reflect therapeutic considerations demonstrated throughout the case study.

1. Consider how Rachel described the way her traumatic experiences impacted her sexuality. What was your reaction to her experiences?
2. What have you been taught about trauma, PTSD and sexuality?
3. What other ways might trauma impact sexual relationships? Could trauma from other contexts (i.e., violence in war, natural disaster) also impact sexuality? In what ways?

4. Consider Rachel's choice not to tell her partner about her traumatic experiences. What do you think about this decision? How might therapy have been different if Rachel had also chosen not to share her experiences with her therapist?
5. Take a moment to engage in self-reflection. What feelings arose for you while you were reading or after you read the case study? How comfortable do you think you would be as the therapist discussing topics from this case? Do you think you would have done things differently than the therapist?

## Conclusion

As with all people, neurodivergent clients should be understood as experts in themselves, their desires, and their needs. As social workers, we should meet all clients where they are at, respect the dignity and worth of all persons, and work to increase their well-being and empower them to lead full lives in accordance with their values (National Association of Social Workers [NASW], 2021). If a client tells us that their neurodivergence, whether from the rainbow spectrum of autism, ADHD, PTSD, TBI, or something else, is impacting their ability to fully enjoy their sex life, we should believe them and work with them to resolve the issue. The infinity sign reminds us that these experiences are constantly flowing and shifting, and we can help support individuals, couples, and groups through these fluxes to live and access their most authentic selves and sexual experiences.

## Resources

Autistic Self Advocacy Network: https://autisticadvocacy.org/
Autistic Women and Nonbinary Network: https://awnnetwork.org/
Brown, F. J., & Brown, S. (2016). *When young people with intellectual disabilities and autism hit puberty: A parents' Q&A guide to health, sexuality and relationships.* Jessica Kingsley Publishers.
Catieosaurus: https://beacons.page/catieosaurus
Children and Adults with Attention-Deficit/Hyperactivity Disorder (CHADD): https://chadd.org/for-professionals/overview/
Davies, C., & Dubie, M. (2012). *Intimate relationships and sexual health: A curriculum for teaching adolescents/adults with high-functioning autism spectrum disorders and other social challenges.* AAPC Publishing.
Downing, M., & Ponsford, J. (2018). Sexuality in individuals with traumatic brain injury and their partners. *Neuropsychological Rehabilitation, 28*(6), 1028–1037. https://doi.org/10.1080/09602011.2016.1236732
Goodall, E. (2016). *The autism spectrum guide to sexuality and relationships: Understand yourself and make choices that are right for you.* Jessica Kingsley Publishers.
Hannah, L. A., & Stagg, S. D. (2016). Experiences of sex education and sexual awareness in young adults with autism spectrum disorder. *Journal of Autism*

*and Developmental Disorders*, 46(12), 3678–3687. https://doi.org/10.1007/s10803-016-2906-2

Lawson, W. (2005). *Sex, sexuality and the autism spectrum*. Jessica Kingsley Publishers.

Little, L. M., Dean, E., Tomchek, S., & Dunn, W. (2018). Sensory processing patterns in autism, attention deficit hyperactivity disorder, and typical development. *Physical & Occupational Therapy in Pediatrics*, 38(3), 243–254. https://doi.org/10.1080/01942638.2017.1390809

Mendes, E. A., & Maroney, M. R. (2019). *Gender identity, sexuality and autism: Voices from across the spectrum*. Jessica Kingsley Publishers.

Neuroclastic: https://neuroclastic.com/

Neurodivergent Rebel: https://neurodivergentrebel.com/

Neurodivergent Sexuality Tumblr: https://neurodivergentsexuality.tumblr.com

Newport, J., & Newport, M. (2002). *Autism-Asperger's & sexuality*. Future Horizons.

Obsessive Joy of Autism

Pelmas, C. (2017). *Trauma: A practical guide to working with body and soul (somatic sex educator's handbook book 1)*. CreateSpace Independent Publishing Platform.

Schmidt, B. J., Döhler, C., & Döhler, D. (2018). *Autism-sexuality-relationships*. BoD – Books on Demand. https://neuromess.weebly.com/blog/economy-of-communication-is-an-autistic-strength

## References

Armstrong, T. (2015). The myth of the normal brain: Embracing neurodiversity. *AMA Journal of Ethics*, 17(4), 348–352. https://doi.org/10.1001/journalofethics.2015.17.4.msoc1-1504

Autistic Self Advocacy Network (ASAN). (2022). *About autism*. https://autisticadvocacy.org/about-asan/about-autism/

Barnett, J. P., & Maticka-Tyndale, E. (2015). Qualitative exploration of sexual experiences among adults on the autism spectrum: Implications for sex education. *Perspectives on Sexual and Reproductive Health*, 47(4), 171–179. https://doi.org/10.1363/47e5715

Bennett, M., Webster, A. A., Goodall, E., & Rowland, S. (2018). Intimacy and romance across the autism spectrum: Unpacking the "not interested in sex" myth. In *Life on the autism spectrum* (pp. 195–211). Springer.

Bertilsdotter Rosqvist, H., & Jackson-Perry, D. (2020). Not doing it properly? (Re)producing and resisting knowledge through narratives of autistic sexualities. *Sexuality and Disability*, 39(2), 327–344. https://doi.org/10.1007/s11195-020-09624-

Blume, H. (1998). Neurodiversity: On the neurological underpinnings of geekdom. *The Atlantic*, 30. www.theatlantic.com/magazine/archive/1998/09/neurodiversity/305909/

Bőthe, B., Koós, M., Tóth-Király, I., Orosz, G., & Demetrovics, Z. (2019). Investigating the associations of adult ADHD symptoms, hypersexuality, and problematic pornography use among men and women on a largescale, non-clinical sample. *The Journal of Sexual Medicine*, 16(4), 489–499. https://doi.org/10.1016/j.jsxm.2019.01.312

Brown-Lavoie, S. M., Viecili, M. A., & Weiss, J. (2014). Sexual knowledge and victimization in adults with autism spectrum disorders. *Journal of Autism and Developmental Disorders, 44*(9), 2185–2196. https://doi.org/10.1007/s10803-014-2093-y

Byers, E. S., Nichols, S., & Voyer, S. D. (2013). Challenging stereotypes: Sexual functioning of single adults with high functioning autism spectrum disorder. *Journal of Autism and Developmental Disorders, 43*(11), 2617–2627. https://doi.org/10.1007/s10803-013-1813-z

Children and Adults with Attention-Deficit/Hyperactivity Disorder (CHADD). (2022). *Understanding ADHD: Overview for professionals.* https://chadd.org/for-professionals/overview/

Colombo-Dougovito, A. M., Dillon, S. R., & Mpofu, E. (2020). The wellbeing of people with neurodiverse conditions. In *Sustainable community health* (pp. 499–535). Palgrave Macmillan.

Crehan, E. T., Rocha, J., & Dufresne, S. (2022). Brief report: Sources of sexuality and relationship education for autistic and neurotypical adults in the U.S. and a call to action. *Journal of Autism and Developmental Disorders, 52*(2), 908–913. https://doi.org/10.1007/s10803-021-04992-z

de Vincentiis, S., Febrônio, M. V., da Silva, C. A. A., Saito, M. I., Takiuti, A. D., & Valente, K. D. R. (2008). Sexuality in teenagers with epilepsy. *Epilepsy & Behavior, 13*(4), 703–706. https://doi.org/10.1016/j.yebeh.2008.05.017

Dewinter, J., Vermeiren, R., Vanwesenbeeck, I., Lobbestael, J., & Van Nieuwenhuizen, C. (2015). Sexuality in adolescent boys with autism spectrum disorder: Self-reported behaviours and attitudes. *Journal of Autism and Developmental Disorders, 45*(3), 731–741.

Downing, M., & Ponsford, J. (2018). Sexuality in individuals with traumatic brain injury and their partners. *Neuropsychological Rehabilitation, 28*(6), 1028–1037. https://doi.org/10.1080/09602011.2016.1236732

Doyle, N. (2020). Neurodiversity at work: A biopsychosocial model and the impact on working adults. *British Medical Bulletin, 135*(1), 108. https://doi.org/10.1093/bmb/ldaa021

Fraser, E. E., Downing, M. G., & Ponsford, J. L. (2020). Understanding the multidimensional nature of sexuality after traumatic brain injury. *Archives of Physical Medicine and Rehabilitation, 101*(12), 2080–2086. https://doi.org/10.1016/j.apmr.2020.06.028

George, R., & Stokes, M. A. (2018a). Sexual orientation in autism spectrum disorder. *Autism Research, 11*(1), 133–141. https://doi.org/10.1002/aur.1892

George, R., & Stokes, M. A. (2018b). Gender identity and sexual orientation in autism spectrum disorder. *Autism: The International Journal of Research and Practice, 22*(8), 970–982. https://doi.org/10.1177/1362361317714587

Gougeon, N. A. (2010). Sexuality and autism: A critical review of selected literature using a social-relational model of disability. *American Journal of Sexuality Education, 5*(4), 328–361, https://doi.org/10.1080/15546128.2010.527237

Hannah, L. A., & Stagg, S. D. (2016). Experiences of sex education and sexual awareness in young adults with autism spectrum disorder. *Journal of Autism and Developmental Disorders, 46*(12), 3678–3687. https://doi.org/10.1007/s10803-016-2906-2

Harden, C. L. (2005). Sexuality in women with epilepsy. *Epilepsy & Behavior, 7,* 2–6. https://doi.org/10.1016/j.yebeh.2005.08.025

Holmes, L. G., Shattuck, P. T., Nilssen, A. R., Strassberg, D. S., & Himle, M. B. (2020). Sexual and reproductive health service utilization and sexuality for teens on the autism spectrum. *Journal of Developmental and Behavioral Pediatrics: JDBP, 41*(9), 667–679. https://doi.org/10.1097/DBP.0000000000000838

Hong, J., Bishop-Fitzpatrick, L., Smith, L. E., Greenberg, J. S., & Mailick, M. R. (2016). Factors associated with subjective quality of life of adults with autism spectrum disorder: Self-report versus maternal reports. *Journal of Autism and Developmental Disorders, 46*, 1368–1378.

Joyal, C. C., Carpentier, J., McKinnon, S., Normand, C. L., & Poulin, M.-H. (2021). Sexual knowledge, desires, and experience of adolescents and young adults with an autism spectrum disorder: An exploratory study. *Frontiers in Psychiatry, 12*. https://doi.org/10.3389/fpsyt.2021.685256

Karan, V., Harsha, S., Keshava, B. S., Pradeep, R., Sathyanarayana Rao, T. S., & Andrade, C. (2015). Sexual dysfunction in women with epilepsy. *Indian Journal of Psychiatry, 57*(3), 301–304. https://doi.org/10.4103/0019-5545.166616

Kim, S. Y. (2019). The experiences of adults with autism spectrum disorder: Self-determination and quality of life. *Research in Autism Spectrum Disorders, 60*, 1–15. https://doi.org/10.1016/j.rasd.2018.12.002

Korchia, T., Boyer, L., Deneuville, M., Etchecopar-Etchart, D., Lancon, C., & Fond, G. (2022). ADHD prevalence in patients with hypersexuality and paraphilic disorders: A systematic review and meta-analysis. *European Archives of Psychiatry and Clinical Neuroscience*. https://doi.org/10.1007/s00406-022-01421-9

Luef, G. J. (2008). Epilepsy and sexuality. *Seizure, 17*(2), 127–130. https://doi.org/10.1016/j.seizure.2007.11.009

Martinson, A. A., Sigmon, S. T., Craner, J., Rothstein, E., & McGillicuddy, M. (2013). Processing of intimacy-related stimuli in survivors of sexual trauma: The role of PTSD. *Journal of Interpersonal Violence, 28*(9), 1886–1908. https://doi.org/10.1177/0886260512469104

National Association of Social Workers. (2021). *NASW code of ethics*. www.socialworkers.org/About/Ethics/Code-of-Ethics/

Neff, M. A. (2021). *ADHD vs. PTSD*. https://neurodivergentinsights.com/misdiagnosis-monday/adhd-vs-or-and-ptsd

Pecora, L. A., Hooley, M., Sperry, L., Mesibov, G. B., & Stokes, M. A. (2020). Sexuality and gender issues in individuals with autism spectrum disorder. *Child and Adolescent Psychiatric Clinics of North America, 29*(3), 543–556. https://doi.org/10.1016/j.chc.2020.02.007

Richardson, J. D., Ketcheson, F., King, L., Forchuk, C. A., Hunt, R., Cyr, K. St., Nazarov, A., Shnaider, P., McIntyre-Smith, A., & Elhai, J. D. (2020). Sexual dysfunction in male Canadian armed forces members and veterans seeking mental health treatment. *Military Medicine, 185*(1/2), 68–74. https://doi.org/10.1093/milmed/usz163

Sala, G., Hooley, M., & Stokes, M. A. (2020). Romantic intimacy in autism: A qualitative analysis. *Journal of Autism and Developmental Disorders, 50*(11), 4133–4147. https://doi.org/10.1007/s10803-020-04377-8

Sander, A. M., & Maestas, K. L. (2014). Sexuality after traumatic brain injury. *Archives of Physical Medicine and Rehabilitation, 95*(9), 1801–1802. https://doi.org/10.1016/j.apmr.2013.06.004

Sapiets, S. J. (2021). *Embracing complexity in research on neurodevelopmental conditions and mental health*. https://kar.kent.ac.uk/id/eprint/93151

Singer, J. (1998). Why can't you be normal for once in your life? From a problem with no name to the emergence of a new category of difference. *Disability Discourse*, 59–70.

Soldati, L., Bianchi-Demicheli, F., Schockaert, P., Köhl, J., Bolmont, M., Hasler, R., & Perroud, N. (2020). Sexual function, sexual dysfunctions, and ADHD: A systematic literature review. *The Journal of Sexual Medicine*, *17*(9), 1653–1664. https://doi.org/10.1016/j.jsxm.2020.03.019

Soldati, L., Bianchi-Demicheli, F., Schockaert, P., Köhl, J., Bolmont, M., Hasler, R., & Perroud, N. (2021). Association of ADHD and hypersexuality and paraphilias. *Psychiatry Research*, *295*, 113638. https://doi.org/10.1016/j.psychres.2020.113638

STAR Institute. (2022). *Your 8 senses*. Sensory Health. https://sensoryhealth.org/basic/your-8-senses

Walker, N. (2021). *Neuroqueer heresies: Notes on the neurodiversity paradigm, autistic empowerment, and postnormal possibilities*. Autonomous Press.

Weaver, T. L. (2009). Impact of rape on female sexuality: Review of selected literature. *Clinical Obstetrics and Gynecology*, *52*(4), 702–711. https://doi.org/10.1097/GRF.0b013e3181bf4bfb

Weir, E., Allison, C., & Baron-Cohen, S. (2021). The sexual health, orientation, and activity of autistic adolescents and adults. *Autism Research*, *14*(11), 2342–2354. https://doi.org/10.1002/aur.2604

World Health Organization (WHO). (2019). *International statistical classification of diseases and related health problems* (11th ed.). https://icd.who.int/

# 5

# ACCESS ISN'T OPTIONAL

Sexuality and Intellectual/Developmental Disabilities

*Shanna Katz Kattari and Kari L. Sherwood*

### Introduction

Intellectual and/or developmental disability is defined as intellectual or cognitive disabilities which begin in childhood (sometimes at or before birth) and impact lifelong learning, sociality, emotionality, and practical living (APA, 2013). Intellectual disabilities often co-occur with other developmental disabilities such as autism (Bryson et al., 2008) and Down syndrome, with Down syndrome being the most common genetic cause of intellectual disability (Boston Children's Hospital, n.d.). Other co-occurring disabilities might include Fetal Alcohol Syndrome, Fragile X Syndrome, and Traumatic Brain Injury. For this reason, we will refer to these conditions as intellectual and developmental disabilities (IDD) throughout this chapter. However, like most cases of identity, there is overlap between experiences. For more information on supporting neurodivergent individuals, check out Chapter 4.

IDD is lifelong and can be genetic, caused at birth, a result of exposure to toxins, or a result of a head injury (CDC, 2022). It can cause a delay in crawling, walking, talking, learning, problems with memory, self-care, and difficulty learning social rules (CDC, 2022). As with other disabilities, children with IDD in the United States (U.S.) are eligible for state-funded early intervention, special education services through their local public school district, and vocational rehabilitation services. The special education law known as the Individuals with Disabilities Education Act (IDEA, 2004) lists "intellectual disability" as one of its 13 disability categories. However, some states such as Michigan list it as "cognitive impairment" (MARSE, 2021). This causes some confusion when it comes to writing policy and providing services for this population. Moreover, different states may support individuals

DOI: 10.4324/9781003308331-8

differently, just as each different country (and sometimes different states, counties, provinces, etc., within these countries) have different policies in place, or not, to support the needs of this group of people.

In the United States, the prevalence of IDD is somewhere between 11 and 13 per 1,000 (~0.01%) for ID and between 46 and 70 per 1,000 (~0.06%) for DD (Anderson et al., 2019). However, there is currently no systematic national collection of prevalence data for IDD, meaning these numbers are likely under reported. Around the world, the prevalence of IDD is approximately 1.0%, with higher rates in low-and middle-income countries (Maulik et al., 2011), though this also could be due to better tracking in these countries. Lack of use of standardized diagnostic assessments across the world is also a challenge in assessing the prevalence of this population.

When treating IDD individuals, it is important to keep in mind their individual strengths, limitations, and needs as these can vary greatly from person to person. There is no one size fits all approach, and much of our work will need to be conducted in tandem with undoing ableism, stigma, and paternalistic beliefs that are often associated with those who are intellectually and/or developmentally disabled.

The American Association of Intellectual and Developmental Disabilities put out a statement that we believe it is important to share in its entirety. While this chapter goes into more details about how to affirm and support the needs of those with IDD, this position statement covers more systemic and foundational beliefs and rights of this population when it comes to sexuality and reproduction:

Every person has the right to exercise choices regarding sexual expression and social relationships. The presence of IDD, regardless of severity, does not, in itself, justify loss of rights related to sexuality.

### All people have the right within interpersonal relationships to:

- Develop friendships and emotional and sexual relationships where they can love and be loved, and begin and end a relationship as they choose;
- Dignity and respect; and
- Privacy, confidentiality, and freedom of association.

### With respect to sexuality, individuals have a right to:

- Sexual expression and education, reflective of their own cultural, religious, and moral values and of social responsibility;
- Individualized education and information to encourage informed decision-making, including education about such issues as reproduction, marriage and family life, abstinence, safe sexual practices, sexual orientation, sexual abuse, and sexually transmitted diseases; and

- Protection from sexual harassment and from physical, sexual, and emotional abuse.

*With respect to sexuality, individuals have a responsibility to consider the values, rights, and feelings of others.*
*With respect to the potential for having and raising children, individuals with IDD have the right to:*

- Education and information about having and raising children that is individualized to reflect each person's unique ability to understand;
- Make their own decisions related to having and raising children with supports as necessary;
- Make their own decisions related to using birth control methods within the context of their personal or religious beliefs;
- Have control over their own bodies; and
- Be protected from sterilization solely because of their disability (AAIDD, 2008).

### Background About IDD and Sexuality

As with most disabilities, biological development and sexual maturity often coincide with their chronological age (American Academy of Pediatrics, 1996). Despite this, intellectually and/or developmentally disabled people are often stigmatized in regard to their sexual development and behavior: for instance, frameworks for people with IDD regarding sexuality often paternalizing (i.e., seeing IDD individuals as precious angels who couldn't possibly be interested in exploring and/or acting upon their own sexualities) or cast IDD individuals as predatory individuals (e.g., those who know not what they do as they seek satisfaction of their basic instincts) (Dotson et al., 2003). People with IDD can also be viewed as only being sexually vulnerable, meaning they are often assumed to only be engaged in sexual experiences if they are being taken advantage of. What is often not assumed is that people with IDD are sexual beings with sexual desires just like the rest of us. They often desire and deserve to engage in sexual experiences of their choosing based on the same legal and cultural norms as their same-age peers.

Affirming sexual education for intellectually and/or developmentally disabled people is necessary to ensure sexual safety, legality, and pleasure, yet is seriously lacking. There is very often a lack of inclusion of people with IDD in sexual education curricula, courses, or presentations. In the 1980s, not even 5% of disabled young people were able to access sexuality education or sexuality counseling services to get accurate information and needed support around their own sexuality (Szasz, 1991). Although there has been progress in the past 30 years, more recent research notes that access to sexuality education varied based on type of disability or impairment. In fact, only 25.0% of those disabled individuals with IDD were able to access such sexuality education compared to 47.5% of their disabled counterparts who have disability types other than IDD (Barnard-Brak et al., 2014). This leaves IDD individuals half as likely to receive sexual education as compared to other disabled individuals – a likely effect of the binarized stigma around IDD individuals and sexuality. When they are included in sexual education, it is often the same pre-packaged curriculum given to all students (with or without disabilities). It is also mostly designed by nondisabled folks who are not able to convey the material in an age- or developmentally appropriate way.

Additionally, sexual assault is often experienced at a high rate by this population, given a variety of factors that increase this risk, including individual factors, factors related to their disability status, and multiple systemic/institutional factors (Burrow et al., 2021). Shapiro (2018) found that intellectually and/or developmentally disabled adults experience sexual assault at a rate of seven times that of adults without disabilities, while (assumptively cisgender) women with IDD experience sexual assault at 12 times the rate of disabled adults. Many of these assaults happen at the hands of caregivers (whether family members or from medical caregivers, in the case of those who have been institutionalized), although sexual violence can also happen from partners, friends, and strangers as well. We think it is important to note this as part of the conversation, and the need for individuals with IDD to understand consent, their bodies, their sexuality, and their rights. However, this will not be a main focus of this chapter, as sexual assault is a form of violence and power and therefore should not be considered part of the general sexuality experience, nor should the onus be placed on individuals with IDD to stop the violence perpetuated against IDD individuals.

## How This Impacts Our Clients and Communities

### Policy Issues

In the United States, Canada, the United Kingdom, New Zealand, and Australia, laws regarding the age of consent for sexual activity range from 16 to 18 in most states and provinces, although certain locales offer flexibility for those ages 12–15, when partnering with someone close in age (Gilbert, 2018). Unfortunately, for disabled people, and especially those with intellectual and/or development disabilities, simply reaching a certain age may not be enough for IDD individuals to be viewed as able to give sexual consent. Disability justice advocates and scholars alike have long engaged the tension between protecting disabled people from harm, while also making sure that they are able to explore and engage in their own sexual experiences and desires (McGuire & Bayley, 2011; Stavis, 1991). One way this tension can be seen is through consent-related laws and policies, many of which target disabled people, and specifically those with IDD, through infantilization, assuming inherent heterosexuality and suggesting that all those with IDD are incapable of consenting to sexual activity in any context (Medina-Rico et al., 2018).

These policies are incredibly harmful, often preventing youths and adults with IDD from being to access information on their own bodies, puberty, and their own sexual desires, none the less information on consent, communication, pregnancy and STI prevention, and pleasure. Given that many people with IDD have not been allowed bodily autonomy and consent, especially those who have been warehoused or otherwise placed in residential treatment spaces, the need to access information on what consent is, what is (and is not) normal for their bodies, and how to understand and navigate their desires is especially crucial, both for preventing sexual assault and in supporting their own bodily autonomy.

In the case of disabled young people who are placed in pull-out learning spaces (in which disabled students are "pulled out" away from their nondisabled peers), the vast majority may never have access to medically accurate sexuality education. On the other hand, those who are in more integrated mainstream education settings may be asked not to attend during the day(s) when such education is be offered to their nondisabled peers. All in all, those with "mild" IDD who are in integrative learning space actually have had less access to sex education than their peers in pull out spaces (Barnard-Brak et al., 2014). Even if they are included in spaces where they are allowed to attend sexuality education sessions, intellectually and/or developmentally disabled people may not be offered appropriate accommodations to engage with this material, rendering it inaccessible. Even when they do have the opportunity engage with comprehensive sexuality education, these disabled youths (as well as adults) are still less likely to be able to access to information on sexual pleasure, and might find their sexuality education experience is more focused on pregnancy and STI prevention as compared to the general population (Tepper, 2000; Turner & Crane, 2016).

### *IDD Specific Sexuality Training*

To design sexuality education for people with IDD, it must be tailored to their needs utilizing a universal design for learning model. It is also helpful if the instruction be as explicit as possible, without making assumptions or using figurative language. In addition to basic sexuality topics found in general sexuality education courses, people with IDD may also benefit from additional topics such as dating, how to proposition someone (or not) during an encounter, and legal and social guidelines for sexual behavior (Walker-Hirsch, 2007).

To address these gaps, curricula have been developed that are specifically designed to meet the needs of those with IDD. For example, RespectAbility offers *Sexual Education Resources* for young adults with IDD. ElevatUs Training provides a *Sexuality Education for People With Developmental Disabilities Curriculum*. In addition, the Center for Parent Information and Resources (2018) offers *Sexuality Education for Students With Disabilities* and the Better Health Channel has a fact sheet on *Cognitive Disability and Sexuality*. Human Relations Media produces a puberty workshop and curriculum for middle schoolers, which could be adapted or supplemented to cater to people with IDD. See the Resources section for more information and links to each of these curriculums.

Some examples of helpful information we would like to make sure we include are the *Better Health Channel* (Australian), that has a whole subsection of cognitive disability and sexuality (n.d.), breaking down a variety of areas for parents, educators, and caregivers of intellectually and developmentally disabled people that covers basic information on everything from body image to reproductive rights, and consent to pregnancy and parenthood. It also discusses sexual assault, which is an important topic for any conversation around sexuality, but especially for those with IDD, who experience high rates of sexual assault (Burrow et al., 2021).

ElavatUs (n.d.) has an entire sexuality education curriculum designed for those with IDD, including very specific lesson plans on topics such as what is appropriate for public versus private time, moving from friend to partner/sweetheart, communication tips, taking care of your body, and more. This is designed for groups of people with IDD, and is excellent for clinicians running small groups in their practice, or educators offering ongoing sex education programing to students with IDD.

There are also opportunities for providers, caregivers, and parents to understand the basics of sexual health when supporting those with IDD. The Maryland Center for Developmental Disabilities at the Kennedy Krieger Institute (n.d.) offers this workshop for providers:

**Sexual Health and Intellectual and Developmental Disabilities 101: A Workshop for Providers**
For sexual health to be attained and maintained, the sexual rights of all persons must be respected, protected, and fulfilled. People with intellectual and developmental disabilities (IDD) are often left out of the conversation about sexuality, almost as if they were incapable of having thoughts, feelings, and needs. In reality, they, too, are sexual beings who need information and skills for making healthy decisions about sexuality. This workshop will help providers who work with people with IDD become more comfortable talking about this topic with people with IDD and their

parents and caregivers. Attendees will also learn how to help people with IDD have safe and satisfying relationships.

Equally as important (and perhaps more importantly) is offering information and trainings to those with IDD themselves. The same center offers this self-advocacy workshop for those with IDD (The Maryland Center for Developmental Disabilities at the Kennedy Krieger Institute, n.d.):

**What Is Sexual Health? Understanding Healthy Relationships, Sexual Self-Advocacy and Making Informed Choices: A Workshop for People With Disabilities, Ages 18 Years and Up**
People with intellectual and developmental disabilities are often left out of the conversation about sexuality, almost as if they were incapable of having thoughts, feelings, and needs. In reality, they, too, are sexual beings who need information and skills for making healthy decisions about sexuality. This workshop is designed to help participants understand what sexual health is, learn how to have healthy relationships, know their rights and the meaning of sexual self-advocacy, and make informed choices.

Unfortunately, workshops and trainings like these are few and far between. Ergo, providers, caregivers, parents, partners, and intellectually and/or developmentally disabled individuals must truly search to access these opportunities. To be an inclusive and affirming practitioner, you must seek out these opportunities, know your local resources, and advocate for your overseeing body (whether as a social worker, educator, psychologist, case manager, or healthcare professional) to offer more of these trainings, particularly ones that center the lived experiences of people with IDD and how they would like their sex education to look.

One important resource is finding local sex therapists, sex educators, or other clinicians who specialize in working with people with IDD. While there may not be any in your specific town or city, one benefit of the pandemic has been to increase access to virtual therapy and other services, so currently, anyone in your state with this specialty should be able to support and serve individuals with IDD and their partners. Of course, if you have a client who does not find virtual environments to be supportive, finding someone more local would be important. Even if you cannot find someone local who advertises as such, asking around at your local Center for Independent Living, or even asking IDD supportive sex therapists or sex educators from elsewhere for their recommendations may help you find someone that you may not yet be aware of. Willingness to do this extra legwork is crucial for supporting your clients with IDD; simply sending someone with IDD to a sex therapist or sex educator without knowledge of and an

IDD-affirming practice could do more harm than good, as the information or experience will likely not be useful to the person, and could trigger issues of anxiety and/or inadequacy (i.e., for not having previous sexual experiences, not understanding the content, feeling like they need their sexuality to look a certain way).

## Best Practices for Working With Intellectually and/or Developmentally Delayed People

According to the National Down Syndrome Society, the following areas are crucial in supporting the healthy sexuality of those with IDD or cognitive impairment: adult self-care, anatomy and physiology, empowerment and self-esteem, relationships, social skills, and social opportunities. When creating a treatment plan, a case management plan, or curricula for your practice, we encourage you to make sure that all of these six areas are addressed. If you are developing a program, curricula beyond a single day or workshop, etc., it would be a best practice to run your ideas by people with IDD (including a subpopulation you work with, such as BIPOC with IDD, LGBTQIA2S+ people with IDD, and young people with IDD). Community input, not just from parents/caregivers/providers, is absolutely crucial in developing affirming and culturally responsive programming to serve your clients, residents, and/or patients.

In an article written by Katherine McLaughlin of Planned Parenthood of Northern New England in 2003, here are some thoughts about age-appropriate sexuality-related topics that should be taught to intellectually and/or developmentally disabled young people:

### Ages 0–8:

- Accurate names for body parts and their functions
- That sexual body parts are private
- The distinction between public and private places
- Similarities and differences between boys and girls
- Body image – That bodies are different and good just the way they are
- People have the right to refuse touch from anyone at any time
- Masturbation can be pleasurable and should only be done in private
- If someone tries to touch your private body parts, say "no," leave, and tell an adult right away
- Where babies come from (in simple terms)

### Ages 9–13:

- Body changes
- Body hair

- Menstruation – what it is and how to deal with it (girls may need more information on using and changing pads/tampons, what to do if it happens at school, etc.)
- Breast development (some boys grow breast buds that go away in a year or so)
- Vaginas lubricating//penis and testicle growth
- Erections and "wet dreams" – what they are and that they're normal
- Hygiene – pimples, body odor, etc.
- Masturbation – what it is and that it should only be done in private
- Reproduction and pregnancy – what intercourse is, and that it is for consenting adults
- The changes of puberty happen at different rates for different people
- They have the right to refuse touch from anyone at any time
- Body image
- Gender roles and stereotypes

### Ages 14–20:

- Reproduction, pregnancy, and birth
- Sexually transmitted infections (STIs)
- Birth control and condom use
- How to say "no" to unwanted sexual contact
- Respecting personal space
- Romantic relationships and friendships
- Body image
- Gender roles and stereotypes

Almost 20 years later, these topics are still applicable, though we as authors would suggest a bit of a more robust conversation about sex differences, gender, gender roles, and stereotypes (including transgender and nonbinary people, and how no one needs to adhere to such roles), and more information about sexual diversity (bisexual, lesbian, gay, pansexual, queer, asexual people, etc.). It should also be noted that despite this nicely inclusive list, there is still little to any suggestion about sexual pleasure outside of masturbation, and no discussion of active consent. This list is an excellent starting point for conversations that should be happening with young people with IDD, yet should also make sure to affirm pleasure and desire, and some of the ways that active consent (i.e., yes means yes) might look like. Additionally, while these age categories may be a useful guide, as we discussed earlier, there are very low rates of sex education among those with IDD, so it is likely that adults with IDD have not been able to access this information, and therefore, you should think about including these topics when working with adults as well.

It is important to understand what knowledge someone may already have about sexuality, puberty, sexual health, etc. There is an example of a general sexual knowledge form in the resources section that can be used as a jumping off point. Given that it is not particularly inclusive of LGBTQIA2S+ individuals (including using the word homosexual), sex workers, etc., and has a question asking what a virgin is, we would encourage you to create your own such form to use in your practice. Again, this is a great opportunity to consult with people with IDD in your own area to make sure it is useful. Additionally, including local language that may differ across regions (i.e., in the U.S., fanny means back side, while in the United Kingdom, it means vulva) will ensure that it is more responsive to those in your own area of practice.

## Case Study

Amari is a 34-year-old, Black nonbinary man, with IDD, who uses he/they pronouns. Amari is very social, and has a partner, Makena, who they have been dating for two years. Makena is a 32-year-old, Black, cisgender woman who uses she/her pronouns. She does not have IDD but is autistic. Amari and Makena would like to have sex but they both want to make sure they ask for consent from one another, and Makena wants to make sure she asks for Amari's consent in a way that meets their needs. Makena reaches out to her therapist, who she has been seeing for the past year, to help her with this.

Makena's therapist, Dr. Onai, meets with Makena to discuss her concerns. Coincidentally, Dr. Onai, has just read a paper on this exact topic. The paper was written by Esmail and Concannon (2022), who specialize in occupational therapy. The paper suggests several different approaches for obtaining sexual consent, but Dr. Onai is particularly interested in the person-centered approach for Makena and Amari. Dr. Onai asks Makena if she would be comfortable bringing Amari in with her for a few sessions as the person-centered approach requires Amari's participation. As mentioned in the paper read by Dr. Onai, "Discussions with the people themselves will enable a better understanding of both their sexuality and cognitive disabilities, which are essential for determining their preferences." Makena agrees and brings Amari with her to the next week's session.

Central to the person-centered approach is (1) open communication, (2) committee approach, (3) capacity assumed, (4) withhold bias, and (5) tracking. So that Makena and Amari can both become familiar with this approach, Dr. Onai provides them each with a copy of the paper and explains each step to them. One step he emphasizes is tracking. He explains to them that tracking means readdressing consent periodically as Amari's (and Makena's) preferences could change over time.

Next, Dr. Onai shares with Makena and Amari the legal criteria of consent. This may have been covered in sex education classes either of them attended in the past. However, since they are both in their thirties now, Dr. Onai feels it is important to reiterate. The three legal criteria of consent include knowledge, understanding, and voluntariness. The report Dr. Onai shared with the couple includes a basic skill check.

1) Knowledge of body parts and sexual relationships and acts.
2) Knowledge of consequences from sexual relationships.
3) Understanding of appropriate sexual behavior and context for it.
4) Understanding of the voluntary nature of a sexual relationship.
5) Ability to recognize abusive situations.
6) Ability to be assertive in such situations to reject unwanted advances.

The report also includes measures to check for the aforementioned areas, as well as a list of interventions the couple can choose to utilize. Dr. Onai researches the following checklists:

- Sexual Consent and Education Assessment (SCEA; Kennedy, 1999)
- Sex Knowledge, Experience and Needs Scale for People with Intellectual Disabilities (SexKEN-ID; McCabe, 1994)
- Tool for the Assessment of Levels of Knowledge Sexuality and Consent (TALK-SC; Hingsburger et al., 2014)

With Amari's consent, he decides to use the TALK-SC as it is publicly available, easy to find, and has everything he needs for Makena and Amari's situation. The measure is administered in two parts: (1) an assessment administered with Amari and (2) an interview with a family member or friend of Amari's (someone other than Makena). As intended, once scored, these measures provide Dr. Onai with the information he needs to proceed. Amari scored just below the required passing score (70%). For this reason, Dr. Onai determines that Amari is in some need of further retraining and selects the *Living Your Life – The Sex Education and Personal Development Resource for Special Education Needs* (Bustard, 2003) intervention to use with Amari and Makena.

Once Amari and Makena have gone through the curriculum with Dr. Onai, Amari is given the TALK-SC again, using only the assessment portion this time. Amari passes the TALK-SC with a score of 83%. Dr. Onai then feels comfortable that Amari can legally and comfortably provide active and ongoing consent for sexual encounters.

## Case Study Questions

After reviewing Amari and Makena's case, take some time to contemplate the following questions, which reflect therapeutic considerations demonstrated throughout the case study.

1. Do you agree or disagree with Dr. Onai's approach to Amari and Makena's situation? Why? What would you have done differently, if anything?

2. Are you familiar with any other strategies or approaches other than the one's suggested? If so, what are they and would you prefer to use one over the other? Why or why not?
3. What have you learned about providing consent with individuals with IDD? Will this be helpful in your work? Why or why not?
4. Take a moment to engage in self-reflection. What feelings arose for you while you were reading or after you read the case study? How comfortable do you think you would be as the therapist discussing topics from this case? Do you think you would have done things differently than the therapist?

## Conclusion

In supporting individuals with IDD regarding their sexuality, it is clear that we must engage in dismantling not only "normal" ableism and stigma but also additional levels of oppression that are specific to those with IDD, including misconceptions of the capacity to consent, being unable to ever understand sexuality concepts including about their own bodies and experiences, and of course, the ever present parentification of disabled adults that is especially present within this subpopulation. Threading the needle between accurately assessing someone's ability to communicate and understand the information presented to them and an individual's own self-determination and rights to their own sexuality and experiences can be difficult yet is a crucial need for this group of people. As George Turner points out in his recent chapter "A Vision of Justice: Seeing the Sex-ABILITY of People With Intellectual Disabilities," intellectually and/or developmentally disabled people may be just as interested (if not more!) about discussing the concept of and learning the components of hooking up than they are about learning house cleaning skills (2021). We must make space for the sexuality explorations of all people, and ensure we are providing individually appropriate, affirmative, and medically accurate information about bodies, consent, desire, safety, and more, while empowering these individuals to explore in ways that feel comfortable and appropriate to them.

## Resources

Better Health Channel. (2019). *Cognitive disability and sexuality*. www.betterhealth.vic.gov.au/health/ConditionsAndTreatments/intellectual-disability-and-sexuality

Blue Seat Studios' Tea and Consent Video: https://vimeo.com/126553913

Brown, F. J., & Brown, S. (2016). *When young people with intellectual disabilities and autism hit puberty: A parents' Q&A guide to health, sexuality and relationships*. Jessica Kingsley Publishers.

Bustard, S. (2003). *Living your life: The sex education and personal development resource for special needs education* (Rev. ed.). The Ann Craft Trust UK Brook Publications.

Center for Parent Information and Resources. (2018). *Sexuality education for students with disabilities*. www.parentcenterhub.org/sexed/

ElevateUs Training. (n.d.) *Curriculum: Sexuality education for people with developmental disabilities*. www.elevatustraining.com/workshops-and-products/sexuality-education-for-people-with-developmental-disabilities-curriculum/

General Sexual Knowledge Questionnaire (note; NOT inclusive of LGBTQIA2S+ individuals, sex workers, etc.): www.midss.org/sites/default/files/questionnaire_gsq_plcopy.pdf

Kennedy Krieger Institute. (n.d.). *Sexuality and adults with developmental disabilities*. www.kennedykrieger.org/stories/making-difference/inspiring-stories/sexuality-and-adults-developmental-disabilities

RespectAbility. (2022). *Sexual education resources*. www.respectability.org/resources/sexual-education-resources/

Scarleteen. http://scarleteen.com

Sexuality and U. (2012). *Teaching sex ed for youth with intellectual disabilities*. www.sexualityandu.ca/teachers/teaching-sex-ed-for-youth-with-intellectual-disabilities.

The SHEIDD Project. www.ohsu.edu/university-center-excellence-development-disability/about-sheidd-project

SHEIDD Report: https://multco-web7-psh-files-usw2.s3-us-west-2.amazonaws.com/s3fs-public/in_their_own_words_SHEIDD_report.pdf

Silverberg, C. (2013). *What makes a baby*. Seven Stories Press.

Silverberg, C. (2015). *Sex is a funny word: A book about bodies, feelings, and YOU*. Seven Stories Press.


## References

American Academy of Pediatrics Committee on Children with Disabilities. (1996). Sexuality education of children and adolescents with developmental disabilities. *Pediatrics*, 97(2), 275–278. https://doi.org/10.1542/peds.97.2.275

American Association on Intellectual and Developmental Disabilities. (2008). *Position statement: Sexuality*. www.aaidd.org/news-policy/policy/position-statements/sexuality

American Psychiatric Association. (2013). *Diagnostic and statistical manual of mental disorders: DSM-5* (vol. 5). American Psychiatric Association.

Anderson, L. L., Larson, S. A., MapelLentz, S., & Hall-Lande, J. (2019). A systematic review of US studies on the prevalence of intellectual or developmental disabilities since 2000. *Intellectual and Developmental Disabilities*, 57(5), 421–438. https://doi.org/10.1352/1934-9556-57.5.421

Barnard-Brak, L., Schmidt, M., Chesnut, S., Wei, T., & Richman, D. (2014). Predictors of access to sex education for children with intellectual disabilities in public schools. *Intellectual and Developmental Disabilities*, 52(2), 85–97. https://doi.org/10.1352/1934-9556-52.2.85

Better Health Channel. (n.d.). *Cognitive disability and sexuality*. www.betterhealth.vic.gov.au/health/ConditionsAndTreatments/intellectual-disability-and-sexuality

Boston Children's Hospital. (n.d.). *What is Down syndrome?* www.childrenshospital.org/conditions/down-syndrome

Bryson, S. E., Bradley, E. A., Thompson, A., & Wainwright, A. (2008). Prevalence of autism among adolescents with intellectual disabilities. *The Canadian Journal of Psychiatry*, 53(7), 449–459. https://doi.org/10.1177%2F070674370805300710

Burrow, C., Miller, A., Meadours, J., Davis, L. A., & VanMattson, S. (2021). *Sexual assault prevention and response for people with IDD: A gap analysis framework*. https://selfadvocatecentral.org/wp-content/uploads/2021/11/SAPR_GapAnalysis Framework_TCDD-1.pdf

Bustard, S. (2003). *Living your life: The sex education and personal development resource for special needs education* (Rev. ed.). The Ann Craft Trust UK Brook Publications.

Center for Parent Information and Resources. (2018). *Sexuality education for students with disabilities*. www.parentcenterhub.org/sexed/

Centers for Disease Control and Prevention. (2022). *Facts about intellectual disability*. www.cdc.gov/ncbddd/developmentaldisabilities/facts-about-intellectual-disability.html

Dotson, L. A., Stinson, J., & Christian, L. (2003). People tell me I can't have sex: Women with disabilities share their personal perspectives on health care, sexuality, and reproductive rights. *Women & Therapy*, 26(3–4), 195–209. https://doi.org/10.1300/J015v26n03_02

ElevateUs Training. (n.d.). *Curriculum: Sexuality education for people with developmental disabilities*. www.elevatustraining.com/workshops-and-products/sexuality-education-for-people-with-developmental-disabilities-curriculum/

Esmail, S., & Concannon, B. (2022). Approaches to determine and manage sexual consent abilities for people with cognitive disabilities: Systematic review. *Interactive Journal of Medical Research*, 11(1), e28137. https://doi.org/10.2196/28137

Gilbert, J. (2018). Contesting consent in sex education. *Sex Education*, 18(3), 268–279. https://doi.org/10.1080/14681811.2017.1393407

Hingsburger, D., Beattie, K., Charbonneau, T., Hoath, J., Ioannou, S., King, S., & Woodhead, S. (2014). *Tool for the assessment of levels of knowledge sexuality and consent (TALK-SC)*. Vita Community Living Services and The Center for Behavioural Health Sciences. https://sbrpsig.files.wordpress.com/2018/05/talk-sc.pdf

Individuals With Disabilities Education Act. (2004). 20 U.S.C. § 1400.

Kennedy, C. H. (1999). Assessing competency to consent to sexual activity in the cognitively impaired population. *Journal of Forensic Neuropsychology*, 1(3), 17–33. https://doi.org/10.1300/J151v01n03_02

The Maryland Center for Developmental Disabilities at the Kennedy Krieger Institute. (n.d.). *Community and professional development training program*. www.kennedykrieger.org/sites/default/files/library/documents/community/maryland-center-for-developmental-disabilities-mcdd/16614_2020MCDDCommunityAndProfessionalDevelopmentTrainingProgramCatalog_IA1.pdf

Maulik, P. K., Mascarenhas, M. N., Mathers, C. D., Dua, T., & Saxena, S. (2011). Prevalence of intellectual disability: A meta-analysis of population-based studies. *Research in Developmental Disabilities*, 32(2), 419–436. https://doi.org/10.1016/j.ridd.2010.12.018

McCabe, M. (1994). *Sexuality knowledge, experience and needs scale, for people with intellectual disability: Sex ken-ID*. Deakin University, School of Psychology.

McGuire, B. E., & Bayley, A. A. (2011). Relationships, sexuality and decision-making capacity in people with an intellectual disability. *Current Opinion in Psychiatry*, 24(5), 398–402. https://doi.org/10.1097/YCO.0b013e328349bbcb

McLaughlin, K. (2003). *Tips for talking about sexuality*. Retrieved Mary 15, 2022, from https://familyvoicesofca.org/wp-content/uploads/2017/12/GULPNewlsletter.pdf

Medina-Rico, M., López-Ramos, H., & Quiñonez, A. (2018). Sexuality in people with intellectual disability: Review of literature. *Sexuality and Disability, 36*(3), 231–248. https://doi.org/10.1007/s11195-017-9508-6

Michigan Administrative Rules for Special Education (MARSE). (2021). MARSE R 340.1705: Cognitive impairment; determination. Rule 5.

RespectAbility. (2022). *Sexual education resources*. www.respectability.org/resources/sexual-education-resources/

Shapiro, J. (2018, January 8). *The sexual assault epidemic no one talks about*. National Public Radio. www.npr.org/2018/01/08/570224090/the-sexual-assault-epidemic-no-one-talks-about

Stavis, P. F. (1991). Harmonizing the right to sexual expression and the right to protection from harm for persons with mental disability. *Sexuality and Disability, 9*(2), 131–141. https://doi.org/10.1007/BF01101738

Szasz, G. (1991). Sex and disability are not mutually exclusive. Evaluation and management. *Western Journal of Medicine, 154*(5), 560. https://pubmed.ncbi.nlm.nih.gov/1830986/

Tepper, M. S. (2000). Sexuality and disability: The missing discourse of pleasure. *Sexuality and Disability, 18*(4), 283–290. https://doi.org/10.1023/A:1005698311392

Turner, G. W. (2021). A vision of justice: Seeing the Sex-ABILITY of people with intellectual disabilities. In S. J. Dodd (Ed.), *The Routledge International Handbook of social work and sexualities* (pp. 285–299). Routledge.

Turner, G. W., & Crane, B. (2016). Pleasure is paramount: Adults with intellectual disabilities discuss sensuality and intimacy. *Sexualities, 19*(5–6), 677–697. https://doi.org/10.1177%2F1363460715620573

Walker-Hirsch, L. (2007). *The facts of life . . . and more: Sexuality and intimacy for people with intellectual disabilities*. Paul H. Brookes Publishing Co.

# 6
# SEXUALITY, HEARING LOSS, AND D/DEAF INDIVIDUALS

*Kari L. Sherwood, Shanna Katz Kattari, and Alison Wetmur*

### Introduction

Approximately two to three out of every 1,000 children born in the United States have some form of hearing loss (NIDCD, 2021). Acquired hearing loss can be present during any point in the lifespan, with causes ranging from genetic factors to infections, and also external stimuli such as loud sound exposure. However, the National Institute of Deafness and Other Communication Disorders (2021) ranks age as the strongest predictor of hearing loss among adults. Some of the most common causes of hearing loss in adults include chronic diseases, smoking, otosclerosis, age-related sensorineural degeneration, and sudden sensorineural hearing loss (WHO, 2023).

Hearing loss is defined as a hearing threshold of 20 decibels (dB) or less in both ears, and can be categorized as mild, moderate, severe, or profound (World Health Organization [WHO], 2022). Those with hearing loss greater than 35 dB in their better hearing ear are considered to have disabling hearing loss (WHO, 2022). The World Health Organization considers a person to be hard of hearing (HoH) if they fall within the mild-severe range, and those who fall within the profound range are often considered to be deaf. The same organization notes that more than 5% of the world's population is estimated to be deaf, and more than 2.5 billion people will have some hearing loss by the year 2050 (WHO, 2022). Nearly 80% of the world's hearing loss population live in low- and middle-income countries (WHO, 2022), who may have less access to support regarding their sexuality health and sexual experiences.

In American Deaf culture, "little d" deaf signifies a severe to profound audiological hearing loss; "big D" Deaf means a person who has a hearing loss and identifies with the American Deaf community and uses American

DOI: 10.4324/9781003308331-9

Sign Language (ASL) (Bauman & Murray, 2014). For the purposes of this chapter, we will be using d/Deaf to honor the diversity of identities and presentations of such that exist within and across this population of individuals, except when citing research with a particular subset. As with some other disability groups (i.e., "spoonies" or neurodivergent culture), there is a significant subset of deaf individuals who consider themselves a separate community, often known as "Deaf culture." Deaf culture and the connected community are a group of Deaf individuals (note the capitalization) who "view themselves as a unique cultural and linguistic minority who use sign language as their primary language" (NDC, 2019). In the United States, the dominant sign language is American Sign Language (ASL). Other countries and regions may use one of over 300 other versions of sign language (Sign Solutions, 2021). Many Deaf individuals who are part of Deaf culture do not consider their deafness or HoH status to be a disability, but rather, simply a facet of human diversity that requires the learning of another language, in this case, sign. Bauman and Murray introduce the concept of Deaf Gain, which explores all of the benefits d/Deaf people offer to our society, and reframes deafness not as a negative experience, but as sensory and cognitive diversity that can contribute to the betterment of human kind (2014).

Hearing loss impacts communication and oral speech and is often tied to concerns related to social isolation, education, and employment (WHO, 2022). Most of the hearing world does not know ASL, which often limits communication between Deaf and hearing people. A lack of access to those who communicate via sign, and an unwillingness of society to move toward captioning all events, movies, meetings, and other interactions, can make it challenging or even impossible for many d/Deaf and HoH individuals to engage both personally and professionally, often resulting in social isolation. Language deprivation is a huge issue among deaf and HoH young people (and continues to impact them as they become deaf/HoH adults), which has lifelong implications in communication, and is the reason why education is often abysmal for d/Deaf people and why there are incredibly high rates of unemployment in this population. Deaf individuals also have higher unemployment rates than hearing individuals, due to the aforementioned communication difficulties, audism (oppression that values hearing and speaking verbally over other forms of communication [Humphries, 1977]) and their access needs not being met (Haynes, 2014; O'Connell, 2022; Punch, 2016).

Cochlear implants (CIs) are a hot topic of debate among the d/Deaf community. CIs are implanted via a surgical procedure where a doctor threads a wire through the cochlea and connects it directly to the auditory nerve, bypassing damaged inner ears. They are by nature invasive and require years of speech and auditory therapy to use successfully. Most people in the Deaf community, and their allies, feel that CIs should not be viewed as a compulsory solution for those born with hearing loss because it often isn't a solution.

As noted earlier, people who receive CIs require intensive post-surgical care for optimal success, and vary in effectiveness. Children as young as 10–12 months of age can receive CIs with their parents' consent (Boston Children's Hospital, 2022). Often, the decision is made by the child's hearing parents, who may not be aware of the benefits of teaching their child sign language or the importance of their child's connection to Deaf culture. Parents may assume a cochlear implant will allow their child to hear as they do, which is not the case. Cochlear implants do not provide "clear and unambiguous access" to sound (NAD, 2014). Furthermore, not learning sign language delays a d/Deaf child's language acquisition (NAD, 2014).

In this chapter, we recognize that some people have cochlear implants, while others don't. Some who have them may regret it, and some who don't may want them. There is no one way to be d/Deaf. Some people use cochlear implants, some use hearing aids or other auditory devices, and others opt to not use any auditory technology. Access to this technology and the medical field's problematic approach of pressuring all parents of all deaf children to get cochlear implants is challenging, highly politicized, and the core of the audist/ableist medical model. That said, those with such technology, which is not limited to CIs and can including hearing aids, may have different experiences than those without, from access to Deaf culture, communication on dates and during sex, and the ability to receive comprehensive and medically accurate sexuality education. This is again tied to language deprivation. Similarly, some people who are d/Deaf sign, while others use other forms of augmentative and alternative communication (AAC) including body language, facial expressions, symbol boards, and even AAC apps on mobile devices in order to communicate. There is no one right way to communicate, spoken, written, signed, or otherwise, and we honor all forms of communication used by this population.

### What Do We Know When It Comes to d/Deaf Sexuality?

Disability sexuality, in general, is shrouded in myths and misconceptions, or "mythconceptions" (Watson, 2002). Job (2004) used Griffiths' proposed model of mythconceptions (Watson, 2002) as a framework for examining d/Deaf sexuality, with the following indicated as d/Deaf sexuality specific mythconceptions:

- Deaf people are not sexual and should be treated as eternal children;
- Deaf people should live in environments designed to restrict/inhibit their sexuality and sexual desires, in order to protect both themselves and others;
- Deaf people should not have access to sexuality education, because it will result in inappropriate behavior;

- Deaf people should be sterilized (with or without consent) or encouraged not to have children for fear they will have d/Deaf kids;
- Deaf people are different sexually from hearing people. They have an increased likelihood developing aberrant, unusual, or perverse sexual behavior;
- Deaf people are promiscuous, oversexed, and sexually indiscriminate; they can be dangerous, and you should not allow your kids around them;
- Deaf people cannot benefit from sexuality therapy or counseling (Job, 2004; Meehan, 2019).

According to Joharchi and Clark (2014), these mythconceptions are in line with the majority of the existing literature on d/Deaf sexuality. They, however, call for an adjustment to this trend toward a focus on sexual satisfaction among d/Deaf individuals.

This is particularly important, because the Traditional Sexual Script, or sexual behaviors, may differ for hearing and d/Deaf individuals (Gilbert et al., 2012). For instance, much of d/Deaf sexual satisfaction is experienced through four of the senses (sight, touch, smell, and taste). Reliance on these four senses may heighten sexual experiences in some ways. For example, facial expressions and body language, rather than auditory language, are used much more frequently to connect with partners. Some d/Deaf individuals also use audiological devices and are able to hear some sounds, which also will add to their experiences. Deaf individuals may also be more sensitive to touch, may prefer to be intimate with the lights on so as to access and activate further stimuli, and may prefer using a variety of sign language or other nonverbal communications during sexual interactions. In Ireland, a qualitative study found that deaf women were not just resilient but actively flourishing in their intimate relationships, even though many had not had access to comprehensive and accessible education on sexuality (Meehan, 2019). As with any marginalized group, d/Deaf people are creative, scrappy, and often come up with innovative solutions to getting their sexual and relationship needs met.

When it comes to education, sexual education often does not meet the access needs of d/Deaf individuals. One of the primary reasons for this is communication barriers. Contributing to this is the fact that approximately 90% of parents of d/Deaf children are hearing (NIDCD, 2021) and only 31% regularly sign with their children in their own homes (Gallaudet Research Institute, 2011). In addition, most sexual education resources and products are developed by hearing individuals. Sexuality education videos frequently don't have captions, or worse, they have them available and the educators do not turn them on (Meehan, 2019). Furthermore, the content is not culturally responsive to the d/Deaf community, which has its own culture and norms.

One survey by Deafax, an organization in the United Kingdom, found that 35% of d/Deaf respondents received no sexual education, while the other 65% reported their sexual education was inaccessible (Deafax, 2012). Nearly half of the respondents in this study shared that they had learned about sex from various forms of media. In Columbia, a study of deaf youth found that the majority of them had learned about sex from pornography, rather than from any type of formal sex education, or even from their peers (Gil-Cano et al., 2019). A recent study in Ethiopia with deaf women found that they too had not had access to basic knowledge about sexual and reproductive health, including their own, which prevented them from being able to make informed decisions around their own sexuality (Boersma et al., 2019). This lack of access to sexual education puts the general d/Deaf community at risk.

Moreover, this can be even more challenging for lesbian, gay, bisexual, transgender, and queer (LGBTQ) d/Deaf individuals. A study in South Africa found that due to the lack of sex education and conversations about sexual orientation and gender, most LGBTQ Deaf students did not come out and get to embrace their identities until after they had left school (Hopkins, 2021). This study, like previous research, called for more Deaf-inclusive sex education in schools, as well as suggested the need for queer- and trans-affirming resources within the Deaf community. In the Philippines, a study of d/Deaf LGBTQ youth noted that, while they had different ideas of meaning-making regarding sex through sign than their hearing peers, they were not as familiar with their HIV and other risk (Gomez & Geneta, 2021).

Another challenge in serving this population is the fluid space it occupies between being part of the disability community (or not), being its own culture (though not all individuals may consider it such), and simply being a linguistic minority. This can mean that some sexuality education will be provided in traditional school settings, where there may be only a few d/Deaf students in the program who are only given information that is pertinent to hearing students, while some d/Deaf students in d/Deaf only schools may not have access to any sexuality education at all, even as others have excellent, comprehensive, and supportive sexuality education specifically exploring their own experiences as d/Deaf sexual beings. Few adult sexuality classes include signed interpretation or live captioning options (though interestingly, American Sign Language interpretation is much more common in U.S. kink education spaces than it is in U.S. vanilla-/non-kink-centric sex education spaces), meaning that it may be just as complicated for d/Deaf adults to access affirming and accurate sexuality education as adults.

Like other disability groups, the d/Deaf community is subject to higher rates of sexual abuse. As many as 45% of d/Deaf children are involved in unwanted sexual experiences, and as many as 39% experience sexual abuse with physical contact (Wakeland et al., 2018). Perhaps even more concerning, as many as 69% of d/Deaf adults have reported being sexually assaulted, which is significantly higher than the general population (Smith & Pick, 2015).

One of the biggest challenges informing the needs and desires related to sexuality and sexuality/relationship education among the d/Deaf community is a deep dearth in research related to the Deaf experience that is not medical or pathological in nature. Since d/Deaf lives are largely absent from the current literature, it is not surprising that much of the extant research was conducted over two decades ago (Suter et al., 2012). While key points of these studies may still stand, much has changed in the world of sexuality since the early 2000s, from different types of contraception and birth control, to new thoughts on active consent, to emerging language surrounding sexuality and gender and new challenges such as navigating sexting and social media. The lack of understanding about the needs of d/Deaf individuals when it comes to sexuality education, therapy, and other supports, as well as specific in-group challenges can make it hard to provide specialized care, counseling, and education that meets the needs of this population.

**Best Practices**

Given that we live in an ableist and audist society, you may need to do an accessibility audit of your practice. Those of us who are hearing may not even realize how inaccessible our practice spaces (both physical and accessible) may be to those who are d/Deaf. Are you and your staff trained on how to use relay services to speak with d/Deaf people through telephone? How friendly is your office or organization when it comes to welcoming d/Deaf individuals? Is your chair clearly facing where people sit, and is the room well-lit and quiet? Do you have masks that allow for lip reading for those who do, and have pens and paper handy for written communication? Do you have ways to connect that don't involve using phone calls and leaving messages? If you show videos, are they captioned? Do you ensure you include and at times center experiences of d/Deaf people in your education, therapy, or other practice (i.e., getting trained by d/Deaf educators, having media materials that showcase members of this population)? Do you have resources in your area of d/Deaf affirming places, and potential places to refer out to d/Deaf sexuality educators, counselors, therapists, and other providers?

Make sure you have a list of local interpreters/organizations/agencies where you can hire people to interpret and/or offer live captioning to facilitate communication with specific clients or communities. Knowing about them BEFORE you need them, rather than having to look them up last minute, will improve things for everyone. Ensure you have a budget put aside for interpretation and/or captioning, and that the cost is not passed on to d/Deaf individuals, which is illegal in the United States and some other countries.

Part of supporting d/Deaf students, clients, and/or patients' sexuality means being ready to talk dating. Dating can be hard for anyone, and it can be even more complicated in inter-abled relationships, in this case, between a hearing person and a d/Deaf person. Be prepared to chat with clients about what dating while Deaf might look like; do they have preferences toward only dating other d/Deaf people? And if so, how might they go about that? If not, how will they navigate potential communication barriers? Communication access is often a determining factor in partners. Also, the d/Deaf community is small and quite open about their lives – some members of the community don't mind or don't see the openness as a hardship, while other d/Deaf people will specifically seek partners outside of the Deaf community.

Holding judgment-free space for these conversations and allowing people to think through their wants and needs when it comes to dating (and sex!) can be incredibly helpful. You may also want to offer space to provide some education on different behaviors, potential risks, and ways to reduce them, whether that is getting tested together for sexually transmitted infections, discussion what type of protective methods they might choose to use, and how to navigate clear and active consent. Due to language deprivation and missing out on incidental learning means that some d/Deaf people may arrive in the office with only a rudimentary sexual educational past.

Encourage clients to figure out what works best for them and their communication needs, and that there is no one "right" way to have sex. While often times, sexual and intimate activities occur in the dark, or dimly lit spaces, remind them that they can add little additional (or a lot!) light in order to be able to sign and see their partner(s) signing as well. Since signed languages use the hands as the method of communication, some forethought is necessary to ensure clear communication (Letico et al., 2022). This means that certain positions where one is using both hands to support themselves, or certain activities, such as using cuffs or rope for bondage, can limit an individual's ability to communicate with their partners. Such an issue can be challenging both for consent, and for pleasure. Working with d/Deaf individuals to think about what positions and activities might work best for signing before they are in the throes of passion can help them plan ahead for optimal communication.

Pro-tactile signing is often used by the Deafblind community (Willoughby et al., 2018). However, d/Deaf people may also find it useful and effective to use during intimate and sexual times, as it does not require lighting or visual contact in order to communicate. Individuals may also take some ideas out of the kink community's playbook for communication while one partner cannot speak (i.e., if they are gagged), by figuring out ways to communicate that might involve a specific body movement, dropping a scarf or ball held in a hand in order to stop an activity, etc. As with figuring out positions that allow for good communication if signing, those who use AAC devices should be encouraged to use them in bed (or on the couch, the floor, the kitchen counter, etc.) so that they too can continue to communicate throughout any sexual exploits.

Those who use hearing technology may choose to use it during intimate and sexual exploration in order to pick up different noises that may occur. Conversely, hearing those noises, particularly if they are new or different, could be a sensory trigger, or even just generally off putting. Some individuals using hearing tech may opt to take it off during sexual play time in order to just feel quiet again. Professional switch and Deaf porn performer Rita Seagrave shared at a Femina Potens spoken word poetry night in 2010 that when she was topping someone, she'd enjoy "taking her ears off" and playing with her deafness as part of her kink play ("Oh no! I guess I can't hear you when you scream!"), and that when she was bottoming, being able to have complete silence while she was tied up was incredibly meditative and grounding. Reminding clients that they can try different things, that it is ok if some of them don't work out, and that experimentation and exploration is part of healthy sexuality can help to normalize innovation and creativity when it comes to engaging behind closed doors.

**Class Activity**

Knowing that the many d/Deaf individuals are learning about sex from the media, take 20–30 minutes by yourself or in a small group to seek out portrayals of d/Deaf and HoH relationships and sexuality. You can look up TV shows, movies, podcasts, books, comics, YouTubers, TikTokers, other content creators, etc. Check out and "consume" some of this media, and then answer the following reflection questions.

- How easy or challenging was it to find d/Deaf representation when it comes to sexuality and relationships?
- How was d/Deaf sexuality and relationships portrayed in the media that you found?
- If you looked at TV and/or movies, were the characters played by actual d/Deaf people? How do you know?
- What messages did you get about d/Deaf sexuality and relationships from this media?
- What important sexuality-related messages are missing?
- If you were working with a d/Deaf young adult (think ages 16–25), how might you support them in translating these messages into effective skills they can use in their own intimate and/or sexual experiences?

## Conclusion

Being d/Deaf can be an identity, a culture, and/or a disability, depending on the individual. Always honor how someone identifies themselves and their relationship to their hearing status, as well as recognize that across the d/Deaf communities, there are many ways people opt to communicate, from hearing technology to signing to using AAC – all of these are valid. When it comes to sexuality and this population, there is a huge gap in the research, especially regarding positive sexuality and sex education experiences, and many d/Deaf individuals are only accessing information about sex and sexuality from the media and their peers. Offering accurate, accessible, and affirming information about sexually, relationships, intimacy, and sexual health is a great start, while brain storming ways to make communication during sex effective can support your clients in exploring how to make their sexual interactions work for best them. Finally, connect with d/Deaf-created resources, including sex educators and sex therapists, referring out as needed.

## Resources

### General

Hard to Hear: Access to Sexuality Resources in Deaf Communities – https://journalofsexuality.weebly.com/uploads/3/0/3/0/30308803/7._hard_to_hear.pdf
Jooux Deaf Sexuality Wellness Center – https://jooux.com/
Sexual Health Video Library for Use by Deaf Communities – www.cdc.gov/prc/resources/tools/sexual-health-video-for-deaf-communties.html

### Deaf Organizations

Center for Deaf Health Equity: https://deafhealthequity.com/resources/ – Resources page
Deafax: www.deafax.org/ – U.K. based organization
DeafHope: www.deaf-hope.org/ – Working to end domestic and sexual violence in Deaf communities
Rooted in Rights: https://rootedinrights.org/video/deaf-access-to-sex-ed-with-bethany-gehman/
National Deaf Center: https://learn.nationaldeafcenter.org/ – U.S. based organization

### Deaf and HoH Creators/Sites

Chella Man
Deaf Sex Education Tumblr: https://deafsexeducation.tumblr.com/
Jessica Kellgren-Fozard
Liam O'Dell
Nyle DiMarco

## Deaf-Inclusive Porn

Crash Pad Series Episode 71 (Deaf queer performer) https://crashpadseries.com/queer-porn/episode/episode-71-asteroid-and-peyton/

Kink.com Performer Rita Seagrave (Deaf performer). www.kink.com/model/19119/Rita-Seagrave

## Books

Miller, C., & Clark, K. (2019). Deaf and queer at the intersections: Deaf LGBTQ people and communities. In I. W. Leigh & C. A. O'Brien (Eds.), *Deaf identities: Exploring new frontiers* (pp. 305–335). Oxford University Press.

## Podcasts

What the Deaf? www.whatthedeaf.com/

## Deafblindness Resources

http://documents.nationaldb.org/products/sex-ed.pdf

## Sexuality Education for the Student With Deafblindness – Video

The topic of this video is *Issues in Sexuality and Deafblindness: Modesty, Appropriate Touch, and Menstruation.* https://library.tsbvi.edu/Play/7604

## References

Bauman, H. D. L., & Murray, J. J. (Eds.). (2014). *Deaf gain: Raising the stakes for human diversity*. University of Minnesota Press.

Boersma, J. M., Tardi, R., Lockwood, E., & Ayansa, W. G. (2019). Informed sexuality: The influence of lack of information on the sexuality, relationships and reproductive health of deaf women in Addis Ababa. In *Diverse voices of disabled sexualities in the global south* (pp. 167–184). Palgrave Macmillan.

Boston Children's Hospital. (2022). *What are cochlear implants?* www.childrenshospital.org/treatments/cochlear-implants

Deafax. (2012). *Education & advice on relationships & sex for deaf people*. www.deafax.org/_files/ugd/9cecfb_351a5c04e9fc489b83870a52e1fecd6f.pdf

Gallaudet Research Institute. (2011). *State summary report of data from the 2009–10 annual survey of deaf and hard of hearing children and youth*. GRI, Gallaudet University.

Gilbert, G. L., Clark, M. D., & Anderson, M. L. (2012). Do deaf individuals' dating scripts follow the traditional sexual script? *Sexuality and Culture, 16*, 90–99. http://dx.doi.org/10.1007/s12119-011-9111-4

Gil-Cano, P. A., Navarro-García, A. M., Serna-Giraldo, C., & Pinzón-Seguro, M. (2019). Sexualidade: as vozes de um grupo surdo de Medellín (Colômbia). *Revista facultad nacional de salud pública, 37*(2), 107–115.

Gomez, M. G. A., & Geneta, A. L. P. (2021). Curbing the risks: Toward a transdisciplinary sexual health literacy program for young adults who are deaf and LGBT+. *Sexuality and Disability, 39*(1), 195–213.

Haynes, S. (2014). Effectiveness of communication strategies for deaf or hard of hearing workers in group settings. *Work, 48*(2), 193–202.

Hopkins, C. M. (2021). *School experiences of queer youth who are deaf* (Doctoral dissertation). University of Johannesburg (South Africa). ProQuest Dissertations & Theses Global. (2642946164).

Humphries, T. (1977). *Communicating across cultures (deaf-hearing) and language learning*. Union Institute and University.

Job, J. (2004). Factors involved in the ineffective dissemination of sexuality information to individuals who are deaf or hard of hearing. *American Annals of the Deaf, 149*(3), 264–273.

Joharchi, H. A., & Clark, M. D. (2014). A glimpse at American deaf women's sexuality. *Psychology, 5*(13), 1536. http://doi.org/10.4236/psych.2014.513164

Letico, V., Iliadis, M., & Walters, R. (2022). De (a) fining consent: Exploring nuances of offering and receiving sexual consent among deaf and hard-of-hearing people. *Criminology & Criminal Justice*. https://doi.org/10.1177/17488958221120887

Meehan, G. P. (2019). *Flourishing at the margins: An exploration of deaf and hard-of-hearing women's stories of their intimate lives in Ireland* (Doctoral dissertation). National University of Ireland, Maynooth (Ireland). ProQuest Dissertations & Theses Global. (2311375349).

National Association of the Deaf. (2014). *Position statement on early cognitive and language development and education of deaf and hard of hearing children*. www.nad.org/about-us/position-statements/position-statement-on-early-cognitive-and-language-development-and-education-of-deaf-and-hard-of-hearing-children/

National Deaf Center. (2019). *The deaf community: An introduction*. www.nationaldeafcenter.org/sites/default/files/The%20Deaf%20Community-%20An%20Introduction.pdf

National Institute on Deafness and Other Communication Disorders. (2021). *Quick statistics about hearing*. www.nidcd.nih.gov/health/statistics/quick-statistics-hearing

O'Connell, N. (2022). "Opportunity blocked": Deaf people, employment and the sociology of audism. *Humanity & Society, 46*(2), 336–358.

Punch, R. (2016). Employment and adults who are deaf or hard of hearing: Current status and experiences of barriers, accommodations, and stress in the workplace. *American Annals of the Deaf, 161*(3), 384–397.

Sign Solutions. (2021). *What are the different types of sign language?* www.signsolutions.uk.com/what-are-the-different-types-of-sign-language/

Smith, R. A. E., & Pick, L. H. (2015). Sexual assault experienced by deaf female undergraduates: Prevalence and characteristics. *Violence and Victims, 30*(6), 948–959. https://doi.org/10.1891/0886-6708.VV-D-14-00057

Suter, S., McCracken, W., & Calam, R. (2012). The views, verdict and recommendations for school and home sex and relationships education by young deaf and hearing people. *Sex Education, 12*(2), 147–163.

Wakeland, E., Austen, S., & Rose, J. (2018). What is the prevalence of abuse in the deaf/hard of hearing population? *The Journal of Forensic Psychiatry & Psychology, 29*(3), 434–454. https://doi.org/10.1080/14789949.2017.1416659

Watson, S. (2002). *Sex education for individuals who have a developmental disability: The need for assessment* (Unpublished master's thesis). Brock University, St. Catherines, Ontario, Canada.

Willoughby, L., Iwasaki, S., Bartlett, M., & Manns, H. (2018). Tactile sign languages. *Handbook of Pragmatics, 21*, 239–258.

World Health Organization (WHO). (2023). *Deafness and hearing loss.* www.who.int/news-room/fact-sheets/detail/deafness-and-hearing-loss

# 7
# "LOVE IS MERELY A MADNESS"
## Sexuality and Madness in a Cisheteropatriarchal Culture

*Laura Yakas*

### Introduction: The Journey

This chapter is an autoethnographic journey through two of my passions: madness and sexuality. In Part 1, I connect madness and sexuality by (1) exploring how constructs like "normalcy" and "pathology/madness" are rooted in **sanism** in my cultures (the United States and Aotearoa/New Zealand) and (2) exploring how sexual diversity (i.e., sexualities that diverge from cisheteronormativity) have been pathologized as "madness" across time. Then in Part 2, I use evolutionary biology to support an argument I develop in Part 1 that **sexual diversity is not pathological – pathologizing sexual diversity is pathological**. Finally, in the conclusion, I reflect upon some of my (and my Mad peers') experiences at the intersection of madness and sexuality. Periodically woven throughout the chapter, I also include mad/queer-affirming reflection activities and practice ideas. Thank you for joining me on this journey!

### Part 1: Pathologization Can Be Pathological

I've been studying "pathologization" since I first heard the word and realized my entire life had been shaped by it. Pathologization derives from the Greek word "pathos," which means not only "to suffer" but also just "to experience." Through the melding of languages, English attached to the "suffering" element, and pathologization came to mean viewing something as a *problem*, specifically a *medical* problem (Liebert, 2014). Put simply, pathologization means to view devalued traits as "illness" or "disorder." And when we're talking specifically about devalued mental/behavioral traits, "madness" is the

DOI: 10.4324/9781003308331-10

historical term (and slur) for what we now call mental illness or disorder. Madness is not a term one commonly hears today – unless one is enmeshed in the Mad Justice movement and/or mad studies. Some of my ancestors and peers in this world include Chamberlin, 1978; LeFrançois et al., 2013; Russo & Sweeney, 2016; Beresford & Russo, 2022. Here, "madness" is reclaimed and used in lieu of "mental illness" to signal that one refuses to be pathologized. Here, I discovered I was a patholo*gized* person (Mad), not a patholo*gical* person (mentally ill).

---

**Mad-Affirming Reflection Activity: Pathological or Pathologized?**

- To the mainstream medical model, **mental illness = patholog*ical* mental/behavioral traits.**
- To the Mad Justice movement, **madness = patholog*ized* mental/behavioral traits.**

I invite you to ponder this distinction, and practice reframing clinical language to reflect it! For example:

- "They have schizophrenia." – "They've *been labeled with* schizophrenia."
- "They're symptomatic." – "They're having experiences that are pathologized in their culture."
- "They suffer from anxiety" – "They *navigate* the world with anxiety."

How does it feel to reframe these common phrases so they are not pathologizing? How could you see this playing out in your practice?

---

The problem with pathologization is that it can be easily wielded as a tool for social control – a point which Michel Foucault is well known for making in works like *Madness: The Invention of an Idea* (2011/1962) and *History of Sexuality: Volume I* (1990/1976). To name this process of when pathologization is used for social control, today we have two words: **ableism and saneism**. Ableism has been well defined earlier in the introduction to this book. Saneism is a variant of ableism specific to the oppression of madness (Simmons University, n.d.). Saneism happens when a culture pathologizes mental/behavioral traits as **mad** (i.e., "abnormal" or "disordered") instead of recognizing that they reflect **natural neurodiversity** (i.e., variation in neurocognitive functioning [Walker, n.d.]), and/or **natural trauma responses** due to life in a violent/oppressive culture (e.g., internalizing responses like depression, externalizing responses like addiction). Saneism is **epistemic oppression**, what happens when a group of people are viewed as incapable of legitimate thought or knowledge production (colonialists were major epistemic oppressors – it's easier to justify eradicating people when they're dehumanized as "cognitively inferior," and Maria Liegghio [2013] made the astute connection between this and saneism). **Saneism is a violent cultural project** of deciding what's "normal" and enforcing that through stigmatizing labels and coercive treatments aiming to "cure," and therefore eradicate, madness – and by extension, Mad people. (Note: henceforth, I will interchangeably use "Mad" and "Mad/neurodivergent" to refer to anyone who has been pathologized by saneism.)

> **Mad-Affirming Practice Idea: A Healing-Centered Approach**
>
> While pathologization is often a tool for saneist social control (nuance alert!), it *can* be a tool for healing if we know how to wield it. A healing-centered use of pathologization can help us identify when and how behaviors hinder survival/thriving, which can help us intervene! As noted, much of what our system calls "mental disorder" describes a complex combination of **neurodiversity** (which should *not* be pathologized, but affirmed and accommodated [Price, 2022]) and **trauma responses** (which *can* be productively pathologized in a healing-centered way). So the goal of mad/neurodiversity-affirming therapy is to support folks in (1) learning to embrace and thrive in their **neurodivergence** and (2) healing from **trauma and internalized saneism** (Walker, n.d.). This starts with our assessment questions. Saneism pushes us to ask the pathologizing question *"What's wrong with you?"* instead of **healing-centered questions** like:
>
> - *What happened to you? What wounds and unmet needs have you (and your ancestors) experienced, and how has systemic oppression shaped these experiences?*
> - *How have these experiences shaped you? What trauma responses are part of your life now, and how do these help and hinder your survival/thriving?*
>
> Pathologizing questions can lead to saneist harm. But healing-centered questions can help us understand and address barriers to thriving. Here are two personal examples to illustrate this distinction:
>
> 1) I was labeled with "bipolar disorder." I now reject this because I view my sensitivity, intensity, and breadth in experiential capacity not as "disorder" but as valid (and misunderstood) **neurodivergence**. Pathologizing my

fundamental way of being was *harmful*. It convinced me *I* was the problem ("there's something wrong with me/my brain!") when the problem was saneism – I was *pathologized*, not *pathological*!

2) I was labeled with varying "eating disorders" – a reflection of **trauma and internalized fatphobia**. Pathologizing these behaviors in a healing-centered way (i.e., identifying them as coping mechanisms that were hindering to my survival/thriving) was an important step on my recovery journey (thanks to my friend and fellow Mad liberationist Shira for her role in this journey [see Collings, n.d.])!

In my social work classes, I define healing as *"identifying the wounds and treating them, identifying the needs and meeting them, and identifying the strengths and greeting them."* Without **healing-centered questions**, we may not be able to identify all the valuable (and often intergenerational) context that help us engage in **healing-centered interventions**, and may instead fall prey to saneist violence! When my neurodivergence was pathologized as "disorder," treatment was coercive, invalidating, and framed violently: something was "wrong" with me (and due to epistemic oppression, if I protested, it only became further proof!), so I needed to be changed, fixed, normalized. Pills to "correct imbalanced chemistry," Cognitive-Behavioral Therapy/CBT to "correct wrong thinking." But when practitioners viewed me as a neurominority in a world built for neurotypicality, or as someone reacting normally to trauma and oppression, interventions became healing centered.

Even the same tool of CBT can be wielded differently (instead of "correcting wrong thinking," what about "liberating from hindering thoughts of internalized saneism"?). Thanks to mad/neurodiversity-affirming interventions (some from within the mental health system, most from beyond it), I have now developed (1) skills that help me navigate and thrive in my neurodivergence and (2) a sense of Mad Pride and community that helps me heal from and buffer against the world's saneism.

Some interventions did involve **changing myself** (e.g., *Internal Family Systems* therapy helped me explore, nurture, and reintegrate wounded parts of myself; *trauma-sensitive yoga* helped my nervous system heal and become less reactive; *non-violent communication* helped me understand and communicate about needs and boundaries; enmeshing in *Mad Justice* helped me liberate from internalized saneism and develop fierce self-advocacy skills; reimagining my madness through *Māori cosmology* helped me liberate from internalized saneism and colonialism [thanks to Niania & Bush, 2016]).

However, most interventions involved **changing my environment** – educating my loved ones who weren't aware of saneism, seeking new loved ones who were, and together co-creating a mad-affirming (and mad-centric) microworld I could thrive in as my authentic self. A world where my access needs are

> met, as well as my deeper spiritual needs for purpose and belonging. Speaking of, my dissertation revolved around Mad folks' building mad-centric microworlds to meet their needs for purpose and belonging in a wider world that denies this – a classic example of research as "me-search!" (Yakas, 2017, 2018).

When wielded appropriately, pathologization *can* be a tool to facilitate healing. But historically, my culture's mental health system has used pathologization as a tool for saneist social control. Foucault called this "biopower" (1976, 1990) – when groups with state-sanctioned power (e.g., physicians, politicians) exert control over the population by defining and policing health. Everything my culture defines as "healthy/normal" and "unhealthy/pathological" was determined by powerful groups maintaining a status quo (of power imbalances) – and this includes sexuality. Sexuality has been pathologized ever since pathologization became my culture's go-to tool for making sense of behaviors we don't understand or value. For generations, state-sanctioned "experts" have asserted there are healthy/normal and unhealthy/pathological sexualities (De Block & Adriaens, 2013). Here are some intersectional examples:

- Saneism and heterosexism intersected when homosexuality was pathologized as an official "mental disorder" (Drescher, 2015).
- Saneism, cisheterosexism, mononormativity, and colonialism intersected when Indigenous sexualities (which embraced non-monogamy and queerness) were pathologized and subjugated (see Chapter 7).
- Saneism and erotophobia intersected when labels like "nymphomania" and "satyriasis" were developed to pathologize "excessive sexual drive." In today's ICD, these terms persist (WHO, 2019). In the DSM they've been replaced by "sex addiction," "compulsive sexual behavior," and "hypersexuality" (Kühn & Gallinat, 2016).
- Saneism and racism intersected in the hypersexualization of enslaved Africans, a dynamic that continues to harm Black people today (Chideya, 2007).
- Saneism and kinkphobia intersected in the pathologization of kink (see Chapter 22).
- Saneism and transphobia intersected in the pathologization of gender variance via historical labels like "gender identity disorder" and "transsexualism," which have been replaced with "gender dysphoria" (DSM-5) and "gender incongruence" (ICD-11) (WHO, n.d.) – for more information, see Chapter 18.

In summary, besides the idealized white cishet baby-making marriage, most sexual behaviors have been pathologized at some stage of my cultural history. This is why my culture is aptly called **sex negative** – a term that describes cultures where sex is viewed as inherently problematic (i.e., dangerous, sinful, pathological) except when socially sanctioned (e.g., through monogamous marriage) (Jorgensen, 2016). Now remember my healing-centered approach to pathologization from earlier, and let's use pathologization as a tool to help identify behaviors that hinder survival and thriving. Here is the absurdity I see: my culture's history of pathologizing natural **sexual diversity** has profoundly hindered our collective thriving, creating a world of pervasive **sexual violence** – so couldn't we say **pathologization itself can be pathological?** That charlatans who promote "conversion therapy" are **pathologically pathologizing?**

> **Mad/Queer-Affirming Reflection Activity: "Pathological Pathologizing" or "Healing-Centered Pathologizing?"**
>
> How have you witnessed sexual behavior being pathologized? Now we have language for it, can you distinguish between moments when it was **pathological pathologizing** (i.e., pathologization as a tool to assert cisheteronormativity), and moments when it was **healing-centered pathologizing** (i.e., pathologization as a tool to identify behaviors that hinder survival/thriving)? How can you tell the difference?

Allow me to define two terms I just used, as not everyone uses them the same way. I define **sexual violence** broadly as *any* kind of violence pertaining to sex and sexuality. Rape is sexual violence. So is homophobia and sex negativity. Slut-shaming, abstinence-based sexual (mis)education, and conversion therapy are sexual violence. And when I say **sexual diversity**, I mean sexual behavior that has been pathologized in my cultures, such as queer, kinky, and non-monogamous sexualities. The word "diversity" helps reframe the dominant narrative, highlighting that what the culture calls "pathology" (i.e., *outside* the range of normal human diversity) is often actually "stigmatized diversity" (i.e., completely *within* the range of normal human diversity, except people in power don't believe/want that to be true). While a pathological pathologizer might say "queerness goes against nature," in fact it's the *opposite* – queerness is an integral *part* of nature, and any attempt to deny or repress it goes against nature! To demonstrate, let's take a quick trip through evolutionary anthropology.

## Part 2: Queerness Is [and Always Was] Natural

In an earlier draft of this chapter, I had 1,500 painstakingly polished words dedicated to explaining why and how human queerness had evolved but realized an edit based on some corrections in my conclusions would benefit us all. I relied heavily on a book called *The Evolution of Beauty* by Richard Prum (2017), who theorized that human queerness may have evolved as a byproduct of his "female sexual autonomy hypothesis." In brief, the hypothesis is: male sexual coercion is common in animals, but females prefer sexual autonomy, and when females assert that autonomy by choosing to mate with less coercive (i.e., friendlier, less aggressive) males, over time this can facilitate more sex equality and more pleasure-focused sexual behaviors in the whole species. He proposed that human queerness may have been a byproduct of this process, and it was a compelling argument – it felt affirming that queerness met criteria for his definition of evolutionary "beauty" (i.e., things that evolve for pleasure/thriving reasons more than for functional/survival reasons)!

As a cultural anthropologist, I knew I was a little out of my element in the realm of evolution. So, I shared the chapter with my friend Rachna; a biological anthropologist who recently published about chimpanzee queerness with our other friend Aaron (Sandel & Reddy, 2021). With a mixture of relief (at avoiding an embarrassing publishing moment) and grief (at culling 1,500 painstakingly polished words), our discussion helped me realize something not only harrowing but also liberating: while Prum's hypothesis that queerness is evolutionarily "beautiful" may be valid, there was an epic problem in the way I had framed my interpretation. Whether or not Prum intended me to (he didn't say this explicitly), and whether or not I realized I was doing it (I did not), I had fallen prey to a pervasive fallacy in the study of animal sexuality: **I had assumed that queerness evolved from a heterosexual origin point.** And as logical as that may seem (to scientists steeped in cisheteronormative cultures, like myself) that actually may not be the case! In a paradigm-busting article, Julia Monk et al. (2019) challenge this assumption and call attention to the cisheteropatriarchy that has fueled it. Instead of starting with the assumption that animal sexuality began as heterosexual (which they call "different-sex sexual behavior" to avoid anthropomorphism) and that non-reproductive sexual behavior (like queerness) evolved from that starting point, they assert that **animal sexuality was *always* queer**. "We propose that indiscriminate sexual behaviour, or sexual behaviour without sex-based mate identification . . . is the most likely ancestral condition of sexually reproducing animals" (p. 1623). (Incidentally, I *love* this as a broad definition of queerness: sexual behavior that doesn't "discriminate" by sex/gender. I've been shamed for such "indiscriminate" behavior, and now I feel validated and proudly united with my queer animal kin!)

Why do they propose this? Because of how astoundingly *pervasive* queerness is throughout the animal kingdom! They review a vast literature of "indiscriminate sexual behavior" in over 1,500 animal species. If you want a more playful account of this literature, Rachna recommends the 2022 book *Queer Ducks (and Other Animals)* by Eliot Schrefer and Jules Zuckerberg. They note that biologists of the past have been woefully limited by cisheteronormative biases. These biases not only prevented biologists from *acknowledging* animal queerness (e.g., failing to notice it when it was present, or choosing to deemphasize it because it seemed shameful or irrelevant), but it also distracted those who *did* acknowledge it from one of the key principles of biology: the principle of parsimony, which "tells us to choose the simplest scientific explanation that fits all the evidence" (Berkeley University, n.d.). Instead of assuming that 1,500 different species independently evolved queerness from a heterosexual starting point, it is more *parsimonious* to assume that queerness *was* the starting point. They worded this well, so I'll include an extended quote:

> If any other trait had been observed in such a diverse array of taxa as same-sex behavior, it likely would be widely accepted that the trait was an ancestral condition present in some of the earliest animal clades. The notion that same-sex behavior has arisen convergently in so many different lineages only makes intuitive sense from a heteronormative world view in which "heterosexual" behaviour is framed as the "natural order" for sexually reproducing species, and "homosexuality" is viewed as a recent aberration whose existence must be explained and justified.... The notion that same-sex behavior is a recently evolved and distinct phenomenon from "heterosexual" sex, rather than one component of the messy and tangled spectrum of behaviours, traits and strategies we clumsily refer to as "sex" and "sexual behaviour," is symptomatic of the kinds of binary essentialism that hinder not only social liberation and equity, but also scientific discovery.
>
> *(p. 1629)*

This is an even more liberating argument than my original one. The notion that queerness evolved from heterosexuality as a byproduct of our ancestors' search for pleasure and autonomy felt affirming. But the notion that queerness didn't evolve from heterosexuality at *all*, but that sexuality was *always* queer? That's even more affirming!

---

**Queer-Affirming Reflection Activity:**

I invite you to reflect upon the immensity of this idea: **Queerness is and has always been natural.** Perhaps say this aloud, and notice how you feel (without judgment). Warm feelings, like validation, vindication, and hope? And/or critical feelings, like suspicion (about the science), or maybe some internalized queerphobia pushing back? Where do you think those feelings come from? How might they impact your relationships with your clients and your communities, if at all?

One point that struck me as powerfully true in Prum's book (and about this I am confident, because it's in the realm of cultural anthropology!) is the assertion that cisheteronormativity has skewed our species toward less visible queerness than one would expect. In his words, "the capacity for broad, nonexclusive . . . sexual attraction should be quite common in humans, if not ubiquitous" (2017, p. 314). Based on mountains of evidence, queerness really should be a majority behavior, not a minority behavior. And yet, that is not what we see today (at least on the surface). We see counterintuitive evidence like 80% (a clear *majority*) of respondents are identified as "heterosexual" in a recent global survey (Boyon, 2021). In making sense of this, Prum turns to **social constructionism** by noting that cisheteropatriarchy can explain why we see less queerness than expected. **The *idea* of cisheteronormativity quite literally *became* reality** – without this (dare I say pathological) attachment to an *idea*, who knows what kind of funky queer utopia we might have had?!

And if we allowed (or encouraged) the cultural traditions of cisheteropatriarchy to die out, what kind of funky queer utopia could we *still* have? I didn't always believe this was possible, because let's be real: the study of violence and oppression can easily render one cynical (especially when one is harmed daily by the forms of violence and oppression they study, like me studying cisheteropatriarchy and saneism!). Violence just seemed so . . . *inevitable*. Especially hierarchical violence (like cisheteropatriarchy and saneism), which so often becomes a complex and cyclical cluster-fuck of self-fulfilling prophecies. But my cynicism was checked thanks to the work of anthropologist and neuroscientist Robert Sapolsky. For decades he studied baboons, bearing witness to their (seemingly) innate and inevitable hierarchical violence. And in 1982, one of the baboon troops he was following experienced a profoundly illuminating tragedy: all the dominant males died at once, after eating (and in true dominant male fashion, preventing anyone *else* from eating) infected food from human trash bins. In the ensuing power vacuum, subordinate males who'd spent their lives prioritizing friendship as a pleasing escape from routine violence, stepped into dominance. And Sapolsky watched as the entire troop became *peaceful* (a peaceful baboon troop? Serious oxymoron alert!) . . . *and* continued to be for subsequent generations (Sapolsky & Share, 2004). The Keekorak baboons revealed that **hierarchical violence is a learned behavior** – shaped by biology, of course, but not a given. Any animal with a culture can change its culture.

And this inspires me to reflect on changes I've already witnessed in my culture, not only as an anthropologist but also as a person enmeshed in it. For example, we're in a much more queer-affirming world than I was raised in, not only in terms of structural things, like changes in how our mental health system views queerness, but also in terms of the visible queerness I see all around me. It's not only in the queer-centric communities I choose to enmesh in but also in the mainstream culture too (e.g., my Netflix watch list is a cornucopia of queerness). That same global survey I just mentioned where 80% were identified as heterosexual also noted that younger generations are increasingly more likely to be identified as queer (Boyon, 2021). This doesn't mean they *are* queerer: it means they (finally) live in a world where they have *permission* to be queerer. So, although I will always validate any and all cynicism about humanity (my latest stand-up comedy show was literally titled *Miss Anthropy*), this big picture view suggests that Dr. King Jr. was onto something when he said, "the arc of the moral universe is long but it bends toward justice" (Smithsonian, n.d.).

## Conclusion: "Love Is Merely a Madness"

As Shakespeare wrote in *As You Like It*:

> Love is merely a madness; and, I tell you, deserves as well a dark house and a whip as madmen do; and the reason why they are not so punish'd and cured is that the lunacy is so ordinary that the whippers are in love too.
>
> *(n.d., Act III, Scene II)*

The character speaking these words (Rosalind) feels that romantic love is excessive and overly glorified in her culture (the comedy is that the audience already knows she is in love herself and overcorrecting in her attempt to hide it!). Dorothy Tennov called this kind of mad romantic love **"limerance"** – an "uncontrollable, biologically determined, inherently irrational, instinct-like reaction" (1998/1979, p. 266), which Wikipedia (of all places) summarizes *perfectly* as "an involuntary state of intense desire." And Rosalind's observation is astute: because it's not "abnormal," we don't define this experience as "mental disorder" – even though it overlaps immensely with experiences we *do* define as disordered!

I *love* this quote. Not only does it resonate with my eternal state of being (the concept of limerance makes me feel *so* seen!), but it also exposes what I see as the two greatest flaws of my culture's mental health system: (1) it constructs madness as *aberrant* to humanity, when really it's *integral* to humanity (just like love is) and (2) it individualizes problems that are actually cultural. Let me unpack that: Rosalind's words suggest that love (by which she means limerance) is madness, but a *normal* madness, a madness too universal to be *pathologized* (or "punish'd and cured"). In 2002, psychiatrist Alvin Poussaint wrote an article about whether racism should be counted as madness:

> After several racist killings in the civil rights era, a group of Black psychiatrists sought to have extreme bigotry classified as a mental disorder. The association's officials rejected the recommendation, arguing that *because*

*so many Americans are racist, even extreme racism in this country is normative – a cultural problem rather than an indication of psychopathology.*
(p. 4, emphasis mine)

So according to the mental health system, it can't be madness/psychopathology if it's also "normal." The logic is that "abnormality" is the marker of pathology. Individuals can stand out as "abnormal" (and therefore mad/pathological) within their culture – but if/when an entire culture normalizes a behavior, even an undeniably destructive behavior (like racism), that's beyond the scope of the mental health system. Which is utterly absurd to me: the system only responds to madness at the individual level, yet individual people's madness is shaped *by* and *in* their culture. We pathologize individual-level behaviors like depression, but normalize the cultural-level behaviors like racism which can *cause* individual-level behaviors like depression. As liberation psychologist Sanah Ahsan wrote: "If a plant were wilting, we wouldn't diagnose it with 'wilting-plant-syndrome' – we would change its conditions. Yet when humans are suffering under unliveable conditions, we're told something is wrong with us" (2022, para. 4, emphasis mine).

---

**Mad-Affirming Reflection Activity: Satirical Anti-Saneist Reframes!**

Imagine: what if the mental health system *did* pathologize cultural problems? Years ago, I saw a satirical parody of a public health poster, one you might also have seen. On the left, a stock image of a person in scrubs holding a clipboard. At the top, in large letters, "Feeling Sad and Depressed?" In slightly smaller letters below, "Are you anxious? Worried about the future? Feeling isolated and alone?" And below that, the punchline: "You might be suffering from CAPITALISM!" Complete with fine print: "Symptoms may include homelessness, unemployment, poverty, hunger, feelings of powerlessness, fear, apathy, boredom, cultural decay, loss of identity, extreme self-consciousness, loss of free speech, incarceration, suicidal or revolutionary thoughts, death." It was one of those *it's funny because it's true* moments (research confirms these harms of capitalism, e.g., Prins et al., 2015). Satire can be informative and cathartic, so I invite you to try it! In my recent comedy show *Miss Anthropy*, I spoke humorous truth to power: *am I "suffering from a shit brain that can't do serotonin right?"* or am *I "suffering from saneism. . .?"*

Please think about one or two ways that we frame mental illness/Madness in our society and think about a satirical way that you could offer a reframe. If you're an artsy person, consider creating a virtual or physical piece to accompany your satire. Then think about how you might be able to use satire with your clients.

My life has been shaped by limerance – by involuntary (and often unwanted) intense desire for another. From my early childhood, when I stole the discarded sock of a boy, I liked and fashioned it into a cherished bracelet, to my early adulthood, when limerance drove me (more than once) to the brink of suicide. Yet my romantic and sexual voracity didn't remain in the realm of "normalized" madness that Rosalind described. No. Using her words, I was "punish'd and cured." My sexual behavior was pathologized as "risky" and "self-harming." Clinicians viewed me as sexually "indiscriminate" – but not in the queer-affirming way that Monk et al. (2019) defined it (as described earlier), in a pathologically "hypersexual" way that was quintessentially "bipolar." And because I believed this pathologizing narrative, I soaked in the shame of "there's something (*so-many-things*) wrong with me" for decades. *Immense* collective (and ongoing) labor has gone into healing the damage of that pernicious internalized saneism and queerphobia.

Looking back, with compassion for the clinicians who harmed me (who were doing their best with the tools our flawed system provided), I see their point. It wasn't just that I loved sex and had lots of it. My sexual behavior was deemed "risky" and "self-harming" because it *was*. To apply the "healing-centered pathologization" concept I shared earlier: some of my romantic and sexual behavior *did* hinder my survival and thriving. In my other co-authored chapter (see Chapter 21), we talk about Critical Non-monogamy and how liberating it can be – but before I learned to be an "Ethical Slut" (Easton & Hardy, 1997), I was an *Un*ethical Slut. I fucked in ways that harmed myself and others, in ways I'd acquiesce to calling "addictive," assuming a trauma-informed model that recognizes addiction as a trauma response (Maté, n.d.). *Of course* my sexual behavior was sometimes pathological – I'd been raised in a sexually violent culture, and had not (yet) learned how to do sex safely or sanely!

Which connects to a frustrating paradox: some folks are labeled Mad *because* of their sexuality, while others are desexualized, *because* they're labeled Mad (Kattari et al., 2021). For my dissertation research, I worked in a psychosocial clubhouse alongside Mad/neurodivergent folks who were deeply mired in the mental health system (i.e., dependent on Supplemental Security Income/SSI; subject to forced treatment regimes). There I learned that some institutional spaces (e.g., group homes) actually *prohibit* Mad folks from having sex! This irked me, though I couldn't articulate *why* until I read an article that explored this later on.

In their study of a long-term care facility, Evans et al. (2019) found:

> [C]linicians responded to residents' sexuality from a discourse of risk. The resident became an object to be monitored and protected rather than a subject with sexual desire and agency. This paternalism also showed itself in relation to a "no-sex on-site" rule that allowed for a shift of risk from the organization to the resident. Residents, rather than having a relatively

safe place to have sexual relations, were required to find a place elsewhere, potentially unsafe, outside the facility.

*(p. 1)*

The issue I couldn't yet articulate was *paternalism*: the irony of trying to protect folks from sexual violence by limiting their sexual autonomy (which is *also* sexual violence).

I share the desire to protect Mad/neurodivergent folks (*all* folks) from sexual violence, but as this chapter has relayed, sex is inherently "risky" in a sexually violent culture. What I needed is what I imagine many folks need: not to be pathologized for our sexuality or desexualized for our madness, but to be validated and empowered with the skills to *thrive* in our madness and sexuality. I am grateful to be part of a mad-/queer-affirming micro-world (alongside many of the other authors in this book!) where this is not only possible but also *normal*. In fact, sometimes I even *forget* that my culture has a poisonous mainstream, because I am happily paddling in the metaphorical side-streams where the water feels great.

### *Acknowledgments*

*Let me acknowledge my peers, who provided invaluable feedback labor on this chapter (special thanks to sex therapist Dorian Stein and biological anthropologist Rachna Reddy!), and the innumerable ancestors who have supported my learning/healing journey in un-citable ways.*

### Resources

- This essay reframes the DSM-5 criteria for "Autism Spectrum Disorder" https://autietraumageek.medium.com/a-neurodiversity-paradigm-breakdown-of-the-dsm-criteria-for-autism-bb524291298b
- The Power Threat Meaning Framework offers a similar trauma/oppression-informed assessment practice to what I've developed/shared here: www.bps.org.uk/member-networks/division-clinical-psychology/power-threat-meaning-framework
- Therapist Neurodiversity Collective educate about Neurodiversity-affirming practice: https://therapistndc.org
- Fireweed Collective and Project LETS educate about saneism and offer Mad-affirming peer support spaces (valuable for liberating from internalized saneism!): https://fireweedcollective.org; https://projectlets.org
- This essay by Stella Akua Mensah connects anti-saneism to abolitionism: https://disabilityvisibilityproject.com/2020/07/22/abolition-must-include-psychiatry/

- Nick Walker's concept of "neuroqueer" means to simultaneously liberate oneself from saneism *and* cisheteropatriarchy – which totally jives with this chapter! https://neuroqueer.com
- Devon Price's book *Unmasking Autism* is an excellent resource for understanding and resisting saneism. It covers a lot; from the history of pathologizing neurodivergence, to Mad/neurodivergent activism and self-advocacy, to affirming neurodivergence (i.e., reframing it as strength not pathology) and healing from internalized saneism, to building communities and cultures that are more accessible and accommodating of neurodivergence (and of disability more broadly).
- For my research on Mad empowerment via purpose and belonging, see *Work is Love Made Visible: Purpose and Community in Clubhouses*: https://dsq-sds.org/article/view/6096/4826 and *Tackling Timelessness*: https://www.anthropology-news.org/articles/tackling-timelessness/
- For more on affirming neurodivergence and sexuality, see Chapter 4.
- There's much more I could share if I had endless space – but please feel free to email me with questions or invite me to facilitate a workshop! At the University of Michigan, my *Mental Healthcare Without Saneism* class is a hit, one I'm happy to take on tour! It covers a spectrum of practices, from more radical forms of anti-saneism (e.g., psychiatric abolition) to forms that can exist within the saneist mental health system (e.g., mad/neurodiversity-affirming healing-centered practice!).

## References

Ahsan, S. (2022, September 6). I'm a psychologist – and I believe we've been told devastating lies about mental health. *The Guardian*. www.theguardian.com/commentisfree/2022/sep/06/psychologist-devastating-lies-mental-health-problems-politics

Beresford, P., & Russo, J. (2022). *The Routledge international handbook of mad studies*. Routledge.

Berkeley University. (n.d.). *Reconstructing trees: Parsimony*. https://evolution.berkeley.edu/phylogenetic-systematics/reconstructing-trees-cladistics/reconstructing-trees-parsimony/

Boyon, N. (2021). *LGBT+ Pride 2021 global survey* [PowerPoint Slides]. IPSOS. www.ipsos.com/sites/default/files/ct/news/documents/2021-06/LGBT%20Pride%202021%20Global%20Survey%20Report_3.pdf

Chamberlin, J. (1978). *On our own: Patient-controlled alternatives to the mental health system*. Hawthorn Books.

Chideya, F. (Host). (2007, May 7). Sex stereotypes of African-Americans have long history [Audio]. *NPR*. www.npr.org/templates/story/story.php?storyId=10057104

Collings, S. (n.d.). The social model of disability and eating disorders. *RDs for Neurodiversity* [Blog]. www.rdsforneurodiversity.com/blog/the-social-model-of-disability-and-eating-disorders

De Block, A., & Adriaens, P. R. (2013). Pathologizing sexual deviance: A history. *Journal of Sex Research*, *50*(3–4), 276–298. https://doi.org/10.1080/00224499.2012.738259

Drescher, J. (2015). Out of DSM: Depathologizing homosexuality. *Behavioral Sciences*, *5*(4), 565–575. https://doi.org/10.3390/bs5040565

Easton, D., & Hardy, J. (1997). *The ethical slut: A practical guide to Polyamory, open relationships, and other freedoms in sex and love*. Greenery Press.

Evans, A., Holmes, D., & Quinn, C. (2019). Madness, sex, and risk: A poststructural analysis. *Nursing Inquiry*, *27*(4), 1–8. https://doi.org/10.1111/nin.12359

Foucault, M. (1990). *The history of sexuality, Vol. 1: An introduction*. Vintage. (Original work published 1976).

Foucault, M. (2011). *Madness: The invention of an idea*. Harper Perennial. (Original work published 1962).

Jorgensen, J. (2016, August 12). The sex-negativity mind-set in academe (essay). *Inside Higher Ed*. www.insidehighered.com/advice/2016/08/12/sex-negativity-mind-set-academe-essay

Kattari, S. K., Hecht, H. K., & Isaacs, Y. E. (2021). Sexy spoonies and crip sex: Sexuality and disability in a social work context. In S. J. Dodd (Ed.), *The Routledge international handbook of social work and sexualities*. Routledge.

Kühn, S., & Gallinat, J. (2016). Neurobiological basis of hypersexuality. *International Review of Neurobiology*, *129*, 67–83.

LeFrançois, B. A., Menzies, R., & Reaume, G. (Eds.). (2013). *Mad matters: A critical reader in Canadian mad studies*. Canadian Scholars' Press.

Liebert, R. (2014). Pathologization. In T. Teo (Ed.), *Encyclopedia of critical psychology*. Springer.

Liegghio, M. (2013). A denial of being: Psychiatrization as epistemic violence. In B. A. LeFrançois, R. Menzies, & G. Reaume (Eds.), *Mad matters: A critical reader in Canadian mad studies* (pp. 122–129). Canadian Scholars' Press.

Maté, G. (n.d.). *Addiction*. https://drgabormate.com/topics/addiction/

Monk, J. D., Giglio, E., Kamath, A., Lambert, M. R., & McDonough, C. E. (2019). An alternative hypothesis for the evolution of same-sex sexual behaviour in animals. *Nature Ecology & Evolution*, *3*, 1622–1631. https://doi.org/10.1038/s41559-019-1019-7

Niania, W., & Bush, A. (2016). *Collaborative and indigenous mental health therapy: Tātaihono – Stories of Māori healing and psychiatry*. Routledge.

Poussaint, A. F. (2002). Is extreme racism a mental illness? Yes: It can be a delusional symptom of psychotic disorders. *The Western Journal of Medicine*, *176*(1), 4. https://doi.org/10.1136/ewjm.176.1.4

Price, D. (2022). *Unmasking autism. The power of embracing our hidden neurodiversity*. Monoray.

Prins, S. J., Bates, L. M., Keyes, K. M., & Muntaner, C. (2015). Anxious? Depressed? You might be suffering from capitalism: Contradictory class locations and the prevalence of depression and anxiety in the USA. *Sociology of Health & Illness*, *37*(8), 1352–1372. https://doi.org/10.1111/1467-9566.12315

Prum, R. O. (2017). *The evolution of beauty: How Darwin's forgotten theory of mate choice shapes the animal world-and us*. Doubleday.

Russo, J., & Sweeney, A. (Eds.). (2016). *Searching for a rose garden: Challenging psychiatry, fostering mad studies*. PCCS Books.

Sandel, A. A., & Reddy, R. B. (2021). Sociosexual behaviour in wild chimpanzees occurs in variable contexts and is frequent between same sex partners. *Behaviour, 158*, 249–276. https://doi.org/10.1163/1568539X-bja10062

Sapolsky, R. M., & Share, L. J. (2004). A pacific culture among wild baboons: Its emergence and transmission. *PLoS Biology, 2*(4), e106. https://doi.org/10.1371/journal.pbio.0020106

Schrefer, E., & Zuckerberg, J. (2022). *Queer Ducks (and other animals): The natural world of animal sexuality.* Katherine Tegen Books.

Shakespeare, W. (n.d.). *As you like it.* The Complete Works of William Shakespeare. http://shakespeare.mit.edu/asyoulikeit/full.html

Simmons University. (n.d.). *Anti-sanism.* https://simmons.libguides.com/anti-oppression/anti-sanism

Smithsonian. (n.d.). *Dr. Martin Luther King Jr.* www.si.edu/spotlight/mlk

Tennov, D. (1998). *Love and limerence: The experience of being in love.* Scarborough House. (Original work published 1979).

Walker, N. (n.d.). *Neurodiversity.* www.autisticuk.org/neurodiversity

World Health Organization. (n.d.). *Gender incongruence and transgender health in the ICD.* www.who.int/standards/classifications/frequently-asked-questions/gender-incongruence-and-transgender-health-in-the-icd

World Health Organization. (2019). *International statistical classification of diseases and related health problems* (11th ed.). https://icd.who.int/browse10/2019/en#/F52.7

Yakas, L. (2017). "Work is love made visible": Purpose and community in clubhouses. *Disability Studies Quarterly, 7*(4). https://dsq-sds.org/article/view/6096/4826

Yakas, L. (2018, November 29). Tackling timelessness. *Anthropology News.* https://doi.org/10.1111/AN.1046

# 8
# BLINDNESS AND SEXUALITY

*Robin Mandell and Hillary K. Hecht*

## Introduction

### What Is Blindness?

Globally, more than 250 million people live with blindness or visual acuity loss (Flaxman et al., 2021). Blindness is the condition of having significantly impaired vision to some legal or social standard, and it refers to a broad range of conditions from total lack of eyesight to diminished eyesight in one or both eyes (Signes-Soler et al., 2017). Blindness is caused by injury or disease in the eye, optic nerve, or brain, and can be congenital or acquired at any point in childhood, adulthood, and older adulthood. The amount of eyesight a blind person has can be static or can vary; vision can be stable or can deteriorate over time.

Nations (political entities), jurisdictions (geographic locations), clinics or social services (organizations), and social communities set distinct criteria and thresholds for defining blindness or vision impairment (Ray et al., 2016; Resnikoff & Keys, 2012). Definitions vary based on *why* sight is being measured (i.e., for access to social services, evolving individual social identity, clinical response), and the dimension of vision being measured (i.e., visual clarity or acuity, visual field or peripheral range, color perception; Ray et al., 2016). Criteria help structure standards for providing clinical and legal services, resources, and benchmarks, as well as create a shared language around which aspects of blindness are being discussed. People may self-identify into blindness without measurement related to any organization's formal definition.

There is no single way to be blind, and no two blind people have the exact same shared experience with their sight. It is important to remember that vision and vision loss are spectrums, like many facets of human experience. Like many traits a person carries, blindness also crosses social identity and culture, and blind people hold a bevy of identities. Shared language around disability and blindness is one important way to ensure that a blind patient or client is being understood and treated as effectively as possible. In this chapter, we will use a number of terms to refer to blind people. *Blind or visually impaired* (BVI) persons is the term we will use to refer to anyone who experiences blindness. *Sighted* and *nondisabled* refer to people with privileged, seeing identities.

## What We Know?

Often, sighted people struggle to imagine how blind people do things. It is commonly stated, uncited, that 80% or 90% of how people take in information is visual, by capacity of the human brain or socially how we interact with the world. The modality of processing information affects the ways blind children develop (Levtzion-Korach et al., 2000), and how adults adjust to their world after sight loss of any amount (Cappagli et al., 2017). As BVI children grow, they may interact with therapists and specialized teachers to develop skills including navigating social situations, reading, and writing. Learners do not have the same opportunities to observe from watching as sighted children do, so they use alternative techniques, like tactical enlarged pegboard Braille (Barlow-Brown et al., 2019). Comparably, adults who lose sight later in their lives frequently benefit from skills-retraining to relearn how to complete daily living activities (cooking, reading, computer skills, job tasks, and navigating public transportation) for which they previously used their vision now using new skills and adaptive tools (Wolffe & Erin, 2020).

A common idea that people fear blindness more than they fear death, drowning, or life-threatening experiences speaks to the misinformation sighted people have about the experience of BVI people, and how poorly designed communities are accessible to the way people live, work, and play (Ferguson, 2001). In the U.S. during the late-2000s, of all the things people most feared, blindness was the only one that was not actually life-threatening (Flaxman et al., 2021; Going Blind, 2018; The Association for Research in Vision and Ophthalmology, 2014). While sighted people may assume that BVI people long to be sighted, or seek cures or "fixes" to their vision, this is not necessarily a desire nor goal. Alongside the social model of disability, it is the act of navigating a world which assumes sight and does not adequately support people navigating without sight that is disabling (Whitburn & Michalko, 2019).

### *What Providers Should Know?*

Unless you are providing vision- or blindness-related services, it is not important for you to know what caused your client's vision impairment or blindness, to ask how much or little eyesight your client has, nor pressure clients to disclose personal medical information (Heydarian et al., 2021). Refraining from asking about your client's blindness isn't about sparing feelings, rather, returning privacy and agency to allow clients to tell you what they need. BVI people experience frequent invasion in the form of random offers of help, questions about the cause or duration of blindness, inquiries into how we complete daily activities, expressions of surprise or admiration, and prayers, blessings, even disbelieving self-referent comments such as "I'd break my neck if I was walking around like you are." None of these are ok to ask of anyone, as they undermine the humanity and sexual agency of blind people. We strongly recommend you deprioritize your own curiosity, and contextualize offering your services with accommodations that your clients have the capacity to receive and use.

It is disruptive to consultation and treatment when providers ask disability-related questions that are not relevant to the service. I (Robin) recall when a doctor used five of the 15 allotted minutes of a medication follow-up visit to ask about how I cook while blind, which was obviously irrelevant to my care. A common frustrating experience occurs when providers display boundary-crossing and countertransference when intending to support disabled clients. Focusing on a patient or clients' goals of care will help you best support that person in getting what they want and need.

### **Blindness and Sex**

Blindness may feel connected to individuals' sexualities in a myriad of ways, to a range of extents, or not at all. For example, scholars explore through film the effects of blindness on masculinity and sexuality (Noson, 2017). Blind people are frequently treated as nonsexual at best, and infantilized at worst (Ubisi, 2020). A common ableist myth is BVI people are often thought of as having bigger things than sex to worry about (Kaufman et al., 2007).

We are predicating this discussion on the knowledge that blind people can and do have sex. Comparable to the broad spectrum of human sexuality experiences, BVI people occupy all aspects of asexuality spectrums, participate in BDSM/kink communities, are unhappily celibate, or seeking more romantic, long-term, or short-term sexual connections. Blind people are happily and unhappily dating, married, or coupled, and having children with and without assisted reproductive methods. Blind people span the LGBTQIA2S+ umbrella in marginalized sexuality and/or gender identities. Likewise, people with marginalized sexual orientation and gender identities have a wide range of experiences with vision that evolve over their life courses. One common frustration is many dating websites and mobile phone apps are inaccessible or difficult to use with screen readers, adaptive, or assistive technologies, therefore excluding BVI people from these fora (Bennett et al., 2021; Mazur, 2022). Acknowledging the sexual and gender diversity that exists in the blind community can help check assumptions to better serve the BVI clients you encounter in your practice.

Everyone uses their senses to experience and participate in sexuality and expresses their sexuality to others. For many, touch, smell, hearing, taste, and yes, sight, collaborate to allow us to interact with the world and each other. When any sense is not available to us, we rely on others to communicate about desire, consent and interact sexually. For some people, the way they experience and engage with solo or partnered sexual encounters may be influenced by how they use their vision, and which senses are heightened during their experiences. BVI individuals skillfully communicate complex, and evolving nonverbal information about desire and consent.

Much like everyone, our sexual desires and needs ebb and flow over time. As a sexuality writer, I (Robin) once wrote on my blog about a blind person desiring more sexual activity with a wider array of partners than was safe or feasible while seeking treatment for a health concern (Mandell, 2017). My friend shared this poignant thought:

> Maybe you think giving up a friends-with-benefits arrangement isn't as big a deal as, oh, having to quit your job for health reasons, or learning that there aren't any more treatments to try, or . . . and you'd be right, mostly, for some people, some of the time.
>
> *(Mandell, 2017)*

We, the blind community, ask providers: "We need you to believe in our intimate relationships, because so many people don't" (Mandell, 2017). Sexualities can be a big part of our identities, our lives, and how we spend time and relate to the people in our lives. Interruptions to these, related to vision, or any other reason can shake our core identities, or leave us feeling unfulfilled and un-whole. "Maintaining as much of who you are becomes a lifeline, one of the things that helps you feel human when you can't rely on your body to do the same thing from one day to the next" (Mandell, 2017). Likewise, acquiring a disability may necessitate big shifts in how an individual thinks, feels, and cares for themselves, as well as how they relate to others. Communicating clearly about changing physical and mental experiences with intimate partners, with family and friends, with caretakers and with providers, can be difficult in the best of times, and even more so when the changes are introducing difficulties into any facet of life. In communities with less openness of talking about sex and relationships, this can be even more strained and can create embarrassment around asking for help or support. For providers, asking open questions, or even offering the topic as an option for conversation, can invite clients to re-introduce the topic when they are ready to talk about it and ask for support in that domain of their life.

### *Identities of Partners*

One big question that people hold strong opinions about is whether to have a sighted or blind partner (Hammer, 2019).

> When a visibly disabled and visibly nondisabled partner go out together, they're rarely read as lovers or spouses. The visibly nondisabled partner might feel resentful about being mistaken, by servers in restaurants, or, yes, staff in doctor's offices or hospitals, for their partner's nurse, paid caregiver, or non-romantic family member.
> 
> *(Mandell, 2017)*

Dating disabled or nondisabled people may be a strong criterion for people seeking romantic or sexual connections, or may be a passing detail that combines with many traits to define how well the partnership meets the needs of the people involved. Notably, bodies change over time, so a person's nondisabled status at the start of the relationship may not remain true throughout its duration.

Whether actively encouraging or discouraging, sighted people have opinions of whether they imagine a sighted or blind person as ideal sexual or romantic partners for themselves and for their BVI loved one. They also hold strong assumptions about the implications of pursuing relationships with people with disabilities or impairments differing from those that BVI people experience. Unless BVI individuals explicitly solicit advice or opinions from their sighted family or friends about their dating lives, opinions about partners' identities may not be welcome nor helpful! For providers, holding space for the way evolving disabilities impact relationships can inform how to offer appropriate responses to what supports your client wants toward their loving relationship.

### *Sexual Education and Sexual Health*

Everyone deserves access to accessible sexual education, sexual health, and sexual healthcare (Raven & Avilla, 2021). Sexual health education can and should start early, in age appropriate and accessible ways for young people to learn about consent, pleasure, safety, and emotional and physical health concerns. People might learn about sexual health in an education setting, a community or family setting, a clinical setting, and probably a combination of many of these settings (Raven & Avilla, 2021). Providers and sex educators should strive to serve BVI and disabled people, as everyone should be able to learn about sexual health that is relevant and specific to the experiences they desire to and are already having.

Accessible and inclusive sexual education can help BVI folks practice communicating what they want their partners to know, how to express their own thoughts and desires, and how to communicate about their own evolving identities. Supporting BVI children in obtaining their emerging autonomy can facilitate them becoming safe, autonomous adults who have practice assessing risk and making decisions about their lives. Helping BVI people of all ages find the sexual safety information that they seek to make informed decisions, define priorities, and protect their own privacy extends sexual autonomy comparable to other sexual education learners. In most scenarios, providers need not have detailed insight into their clients' inner lives in order to provide safe and affirming care.

When it comes to sexual activities, let's be clear; the mechanics of sex are not a barrier for blind people. In spite of the commonness of questions about how blind people have sex, blind people are only limited by their level of knowledge about the human body. However, many people who have been blind from birth or early childhood are sometimes challenged by a lack of access to early sexuality education. As dicey, inadequate, and filled with knowledge gaps as general sexuality education in public schools is for all children and teens, blind people often don't have access to even that. They are often pulled out of physical education/gym classes, both because these classes are (inaccurately) considered inherently unsafe, are inaccessible, and because time is needed in the school day to teach blind children specialized skills such as walking with a white cane, learning Braille, and other hands-on skills that aren't taught in mainstream classrooms. Being excluded from gym class often means automatic exclusion from the health education (including sexuality education) portions of class. Additionally, blind children may not have access to more clandestine methods of learning, such as reading sexuality-related books in the library, finding an adult's hidden stash of erotic magazines, or even studying the diagrams on a tampon or information on a condom box.

### Flirting and Dating

When it comes to flirting and casual dating, much of sighted flirting is inaccessible as it relies on meaningful glances and gazes. A lot of casual connections happen in noisy clubs and bars where it is inaccessible to communicate verbally. Here, it can be difficult for many blind people to stay oriented to their surroundings, let alone find and connect with people they are interested in. Within queer communities, BVI members discuss the exuberance they feel in finding intersecting queer and BVI communities, advocating for their being perceived as desirable, sexual members of their queer spaces (Wolfe, 2020).

> "Often, gay people know so little about blindness," Lopez Kafati said. "They think we can't have sex!" Gay men communicate so much nonverbally – through a wink or a nod – and he can't see to respond. This makes Lopez Kafati feel excluded from the gay community.

This is evidenced by Kafati's experiment disclosing and not disclosing his blindness on dating app (Wolfe, 2020). However, some have welcoming experiences, including memoirist and disability rights advocate Belo Miguel Cipriani, who was active in the gay dance club scene in San Francisco before he lost all his sight in his mid-20s. After a period of focused rehabilitation, Cipriani resumed his dating life as he had before and writes of the chaos that ensued (Cipriani, 2018).

Blind-inclusive flirting and dating may contain more audio and text communication, focusing on sharing what each person likes about the other. Distinct from a platonic or professional caretaking relationship, a flirtatious or dating relationship will highlight to the people in the relationship, and hopefully to friends, family, and bystanders, how each person supports and cares for the other. Romantic indicators, like hand-holding, are one way BVI people communicate nonverbally to others about their partnerships, even when bystanders misread those relationships, desexualizing BVI individuals and invalidating their partnerships (Godin, 2018). Instead of assumptions about BVI acquaintances, as "a cashier with whom we'd struck up a strange friendship – she often gave me candy meant for children – finally screwed up her nerve to ask, 'So you are brother and sister?'" (Godin, 2018), providers can practice using open phrases like "who's here in the room with you today?", "what role does that person play in your life?", or "how do you take care of each other in your relationship?" to give affirming space for clients to define and celebrate their relationships.

### *Reproduction, Pregnancy, and Parenting*

Blind people face stereotypes and incorrect assumptions from sighted people about their desires, willingness, and ability to reproduce, carry, and parent children (Frederick, 2015). It's a social (and nosey!) habit in the U.S. to ask adults when they're going to have children. The culture is one of active encouragement toward parenthood (Brunet, 2020). Disabled people are often left out of this cultural habit, are assumed to not be parents, or actively discouraged from parenting (Frederick, 2015). In reality, blind and visually impaired people have varied and complex relationships to parenting, with a range of desires on when and how they wish to reproduce, if at all. BVI people make for warm, loving, and supportive parents, and use many tools and techniques to safely raise their children, as all parents do.

Asking invalidating questions as "[A]re you fit to have a child? Should you be having a child? Would you be able to take care of the child?" are as offensive and irrelevant to BVI as to any prospective parents (Vishwanathan & D'Souza, 2022). Invasive questions BVI parents receive about whether and how they have sex, praising of young sighted children for "taking care of" a blind parent, to taking pictures of a blind caretakers and children without permission perpetuate ableist eugenicist beliefs regarding disabilities and expectations for how humans are and ought to be in societies. BVI activists share:

> [F]or someone who's lived with a disability their whole life, like someone who's known, they've had cerebral palsy or ADHD, or being born blind, or with low vision, that's a part of who they are, that's the only normal they have known . . . ?

And this will be as (un)related to their preparation for parenthood as anyone's relationship to their physical selves (Vishwanathan & D'Souza, 2022).

All these take not only an emotional toll but also a legal one. Custody disputes are often settled with a simple mention of disability, giving custody to the nondisabled parent without investigating whether being with the disabled parent would actually be the best option for the child(ren). Sometimes, it doesn't even get that far, and babies are removed from their disabled parents at or shortly after birth. In a 2010 case in Missouri, United States, a blind couple's newborn was removed and placed into foster care shortly after birth (Smith, 2014; Wunder, 2010). Parents and child spent over two months apart before permanent reunification. The removal was made based on hospital staff's mistaken belief that blind people cannot safely care for children, and on a lack of training to provide the teaching and coaching all new parents need (Smith, 2014; Wunder, 2010). This horrifying use of legal courts to invalidate disabled parents as viable and loving caregivers has a long history, in many places (Wheatley, 2010). All new parents – BVI and sighted – learn as they go. "Over 4.1 million parents in the U.S. are disabled, and have a child under 18 living with them. In other words, disabled parents aren't rare, and most of them have been able to parent their own children just fine" (Mandell, 2017). Many supporters including healthcare providers, therapists, and community groups can legally advocate on behalf of BVI parents to raise their children as they choose. Online resources such as Disability, Pregnancy & Parenthood in the United Kingdom, connect disabled parents directly to discuss what they are experiencing, how they navigate parenting, and to promote peer-to-peer skill sharing (2022; Frederick, 2015).

## What Can We Do?

### *Acknowledging Abuse*

We need you to know that many of us have, or will experience abuse, sometimes in care settings (Poche, 2021). What do you do when your abuser is also your care provider, someone who bathes you, or dresses you, or whose assistance you need if you want to leave the house or communicate with other people? What do you do if people constantly tell you not only how good a person your abuser is but also how courageous and wonderful they are for helping you? What do you do when your abuser doesn't treat you like a human being, but neither does much of the rest of the world? These questions can come up among intimate partner relationships, when receiving care from "trusted" professionals, or in other relationships BVI people experience. This, in concert with inaccessible spaces may lead to social isolation and hesitation in entering new intimate relationships (Kelley & Moore, 2000).

Disabled women have been found to experience abuse for longer periods of time and from a larger number of abusers than nondisabled women who experience physical or sexual abuse (Center for Research on Women with Disabilities, 2022). Many children with disabilities are at higher risk of abuse, because they come into contact with more adults who can claim the right to take them into private spaces without being asked questions. Disabled children's exposure to a greater number of people than nondisabled children are usually exposed to – medical specialists, nurses, physical, occupational, and speech therapists, educational assistants and support workers – may account for the higher incidence of physical and sexual abuse they, as a group, typically experience (Kaufman et al., 2007). Providers who acknowledge former harms done by former providers or BVI community members can create an opportunity but not an obligation for clients to share their experiences, and take active steps to build trust and make amends for previous harm. These actions can allow BVI clients access to affirming services free from abuse, allowing the clients space to safely ask for and receive help. You as a provider might be a BVI's first, and only, line of defense to cope with or get out of an abusive situation. Your patients and clients may also have deep and complicated histories of abuse. Please, don't be afraid to ask, and also, don't push too hard.

If disabled clients are going to trust you enough to talk about sex and sexuality, we need to feel safe in your office or classroom. It means helping you understand the disability-related stresses we carry into our appointment with you, whether we're seeing you for a routine physical, grief counseling, sexuality education, or to get forms filled out that will make our lives as disabled people easier. Knowing that we can share as much as we're comfortable sharing of our feelings about and experiences of sex, as well as our broader interaction with our sexualities with a healthcare provider who will use the information to help, not judge us, can save folks a lot of worry and heartache. One of the biggest struggles people have around their sexuality, or how they express themselves sexually, is feeling sure they're alone in their experiences or desires (Mandell, 2017). We support BVI clients by validating their experiences and desires and connecting them with other people who may share related experiences.

### Social Energy

Social exhaustion is an experience that many BVI and other disabled people feel after a day out in public that includes routine disability-related conversations (Hingsburger, 2015). Social exhaustion can come from the highly emotionally charged discussions with strangers who come up to us out of the blue and ask to pray with us, or being stuck next to someone on the bus who wants to tell us all about all disabled people they've known, or responding to people's anger because we don't fit their definition of a disabled person (i.e., a wheelchair user who stands up to take something off a high shelf, or a blind person carrying a cane who reads a print sign). Social exhaustion stems from experiences of condescension, or gushing claims of how much they admire us. It comes from random, uninvited pats on the head, shoulder, back, or hand from strangers. Social energy is depleted by having one's arm, or mobility aid grabbed without permission by someone who "just wants to help" but instead scares us half to death, throws off our already unsteady balance, or disorients us by dragging us across a street we never intended to cross. For visibly disabled people, the interactions with strangers can be constant, and tedious, especially so for the congratulations or praise for doing everyday activities.

As a reminder, when encountering BVI people within or outside of your practice, you can affirm their right and autonomy to move through the world using the following tools:

- Speak directly to the person you are addressing, even if we're with a visibly able person and even if that person is speaking for us
- Ask directly what kind of help we need and want
- Do not touch someone until they invite you to do so
- Speak in a respectful tone of voice, addressing the person by name or asking their name and offering your own name
- Do not use terms of endearment
- Treat people respectfully, regardless of age, extending the same autonomy to both BVI adults and BVI children

**Class Activity**

Imagine you are providing care to a new client or patient, and you learn before your first appointment with them that they are blind. Write at least three responses to each of these questions:

1. What do you need to do to prepare to meet this client for the first time?

    a. Who on your care team can support you in making these preparations?

2. What questions do you need to ask this client during your first meeting that are relevant to the care or services you provide?

    a. How will you find out your client's primary goals for their appointment?

3. Name three things you are curious about, but are not appropriate nor necessary to this appointment.

    a. Where else could you find out that information without taking time away from this client's appointment (i.e., if you are curious how a client puts their socks on in the morning, where could you find that out?)?

4. Name three steps you can take to build rapport with this client.

    a. For example, when a blind patient first met their primary care physician, the provider asked them what the best way would be for her to send the patient's test results. She did not automatically assume, as others providers had, that someone would read the results to the patient. This went a long way toward helping the patient trust their doctor, and interact with care in an accessible way.

Once you have your plan together, practice asking these questions out loud to a classmate. How is your tone building rapport? How are you helping your client feel comfortable? What are any adjustments to your scripts that you might want to make?

**Conclusion**

In this chapter, you have gained new knowledge around blindness and sexuality and have been introduced to tools that allow you to check assumptions that you hold about BVI people, and affirm your BVI clients in their sexual desires and sexual health. You have had the opportunity to practice verbalizing respectful questions to affirm your clients' lived experience, support their goals for care or services, and reflect on your own feelings and relationship to your sight. Thank you for co-creating with us a more blind-affirming society across all aspects, including sexuality, to support the BVI people in your life and your community.

## Resources

1. Writing resources
   a. American Foundation for the Blind. (n.d.). *Low vision and legal blindness terms and descriptions*. The American Foundation for the Blind. www.afb.org/blindness-and-low-vision/eye-conditions/low-vision-and-legal-blindness-terms-and-descriptions
   b. National Center on Disability and Journalism. (2021, August). *Disability language style guide*. Walter Cronkite School of Journalism and Mass Communication at Arizona State University. https://ncdj.org/style-guide/
   c. Lee, S. Y., & Mesfin, F. B. (2022, January/August). Blindness. In *StatPearls* [Internet]. StatPearls Publishing. www.ncbi.nlm.nih.gov/books/NBK448182/

2. Media and Entertainment
   a. Mandell, R. (2015). *Ready sexy able* [Blog]. https://readysexyable.com/ready/
   b. Blind LGBT-Pride International. (2020). *ACB Radio mainstream* [Podcast]. https://blindlgbtpride.org/pride-connection/
   c. Kelly, N., & Tuberty, S. (2019). *Disarming disability podcast* [Podcast]. www.disarmingdisability.com
   d. Guter, B., & Killacky, J. R. (Eds.). (2014). *Queer crips: Disabled gay men and their stories*. Routledge.
   e. Downes, J. C. (2014). *An investigation into the experiences and identities of visually-impaired gay men in 'gay spaces'*. KDP Publishing.
   f. Cipriani, B. M. (Ed.). (2018). *Firsts: Coming of age stories by people with disabilities*. Oleb Books.
   g. Luczak, R. (2007). *Eyes of desire 2: A Deaf GLBT reader*. HandtypePress.
   h. Rainey, S. S. (2011). *Love, sex, and disability: The pleasures of care*. Lynne Rienner Publishers.
   i. Kaufman, M., Silverberg, C., & Odette, F. (2016). *The ultimate guide to sex and disability: For all of us who live with disabilities, chronic pain, and illness*. Cleis Press.

## References

The Association for Research in Vision and Ophthalmology. (2014, September 18). *The association for research in vision and ophthalmology-new poll: Americans fear blindness more than loss of other senses, strongly support more funding for research*. www.arvo.org/About/press-room/press-room/2014-press-archive/new-poll-americans-fear-blindness-more-than-loss-of-other-senses-strongly-support-more-funding-for-research/

Barlow-Brown, F., Barker, C., & Harris, M. (2019). Size and modality effects in Braille learning: Implications for the blind child from pre-reading sighted children. *British

*Journal of Educational Psychology, 89*(1), 165–176. https://doi.org/10.1111/bjep.12229

Bennett, C. L., Gleason, C., Scheuerman, M. K., Bigham, J. P., Guo, A., & To, A. (2021, May). *"It's complicated": Negotiating accessibility and (mis)representation in image descriptions of race, gender, and disability*. Proceedings of the 2021 CHI Conference on Human Factors in Computing Systems, pp. 1–19. https://doi.org/10.1145/3411764.3445498

Brunet, S. (2020). Disability and the desirability politics of motherhood. *Knots: An Undergraduate Journal of Disability Studies, 5*(1).

Cappagli, G., Cocchi, E., & Gori, M. (2017). Auditory and proprioceptive spatial impairments in blind children and adults. *Developmental Science, 20*(3), e12374. https://doi.org/10.1111/desc.12374

Center for Research on Women with Disabilities. (2022). *Abuse*. Baylor College of Medicine. www.bcm.edu/research/research-centers/center-for-research-on-women-with-disabilities/a-to-z-directory/national-study-of-women-with-physical-disabilities/abuse

Cipriani, B. M. (Ed.). (2018). *Firsts: Coming of age stories by people with disabilities*. Oleb Books.

Disability, Pregnancy & Parenthood. (2022). *Ask the community*. www.disabledparent.org.uk/ask-the-community

Ferguson, R. J. (2001). We know who we are: A history of the blind in challenging educational and socially constructed policies: A study in policy archeology. *Caddo Gap Press, 16*(4), Portland, Oregon. https://www-proquest-com.libproxy.lib.unc.edu/trade-journals/we-know-who-are-history-blind-challenging/docview/199594426/se-2?accountid=14244

Flaxman, A. D., Wittenborn, J. S., Robalik, T., Gulia, R., Gerzoff, R. B., Lundeen, E. A., Saaddine, J., Rein, D. B., & Vision and Eye Health Surveillance System Study Group. (2021). Prevalence of visual acuity loss or blindness in the US: A Bayesian meta-analysis. *JAMA Ophthalmology, 139*(7), 717–723. https://doi.org/10.1001/jamaophthalmol.2021.0527

Frederick, A. (2015). Between stigma and mother-blame: Blind mothers' experiences in USA hospital postnatal care. *Sociology of Health & Illness, 37*(8), 1127–1141. https://doi.org/10.1111/1467-9566.12286

Godin, M. L. (2018, July 17). Are blind people denied their sexuality? The contortions that people will undergo to desexualize me, a blind woman, can be overwhelming. *Catapult*. https://catapult.co/stories/are-blind-people-denied-their-sexuality

Going Blind. (2018, February 6). *Salient facts about vision loss*. https://goingblindmovie.com/salient-facts-about-vision-loss/

Hammer, G. (2019). *Blindness through the looking glass: The performance of blindness, gender, and the sensory body*. University of Michigan Press. https://doi.org/10.3998/mpub.9271356

Heydarian, N. M., Hughes, A. S., Morera, O. F., Bangert, A. S., & Frederick, A. H. (2021). Perspectives of interactions with healthcare providers among patients who are blind. *Journal of Blindness Innovation and Research, 11*(2). https://nfb.org/images/nfb/publications/jbir/jbir21/jbir110203.html

Hingsburger, D. (2015, February 26). *28:7:1. of battered aspect*. https://davehingsburger.blogspot.com/2015/02/2871.html

Kaufman, M., Silverberg, C., & Odette, F. (2007). *The ultimate guide to sex and disability: For all of us who live with disabilities, chronic pain, and illness*. Cleis Press.

Kelley, S. D., & Moore, J. E. (2000). Abuse and violence in the lives of people with low vision: A national survey. *RE: View*, *31*(4), 155. http://libproxy.lib.unc.edu/login?url=www.proquest.com/scholarly-journals/abuse-violence-lives-people-with-low-vision/docview/222964598/se-2

Levtzion-Korach, O., Tennenbaum, A., Schnitzer, R., & Ornoy, A. (2000). Early motor development of blind children. *Journal of Pediatrics and Child Health*, *36*(3), 226–229. https://doi.org/10.1046/j.1440-1754.2000.00501.x

Mandell, R. (2017, November 10). The erasure of sexuality in the health care system. *Ready Sexy Able*. https://readysexyable.com/ready/2016/08/25/the-erasure-of-sexuality-in-the-healthcare-system/

Mazur, E. (2022). Online dating experiences of LGBTQ+ emerging adults with disabilities. *Sexuality and Disability*, *40*, 213–231. https://doi.org/10.1007/s11195-022-09726-2

Noson, K. (2017). Blind sexualities: Blindness and the Gaze in the films of Dino Risi. *The Italianist*, *37*(2), 192–211. https://doi.org/10.1080/02614340.2017.1332723

Poche, K. (2021, July 5). Months after national federation of the blind's abuse scandal, survivors want accountability. *Gambit Best of New Orleans*. www.nola.com/gambit/news/the_latest/months-after-national-federation-of-the-blind-s-abuse-scandal-survivors-want-accountability/article_76dc57ac-d9cd-11eb-9774-170c894da208.html

Raven, B., & Avilla, D. (2021). Sexual education and the LGBT+ community: The impact of information sources on sexual outcomes. *UC Merced Undergraduate Research Journal*, *13*(2). https://escholarship.org/uc/item/9br4z6jv

Ray, P. L., Cox, A. P., Jensen, M., Allen, T., Duncan, W., & Diehl, A. D. (2016). Representing vision and blindness. *Journal of Biomedical Semantics*, *7*, 15. https://doi.org/10.1186/s13326-016-0058-0

Resnikoff, S., & Keys, T. U. (2012). Future trends in global blindness. *Indian Journal of Ophthalmology*, *60*(5), 387–395. https://doi.org/10.4103/0301-4738.100532

Signes-Soler, I., Hernández-Verdejo, J. L., Estrella Lumeras, M. A., Tomás Verduras, E., & Piñero, D. P. (2017). Refractive error study in young subjects: Results from a rural area in Paraguay. *International Journal of Ophthalmology*, *10*(3), 467–472. https://doi.org/10.18240/ijo.2017.03.22

Smith, S. E. (2014, November 7). The fight for reproductive rights too often excludes disabled parents. *Rewire News Group*. https://rewirenewsgroup.com/article/2014/11/07/fight-reproductive-rights-often-excludes-disabled-parents/

Ubisi, L. (2020). Using governmentality and performativity theory to understand the role of social attitudes in young people with visual impairment access to sexual and reproductive health services. *Gender & Behaviour*, *18*(2), 15399–15408. http://hdl.handle.net/2263/81284

Vishwanathan, Y., & D'Souza, C. (2022). *Importance of sex positive therapy spaces for people with disabilities* [Video]. YouTube. www.youtube.com/watch?v=_C4unG67ccY Transcript. https://docs.google.com/document/d/1B0-BhT0aYbtFdqcey7Zbcj8qsoeTH3czs02W5En6YmI/edit

Wheatley, E. (2010). *Stumbling blocks before the blind: Medieval constructions of a disability*. University of Michigan Press.

Whitburn, B., & Michalko, R. (2019). Blindness/sightedness: Disability studies and the defiance of di-vision. In N. Watson, A. Roulstone, & C. Thomas (Eds.), *Routledge handbook of disability studies* (2nd ed., pp. 219–233). Routledge, Taylor & Francis Limited. https://doi.org/10.4324/9780429430817

Wolfe, K. (2020, September 25). Blind and queer and finding community: A look at the unique struggles, triumphs of the visually impaired. *Washington Blade: LGBTQ News, Politics, LGBTQ Rights, Gay News*. www.washingtonblade.com/2020/09/25/blind-and-queer-and-finding-community/

Wolffe, K., & Erin, J. (2020). Transition education for adolescents who are blind or have low vision. In K. A. Shogren & M. L. Wehmeyer (Eds.), *Handbook of adolescent transition education for youth with disabilities* (2nd ed., pp. 458–479). Routledge. https://doi.org/10.4324/9780429198342

Wunder, G. (2010, November). Whose child is this if mom and dad are blind? *Braille Monitor*. https://nfb.org/images/nfb/publications/bm/bm10/bm1010/bm101002.htm

# 9

# NO SPOONS FOR SPOONING

Navigating Sexuality, Chronic Illness, and Chronic Pain

*Shanna Katz Kattari*

## Introduction

Globally, approximately one-third of adults lived with multiple chronic conditions, although this of course varies country to country (Hajat & Stein, 2018). According to the United States (U.S.) Centers for Disease Control and Prevention (CDC), six out of ten adults in the U.S. live with a chronic disease, with 40% of all adults having two or more chronic diseases. According to the CDC, "Chronic diseases are defined broadly as conditions that last one year or more and require ongoing medical attention or limit activities of daily living or both" (United States Centers for Disease Control and Prevention, 2022, para. 1). The National Library of Medicine (2020) lists some examples of chronic illness and disease, including Alzheimer disease and dementia; arthritis; asthma; cancer; COPD; Crohn's disease; Cystic fibrosis; diabetes; epilepsy; heart disease; HIV/AIDS; mood disorders (i.e., bipolar, cyclothymic, and depression), multiple sclerosis; and Parkinson's disease. Missing from this list are many illnesses that tend to target those assigned female at birth, and those illnesses more specific to Black and other racialized individuals, indicating perhaps some implicit sexism and racism, so to this extant list, I will also add fibromyalgia; Sickle cell anemia; chronic migraine; Ehlers-Danlos syndrome (EDS); postural orthostatic tachycardia syndrome (POTS)/dysautonomia, mast cell activation syndrome (MCAS), Grave's disease, Sjoren's disease, chronic fatigue syndrome/myalgic encephalomyelitis; cellulitis, chronic kidney disease, ulcerative cystitis, Celiac disease, Hashimoto's disease, and many and many more (for a potentially more extensive list, consider many of the other items on Scotland's National Health Service's [NHS] site, n.d.).

DOI: 10.4324/9781003308331-12

Based on a recent paper by El-Metwally et al., "Chronic pain can be constant or intermittent; that usually persists for a prolong period of time and is not always attributed to a specific cause" (2019, p. 1). When looking at the global prevalence of chronic pain, studies have ranges of between 10.1% and 55.2% of the population, resulting in a weighted mean prevalence of 30.3% of all people worldwide experiencing chronic pain of some sort (Elzahaf et al., 2012). There is also a lot of cross over between chronic illness and chronic pain – for example, while things like back pain is clearly delineated into the pain category, things like endometriosis, fibroids, polycystic ovarian syndrome, and even things like arthritis and fibromyalgia can be counted as both chronic illness AND chronic pain. Ergo, for the purposes of this chapter, I will speak to best practices that support people who are chronically ill and experience chronic pain, as well as those of us who are the lucky ones who live with both.

As the CDC noted, many people have more than one chronic illness or disease – some of the communities have spoken to the idea that chronic illness diagnoses are like Pokémon – "you've gotta catch them all!" (Stanton, 2017). However, in reality, many of these illnesses and medical conditions do come in clusters, such as EDS, POTS, and MCAS (Cheung & Vadas, 2015). Also, while the medical profession tries their best, many of us run into the issue of having to go through multiple diagnoses as we go on a journey to figure out "what is wrong" with us (in quotations because while pain and illness may not be things most people desire to navigate in their lives, it is not an indication that anything is indeed wrong with us), and then to be told, in many cases, that there is little to be done to care for us or support our needs and manage our pain, or that research is years away.

I would be remiss writing this chapter in early 2023 if I did not name the elephant in the chronic illness conversation room – COVID-19. This pandemic, which is ongoing, despite so much mainstream and institutional sentiment, has wreaked havoc when it comes to chronic illness. First, knowing that getting COVID as someone with extant chronic illness(es) could be a death sentence (Antony et al., 2020), so many chronically ill individuals have had to make the choice to isolate for literal years on end while the world moved on without them (I count myself at least partially among this group, having prepared this book in almost totally isolation from everyone except my partners), and going to risk their literal lives for their jobs, their families, and their social connection. Even routine medical care for those of us with chronic conditions has been made more difficult (Chudasama et al., 2020). Long COVID, sometimes referred to as post-COVID syndrome, has been and continues to be a mass disabling event internationally (Lowenstein & Davis, 2021), resulting in scores more of individuals who now navigate chronic illness with little support or infrastructure to support them. In coming years, it is likely that this number will increase due to the removal of almost all prevention strategies, so all health and human service professionals should be better prepared to support and affirm all the needs, including sexuality-related needs, of those with chronic illness and chronic pain.

Because of the challenges with having illnesses or pain that is persistent, and for which there is likely not a solution or treatment that is clear, life can be incredibly exhausting for this population, on top of the fatigue already inherent with many of these conditions. People with chronic illness and/or chronic pain often become their own healthcare case worker and advocate; managing multiple specialists, appointments for physical/occupational/behavioral therapy in addition to their primary care provider and specialists, reading new studies, trying non-Western approaches to care such as acupuncture (Vickers et al., 2018), supplements, rolfing (Jones, 2004), and inversion chairs. They connect with communities online to try and understand what is happening to their bodyminds, to learn new ways to navigate their realities, and to form connections with those who have similar lived experiences. Yet they are often the ones teaching their providers about their chronic conditions, asking for the newest modality or intervention to see if it will be effective for them.

Unsurprisingly, this leaves little space and time for both those with these conditions and their providers to explore ways to support their sexuality. At a G-spot class I taught once, I had a participant tell me that she was a breast cancer survivor, and was recovering from a double mastectomy. After this, she struggled with her body image, and feeling sexy and desirable, and despite her husband being incredibly supportive, she just didn't feel up to being sexual with him, or at all. When she asked her oncologist about this, he told her "You just survived cancer; I cannot believe you're even thinking about sex." When I share this study in workshops and trainings, I see many nods and have heard that this is not an infrequent occurrence with survivors of cancer, or those currently navigating cancer treatment, when they ask their providers for help in navigating changes in their body image, sex drive, and desires. Similarly, those with chronic pain are often pushed to focus on working toward increased function in their activities of daily living, to the detriment other areas of their health, including their sexual health needs (Grabovac & Dorner, 2019). There is also a push for measurement of sexual function, as compared to sexual pleasure and agency, which is a different concept totally.

With these types of interactions being unfortunately commonplace within medical/health interactions, those living with chronic illness and chronic pain often are unsure of where to turn to get information and support about sexuality, and may be stigmatized when they do. While Miriam Kaufman, Cory Silverberg, and Fran Odette's 2007 book *The Ultimate Guide to Sex and Disability: For All of Us Who Live With Disabilities, Chronic Pain, and Illness* has been an incredible asset, and more recent conversations in the form of books, podcasts, and other resources have become more commonplace; often chronic pain and chronic illness are still left out of conversations around sexuality and disability or offer only very dated information. Therefore, people with these lived experiences often have no access to recent information and current support and may turn to therapists, educators, friends, partners, etc., for information, or in many cases, may just shut down around their sexuality out of exhaustion, fear, shame, or just not knowing how to proceed. Obviously, there is no one solution we can offer. However, in my years of practice, I have found some concepts that are useful, I've modified existing modalities, and I've collected really creative tools that chronically ill people and those in chronic pain have created to make their sex lives as robust as they desire and would like to share these with you.

## Theories, Modalities, and Tools for Practice

### Spoon Theory

Spoon theory is a concept created by Christine Miserandino to more clearly explain some of the challenges experienced by people who live with chronic pain and/or chronic illness (2017). In her story, she talks about an experience in which she was at a diner with a friend, and that friend asked for more information as to what it is like to be chronically ill; in Christine's case, with Lupus. Her friend further explained that she had been socialized at least in some way to understand what it meant to be a wheelchair user, or to be Deaf, but really had no concept of what it meant to move through the world with illness or pain that has not expectation of ending. Miserandino grabbed up all the spoons on the tables in the diner, showed this spoon bouquet to her friend, and detailed how she went through her day, using the spoons as a stand in for capacity.

When I share this story during trainings, I think about some of my first times navigating chronic illness and chronic pain when I was in my early 20s living in Philly. Starting my day, I'd have to decide whether to take a quick shower (one spoon), wash my hair and do my make up (two spoons, but I looked good and felt happy about that), or just toss on new clothes and walk out the door (no spoons!). Every morning, I'd have to decide between the more environmentally friendly (and fiscally smart!) option of taking the train, during which I had to walk to the station, stand to wait for the train, wait to see if someone would let me have a seat on it (because I don't "look" disabled), then walk to my office, all of which would take five spoons; or to take my car (which required a car payment, insurance, gas, cost of parking both at my apartment and downtown by my job, as well as an hour driving on the highway in traffic), but which only took one spoon. Throughout the day, I had to make decisions, such as a high spoon usage collegial lunch with co-workers versus a low spoon, isolating lunch in the break room with a frozen meal. By the time I go to the end of the day, my decision was whether to just heat up leftovers and watch a Netflix DVD with my partner (usually one spoon, which sometimes meant I'd have an extra spoon to carry over to the next day) or to have a fun date, intimate connection, and sometimes sexual adventures, which usually meant pulling an extra spoon or two from the following day. Heck, now, with my cadre of illnesses and pain, choosing to have sex with a partner could set off an illness flare that could last a week.

I hope you are seeing how the spoon theory analogy could be used to support individuals with chronic pain and/or chronic illness in a myriad of ways. First, having shared language to use with partners (as well as family and friends for that matter) allows for more kind and nuanced conversations where people can assume best intent. For example, rather than saying "No, I don't want to have sex tonight; I have a headache" (which is not only a completely valid statement but also one that has been socialized into being viewed as a rejection), someone could say "Oooh, I wish I could do that, but I'm low on spoons today." This reframe then opens up the conversation; the partner who was initiating can then come back with "thanks for letting me know; perhaps a massage might feel good?" or "noted! Would you feel up to sending some sexy text messages back and forth, or to watching me masturbate in front of you?" Similarly, when dating, if someone says "I'm sorry I have to cancel; I'm out of spoons," their date could offer a lower spoons date, a reschedule, or even just sending over an ice pack or some soup, rather than feeling that the person asking for their needs to be met is "checking out" of their interactions.

It makes tangible the amorphous concept of capacity, energy, and sometimes even ability to do a certain thing in a certain way. When you share this tool, you can also adapt it to meet your clients where they are at. Over the years, I've had students and clients use the terms "battery power" (in relation to what percentage of battery power they have left), hit points (a common measurement in Dungeons & Dragons, as well as other table top role-playing games), and other analogous concepts that make more sense to them. The key is the shared language that allows for chronically ill people and those with chronic pain to communicate their needs and capacity without feeling like they have to constantly detail their pain, their illness, and their symptoms in order to be understood and validated.

The spoon concept has become incredibly popular in many chronic illness and chronic pain communities, with swaths of individuals, myself included, identified as "spoonies" (i.e., those whose days are measured in spoons). There are support spaces such as the Tarnished Spoonies group on Facebook, and #SpoonieChat on Twitter where individuals with these lived experiences can come together in community, ask questions, share resources, and even complain about various challenges or interactions. While the spoonie concept is just now starting to enter the academic literature, mostly around support, accommodations, and reducing burn out risk (McGuinness, 2021), in work (Huitson, 2022), educational (Beam & Clay-Buck, 2018), and parenting (De León-Menjivar, 2022) settings, it is in common use in disability and chronic illness spaces. Having trained literally thousands of therapists, educators, counselors, and researcher on sexuality and disability over the past 15 years, this is one of the concepts I get told is most useful, both for the learners themselves to reframe disability and for their students, clients, patients, and even their partners.

### Sensate Focus Exercises

Sensate focus exercises were originally created by Masters and Johnson in 1970 and then further updated by Kaplan a few years later in 1974 (Weeks & Gambescia, 2010). Originally, they were designed with the goal of fixing "sexual problems" and, later on, framed as a way to increase sexual function. Based loosely on some facial tracing exercises that Johnson remembers from her childhood (Weeks & Gambescia, 2010), the goal of these exercises is to re-set sexual interactions between partners, re-focusing on different sensations, and disrupting existing (and sometimes unproductive or even harmful) sexual scripts in lieu of figuring out what each person in a relationship finds pleasurable and desirable, without focusing on traditional sexual functions/interactions.

It continues to be a popular modality used by sexuality-focused clinicians. A 2014 study found that 41.5% of clinical sexologists often use sensate focus with a multitude of clients, with an additional 43.08% using the techniques sometimes, in a sample of 94 sexologists (Weiner & Avery-Clark, 2014). There have been a number of critiques of the original model, from discussion on what is meant by sex being labeled as a "natural function" to conversations on "non-demand touching."

There have been previous attempts at engaging various disabled folks with sensate focus as a practice. Mitchell Tepper wrote about ways to integrate this work with disabled people in 2000, following a case study by Bell et al. in 1999 that detailed the experience of a married couple with learning disabilities that used sensate focus to try and improve their sexual interaction. Another publication in 2000 authored by Gallo-Silver focused on the use of sensate focus exercises that can be used specifically with those who are navigating cancer, and their partners. Later on, Melby published a case study featuring an autistic man and his allistic sex therapist partner, who used various modalities, including bodymapping in order to engage each other differently (2011). However, there are not full studies on the efficacy of using the traditional sensate focus methods with disabled and chronically ill people generally. Moreover, the traditional model of sensate focus is very cis-heterocentric and monogamous-centric, with the end goal being penis in vagina intercourse between only two partners. Ergo, while this original modality has been and continues to be useful to many, it is not always as inclusive as one might hope, and simply is not the right fit for all individuals.

Over the years, I have come up with adapted versions that are teachable and more applicable, both for practitioners and for clients/students themselves. I've found that these are particularly useful for those with chronic illness, chronic pain, and those with newly acquired disabilities or impairments. As one's bodymind changes, there is often a sense of loss and/or grief that accompanies it (Stephenson & Murphy, 1986), and this is not limited to the nonsexual parts of oneself. Sexually, things that used to feel good may not, activities that used to be energizing may now exhausting, and even body parts that used to work a certain way (i.e., erect penises, vaginas that can create comfortable, natural lubrication) now may be very different than before, or than one would want. Using these modified exercises can allow a re-set of sorts, to help people feel more comfortable with their bodyminds as they are as compared to how they used to be, and to help individuals find types of sensual and/or erotic touch that actually feel affirming to them.

*Modified Sensate Focus Exercises*

There are several stages that the individuals participating in the exercise will go through, and they can decide how long the stages will be. Many proponents of sensate focus suggest certain stages taking up to a month each; I recognize that in today's world, spending a month only touching your partner(s) (intentionally) above the neckline might feel like a lot, so I generally suggest people commit at least a week to each stage. The key here is that the things you do with each other in each stage are done during intentional intimate time together – I want to be clear I am not suggesting you don't hug your partner(s) during the first stage, for example.

**Stage One:** Take turns, one at a time, touching and exploring each other above the neck. The first person who is going to receive touch should get into a comfortable position so that they can be comfortable while the focus is on them. Their partner(s) can use their fingers, hands, cheeks, lips, or whatever feels best to touch their face, hair, and neck. Explore everything (with consent!), be open to both giving and receiving feedback. Once everything has been explored, switch! You can do this as many times as you'd like during the week, but there should be no intentional sensual or sexual touching below the shoulders during this week.

**Stage Two:** Again, you'll take turns, but this time, everything on the body above the waist is fair game. One partner will get comfortable while the other(s) touches and explores in a sensual way with any parts of their body. While it is fine to touch, caress, lick, suck, fondle, etc., anything above the waist, and either person may become aroused during this process, the goal is not to focus on arousal; everything should be explored (with consent!) with equal interest, not just the parts that result in arousal. Again, you can do this as many times as you'd like during the week, but there should be no intentional sensual or sexual touching below the waist during this week.

**Stage Three**: Now anywhere on the body can be touched, including the genital area, but again, the goal is simply exploration of all areas without intent of arousal or orgasm – you're just feeling things out (literally) to try and better understand what types of touch feel good, bad, arousing, off putting, interesting, etc. Similarly, you should take turns on this, and like the previous weeks, there should be no (intentional) orgasms, and the focus is not on causing arousal, nor should it be on the genitals. Again, this is the only sensual or sexual touch that happens this week.

**Stage Four**: This week, you can add in a focus of sensual touch on the genitals, ideally with a body-friendly lubricant (I'd suggest a good quality water-based lube like Sliquid or a silicone-based lube like Pjur or Eros; stay away from oil if there is any plan for internal stimulation). Like before, you focus on one person at a time, taking turns. The goal of the touch is sensual, NOT sexual. Like previous weeks, it is ok if a person becomes aroused, but the focus is not on orgasm. This week can include penetration if the person being focused on desired it, but without an intent for orgasm – this is a focus on sensual interactions only. If someone may need vaginal dilation for a variety of reasons, this can be a part of that as well. Once you both feel the exploration is in a good place for completion for that session, you should switch.

**Stage Five**: NOW you can focus on BOTH sensual and sexual pleasure. Anything goes! Make intentional time to connect, and using all you have learned over the last four weeks (or months if you decided to go with that unit of time), and connect together. Focus on being sensual (as well as sexual if you desire). Break those previous patterns; maybe someone gets the most sexual pleasures from their nipples and doesn't care about clitoral stimulation. Perhaps someone else wants oral sex without penetration and that's their number one opportunity for sexual pleasure. Who knows – only you do, because you and your partner(s) are on that journey together!

*Bodymapping*

Bodymapping is another way to talk about sensate focus work. Some therapists have used a physical representation of bodymapping either before or after doing the full exercises as a way to visually represent each person's body. Ordinarily, this type of bodymapping is done by having a person lie on a large sheet of paper, and having a partner or other support person trace their body. Then, they switch roles, and each person takes time to label different body parts and they name they'd like used for them, as well as making clear the areas in which they'd like to be touched, and how they would like that touch to happen. Additionally, they may choose to delineate areas that they would not like touched, and are hard limits for them – this piece can be particularly empowering for trauma survivors, who may feel a sense of regaining control by being explicit here.

However, not all bodies are suited for lying on the ground on a piece of paper; I know mine certainly is not! It is completely acceptable to use a drawing of a person, or even an image you find online, and use that to label areas. Similarly, not everyone can hold a pen or use a computer, so it may need to be a supported team effort for some people in attempting this activity. I constantly remind people that there is no wrong way to do this, just as there is no wrong way to have a body (so perfectly stated by Glenn Marla!), and that any way that individuals and their partners can use bodymapping to re-envision how they view their body, how they'd like it touched, and in what ways, and to communicate that with one another, is a successful use of this activity.

### Other Tools

One of the biggest things I have found in working with chronically ill people and those with chronic pain is that many of them need help in flipping the script in order to find out what actually works for them and getting their needs met. Like with other types of disability discussed in this book, part of this is lack of education and little to no visibility on what happy, healthy sexuality with chronic illness and/or chronic pain looks like – we don't see people like us getting it on in the media, or in porn, or even in most erotica. Rather, we have to create these affirming worlds for ourselves.

People have this idea that all sex is supposed to be magically beautiful, on satin sheets, with rose petals falling from the sky, while Seal or Harry Styles plays on the speakers, and both/all partners orgasms simultaneously. That is, in fact, very rarely (if ever), the case. As practitioners, we must disrupt this narrative and remind folks that sex is a real experience between real people. First, simultaneous orgasm is a cis-heteronormative ableist pipedream that rarely happens in the real world, and is not any more exciting than any other form of pleasurable experiences. Encouraging people to re-think not only the "bases" or "stair step" model of sex (in which the "natural" progression of sex is seen as kissing → manual stimulation → oral sex → intercourse) and focus on doing what feels good to them and their partner can be a radical process for them. It takes time to deconstruct all they have been taught about what "good" or "real" sex is, but once they are able to engage those thoughts, the world is their sexual oyster.

Sometimes, this is as easy as offering the suggestion that people use their ice packs, ice masks, heating pads, fuzzy socks, C-shaped/U-shaped/lumbar pillows, etc. during sex. Reminding individuals that being as comfortable as possible during sex is not only acceptable but also actively encouraged can be incredibly freeing to them. Similarly, people may feel like they have to be able to get into certain positions in order to be desirable or to have hot sex – I encourage them to think about how they can get most comfortable in a position that they can be in for a period of time (such as with restorative yoga practice), and then figure out what feels good and how they can be sexual from there. I suggest getting lots of fun sizes and shapes of pillow they can use to support their back, their heads, their limbs, etc. during sexual play time; there is no rule saying you cannot be comfortable and sexy at the same time!

Similarly, adding in some sex toys might be a great option here. For individuals with a penis who are not experiencing erections in the way that they would like, using a penis pump and ring (often called a cock ring) can allow them to get semi-erect in order to enjoy fellatio or manual stimulation. These same people can use something like the Spareparts Deuce harness, which is specifically designed for penis possessors who would like to wear a strap on over their original equipment in order to penetrate their partner(s). For someone who may have fatigue, using a high harness like those from Sportsheets, or a dildo with a handle on it, like those offered by Tantus, can be a nice alternative. A vibrator that can be worn, like the We-Vibe, and then be hands free (unless you're using the remote function!) can also be a nice low energy pleasurable activity. If someone is kinky (for more, see Chapter 22), using floggers with finger loops rather than handles can reduce fatigue, sensation toys like TENS units, Violet wands, fire play, cupping, etc., can allow an intersection of treating pain with kink play, and being willing to navigate the concept of service as correlated with access intimacy, are all different tools kinky people in this population can use.

Another concern that comes up, especially with those who live with chronic pain, is whether it is ethical to be sexual while on pain management medication. Consent is clearly an important value in all relationships, and so I encourage them to engage with their partner(s) when they are not using such medications to discuss how they would feel about being sexual while they are medicated. Some people may be fine with consenting prior to the medication being taken and just having very clear conversations during sexual time, while others may have additional concerns they'd like addressed. As with all facets of sexuality, communication is absolutely key.

**Reflective Activity**

*Step One*: Make a list of your whole day. Choose a day that is fairly average; not a chill day where you just hangout (unless that is *your* normal), nor one that is extra crowded and overbooked. This list should be detailed; think about activities of daily living (bathing, eating [including food prep], toileting, household chores), about various facets of work and/or school, family responsibilities, interactions with friends, family, co-workers, etc.

*Step Two*: Now assign capacity value to each of these things based on your capacity for an average day. You can use percentage of daily energy, hit points, red/yellow/green, or any other system that works best for you.

*Step Three*: Think about days where you have lowered capacity, due to fatigue, to pain, to feeling less than optimal due to the weather, or any of the other things that can influence the way we are able to show up in the world. Which things would you prioritize? Which would you cut? Which can adapt to take less capacity while still getting your needs met?

*Step Four*: With this enhanced understanding of the process of navigating available capacity with desire and/or need to accomplish or engage certain things, please think about at least THREE different sexual and/or relationship practices (i.e., cooking dinner together, a date night on the town, specific sexual experiences), and list them out. Now for each, list THREE alternative practices and/or adaptations that would use less capacity or spoons while still meeting the underlying sexual and/or relational need.

*Step Five*: Rejoin a small group or full group discussion or in your next therapeutic session. Begin by sharing reflections on the process of having to enumerate your daily tasks/engagement with the world, and then having to think through capacity to accomplish them and potential adjustments you might need to make on more challenging days. Then share out some examples of various adjustments and/or adaptations for relationship and/or sexuality-focused practices. Finally, think through and discuss in your group(s) how you can apply your learnings from this activity to your professional (and/or personal) practice.

## Conclusion

Chronic illness and chronic pain impact an incredible amount of people, and with the ongoing COVID pandemic, these numbers are only increasing. This population is often left out of conversations regarding sexuality, and even many of the conversations about the intersection of sexuality and disability. Using concepts like spoon theory, modified sensate focus exercises (including adaptable bodymapping), and working with your clients and students to really disrupt ideas of what "normative" sex should be and look like can help those you work with in re-taking agency over their sex lives and their sexual pleasure. More so, recognizing that all of us, even those without illness or pain, have to make decisions on capacity and where to put on energy, can help to build empathy and shared understandings, despite having differential experiences of navigating the world.

## Resources

### Podcasts

Sex and Chronic Illness Podcast. https://invisiblenotbroken.com/sex-chronic-illness
Chronic Sex Podcast.
www.chronicsex.org/podcast/
Pleasure Mechanics Episode on Chronic Illness and Chronic Pain.
www.pleasuremechanics.com/turning-towards-pleasure-while-living-with-pain-illness/

### Social Media Accounts to Follow

#### Instagram

@AndGurza
@ChronicallyCandidMemes
@Chronic_Self_Love
@Crutches_And_Spice
@Disabled_Eliza
@GlitterAndYelling
@iHartEricka
@LASpoonieCollectibe
@PinkSaltCollective
@SexForSpoonies
@Spoonie_Love_Notes
@TheChronicIconic
@The_Chronic_Notebook

#### Twitter

@BlackRoundBoi
@Gurza__
@iHartEricka
@Imani_Barbarin
@Hedonish
@TheLLPSx
@TheSeatedView

### Sex Toy and Lube Companies

Aneros.
www.aneros.com/
Earthly Body Massage Candles and Oils.
https://shop.earthlybody.com/
Liberator Sex Furniture.
www.liberator.com/
Sliquid.

https://sliquid.com/
Spareparts Hardwear.
https://myspare.com/
Sportsheets.
www.sportsheets.com/
Tantus.
www.tantusinc.com/
We-Vibe.
www.we-vibe.com/

## References

Antony, A., Connelly, K., De Silva, T., Eades, L., Tillett, W., Ayoub, S., & Morand, E. (2020). Perspectives of patients with rheumatic diseases in the early phase of COVID-19. *Arthritis Care & Research*, 72(9), 1189–1195. https://doi.org/10.1002/acr.24347

Beam, S. N., & Clay-Buck, H. (2018). Low-Spoon teaching: Labor, gender, and self-accommodation in academia. *Tulsa Studies in Women's Literature*, 37(1), 173–180. https://doi.org/10.1353/tsw.2018.0008

Bell, D. M., Toplis, L., & Espie, C. A. (1999). Sex therapy in a couple with learning disabilities. *British Journal of Learning Disabilities*, 27(4), 146–150. https://doi.org/10.1111/j.1468-3156.1999.tb00149.x

Cheung, I., & Vadas, P. (2015). A new disease cluster: Mast cell activation syndrome, postural orthostatic tachycardia syndrome, and Ehlers-Danlos syndrome. *Journal of Allergy and Clinical Immunology*, 135(2), AB65. https://doi.org/10.1016/j.jaci.2014.12.1146

Chudasama, Y. V., Gillies, C. L., Zaccardi, F., Coles, B., Davies, M. J., Seidu, S., & Khunti, K. (2020). Impact of COVID-19 on routine care for chronic diseases: A global survey of views from healthcare professionals. *Diabetes & Metabolic Syndrome: Clinical Research & Reviews*, 14(5), 965–967. https://doi.org/10.1016/j.dsx.2020.06.042

De León-Menjivar, C. (2022). "Dear spoonie mom": Digital open letters as counter narratives for chronically ill mothers. https://constell8cr.com/issue-5/dear-spoonie-mom-digital-open-letters-as-counter-narratives-for-chronically-ill-mothers/

El-Metwally, A., Shaikh, Q., Aldiab, A., Al-Zahrani, J., Al-Ghamdi, S., Alrasheed, A. A., Househ, M., Da'ar, O. B., Nooruddin, S., Razzak, H. A., & Aldossari, K. K. (2019). The prevalence of chronic pain and its associated factors among Saudi Al-Kharj population; a cross sectional study. *BMC Musculoskeletal Disorders*, 20, 1–9. https://doi.org/10.1186/s12891-019-2555-7

Elzahaf, R. A., Tashani, O. A., Unsworth, B. A., & Johnson, M. I. (2012). The prevalence of chronic pain with an analysis of countries with a human development index less than 0.9: A systematic review without meta-analysis. *Current Medical Research and Opinion*, 28(7), 1221–1229.

Gallo-Silver, L. (2000). The sexual rehabilitation of persons with cancer. *Cancer Practice*, 8(1), 10–15.

Grabovac, I., & Dorner, T. E. (2019). Association between low back pain and various everyday performances: Activities of daily living, ability to work and sexual function. *Wiener klinische Wochenschrift*, *131*(21–22), 541–549. https://doi.org/10.1007/s00508-019-01542-7

Hajat, C., & Stein, E. (2018). The global burden of multiple chronic conditions: A narrative review. *Preventive Medicine Reports*, *12*, 284–293. https://doi.org/10.1016/j.pmedr.2018.10.008

Huitson, K. (2022). Chronic illness and resilience in the veterinary industry. *The Veterinary Nurse*, *13*(3), 114–118. https://doi.org/10.12968/vetn.2022.13.3.114

Jones, T. A. (2004). Rolfing. *Physical Medicine and Rehabilitation Clinics*, *15*(4), 799–809.

Kaufman, M., Silverberg, C., & Odette, F. (2007). *The ultimate guide to sex and disability: For all of us who live with disabilities, chronic pain, and illness*. Cleis Press.

Lowenstein, F., & Davis, H. (2021, March 17). Opinion – long Covid is not rare. It's a health crisis. *The New York Times*. www.nytimes.com/2021/03/17/opinion/long-covid.html

Masters, W., & Johnson, V. E. (1970). *Human sexual inadequacy*. Little, Brown and Company.

McGuinness, K. (2021). An evaluation of a tool, based on spoon theory, to promote self-regulation and avoidance of burnout in autistic children and young people. *Good Autism Practice (GAP)*, *22*(1), 59–72.

Melby, T. (2011). Trying to dance, but missing rhythm. *Contemporary Sexuality*, *45*(10), 1–7.

Miserandino, C. (2017). The spoon theory. In L. J. Davis, J. Dolmage, N. Erevelles, S. J. Harris, A. Luft, S. Schweik, & L. Ware (Eds.), *Beginning with disability* (pp. 174–178). Routledge.

National Health Service of Scotland. (n.d.). *Illnesses and conditions*. www.nhsinform.scot/illnesses-and-conditions/a-to-z

National Library of Medicine. (2020). *Living with a chronic illness – reaching out to others*. https://medlineplus.gov/ency/patientinstructions/000602.htm

Stanton, S. (2017). *Loss is the softest word*. https://theduckopera.medium.com/loss-is-the-softest-word-b21b7911315e

Stephenson, J. S., & Murphy, D. (1986). Existential grief: The special case of the chronically ill and disabled. *Death Studies*, *10*(2), 135–145.

Tepper, M. S. (2000). Sexuality and disability: The missing discourse of pleasure. *Sexuality and Disability*, *18*(4), 283–290. https://doi.org/10.1023/A:1005698311392

United States Centers for Disease Control and Prevention. (2022). *About chronic diseases*. www.cdc.gov/chronicdisease/about/index.htm

Vickers, A. J., Vertosick, E. A., Lewith, G., MacPherson, H., Foster, N. E., Sherman, K. J., Irnich, D., Witt, C. M., Linde, K., & Acupuncture Trialists' Collaboration. (2018). Acupuncture for chronic pain: Update of an individual patient data meta-analysis. *The Journal of Pain*, *19*(5), 455–474. https://doi.org/10.1016/j.jpain.2017.11.005

Weeks, G. R., & Gambescia, N. (2010). A systemic approach to sensate focus. In K. M. Hertlein, N. Gambescia, & G. R. Weeks (Eds.), *Systemic sex therapy* (pp. 354–375). Routledge.

Weiner, L., & Avery-Clark, C. (2014). Sensate focus: Clarifying the masters and Johnson's model. *Sexual and Relationship Therapy*, *29*(3), 307–319.

# PART THREE
# Diverse Types of Practice

# 10
# DISABILITY-AFFIRMING SEX THERAPY

*Erin Martinez and Emma Hertzel*

### Introduction

Sex therapy is a specialization within therapeutic practice that integrates psychotherapy approaches with medical and somatic approaches to reduce "dysfunction" and help individuals or couples achieve their goal of sexual experience. The field has changed a great deal over the last century and beginning of the 21st century. The work of William Masters and Virginia Johnson established the field as a more respected field based on data and not just theory (Wylie, 2022). Their research on hundreds of individuals/couples resulted in the *Human Sexual Response Cycle*. The Human Sexual Response Cycle provides stages of biological experiences that include arousal, plateau, climax, and resolution (Perleman, 2012). It can be argued that while this allowed sex therapy to be recognized as more valid, it also highlighted the biological over the relational and psychological. This concept of a "normal" performance means many people exist outside of it, resulting in them becoming othered.

These socially constructed "norms" of human sexual response are also represented in some of the sexual dysfunction diagnoses within the Diagnostic and Statistical Manual of Mental Disorders that is often utilized by mental health professionals. As an example, the diagnostic criteria for Erectile Disorder (F52.21) is "Marked difficulty in maintaining an erection until the completion of sexual activity" (American Psychiatric Association, 2022, pp. 426–427). The idea of *completion of sexual activity* is loosely based on the Human Sexual Response, and the idea that arousal always leads to climax or "completion." When providing sex therapy, we can both benefit from the diagnostic criteria and Human Sexual Response Cycle, and can be incredibly hindered by it. It is necessary and useful to understand the common biological response to arousal and what may occur in the body, yet it is a hindrance to reduce a complex human experience that is spiritual, psychological, and relational to simply performance standards with biological outcomes based on a limited scope of data.

There is tremendous diversity of therapeutic practice strategies and approaches among the small group of mental health practitioners clinically trained as sex therapists. Many sex therapists focus on pleasure versus performance, body uniqueness versus standards of sexual achievement, and expanding the ways that individuals experience connection, sensuality, intimacy and eroticism (Henderson, 2014). In using these standards of treatment, there are several common interventions that offer flexibility in application for disabled clients. In order to effectively illustrate sex therapy practice with disabled clients, we will present the information with two case studies with some reflection prompts following.

## Case Studies

### Case Study #1: Nakita, Spinal Cord Injury With Partial Paralysis

Nakita entered therapy with the presenting problem of major depressive disorder related to chronic health issues. Similar to many clients, Nakita noted the sex therapy certification on the office wall and stated, "well that's cool, we can talk about that stuff too?" This is common for clients to need our *permission* to discuss the topics related to sex, and many therapists often do not open up this conversation directly. Nakita shared in the first session that she had struggled with low mood in her teenage years surrounding some difficult life transitions. She reported generally being "pretty easy-going" up until the paralysis. Nakita was a victim of random gun violence, with a spinal cord injury leaving her paralyzed from the waist down. This experience was traumatic and completely life-changing for her. A great deal of her energy of the last eight months, both in hospitalization and in long-term rehabilitation, has focused on learning to manage her life differently as a homeowner, mother, employee, and partner.

In the second session, Nakita referenced her partner, Rashad, and the stressors that they had faced in the last year. She reflected that sexual intimacy used to be a way that they connected and made it through life's ups and downs together. Although they had participating in penetrative sex (with her receiving) since the shooting/paralysis, they both felt disconnected and a sense of grief because the experience felt so very different. I used a common technique of sex therapy; "tell me about a recent sexual experience." Nakita was happy to oblige. She shared that Rashad felt guilty and disconnected because Nakita was unable to orgasm, and noted that she felt confused on how to express her experience without the physical sensations to accompany the act of sex. Nakita offered a major challenge in my early sex therapy career, "Can you help me have an orgasm again?" Through this chapter we will discuss the work of sex therapy with disabled individuals and reference Nakita's journey.

**Case Study #2: Steve, Spinal Muscular Atrophy, Type 2**

Steve is a 28-year-old man with spinal muscular atrophy. He works from home doing graphic design and social media marketing for a local toy company. He utilizes personal care attendants as well as help from family to attend to his daily needs such as bathing, using the restroom, cooking, and transportation. He has limited movement of his arms. He shared during the sexual assessment that he is able to masturbate on his own, though he doesn't talk about it to his mom or attendants, though expressed "they *have* to know." He shared that he has always felt too shy to show interest in someone, expressing frustration at "forever being in the friend zone." When he finally got the courage to talk about his desire for a partner to his doctor, they suggested a therapist. He was pleased to find a disabled sex therapist that he thought would best understand him and his needs. Steve and I collaborated on a treatment plan that focused on reducing the impact of his own internalized ableism in order to make room for identifying and developing the skills he needed to find a sexual or romantic partner.

## Review of the Literature

Prominent topics at the intersection of sexuality and disability literature include sexual rights, sex education access, sexual satisfaction among disabled populations, and sexual facilitation (Di Giulio, 2003). The literature largely showcases a gap in that most research has a male-centric, cisnormative, and heteronormative focus, neglects racialized individuals, and focuses mostly congenital disabilities rather than acquired disabilities represented (Jungels & Bender, 2015).

Common themes of study in the existing research include the attitudes of parents and caregivers related to sexuality among disabled individuals, usually their children or wards (de Wit et al., 2022). Parents and caregivers often perceived their disabled children and/or wards as asexual, limiting access to resources and support that would allow for the opportunity for the individual to practice sexual expression in a solo or partnered sexual experience. Another common theme of the research is sexual satisfaction, with a focus in areas of sexual disenfranchisement, cognitive-genital dissociation, and sexual rediscovery (Medina-Rico et al., 2018).

## Best Practices

### Sex as It Relates to Identity and Ability/Disability

Disabled clients seeking sex therapy may be coming to sessions with a variety of sexual and relationship concerns that are not different from nondisabled individuals. However, it is often the case that they may have a difficult time seeing themselves as a capable partner in a relationship or even seeing themselves as a sexual person. Disabled clients who were also disabled as young people often share that when they were growing up, they were not included in discussions about romance or sex with their peers and didn't have examples of disabled teens in healthy relationships in the media. Parents, medical professionals, siblings, and mentors often do not encourage disabled teens and young adults to pursue relationships in the same way they do their nondisabled peers. Disabled youths are also sometimes encouraged to "rise above" their disability, thereby minimizing and hiding their disabled selves, which reinforces feelings of shame and invalidation about an important part of their identity.

It is important that therapists help clients view themselves as sexual beings. Therapists must also do the work of educating clients about issues of sexuality and disability, particularly because many clients have been deprived of this information. We can help clients visualize what they desire and what is possible. As therapists, we should help clients with their identity as a disabled person who is ALSO worthy of sexual pleasure.

In one session with Steve (Case #2), we explored how he talks about his disability with friends and family. He shared that it's often something he jokes about as a way to cope and he likes to be positive about it because he "doesn't want to bum people out or upset his parents." I asked him more questions about his childhood and he shared that only in his 20s did he really embrace his illness and identity as a disabled person. He described spending years avoiding talking about it, and realized that there was a lot of shame, sadness, and frustration that he didn't have the skills to deal with effectively. "I didn't want to talk about it with my family. I was worried about making them sad." He said that it's something he can be more open about now, but, upon reflection, "he still feels like he has to keep it light." In subsequent sessions, Steve was able to tap into some of the difficult emotions in a way he hadn't before. We were able to make the connection between his more serious and vulnerable side, and the emotional intimacy and deep connection that he would really want in a sexual partner.

### Exploring and Challenging the Sexual Narrative

Whether a client enters sex therapy as an individual or as part of a couple (or group) dynamic, a crucial element of the work is helping them understand their own sexuality, communicate their wants, dislikes, hopes, goals, and fears related to their own sexual expression and experience of intimacy. Many people absorb the messages of the larger culture, family, religion related to who they should be, how they should present and how they should/should not experience sexual pleasure; this is very common for disabled individuals (Foley et al., 2012).

Prompts that can be used to help explore, and then challenge, the sexual narrative:

- How do you view yourself as a sexual person?
- What experiences or people have influenced that narrative of yourself? This may include pornography, messaging from larger culture, lack of representation in media, etc.
- How do you want to be seen?
- What do you want to experience?

Consider that perhaps this initial assessment phase is helping them read themselves less like a traditional book, and more like the 1980s/1990s *Choose Your Own Adventure* book that allowed the reader to select their own plot through hundreds of prompts within the chapters. As a child/adolescent, we learned to *play* with the plot and take some risks reading these books. We also learned the value of shrugging off the ending if we didn't like where we ended up, and restarting a new adventure. These values of play, exploration, and some risk-taking also feel important to help clients explore in sex therapy, first in their imagination, then their spoken or written word, and then eventually, in their sexual experiences.

A common challenge throughout any initial assessment is "How do you know that?" I use this to bring attention to assumptions about one's body, notice beliefs that have been taught, and may serve as a hindrance or even expectations of themselves, or others that are incorrect, possibly limiting or harmful. Reflecting on the case study, if Nakita (Case #1) is to say, "I can't have an orgasm because I don't feel much at all below the waist," I would ask, "How do you know you can't have an orgasm?" She may have been told this by doctors. She may have images of individuals with paralysis that are not portrayed as sexual people. Whatever the reason, I want Nakita to be thoughtful about how she came to this information, and in that process, she will inherently question the truth of this idea. A follow-up question may be used, "Do you want to keep this as *your* truth?"

As sex therapists, we will work with a belief that there are endless ways to be sexually expressive, and there is never only one correct way to find sexual pleasure. Rather, there are countless ways to experience one's own unique sexual pleasure. Due to the tremendous variance of disabilities and resilience, it is important that we do not have a specific solution for our clients; rather, we must be comfortable working alongside our clients with curiosity and problem-solving to reach sexual solutions.

### *Empowerment and Self-Acceptance*

One of the biggest things that a sex therapist can do for a disabled client is to give them a space to have their own voice. Because disabled people are often left out of the conversation when it comes to sex, therapy may be the first place they can talk about their sexuality (Rocco, 2019). Getting comfortable talking about their sexuality may help them better identify as a sexual person with the same desires as anyone else. Some clients may come to session with a fully developed understanding of their sexuality; therapy will be the first place they can finally articulate everything they have ever thought, but may have been pressured to internalize. Other clients may have come to believe the messages they have received from their environment – that they aren't interested or aren't capable of being sexual. Still others may be somewhere in the middle; starting to understand their sexuality, but feeling nervous to talk about it for the first time. Sex can still feel like a taboo topic, whether or not you are disabled. Validating and reflecting on clients' feelings around *talking* about sex in therapy are a good first step.

---

*Therapist*: How does it feel to talk about sex in this way?

*Steve*: It's good but, it still makes me nervous. I have literally never been asked these kinds of questions before.

*Therapist*: Where do you think the nerves come from?

*Steve*: I still feel like I'm going to be judged. Even though you're disabled and you understand, I still don't feel like I can be seen as someone who is capable of a relationship. Or I don't see myself that way.

*Therapist*: So . . . the nervousness is not just about saying it out loud to someone else, it also runs a bit deeper. What do you think you are needing or lacking that would help you see yourself as a sexual person?

*Steve*: I really don't know. Talking about it for the first time in this way is definitely helping.

> *Therapist:* I am glad. It's also okay to not know yet. As you said, no one has ever asked you this before, so it would totally make sense that you're still developing that part of yourself. And by the way, talking about sex can make anyone nervous!

Feeling seen and validated in this way will empower clients not only to see themselves as sexual but also to talk to family, friends, peers, and their medical professionals about their desires for sex or relationships. Empowering clients will also help them communicate their sexual preferences and needs to partners or caregivers that can help them achieve their goals. For example, a client who wants to use a sex toy, but has limited mobility, may feel empowered to ask for assistance from a care attendant who can help them position the toy in a way that feels safe, respectful, and considerate of the professional relationship.

## *Loss and Grief*

Disabled clients may enter therapy with unresolved grief from lack of experience during adolescence, and feelings of invalidation, being behind, or feeling "othered" by others in their lives. Addressing the grief and trauma from past experience may be a vital part of their therapy as they explore the possibility of what they may have thought was impossible in their youth.

> *Steve:* I don't ever talk about sex with anyone. At least sex involving me.
> *Therapist:* Why do you think that is?
> *Steve:* I don't know. No one ever talked about it with me. Sometimes I would be with a group of guys, and they would be talking about their experiences and cracking jokes, but it seems like whenever they talked about sex or girls, I didn't have anything to contribute and people correctly assumed I didn't, so I didn't. My parents never did. Doctors never did. My health stuff was just about living and surviving.
> *Therapist:* Sex is a part of living too. Unfortunately, many disabled folks aren't included in conversations about sex because they aren't seen as sexual beings with all of the same desires and capability of loving, pleasurable relationships as their nondisabled peers.
> *Steve:* Yes! I agree. I just haven't ever seen myself as someone who could participate in that part of life because no one else has seen me that way and, after a while, you start to believe it about yourself . . . that you're not capable.

This exchange illustrates how an environment of invalidation and lack of representation of healthy and positive relationships with other disabled people lead to Steve's internalized ableism, or his belief that he is inferior sexually to nondisabled people because of all of the stereotypes reinforced by his social environment. Helping clients process these negative beliefs can be the first vital step in helping disabled clients identify people capable of fulfilling romantic and/or sexual relationships.

Grief is part of the disabled experience whether the disabilities are congenital (since birth) or acquired due to injury or illness. For people with acquired disabilities, loss of ability is a pervasive experience that impacts many facets of life, including sexuality. For example, clients with spinal cord injuries may have a loss of sensation in their genitals that impacts their ability to experience orgasm or achieve an erection. Clients and therapists can work together to identify new ways to experience sexual pleasure while combating myths around what is "normal."

For disabled clients with a congenital disability, grief may present as a lack of experiencing what society presents as "normal" romantic and/or sexual relationships, and/or a loss of their own identity as a sexual person. As a client develops skills and a sexual identity through therapy, they may have increased feelings of sadness, anger, and/or grief for what they feel like they didn't get to experience. Clients may say things like "I wish someone talked to me about this when I was a teen," or "I wish I knew then what I know now." Holding space for the grief and honoring the difficult feelings may also be a new experience for disabled people.

*Steve:* When I think about the past and all of the things I missed out on, I feel kind of sorry for myself. I *hate* feeling sorry for myself.

*Therapist:* What you might be feeling sounds kind of like grief. Grief comes in all forms. It's not just about death or losing someone; it can also be about losing out on experience or feeling left behind or left out.

*Steve:* That's it. I never dated as a teen or had a high school sweetheart. And since I'm in my late 20s, I'll never have an opportunity to have those experiences, ever.

*Therapist:* That makes sense. And that's why we treat it like grief. But we can mourn the loss of our past and really honor those feelings while simultaneously working on the present and looking toward the future. No matter what, not having a high school romance does not preclude you from having a romance now or in the future.

When it comes to grief, it's important to sit with the feelings and not try to change them. Disability-related grief can be complex. Many people with disabilities internalize their negative feelings about being disabled in order to reduce experiencing pity from others. Therapy may be the first space in which a disabled client can explore their grief and really sit with their sadness and/or anger. Clients may also come to therapy after experiencing rejection from potential partners and dealing with misconceptions about their sex and relationship potential. It's not uncommon for disabled people entering the dating world to encounter people who say things like "your disability seems like a lot of work," or "I don't think I could handle this." They may also have experienced deeply personal questions about their sexuality before it feels appropriate.

> *Steve:* I've said "yes it works" [referring to his penis] to complete strangers more times than I can count. It's kind of funny to joke about, but, when I sit and think about it, it's kind of messed up and really bums me out. Would you ask a nondisabled person if they're capable of having sex within 10 minutes of meeting them?

Being treated or seen as different by potential partners is a form of rejection that is all too common for many disabled people. Rejection, or being overlooked over and over again, becomes part of the norm for many disabled clients and it often goes unnoticed just how painful it is until a person begins therapy.

## *Collaborative Curiosity*

As mentioned in previous sections, disabled clients may be attending therapy with the belief that they are not worthy or capable of a sexual or romantic relationship. One of the biggest causes of this is a significant lack of representation. Mainstream media has very few examples of positive disability representation. If you don't see what is possible, you don't think you can have it. Invoking a curious mind and encouraging exploration and research is essential. Thankfully, finding examples of disabled people in the media has become much easier in recent years. With a little research, a therapist and disabled client can find positive and healthy disability representation in books, articles, TED talks, and social media. Many disabled social media influencers talk openly about sex, dating, and relationships, and share their experiences on YouTube, Instagram, TikTok, and other social media platforms. Through this evolution toward acceptance and validation, more and more disabled people will be able to see or expand their identity as a sexual person.

A therapist working with disabled clients will benefit greatly by being curious and willing to get outside of their comfort zone about being the expert in the room. Clients and therapists can work together to find and process the content they find. A therapist can ask their client questions about the content and help them identify what is helpful to them. Ask open-ended questions like "What does that mean for you?" and "Why do you like them?" or "What emotions come up for you as you watch this video?" It can be incredibly empowering for a client to see someone like them in a healthy and happy relationship, or talking openly about their sexuality.

In one session, Steve and I went on YouTube together and watched a vlog of an inter-abled couple (a nondisabled person who is dating a disabled person) that he had found as part of his homework assignment. We talked about how he felt about the content and he shared that he felt a mixture of happiness and jealousy. He was able to conclude that his jealous feelings of wanting what they had reaffirmed just how important it was for him to find a partner and how, ultimately, he was happy to see an example of what a relationship could look like for him. This is something that he thought, deep down, wasn't possible.

A therapist's effective use of assessment and treatment planning will help clients identify their challenges while redefining what sex means for them and make goals that focus on sexuality and pleasure instead of "fixing" their problems. Books such as *The Ultimate Guide to Sex and Disability* (Kaufman et al., 2010) can help clients normalize their experiences, learn communication skills, and explore their sexuality in a way that works for them. For example, one goal a client may have might be to gain the confidence to find or purchase sex toys or aids that could help them with either solo or partnered sex. A collaborative therapist will work together with a client to find products that may work for them. See our Resource list at the end of the chapter for ideas!

*Therapeutic Self-Disclosure*

It is sometimes the case that disabled clients will seek out therapists that they can relate to in some way. Disabled therapists often have to navigate if, how, and when to self-disclose their disability to their clients in a way that may be different from their nondisabled colleagues. One therapist decided to include a small paragraph on her physical disability in her website biography as a way to demonstrate an open and accepting discourse on disability, as well as a way for disabled clients to find a therapist that may be able to understand their circumstances. We, as therapists, don't want to give the message that we are avoiding talking about things. It is often our responsibility to set the stage as to how to navigate this. Disabled therapists have a unique opportunity to model how to talk about disability and sexuality in a way that feels authentic, vulnerable, and self-empowered.

For nondisabled therapists, you might encounter a client who may feel like you don't understand their struggle because you aren't disabled. Part of therapeutic self-disclosure is honoring the fact that you, in fact, don't get what it's like to be disabled. This doesn't mean you are less effective than your disabled colleagues. In fact, an honest conversation between a disabled client and their nondisabled therapist might just be the best way for the client to practice how to talk about their disability with others in a way that most accurately mirrors their experiences outside of the therapy office. A therapist can ask honest and reflective questions like "What is it like to talk about your disability with someone nondisabled?" or "What sorts of things would you wish I understood about you?"

Self-disclosure on sex-related issues may pose additional challenges to disabled therapists as more personal questions could cross both professional and personal boundaries. Setting limits, while exploring the reason behind client curiosity in a way that is not invalidating, is important and requires some self-reflection.

### *Bodymapping*

Bodymapping is a standard approach as both an assessment and an intervention (De Jager et al., 2016). Most commonly, an individual would have a blank outline of the front and back of a body. We introduce purpose of this tool which includes reflection on preferences and boundaries about their body, as well as consent and negotiation, and finally, identifying areas for future sexual growth and possibility.

Consider these Body Map modification for disabled clients:

- Blind clients can use a video recording or in-person introduction of their Body Map by identifying their body map and numbering 10: Full Go // 5: Interesting but not sure // 0: Absolute No/Don't Touch!
- Body outlines should replicate an individual's body in shape as well as any mobility aids they use.
- We can ask clients to use color or their own spoken/typed words to identify areas they want to be touched, don't feel too much one way or other, or don't want to be touched. The traditional body map uses the language of green light, yellow light, and red light.

Certainly, we approach this with creativity based on different abilities, remembering that we want clients to complete the map for the front and back of their bodies.

We then work to help the clients describe with us how they want to be touched on this area of their body. It is helpful to introduce the idea of the different purposes of touch, such as affectionate, sensual, and erotic. It is also interesting to explore the different ways they might enjoy touch on different parts of their body. Helping clients think about where deep rubs, gentle caresses, and maybe gripping or biting might belong is really helpful exploration. Of course, this can be vulnerable for clients, and even sometimes embarrassing. It is important to think about the idea that giving space for this conversation may also be new for the client. For some clients, viewing themselves as sexual may feel exciting, emotional, and scary.

The final step is helping the client think about how to communicate their map with a partner if that is their goal.

This tool is especially useful for disabled clients for multiple reasons. It provides an opportunity to think about the body as a unique, individualized map. It is empowering to describe what they do know about their body, and what it needs and wants. I love that it is a time to talk about one's body in a sexy way, often an opportunity under-explored for disabled clients. It also identifies negotiating and communicating about one's body, which part of the general sexual experience, as compared to "an extra thing disabled folks have to do."

A specific goal I hold for disabled clients during the Body Map exploration is to challenge the limitations. For example, "I can't be on top, I can't have penetration, I can't orgasm." I must respect the lived experience that has made this statement a reality AND I can also ask permission to discuss if this needs to be their reality, or if they would like to discuss possibilities and modifications to achieve a different possibility. The sexual experience is so expansive; sexual props for disabilities, expanding the definition of the erotic and the parts of the body that are erotic (beyond genitals), kink, tantric sex, etc. can open so many opportunities for achieving pleasure. The "yellow light" or medium interest or "5" in the numeric rating of the body map is often an area I encourage clients to focus on, and think about what they might explore sexually with this "untapped" part of themselves. It also allows the therapist and client to consider areas of their body they have negative emotions toward or have experienced shame related to this part of their body. Helpful questions:

- Can we discuss that part of your body? (i.e., asking permission)
- What are the experiences that are associated with this part of your body?
- Can you imagine feeling differently about this part of your body?
- How do you feel a sexual partner would view this part of you?

When I introduced the body map to Nakita, she felt open to the tool, but not necessarily hopeful. Nakita identified the first barrier is feeling blocked about viewing herself as sexual, because she didn't "move in sexy, powerful ways anymore." She took the green/yellow/red light instructions very seriously. She identified her nipples, her hair, and her neck as green. She identified her genitals as yellow because she felt indifferent to this part of herself now. She identified her abdomen as red due to scars and reminders of her trauma. When asked about the neck and hair, she noted that she was aware that when a partner pulled her hair during sex, she felt really turned on. She also shared that she fantasized about nipple-play and choking but hadn't tried this with a partner.

These green lights identified by Nakita lead us to begin exploration about kink practice. Nakita purchased nipple clamps and also began to communicate with her partner about her fantasies, and incorporating choking into their intimacy. Nakita had also mentioned not being able to feel powerful anymore in a sexual way. When we explored this, Nakita identified that being in on-top during sex had made her feel powerful, but without the ability to control her legs, she could no longer do this with her partner. This allowed us to begin discussing sexual props as well as new positions to increase movement and positioning for disabled individuals.

### *Incorporating Sexual Props and Toys*

Sex therapists often introduce the idea of sexual props to allow for different positioning and movement. This can enhance solo or partnered intimacy. For some clients, this may be a completely new topic, and description and education about what props and toys are, and specific ways they can be used will be a place to begin. For other clients, there may be familiarity, but their sexual narrative may limit their experimentation; as therapists, we might challenge the narrative. Some clients may want to consider how they communicate with partners, or even caregivers, about purchasing products, storing them in a way that allows privacy, trouble-shooting, preparing for, and using the new tools. It is important to remain informed of these tools as well as quality-/body-friendly products and resources to direct clients to when the topic is covered. See additional information regarding sexual tools in the Resources Section.

### Questions for the Case Studies

Read through the case studies how we both engaged with and supported these clients.

- What did you learn from hearing about Nakita and Steve's experiences in sex therapy?
- What would you do differently or in addition? What things did you feel worked really well?

- On a scale of 1 to 10 (1 being not at all, 10 being completely), how prepared do you feel to see clients with similar experiences to Steve and Nakita?
- What would make you feel more prepared?
- What resources do you have/would you need to have to be able to support clients like Steve and Nakita?

## Conclusion

Sex therapists working with disabled clients would benefit from adapting their practice in a way that is both accommodating and empowering. Clients may come to therapy with unresolved issues such as medical trauma, grief, lack of self-acceptance, trauma from rejection, and a global sense of rejection from society at large. An effective sex therapist may have to dismantle the society-enforced stereotype of sex as a performative act which is dependent on ability, and work redefine sex as pleasure for all, regardless of disability status. Sex therapists may utilize an eclectic approach that incorporates common psychotherapy modalities with sex therapy to address co-occurring concerns that may impact a disabled client's sexual identity. A therapist working with disabled clients must be flexible, open-minded, and be willing to forego the "expert" role in a way that empowers the client to speak honestly and frankly about their disabled identity. Effective use of the assessment and treatment plan that reflect clients' specific goals regarding sex and relationships is a vital first step. It sets the stage for self-acceptance and self-empowerment. Sex therapy values pleasure over performance. We help disabled clients envision the sexual pleasure they want to experience, and move them away from the cultural norms of sexual achievement toward a narrative of their body as sexually capable. Collaboration, creativity, and curiosity are the best tools of our work, so we can imagine with our clients how it could be and the tools we need to apply to reach their sexual pleasure goal.

## Resources

### Examples of Disability and Sexuality in the Media

- Lyric Seal, Asteroid, and others are erotic performers (including wheelchair users, Deaf folks, and Mad individuals) on the porn website Crashpadseries.com
- Queer as Folk (produced by Peacock) is a TV series with a disabled main character and an episode that features an inclusive sex party for people with disabilities.
- Heartbreak High (produced by Netflix) is a TV series featuring a queer autistic main character played by an autistic actress, and has several episodes that include explorations of her relationships and sex.

## Toys, Props, and Mobility Aids

Xes – a Sydney-based shop that designs accessible sex toys for *all* pleasure-seekers. www.xesproducts.com/au

Bump'n – an adaptive "joystick" that makes sex toys more user-friendly for disabled people. https://getbumpn.com

Intimate Rider – a sex chair that helps individuals and couples with limited mobility. www.intimaterider.com/

The Liberator – wedges that are designed to provide support and position enhancement with comfort. www.liberator.com/

## References

American Psychiatric Association. (2022). *Diagnostic and statistical manual of mental disorders* (5th ed. Text rev.). American Psychiatric Association.

De Jager, A., Tewson, A., Ludlow, B., & Boydell, K. (2016). Embodied ways of storying the self: A systematic review of body-mapping. *Forum Qualitative Sozialforschung/Forum: Qualitative Social Research*, 17(2).

de Wit, W., van Oorsouw, W. M. W. J., & Embregts, P. J. C. M. (2022). Sexuality, education and support for people with intellectual disabilities: A systematic review of the attitudes of support staff and relatives. *Sexuality and Disability*. https://doi-org.proxy.lib.umich.edu/10.1007/s11195-021-09724-w

Di Giulio, G. (2003). Sexuality and people living with physical or developmental disabilities: A review of key issues. *The Canadian Journal of Human Sexuality*, 12(1).

Foley, S., Kope, S., & Sugrue, D. (2012). *Sex matters for women: A complete guide to taking care of your sexual self*. The Guilford Press.

Henderson, P. (2014). In praise of "ordinary" sex therapy. *Sexual and Relationship Therapy*, 29(1), 132–134. https://doi-org.proxy.lib.umich.edu/10.1080/14681994.2013.860436

Jungels, A. M., & Bender, A. A. (2015). Missing intersections: Contemporary examinations of sexuality and disability. In J. DeLamater & R. Plante (Eds.), *Handbook of the sociology of sexualities* (pp. 169–180). Springer International Publishing. https://doi.org/10.1007/978-3-319-17341-2

Kaufman, M., Silverberg, C., & Odette, F. (2010). *The ultimate guide to sex and disability: For all of us who live with disabilities, chronic pain, and illness*. Cleis Press, Inc.

Medina-Rico, M., López-Ramos, H., & Quiñonez, A. (2018). Sexuality in people with intellectual disability: Review of literature. *Sexuality and Disability*, 36(3), 231–248. https://doi-org.proxy.lib.umich.edu/10.1007/s11195-017-9508-6

Perleman, R. (2012). Helen singer Kaplan's legacy and the future of sexual medicine. *Journal of Sexual Medicine*, 9, 138.

Rocco, S. (2019). When healthcare providers do not ask, patients rarely tell: The importance of sexual counseling in multiple sclerosis. *Journal of National Medical Association*, 111(6). https://doi.org/10.1016/j.jnma.2019.05.001

Wylie, K. (2022). Masters & Johnson – Their unique contribution to sexology. *BJPsych Advances*, 28(3), 163–165. https://doi-org.proxy.lib.umich.edu/10.1192/bja.2021

# 11
# EXPLORING A METHODOLOGY OF CARE

Creating Research With Disabled Queer Individuals and Community

*Bri Noonan and Elisabeth Z. Lacey*

In writing this chapter, we employed the very methodology that we will discuss within these pages. We had open and honest conversations about boundaries and our other obligations, including our jobs, our research, and our personal lives. We wrote from bed, the kitchen table, our desks, and our doctors' offices. We recognized our positionality in this project and utilized crip-time. We built a major surgery into our writing timeline as well as job changes, teaching schedules, and research complications. The complexities of bringing this chapter to fruition meant that, above all, this chapter was written with care at its center: care for ourselves, care each other as we wrote together, and care for the subject matter itself. Without care, we cannot foster deep relationships or imagine possibilities for a queer, crip future.

Cultivating care in practice means that as researchers and practitioners, we seek to deconstruct traditional research practices and methods that are built on a foundation of transitionary data mining and ableist notions of "usefulness." Instead, this chapter centers a care-full methodology to create more well-rounded research requiring us to interrogate our approaches to time, relationship building, communication, and emotion. A care-full methodology is one rooted in Black feminist scholarship and disability justice; it is queer and fluid. It is an intersectional feminist, disabled, queer framework that allows us as researchers to "create a care-full method through which to reckon with the loss of human life within the dehumanizing confines of the out-put obsessed neoliberal academy" (Ohito, 2020, p. 3). Care needs to be interwoven into how we work together within academic institutions and how we work with our communities. "Emergent research designs allow us to respond to the needs and desires of communities and individuals with whom we work in meaningful ways" (Vanderbilt & Ali p. 75). Such flexibility is critical to a care-full approach. This chapter will provide recommendations and frameworks for how one might approach their own care full research practices. It is also a record of mistakes made, reevaluation, in-the-moment decisions, and changing our minds. These things are necessary when developing a methodology of care.

Academics such as Dolmage (2017) have put forth the idea of universal design – a concept posited as a way for us to pedagogically address the systematic oppression within educational spaces – as a way to "move" through these spaces. How does an academic institution "move" to undo its ableism when it is woven into its very design? The answer lies in how we care. Is our care flexible? Reflexive? Thoughtful? Does it contain movement? We seek to push back against this solution and posit perhaps a universal (but ever changing) starting point for researchers built upon a foundation of care that extends and adapts similarly in caring, thoughtful, collaborative ways.

As the world ungulates both closer together and further apart due to social media, globalization, and violence across and within borders, networks of care are becoming increasingly globalized. Transnational care networks are reinforced through technologies of information becoming increasingly accessible to some, and we can see the care connections between communities in ways that have never been possible. This chapter not only has been written with these new possibilities in mind but also encourages future scholarship on the possibilities for these transnational networks of care among researchers and practitioners. We have the opportunity to practice care and learn not only from those right around us but also from those far beyond our local landscape. As we worked with care to create this chapter, there were times the internalized, ableist guilt left over from a combined nearly three decades entrenched in academic grind culture would find us. It was important that we had each other to talk to, listen to, and lean on. Our care-full practices made us better equipped to be present, to care for ourselves and for each other, and to take care with the material we were writing. We knew from the beginning that, as Lakshmi Piepzna-Samarasinha writes, "Our work needs to be cripped the fuck out" (2018, p. 124), and this work is better for it.

## Background

Because care is multimodal and multidirectional, the literature that we pull from must be intersectional and interdisciplinary. Thus, we offer many perspectives of care in this literature review to set the stage for the variety of possibilities for care. Reflexivity is central to creating a care-full methodology. As feminist researchers, it is crucial to consider our own subject positions, our ethical approaches to research and our role as a researcher and representative arm of an oppressive, white supremacist institution – the academy (Alcoff & Potter, 1993; Collins, 2009). To understand our relational positions in this work means that it is also critical to be reflexive in asking questions of care for our subjects that co-create knowledge alongside us as scholars, and also to ask reflexive questions of the academic institutions we are representing (Mitchell-Eaton, 2019). As researchers and scholars, we occupy ambivalent positions of authority in a hierarchical structure that is recognized as a place of knowledge and expertise – both favored in a modernist, capitalist society – these positions are complex when thinking about our engagement as individuals with the academy and our engagement in our own research. A feminist, disabled, queer reflexivity must extend to include questions of care for those who continue to suffer at the hands of a white supremacist, ableist, cis-hetero capitalist system as well as for ourselves, as researchers open to the witnessing the grief, trauma and realities of this suffering (Thieleman & Cacciatore, 2014). A reflexive feminist methodology also understands that care is reciprocal and multidirectional, yet must also remain sensitive to dynamics of power and hierarchies intrinsic in the relationship of researcher and research participant (Mitchell-Eaton, 2019). All of these things are factors in the foundation of a feminist, disabled, queer methodological framework.

It is also important to take seriously one's ethical orientations and obligations in research. An ethic of care and of personal accountability, as outlined by Patricia Hill Collins (2009) is the foundation of our ethical engagement with various and multiple vulnerable populations (Rowling, 1999). The central principle of an ethic of care rests on three interrelated components: personal expressiveness, emotions, and empathy as central to understanding and validating knowledge. An ethic of caring is also directly enmeshed in an ethic of personal accountability. The central tenet of an ethic of personal accountability is that we are all accountable for our knowledge claims (Collins, 2009). These knowledge claims include the ontological understandings of the world that we, as researchers, bring to our work as well as the public and semi-public knowledge claims that we perpetuate and reproduce in the publication, teaching, and dissemination of our research. That means that as an individual and as the product of an institution of white supremacy, we are responsible for the care of and accountability to the research participants that we interact with throughout the course of research, the assertion of knowledge claims, and beyond. Individual embodiment, context, conduct, and knowledge matter in our work, as does the care that one takes in being with participants who are choosing to be vulnerable with their experiences, and that as researchers, we are vulnerable in return (Mika, 2020). Capacity for empathy, accountability, and contextual awareness are all important for an ethical engagement with others, including an acknowledgment of and a constant negotiation of my status as an "outsider-within" (Collins, 2009). Researchers can recall how the emotions being expressed by another person – during the process of research and data collection – have felt inside our own bodies and experiences, creating a bridge of empathy. We are together in a place of meeting when we share experiences of socialized/normative expectations or assumptions that are designed and upheld through institutionalized oppressions.

A scavenger methodology uses different methods to gather and generate information, methods that might often seem at odds with each other, queering the combination of sites and subjects that are "acceptable" to be studied, and also resisting siloing those studies into disciplinary stalls (Halberstam, 1998). This methodology explicitly focuses on subjects and phenomena that have been deliberately – through systematic deletion or otherwise – marginalized or excluded from "traditional studies" of human behavior. Halberstam further describes this methodology as one that adamantly refuses academic or cultural pressure for disciplinary recognition. While it can be loosely related to the field of cultural studies, a scavenger methodology is reliant on the creativity and the academic process of the researcher/writer. It is queer, also, insofar as it names and performs an analytical function in relation to something other than itself. It is at once "collective and focalized" (Phelan, 2015) to particular articulations of experience, affect and oppression.

In *Critical Youth Research in Education: Methodologies of Praxis and Care*, H. Samy Alim takes up "the gift of a thoughtful, introspective, deeply committed, multivocal approach to research that foregrounds the relationality, mutuality, care, reciprocity, and responsibility in critical qualitative research with youth and their communities" (2020, foreword xiii) and its effects on knowledge production. The goals of care-full methods include embracing emotionally inflected and vulnerable practices that are affirmative in their own vulnerability, cultivating a more empathic researcher who is more highly attuned to both others' emotions and their own, and enabling more intimate connections by removing that which hinders the ability to emotionally engage in research at all. It is a "methodological, reflexive approach" that is invested in uncovering the material, economic, political, and geographical conditions that structure grief as radically uneven and from that, cultivating a critical politics of care which is what animates this method in the field. "Caring with" as opposed to "caring for" or "caring about" means that a researcher can and must engage empathetically with the subject while being careful not to erase differences of power, access and experience (Mitchell-Eaton, 2019). Even when one belongs to the community they research, this acknowledgment of power, access, and experience is necessary. In Brilliant Imperfection, Eli Clare (a queer crip creative) describes being at a podium speaking about the dangers of cure as their friend who had survived cancer is standing in the back of the room: "All at once, my words feel like empty rhetoric. I have no idea what cure means to her" (Clare, 2017). All at once, there is a realization of a need to ask us as a community to reject a binary idea of cure as good or bad, and instead, embrace an anti-binary that broadens to include a myriad of experiences. As researchers who may also belong to the communities we research, we must be especially careful to not hold our own personal knowledge/experiences above the knowledge/experiences of our participants.

## Why Does This Matter? Examining Best Practices

There is a bridge we must continue to build between academia and communities that requires radical shifts in how academic institutions function and how they work with oppressed populations. To be a part of an academic institution and not reckon with and adjust how we conduct research is to not hold the institution and ourselves accountable. Methodologies of care are required in order to bridge these spaces, create impactful research and relationships, and work together against injustice.

We have created a list for researchers and practitioners to consider throughout their working process. We will be using these points to build up a toolkit for care-full thinking and doing. Listing out our strategies in this way has allowed us to more effectively use accessible language and formatting, while also paying homage to a genealogy of scholars/activists/artists that came before us with strategies of their own to plainly talk about these topics. In no way do we think this constitutes an exhaustive list of considerations or tactics. This is an incomplete list, an ongoing project which seeks to move toward more accessible and caring approaches of thinking and doing.

- *Every community needs and wants different things. Every individual needs and wants different things. Sometimes these needs overlap, and sometimes they do not.*
  - Work with communities and individuals to hear what they need and want. Even if you are a member of this community, doing this listening work honors the power imbalances at play when conducting research or providing a service. Do not assume that you know what is wanted or needed from your work.
  - When in doubt, **ask**. These questions can start a conversation about how and why an individual or a community is invested in the work that you are doing.
    - Questions like this can include:
      - "Why was it important to talk to me today?"
      - "Why is this research/art/story important to you?"
      - "How do you see me incorporating your story into my work?"
  - Be transparent with the community or individuals you are working with in order to demonstrate radical care. This can look different for every circumstance. Give care and support to the individuals and communities whose knowledges you are collecting.

- Strategies for transparent care can include:
  - Pre-interview meetings or discussions
  - Previewing questions for discussion, schedule, or plan for the work you will be doing
  - Compensation for time (when possible)
  - Transcript reviews by interview participants
  - After care, including:
    - Check-ins
    - Follow-ups
    - Thank you notes
    - Be flexible when change is needed/wanted. Needs change; wants change.
- *Crip time is #1. Build in time.*
  - Continue to keep an open dialogue within your work/project not only for the individuals and communities you may be working with but also for yourself.
  - Talk with all parties involved in your work and strategize for these possibilities by setting up expectations or ways to manage expectations.
    - Examples of ways to begin a conversation about flexible timelines and expectations:
      - "I understand that a lot of things are changing for you right now, so let's make a plan for how we might tackle unforeseen circumstances like . . ."
      - "I'm working through a lot of moving pieces right now in my research, so I cannot give you an exact date that you will hear from me next. You can expect an email from me in a few weeks, which right now looks like somewhere between 4 and 6 weeks from now. If you need to reach me before then, I will be checking my email daily and available to reply."
  - Care must include acknowledging that some individuals and communities might not be ready or willing to work with you. They may never want to work with you and that has to be okay.
  - Time does not stop, and we must be flexible within the time constraints that everyone lives within. Be reflexive about your own timelines for your work and recognize if/when/how those timelines impact the people you are working with.
  - Resist building a strict timeline for your work. If necessary, think about some alternative strategies to creating timelines beyond deadline-setting. Be reflexive about expectations on yourself and external pressures created by capitalism, racism, ableism, etc.

- Deadline-oriented timelines can make working with disabled and queer individuals and communities extremely stressful, as flexibility is a requirement of operating in crip time. Instead of deadline-oriented timelines, think about using things like:
  - Benchmarks for large project/work sections
    - Create lists or collections of the work you have already done and organize those lists in a way that helps you keep track of the pieces that still need to come together and set timeline accordingly.
    - This can help you to run multiple/ongoing large sections of a project and measure your progress with a little more time flexibility.
    - Reframes measurement from what you need for your work/project to what you have.
  - Percentage goals
    - This can help you to be a little more strategic and targeted with your timeline, while maintaining flexibility for individual tasks that might be required to complete this task.
    - That is, "By week 4 in the semester I would like to have my transcripts 30% completed."
  - If/then timelines
    - Reframes the "procrastination" stigma perpetuated by capitalism and recognizes the invisible physical/mental/emotional labor of processing/resting/recovering/healing.
    - That is, "If I hear back from this archive, then I will be able to complete cataloging that section in three days."
- Any use of these "undated timelines" requires regular and transparent communication with everyone involved in your project/work.
- Recognize that discussing difficult topics with queer, disabled and/or otherwise marginalized people(s) must take time, compassion, space and processing. It is not your responsibility to determine what a difficult topic is, but there are ways to acknowledge this difficulty and care for your participants and yourself.
  - Examples of helpful phrases to encourage taking time and space for heavy processing include:
    - "I understand that anything we are talking about today has the possibility of being really difficult, and I want you to know that we can take a break or stop whenever you need to."
    - "I do not have any specific expectations for our conversation today, so anything that you feel comfortable talking about is okay with me."

- "I'm going to be asking some pretty specific questions in our conversation today. If I ever ask a question or try to clarify something that you are not comfortable talking about in detail, please let me know and I will move on immediately."
  - Establishing a safe word or safe phrase for when uncomfortable situations of disclosure arise might also help participants feel more willing to maintain conversation boundaries that they are most comfortable with.
- No one owes you their full disclosure. Likewise, be intentional and reflexive about what you choose to disclose.
- *Listen more. Talk less.*
  - Deep listening is essential for a care-full methodology.
    - Deep-listening strategies:
      - 80/20 listening
        - Overall, 80% listening and 20% talking where that 20% is mainly follow-up and clarifying questions
      - Emotion-seeking exploration
        - "How did that make you feel?"
        - "I hear that you felt afraid. Can you tell me a little more about that?"
      - Emotional-somatic connection questions
        - "Where did you physically feel that emotion in your body at that time?"
        - "What are you feeling in your body as you describe this to me right now?"
  - Build relationships with people. We listen more deeply to those that we care about.
    - Create memos: make a note of important things to remember about the people you are working with. This can also be a great place to keep track of any follow-up questions or conversations you have.
    - Resist a "usefulness" narrative: when building relationships are central to your methodology of care, not every interaction, conversation, or discussion will be a data point.
- Everyone has personal histories, feelings, stories, and lives that deserve to be heard and honored.

- *We are co-conspirators.*
  - Do not approach this work from an academic standpoint alone.
  - You will be wrong and you should admit it. Researchers are researching to learn!
  - Hierarchies exist and continue to be reinforced. Acknowledging these hierarchies of privilege/access and oppression/barriers is an important first step in disrupting these hierarchies.
  - Care is a two-way street. You may care and be cared-for. These relationships should be multi-directional, not hierarchical, or transactionary.
- *Always make your work accessible.*
  - Writing a paper can be necessary/wanted/fun, but it is not the only way to present or talk about your work.
  - Always ask: "How am I going to relay this information back to the community or individuals whose knowledge/experiences/labor constructed it? What is the format that makes the most sense or is the most wanted/needed?"
  - If the community cannot access what you have done, what was the point? Your work should not live in the academy alone.
  - Ask individuals and communities what format(s) for your work would make the most sense or be the most exciting for them (i.e., news article, social media posts, policy reform, informational material, historical archive, film, podcast).
  - Consider all bodyminds when completing your work. Ways to ensure your work is or could be accessible include:
    - Plain language translations (for any written material)
    - Large print (if material is printed)
    - Open access (for digital content)
    - Captioning, automatic or pre-loaded (for film/video)
    - Readable PDF versions (for screen readers)
    - Image descriptions (embedded in images and/or included in captions)
  - Accessibility is complicated and constantly changing. Maintain an open dialogue with all involved in your work about new or ongoing changes to access needs.

## Two Case Studies for the Practically Inclined

In order to demonstrate the different ways that a care-full methodology can be employed by and with queer and disabled communities, we have chosen to include a case study from each of this chapter's authors' own research work. You will notice that in both case studies, we make mistakes: it is important that a care-full methodology acknowledges that mistakes create the space for us to learn and hone our approaches to care. We chose to include two shorter case studies for a number of reasons: to demonstrate the range of participants with whom a care-full methodology should be considered and employed, to provide readers with a better understanding of the utility of the tools outlined earlier, to provide firsthand accounts of this methodological approach, and to honor the experiences and stories of the participants who have helped us to better understand the importance of care in our research.

*A Case Study for Crip Time Being Superior: Bri*

In the pilot study, "How Do Queer, Chronically Ill Creatives View Art-Making?" I investigated the correlation between queer, chronically ill/disabled folks and art-making. The process included showcasing the participants' artwork in an accessible book, which was intentionally disseminated beyond the academic institution. This research project included a methodology of care directed toward participant care and accessibility. It was important to make sure that the participants felt they had space within the research to ask for what they needed and move at their own pace through the surveys, interviews, and art collection with low stress. In other words, the research was designed to operate within crip time and not the timeline of an academic institution. My pilot study was conducted starting in summer of 2020 and was not completed until April 2021. Often, especially in Master's programs, students are trying to complete their research and graduate within the same semester. Such an accelerated timeline cannot truly demonstrate care within the queer, disabled population. If I had attempted to conduct my research in one semester, I could not have cultivated the relationships necessary nor would this research have been ethical, compassionate, or rooted in a methodology of care. When we as researchers bend to institutional time, it comes with a detriment not only to ourselves and our research results but also to our participants.

It was important to me at the beginning of this research process to inform participants that I was an open and direct communicator. I let them know early and often that if they needed something changed at any point, we could make it happen. Shortly after launching my research project, a participant sent me an email letting me know they couldn't answer one of my survey questions regarding identity in relationship to sex assigned at birth. This allowed me to reflect on my position as a queer disabled researcher, and recognize that even after all the work I had done trying to make sure everything in my study made sense, this question didn't. It enabled me to go back to this person and thank them for pointing this error out and strengthening this research. The response I got from the participant validated this approach of open communication and reflection. They thanked me for not being defensive when approached with an error in my own research. This participant clearly understood the implicit power imbalance between us, and recognized the potential danger in pointing out such an error. That danger, in speaking truth to power, was not lost on me. Community voices are critical for bridging the gaps in knowledge we have and creating better more comprehensive research.

One of the primary considerations in designing compassionate accommodations was that of time. How much time would it take to complete a work of art to be contributed to this book? How much time was needed for conducting an interview? How much time both before and after the interview would a participant need to process that interaction? These temporal considerations included possibilities like having extra time to submit art later in the process, adjusting interview times for both individual and group participation (which was particularly impactful for an international contributor who was working in a vastly different time zone), and allowing participants and contributors time to review the book before anyone else was able to view it. This meant emailing a copy of the book with a set of loose deadlines to accommodate their needs. This email also included information on how to navigate the book to avoid any triggering information; they could use the table of contents to navigate to their specific page without encountering other content. Extra care was taken to work with participants on their art pages as they needed adjustments to make sure their art and voice was portrayed correctly.

It was necessary for myself to make sure I did this research in the most accommodating and open way to allow these participants to feel that their art, voice, and stories were going to be handled with the utmost care. Adopting a methodology of care when working with marginalized communities allows for participants to be more safe in their vulnerability and will likely increase the amount of participants that will want to participate in the study. To further stress this point, one of the main compliments I got throughout this process was thanking me for creating a safe space in which accessibility was central to every step of the process as well as thanks for helping to magnify their voices and stories with their collaboration, feedback, and input. Utilizing this methodology of care allowed myself as the researcher to create meaning-making relationships with the participants rather than to simply assign meaning to their stories.

### *A Case Study for Care-Full Disclosure: Zee*

"Why are you interested in this?"

It always seems as though in the moments that have the biggest impact in my research, I feel the least prepared. This was the case when one of my participants, John – an older, white gay man who had lost his partner to the

AIDS epidemic in the mid-1990s – asked such a question. I was surprised by this question for one major reason: in the handful of research interviews I had completed up to that point, no one had asked me. I have thought about this question in my own, reflexive practice hundreds of times. As a feminist researcher, this is one of the central questions that I ask myself regularly – why am I interested in this? Which, as an academic, quickly becomes waves of: What does it mean that I am doing this work? What does my position and experience bring to this work? How do my social locations and privileges (as a white, queer, disabled, femme person) impact the research that I am doing, the questions that I am asking and the ways that people who participate in this research may or may not feel safe to discuss their answers with me? I have also found that it is very easy to generate complex and nuanced answers that intellectualize what should ultimately be a much more holistically felt question. All of these questions are important, and should be given thoughtful, repeated attention throughout the research process, but somehow, my constant reflection still failed to prepare me for this moment. This person, who had just opened himself and his story up to me so completely, was equally (and justifiably) curious about what I brought to the table.

"Why are you interested in this?"

There was no judgment in his voice when he asked me this question – purely logical curiosity; I have shared with you, and now you will share with me. On the face of it, it makes so much sense and I was ashamed that I had not even thought of a satisfactory way to address that question in the context of an interview. I knew the answer that I gave to my dissertation chair. I knew the answer that I gave to my colleagues and research partners. And yet, none of those seemed to be quite right at this moment. What felt like 300 years stretched out between that question and my answer. I started to feel anxious, even self-conscious. I took a deep breath and sighed before simply repeating the question.

"Why am I interested in this?"

I realized I didn't have a "participant-friendly" version of the story that I wanted to tell, and so I shakily began telling him the story of the time that I was 6 years old and sang at an interfaith memorial service hosted by the local hospice. I had no plans for telling that story, nor did I have plans to tell him about a classmate of mine who had died in middle school, or the unexpected death of a central father-figure in my life. I told him about how each experience of grief that I had witnessed and experienced fundamentally shaped who I am as a person, not just an academic or a researcher. I told him that I wanted to understand those experiences better and be less afraid of them. I think it was the most human (and least academic) answer I'd ever given to that question. I wasn't sure, at first, what he had "wanted" from my answer – was he looking for something specific, for me to say the "right" thing? Would that make him feel satisfied in his participation; would he maybe revoke his participation? I was terrified and relieved when I heard myself stop talking. John considered my answer for a few seconds. He asked several follow-up questions about my experiences and my interests. He was excited about hearing what I had shared and interested in understanding more.

What I couldn't articulate until much later was the discomfort that I felt stepping outside of my "role" as "the removed, but empathetic researcher." I had found safety in the distance between me (the researcher) and "them" (the participants). What I had also failed to acknowledge until this exchange was the immense power imbalance that reinforced my own comfort at the expense of those who were so generously sharing their stories. I thought I had been reflexive "enough" or open "enough" about my own subject positions, but what I had actually done was hide behind the walls that the ivory tower of academia had given me. I neglected to level with John, Wednesday, Mac, Olivia, and everyone who participated in this research as a *human being*. My approach up to that point had not been one of multi-directional care; it had been one of care-as-self-preservation and it was wrong. I realized that while I was never withholding my story from anyone that I interviewed, I was also taking for granted my ability to *not* disclose experiences of pain and loss. I am still practicing what this approach to care-full, empathetic listening in my research means to this day, and I don't always get it right. I also do not disclose my personal stories of love and loss unprompted, but now I am intentional about letting my participants know that I will answer any question that they may have of me. I've started doing this at both the beginning of interviews and the end, and have had many participants take me up on one or the other (sometimes both). It is because of the care John showed to me in asking that I feel much more free and safe to answer and engage when someone asks me:

"Why are you interested in this?"

## Conclusion

The first most critical takeaway from doing research with a care-full framework is that for this work to be successful, it needs to disrupt institutionalized ableism of the academy and operate under a crip-time framework. Building in the time needed to do this important work makes for more comprehensive and impactful results that live beyond the academy. Second, this work requires us to be accountable to ourselves and the individuals and communities we work with. Finally, the impact of queer, crip/disabled/chronically ill care work will extend beyond that of disability justice and queer spaces of research but must imperatively extend to researchers and/or practitioners undertaking this work across other (inter)disciplines and communities. It is important to remain attuned to this, and adjust your approach accordingly. Be gentle with yourself as you move through this work. A care-full approach is also one that more than likely will never look the same twice. It is important to note that while we have already outlined takeaways that are important in our work, you may find in your work a variety of outcomes that both intersect and diverge from what we have found. This flexibility is the very nature of a framework that adapts and morphs across communities and individuals whose specific intersections of existence require nuanced and thoughtful approaches.

The methodologies of care we have explored throughout this chapter are a piece of how we continue to dismantle the systemic oppression within the academic institution. A care-full framework must question the blueprint of universal design, as to believe something is universal is to say one size fits all, and we are not looking to create another concrete methodology which disallows movement and cannot possibly hold all bodyminds with care. Care-full methodologies are consistently in conversation and moving with the flow of the individuals and communities who are participating in the project/work. Care-full methodologies push us as researchers, educators, practitioners, etc. to be in relationship with one another in meaningful ways, to celebrate each other's wants/needs, and allow us to uplift each other up as we experience the ever-changing experience that is being human.

### *Questions and Prompts for Further Discussion*

1. Are there any elements to this methodology that you could see incorporating into your own research practices or the services you provide? If so, what are they and how so?
2. How does being in relationship with individuals and communities in a care-full way change your approach to research and service? What elements of a care-full methodology would you find the most challenging to explore? Why is that the case?
3. Now that you have identified the most challenging elements of a care-full methodology, how would you imagine a creative solution and/or a different future in which you could remove this hurdle?
4. What struck you most about each of the case studies in this chapter? Why did you find that to be important? How could you relate their experiences to your own research and service experiences?
5. Have you ever been a participant in a research study? If so, what elements of a care-full methodology do you wish had been implemented for your body mind's access needs?

### *Roleplay Prompts*

Disclaimer: Just as we try to enact a care-full methodology in our research and work, it is important to approach these roleplay prompts with care. These are not designed to create or foment conflict, and if the roleplay ceases to be a generative space for understanding and reflection, it's okay to bail. Ultimately, listen to your collective bodyminds.

* *Take 3–5 minutes to center your thoughts before engaging in the roleplay prompt. Feel free to reference other sections of this chapter for ideas.*

1. Identify a community that you work with in some way (whether through research or providing services). How would you enter into a conversation with a member or members of that community? How would this change if this is a community you consider yourself to be a member of? Write a care-full introductory statement about your research/work that includes the following:

    a. Your goals for the projects you are working on/service you are providing
    b. Your timeline for these goals
    c. Any emotional, mental, or physical barriers to access that might arise during their participation
    d. How you will mitigate or address any and all barriers to access
    e. A description of the ways that you will be mindful of and responsive to the needs of your participants, particularly in the event that they are triggered or otherwise incapacitated (both from your actions and from external forces)

2. A conflict has come up between you and a participant. With a partner, utilize one of your examples here to work through one of the following conflicts using a care-full methodology.

    a. One of your participants/community members feels uncomfortable with your survey questions and brings this to your attention. How do you work within a care framework to work through this conflict?
    b. A friend comes to you (who is not currently participating in your research/organization) and is upset that you have not asked them to join. As the researcher/provider, you have made a deliberate choice not to directly ask friends and community members that you have relationships with due to the inherent power dynamic as the researcher/provider. How do you sift through this complex conflict in a care-full way?
    c. As researchers and providers, it is important that we do not take up too much space when working with participants. However, a participant has asked you a pointed question about your own experiences as it relates to this research. How do you disclose why this research matters to you utilizing a care-full framework?

## Resources

### Universities and Organizations With Disability Studies/Disability Justice

York University: Graduate Studies in Critical Disability Studies
Lancaster University: Centre for Disability Research
University of Illinois Chicago: Disability and Human Development

Ford Foundation: Disability Futures Fellows
Sins Invalid

## Books/Articles/etc.

*Care Work: Dreaming Disability Justice* by Leah Lakshmi Piepzna-Samarasinha
*Brilliant Imperfection* by Eli Clare
*Exile and Pride* by Eli Clare, Collage
*Counterhegemony, and Community Engagement: Queer Feminist Zine Making as a Process of Generative Failure* by Jessica Pruett
*Queering the Crip or Cripping the Queer? Intersections of Queer and Crip Identities in Solo Autobiographical Performance* by Carrie Sandahl
*Feminist, Queer, Crip* by Alison Kafer
*The Body is Not an Apology* by Sonya Renee Taylor
*On Earth We're Briefly Gorgeous* by Ocean Vuong
*Zami* by Audre Lorde
*Dirty River: A Queer Femme of Color Dreaming Her Way Home* by Leah Lakshmi Piepzna-Samarasinha
*Sitting Pretty* by Rebekah Taussig
*Black Disability Politics* by Sami Schalk
*Bodyminds Reimagined (Dis)ability, Race, and Gender in Black Women's Speculative Fiction* by Sami Schalk
*The Invisible Kingdom* by Megan O'Rourke
*Academic Ableism: Disability and Higher Education* by Jay Timothy Dolmage
*Rest is Resistance* by Trisha Hersey
*Crip Kinship: The Disability Justice & Art Activism of Sins Invalid* by Shayda Kafai
*Just Care: Messy Entanglements of Disability, Dependency, and Desire* by Akemi Nishida
*Crip Theory: Cultural Signs of Queerness and Disability* by Robert McRuer
*Crip Times: Disability, Globalization, and Resistance* by Robert McRuer
*Emergent Strategy: Shaping Change, Changing Worlds* by adrienne maree brown
*Pleasure Activism: The Politics of Feeling Good* by adrienne maree brown
*Disability Visibility: First-Person Stories from the Twenty-First Century* Edited by Alice Wong
*Holding Change: The Way of Emergent Strategy Facilitation and Mediation* by adrienne maree brown
*Pleasure Activism: The Politics of Feeling Good* by adrienne maree brown
*THE CARE WE DREAM OF: Liberatory and Transformative Approaches to LGBTQ+ Health* Edited by Zena Sharman
[Disability Studies Quarterly (DSQ)](#)
[Queer Crip/Chronically Ill/Disabled/Sick Artists](#) – Bri Noonan

## Disability Justice Audit Tool

www.northwesthealth.org/djaudittool

## Instagram Accounts

@nina_tame
@mia.mingus
@crippingmasculinity
@butyoudontlooksickofficial

@deafqueer
@aaron___philip
@theendojournal
@spoonie_village
@ableismistrash
@invalid__art
@thebodyisnotanapology
@sinsinvalid
@disability_visibility
@leahlakshmiwrites
@disabilityjusticecultureclub
@adriennemareebrown

## References

Alcoff, & Potter, E. (1993). *Feminist epistemologies*. Routledge.

Alim, H. S. (2020). Foreword. In Ali, A. I., & McCarty, T. L. (Eds.), *Critical youth research in education: Methodologies of praxis and care*. Essay. Routledge, Taylor et Francis Group.

Clare, E. (2017). *Brilliant imperfection: Grappling with cure*. Duke University Press.

Collins, H. (2009). *Black feminist thought: Knowledge, consciousness, and the politics of empowerment* (2nd ed.). Routledge.

Dolmage, J. (2017). *Academic ableism: Disability and higher education*. University of Michigan Press.

Halberstam, J. (1998). *Female masculinity*. Duke University Press.

Mika, K. (2020). *Vulnerable witness: The politics of grief in the field* (K. Gillespie & P. J. Lopez, Eds.). University of California Press.

Mitchell-Eaton, E. (2019). Grief as method: Topographies of grief, care, and fieldwork from Northwest Arkansas to New York and the Marshall Islands. *Gender, Place and Culture: A Journal of Feminist Geography*, 26(10), 1438–1458. https://doi.org/10.1080/0966369X.2018.1553865

Ohito, E. O. (2020). Some of us die: A black feminist researcher's survival method for creatively refusing death and Decay in the Neoliberal Academy. *International Journal of Qualitative Studies in Education*, 34(6), 515–533. https://doi.org/10.1080/09518398.2020.1771463

Phelan, P. (2015). Hypothetical focalization and queer grief. In R. Warhol (Ed.), *Narrative theory unbound: Queer and feminist interventions* (pp. 78–97). The Ohio State University Press.

Piepzna-Samarasinha, L. L. (2018). *Care work: Dreaming disability justice*. Arsenal Pulp Press.

Rowling, L. (1999). Being in, being out, being with: Affect and the role of the qualitative researcher in loss and Grief Research. *Mortality*, 4(2), 167–181. https://doi.org/10.1080/713685968

Thieleman, K., & Cacciatore, J. (2014). Witness to suffering: Mindfulness and compassion fatigue among traumatic bereavement volunteers and professionals. *Social Work*, 59(1), 34–41. https://doi.org/10.1080/0966369x.2018.1553865

Vanderbilt, S. K., & Ali, A. I. (2020). Community engagement and meaningful trust as bedrocks of well-crafted research. In Ali, A. I., & McCarty, T. L. (Eds.), *Critical youth research in education: methodologies of praxis and care*. Essay. Routledge, Taylor et Francis Group.

# 12

# READY, WILLING, AND ABLE

## Sexuality Education for Disabled Individuals

*Autumn Dae Miller and Tiffini (Tiff) Lanza*

### Introduction

Sexuality education is a human right, not a privilege. It is not for an elite few humans that fit a mold of social acceptance and ability; it exists for a reason and should be offered to everyone. In the same manner that we teach mathematics, where counting acts as the foundation to multiplication or geometry, we can and should be educating all humans with the developmentally appropriate building blocks of sexuality education through the lifespan. For individuals whose intellectual or developmental disability and/or neurodivergence act as a barrier to receiving standard forms of this education, it is socially and developmentally imperative to create educational adaptations of the information in order to meet everyone's needs. Those who have been expected to offer sexuality education often have not had the necessary tools or experience to do this effectively especially for disabled individuals.

### Literature Review

The myth that disabled people lack experiences of sexuality has been debunked (Gomez, 2012). Many children and adults with intellectual and developmental disabilities (I/DDs) and/or autism spectrum disorders (ASDs) can experience delays in developmental milestones or skills that do not arrive with maturation and prompting; however, the sensory awareness of one's sexuality is typically the one area of life that arrives without hesitation (McDaniels & Fleming, 2018). Disabled individuals are often able to experience sexuality in ways such as the sensation of pleasure in nonsexual forms, puberty, attraction, sexual excitement, and a desire to couple (Chrastina & Večeřová, 2020; McDaniels & Fleming, 2018).

DOI: 10.4324/9781003308331-16

Especially in the United States (U.S.), proactive sexuality education – including purposeful lessons and discussions on topics that are comprehensively covered as each layer of information becomes developmentally appropriate – is a taboo and rare commodity (Winges-Yanez, 2014). Disabled individuals are even less likely to have access to comprehensive, developmentally appropriate sexuality education in their lifetime (Black & Kammes, 2021). For those disabled students and adults who are able to obtain sexuality education, proactive human sexuality educational programming is rarely provided; instead, information is offered as a reactive strategy (Friedman & Owen, 2017; Wilson & Frawley, 2016; Winges-Yanez, 2014).

In many cases where disabled individuals are offered sexuality supports and education, the opportunity is given only as a reaction to a sexual boundary violation or legal ramification as a result of a behavior performed by the individual (Friedman & Owen, 2017; Wilson & Frawley, 2016). These situations are often a result of an individual's lack of general sexuality education and a misunderstanding of unsafe, non-consensual, or socially inappropriate interactions (Friedman & Owen, 2017). Along with whatever sanctions have been dictated by the social or legal offense, the disabled individual has to unlearn years of misinformation in order to comprehend the new concepts and social expectations. It is often the case though that – following the performance of a sexual behavior – the punitive measures are the only ones offered, rather than programming focusing on the extensive educational needs that were the original concern (Friedman & Owen, 2017; Wilson & Frawley, 2016).

Impediments to experiencing and learning about human sexuality in general and one's own sexuality in particular are often external factors rather than one's innate inability or desire to understand sexuality (Björnsdóttir & Stefánsdóttir, 2020; Chrastina & Večeřová, 2020). These outside forces may include sociocultural limitations, barriers set by support people or agencies, and inaccessibility to necessary information (Björnsdóttir & Stefánsdóttir, 2020; Chrastina & Večeřová, 2020). Added to the complexity of learning new skills and information, the supports assigned to offer these interventions are not human sexuality professionals trained in the nuances of educating disabled individuals (Blanchett & Wolfe, 2002; Schaefer Whitby, 2020). This can lead to unintentional shaming, misguided and restrictive treatment planning, social isolation, or escalation of behavioral reactions (Schaefer Whitby, 2020).

### *The Facilitators*

Disabled individuals have many facilitators in their lives that could provide developmentally appropriate sexuality education from birth through end of life. There are four distinct types of opportunities where sexuality education programming could occur: caregivers – biological, adopted, bonus, or chosen family members; educators – grade school teachers, paraprofessionals, support aids, professors, or guest lecturers; paid professionals – direct supports, agency administration, or paid clinical professionals; and social informants – peers, social media platforms, general media, and pornography (Chrastina & Večeřová, 2020; Crehan et al., 2022; Kürtüncü & Kurt, 2020; Wilson & Frawley, 2016).

*Caregivers*

Loving someone and wanting to offer them the best possible opportunities in life is a massive responsibility as a caregiver. Raising intellectually disabled or austistic children can feel like an intense responsibility, creating a desire to protect children from all complicated or confusing topics by avoiding subjects or offering misinformation in order to guard children from the truth (Holmes & Himle, 2014). The sentiment comes from good intentions; however, in regard to the subject of human sexuality education, the less one knows, the more vulnerable they are to harm (Travers et al., 2014). Research studies have shown a correlation between a lack of or limited sexuality education and higher rates of sexual trauma and abuse (Sinclair et al., 2015). The likelihood of these experiences increases drastically if an individual is living with a disability (Black & Kammes, 2021). In order to keep disabled children safe from those who would seek to do them harm, caregivers have to be willing to communicate complex concepts with the same frequency and persistence of any other safety skills (Yektaoğlu, 2021).

In circumstances where caregivers are willing to offer sexuality education, they are not offered the tools to teach nor do they have all the necessary information to answer questions that may arise (Kürtüncü & Kurt, 2020). The process of offering these educational interventions becomes daunting as children mature and begin to recognize their desire to keep sexuality information and discussions separate from caregivers due to feelings of embarrassment (Chrastina & Večeřová, 2020). If these caregivers have become the sole keepers of this intimate knowledge, disabled adolescents and young adults may be less and less likely to seek safe and accurate sexuality information. It becomes beneficial – especially as children become adolescents – to have a sexuality educator separate from the caregivers within the home, even with caregivers supporting the interventions that are being taught (Chrastina & Večeřová, 2020).

*Educators*

A lack of healthy sexuality education limits community participation for disabled individuals (McDaniels & Fleming, 2018). Sexuality education in school districts does not have a universal standard, causing great variability in what is offered in each school, district, or region (Saul Butler et al., 2018). The information that is offered is highly influenced by the local culture and religious beliefs (Phasha & Runo, 2017). Some school districts refuse to offer any sexuality education, others are limited to abstinence-only education, while other educators focus human sexuality discussions on friendships versus intimate relationships (Saul Butler et al., 2018; SIECUS, 2011). Schools that are attempting to provide sexuality education continually lack information specific to sexual identity as well as most areas of sexual health and reproduction (Sala et al., 2019).

School teachers, and even professors, are often given the responsibility of acting as the sexuality educator without proper training (Phasha & Runo, 2017). Teachers struggle to grasp the entirety of the material due to limited exposure to these subjects themselves leading to students' questions going unanswered or the perpetuation of misinformation (Blanchett & Wolfe, 2002; McDaniels & Fleming, 2018). Many teachers complete mandatory lessons without having the necessary tools and modified curriculum available; therefore, learning objectives are not being met and topics are missed (Blanchett & Wolfe, 2002; McDaniels & Fleming, 2018).

If schools can afford trained sexuality educators, lessons may be offered as one-time workshops or guest lecturer programs. While the sentiment that something is better than nothing stands behind the motivation for such programming, this is by no means an appropriate amount of time to cover the vastness of topics within human sexuality education nor does it accommodate for the repetition needed for most disabled learners (Hott et al., 2022). These lessons may also be stunted by the school administrators' views around what information is absolutely necessary for their students (Shamrock & Ginn, 2021).

*Paid Supports*

Disabled individuals have access to certain paid supports at each life stage; however, the access to these supports typically relies on having knowledgeable caregivers early in life to set someone up for successful qualification of services as a child or adult (Montgomery County PA, n.d.-a). Some examples of paid services include early intervention services from birth to age five, specialized therapies and clinical support based on individual educational plans (IEPs) as students, insurance plan covered therapies, or government-funded waiver programs as an adult (Montgomery County PA, n.d.-b). These support professionals are asked to educate and support the individuals focusing on sets of goals and objectives developed by the individuals' teams based on assessed need (Office of Developmental Programs, n.d.).

After general health and safety needs, paid supporters tend to focus on building independence skills or problem-solving the challenges faced by those in more of a direct caregiving role including family, friends, or shift worker support professionals (Souza et al., 2021). Paid supporters tend to be more comfortable working on monetary skills, domestic tasks, and behavior modification strategies than topics within human sexuality (Wilson & Frawley, 2016). If paid supporters do work on anything related to human sexuality, it is typically related to general hygiene awareness or the need for personal space when communicating with others; they demonstrate a general reluctance to act as socio-sexual educators (Wilson & Frawley, 2016). Grieve et al. (2009) conducted a comparative study among different types of facilities where staff were asked to report on their beliefs, comfort, and knowledge around human sexuality for the disabled individuals that they supported. The study found a correlation between the level of independence skills supported by the program and the conservative stance of staff around sexuality (Grieve et al., 2009). Nursing facilities had the highest level of conservatism among paid supporters while more independent community living support agencies had significantly lower levels of conservatism; however, these levels were higher than in the general population (Grieve et al., 2009).

Most agencies that offer direct care or clinical support to disabled individuals tend to lack comprehensive human sexuality policies that are regularly updated to match practices and changes in societal understandings and terminology (Chrastina & Večeřová, 2020). While employees at agencies will state the desire to learn more about human sexuality topics in order to support disabled individuals, most do not seek out these trainings (Chrastina & Večeřová, 2020). In fact, even with a basic level of human sexuality training, most paid supporters do not feel confident or comfortable in their ability to assist disabled individuals in this area (Chrastina & Večeřová, 2020). In circumstances where paid supporters have been willing to attempt sexuality education, they are forced to balance a tightrope between protector and caring instructor (Rushbrooke et al., 2014). The education that is offered by a paid supporter will always be tainted by personal beliefs, lack of supervision by managerial supports, awkward professional boundaries or regulations, and social messages especially where there is a lack of clear guidance in an updated agency sexuality policy (Rushbrooke et al., 2014).

Having paid supporters as sexuality educators can also add an additional level of oversight of the disabled individuals they are instructing (English et al., 2018). Many professional goals must be tracked with data and staff are responsible for the health and safety regarding the matter of concern, but when issues of human sexuality are addressed, this oversight can become stifling (English et al., 2018). Someone who has staff at home 24/7, at a place of employment the entire time they attend, and whenever out in the community has no privacy to engage in sexual exploration in a healthy manner (English et al., 2018). This can become an emotional stressor on disabled individuals where sexual expression is now something that has to be rushed, secretive, and potentially quite unsafe (English et al., 2018). It would behoove the opportunities for safe and healthy sexual expression to have the educational components separate from paid supporters who are staffing shifts with an individual on a regular basis so that privacy can be achieved while still meeting the health and safety goals (English et al., 2018).

Outside of the direct paid supporters, clinical staff are often asked to provide sexuality education and programming to disabled children and adults (Schaefer Whitby, 2020). A behavioral specialist has the skills to identify the underlying components of a socially inappropriate or illegal behavior that occurs and to develop interventions to redirect or address those behaviors; however, they do not typically have the skills to properly educate disabled clients in safe and healthy forms of sexual expression (Schaefer Whitby, 2020). There are some behavioral staff who have appropriate training and credentials but these are often difficult to acquire (Schaefer Whitby, 2020). There are disabled individuals and teams that have requested sexuality information from psychologists, psychiatrists, primary care providers, gynecologists, and other medically specialized professionals; however, they do not typically receive extensive training in human sexuality nor would they typically be well versed in models for ongoing educational strategies as this is not their professional focus (Verrastro et al., 2020). While each paid supporter has a role in sexuality education programming and intervention – similar to caregivers – they are best suited to act as reinforcement to direct interventions offered by trained and experienced professionals (Verrastro et al., 2020).

*Social Informants*

Due to the lack of formal sexuality education opportunities, students and adults alike have relied more heavily on accessing the internet to answer questions as they arise (Jones & Biddlecom, 2011). One of the biggest concerns about utilizing the internet for sexual information is the inability of most online consumers to discern research-based factual information from fabrications or opinions (Jones & Biddlecom, 2011). Disabled individuals have fewer opportunities for learning about the use of technology and therefore do not have as much access to social media, online platforms, or training to navigate education they may be searching for in a safe way (Shamrock & Ginn, 2021). Oftentimes, a lack of information around safe internet usage leads to situations that create a need for reactive sexuality education; however, one wrong search term or click on a pop-up ad could lead to legal consequences (Löfgren-Mårtenson et al., 2015). Even when disabled individuals have the availability to use technology to gather sexuality education, they do not always have the necessary privacy to seek out this information (Darragh et al., 2017). Without the necessary personal freedoms to seek out this information while minimizing discomfort, disabled individuals do not get the time or ability to access the online resources that could fulfill their needs (Darragh et al., 2017).

The absence of comprehensive adapted sexuality education for disabled students leads to fewer peer interactions which, in turn, diminishes the chance for disabled individuals to gain sexuality education through social interactions with peers (Gougeon, 2009). Individuals benefit the most from social education and reflection that begins while students are discussing situations that arise naturally beginning at school and continue as adults in social settings or the workplace (Gougeon, 2009). With minimal socialization options, disabled individuals miss out on the chance to negotiate complicated relationship and sexuality concepts that are less scientific and more constructed through experience (Gougeon, 2009). For example, a student may understand the necessity to obtain consent before engaging in sexual activity with another person but may not really know how to engage in those conversations without roleplaying and discussing these aspects with peers.

**Best Practices**

The authors offer the following guidelines to prompt the shift of haphazard and unstructured sexuality education into a best practices model for disabled individuals:

1. Inclusive human sexuality education is not about having one course carved out specifically for disabled individuals; it is about the consistent consideration of the needs of children and adults with a variety of skills and abilities in all sectors of comprehensive programming.
   a. What assumptions are you making about your students or clients and what they know?
   b. Are you offering people education on sensitive topic areas? What does this look like?
   c. Does everyone have equal access to information that could benefit them? If that access is not equal, do you have a plan for how this information will be shared with those who are not readily able to obtain this information and conceptualize it on their own?
2. Human sexuality education is a lifelong learning process and all humans have the right to developmentally appropriate comprehensive sexuality education (Eglseder & Webb, 2017). No one is ever too young, old, or incapable of learning about human sexuality. In fact, it is only the limitations of the educator that stand in the way of offering developmentally appropriate human sexuality education from birth to the end of life and

having it accessible to all audiences. Knowledge should grow and shift focus, as the natural progression of human life does the same. We learn to crawl before we walk, why not use the same colloquial logic for building sexuality skills.
3. The role of the sexuality educator is to provide accurate, current, inclusive, progressive, and skill-adapted interventions (Schaefer Whitby, 2020). Additionally, educators should be providing education through the lens of trauma and culturally informed space. There is no space for judgments, value-based limitations, or program restructuring based on the limitations of the educator's abilities in the best practices of sexuality education (Schaefer Whitby, 2020). Imagine a world where mathematics taught across the lifespan was based on each instructor's opinions on which math skills were the most valuable. If we would not tolerate this level of preferential discernment on all subjects, then it should not be condoned for human sexuality education. Additionally, we have to stop asking people to "fly a plane without a pilot's license." If we want disabled individuals to learn about sexuality in an accurate and appropriate way, then we have to identify trained human sexuality professionals that have extensive experience working with disabled individuals.
4. Sexuality education does not have to sit in isolation with the trained and experienced instructor alone (Schaefer Whitby, 2020). In fact, in order to bring interventions into better understanding, they must be reinforced, normalized, and put into practice. Caregivers, educators, paid supporters, and social informants all have roles to play in human sexuality education. It is up to each set of these individuals to seek out peer-reviewed, factual information and training so that they are less reliant on egocentric thinking and socially constructed understanding of sexuality. Having a foundation steeped in research-based sexuality knowledge allows disabled individuals to absorb less structured forms of sexuality information to formulate their own opinions and values (Shamrock & Ginn, 2021).
5. Even though the political climate of a society can affect how certain aspects of human sexuality are perceived by a culture, it is the ethical duty of the trained sexuality professional to offer sexuality education that does not wax and wane with public opinion.
6. Educators need to be aware of the colonizing practices that have influenced education and continue to be present in how information is provided to individuals. Education was seen through the dominant ideologies that included ableism – excluding opportunities for disabled individuals. Educators need space to recognize and actively decolonize what information they are disseminating so that it is accessible to all individuals without the influence of what was once the dominant ideologies of white, heterocentric, cisgender, nondisabled, Christian, and misogynistic beliefs.

## Classroom Activity: Access-Ability

The following activity was designed for students and emerging professionals. It was created to demonstrate how to adapt and build comfort around offering lessons to disabled learners. It is a two-part activity that offers participants the ability to recognize their values and assumptions about how people learn and will demonstrate that the most effective educators are ones that think beyond their levels of comfort to consider the needs of all students.

### *Part One: Comfortable Teaching*

1. Students will be asked to research one subtopic within *The Circles of Sexuality* (Dailey, 1981; Advocates for Youth, 2007). This model is designed with five main themes of sexuality – sensuality, intimacy, sexual identity, sexual health and reproduction, and sexualization – in addition to their subcategories. These topics can be pre-selected by the presenter and distributed at random, or students may be given carte blanche according to their interests.
2. Once a topic is identified, students should be given concise instructions.
    a. Identify two learning objectives and how they will be measured.
    b. The lesson needs to be 15–20 minutes in length.
    c. Utilize any activities or techniques desired but document all the necessary steps for an educator to be able to pick up and use the lesson plan.
    d. The target audience can be children, youths, or adults. Make sure to clarify at the beginning of the lesson plan.
    e. Note how the classroom will be set up and any materials that will be needed by the educator or the participants.
3. The facilitator of the comfortable teaching activity should give students ample time to complete this assignment.
4. Ask the students to include a title page using appropriate formatting. Students must put the title of their lesson in the header of the main document, but leave their name out of the lesson plan details. This is done to create anonymity.
5. Lesson plans will be submitted to the facilitator with only this individual aware of who completed what lesson plan initially.

### *Part Two: Adaptive Teaching*

1. Redistribute the lessons created, making sure that no one received their original work.
2. Explain that this is the lesson plan the students will be using moving forward. The audience will remain the same; however, all of the participants

have some form of intellectual, developmental, neurodivergence, and/or physical disability. Some participants communicate verbally, a few use communication devices, and at least one of them is unable to read.
3. Their homework is to recreate this lesson plan with as many adaptations to the activities and information as possible in order to best reach their audience.
4. Remind them to revisit the classroom setup, materials, and ways that the objectives were going to be measured as well as the activities themselves.
5. Once the new lesson plans are completed, have everyone reflect on the experience using the following prompts.

   a. In your comfortable teaching lesson plans, what assumptions did you make about your audience?
   b. What skills and abilities were the most challenging for you to accommodate and why?
   c. What did you have to leave out?
   d. Was there anything you added to the lessons because you felt the participants would need to know this information first? Describe your motivation behind those additions.
   e. Would you have preferred doing the adaptations to your own lesson? Why or why not?

The goal of this activity is to educate students and professionals so that they comprehend the need to prepare, practice, and modify rather than forgo teaching complex and rather challenging human sexuality topics. We must equip educators, not only with information about human sexuality but also with the ability to adapt to become capable, accessible, inclusive, and motivated human sexuality educators.

## Conclusion

Anyone and everyone can and should have access to developmentally appropriate, trauma and culturally informed, comprehensive sexuality education. This information should not be dictated by age as developmentally appropriate indicates education from birth to end of life. Having an intellectual or developmental disability or being autistic does not dictate one's capability of understanding sexuality information. The same as any educational program; comprehension and application of topics is less about the subject matter being taught and more about how the information is offered. Disabled individuals would benefit from sexuality education programs created by well-trained and experienced sexuality professionals who understand the nuances of working with disabled clientele. All caregivers, paid supporters, social informants, and other educators involved in this person's life should be seeking out training on human sexuality topics so that they can be reinforcing and offering opportunities to practice skills learned in sessions with the specialized instructors. We – as a society – have to stop expecting untrained individuals to be able to offer sufficient human sexuality training. Moreover, we must stop assuming that single resources, interventions, or reference materials will be enough to equip disabled individuals with all the information they need to have safe and healthy sexual lives.

## Resources

### Websites

- Sex Education Collaborative https://sexeducationcollaborative.org
- Sexual Information and Education Council of the United States SIECUS: Sex Ed for Social Change www.nsvrc.org
- World Association for Sexual Health (WAS) https://worldsexualhealth.net
- Amaze: Age-appropriate info on puberty for tweens and parents https://amaze.org/

### Books

- Couwenhoven, T. (2007). *Teaching children with Down syndrome about their bodies, boundaries, and sexuality: A guide for parents and professionals*. Woodbine House.
- Hartman, D. (2013). *Sexuality and relationships education for children and adolescents with autism spectrum disorders*. Jessica Kingsley Publishers.
- Heighway, S., & Webster, S. (2007). *S.T.A.R.S.: Skills training for assertiveness, relationship-building, and sexual awareness*. Future Horizons, Inc.

### Podcasts and Podcast Episodes

- *Disability After Dark* By: Cripple & Co Productions
- *Sex and Disability* By: Sex and Psychology Podcast, Dr. Justin Lehmiller
- *Sex & Disability* By: Sexology, Dr. Moali
- *Sex and Disability* By: Uncomfortable; Uncomfortable conversations around uncomfortable topics, Debbie Roche
- *Sex and Disability: Breaking the Taboo* By: Better in Bed: A Sex and Sexuality Podcast with Sarasense.

## References

Advocates for Youth. (2007). *Life planning education: A youth development program*. www.advocatesforyouth.org/for-professionals/lesson-plans-professionals/200?task=view

Björnsdóttir, K., & Stefánsdóttir, G. V. (2020). Double sexual standards: Sexuality and people with intellectual disabilities who require intensive support. *Sexuality and Disability*, *38*(3), 421–438. https://doi.org/10.1007/s11195-020-09643-2

Black, R. S., & Kammes, R. R. (2021). Sexuality interventions for individuals with intellectual disability. *Education and Training in Autism and Developmental Disabilities*, *56*(4), 371–393.

Blanchett, W. J., & Wolfe, P. S. (2002). A review of sexuality education curricula: Meeting the sexuality education needs of individuals with moderate and severe intellectual disabilities. *Research and Practice for Persons with Severe Disabilities*, *27*(1), 43–57. https://doi.org/10.2511/rpsd.27.1.43

Chrastina, J., & Večeřová, H. (2020). Supporting sexuality in adults with intellectual disability – A short review. *Sexuality and Disability*, *38*(2), 285–298. https://doi.org/10.1007/s11195-018-9546-8

Crehan, E. T., Rocha, J., & Dufresne, S. (2022). Brief report: Sources of sexuality and relationship education for autistic and neurotypical adults in the US and a call to action. *Journal of Autism and Developmental Disorders*, *52*(2), 908–913. https://doi.org/10.1007/s10803-021-04992-z

Dailey, D. (1981). Sexual expression and ageing. In D. Berghorn & D. Schafer (Eds.), *The dynamics of ageing: Original essays on the processes and experiences of growing old* (pp. 311–330). Westview Press.

Darragh, J., Reynolds, L., Ellison, C., & Bellon, M. (2017). Let's talk about sex: How people with intellectual disability in Australia engage with online social media and intimate relationships. *Cyberpsychology: Journal of Psychosocial Research on Cyberspace*, *11*(1). https://doi.org/10.5817/CP2017-1-9

Eglseder, K., & Webb, S. (2017). Sexuality education and implications for quality of care for individuals with adult onset disability: A review of current literature. *American Journal of Sexuality Education*, *12*(4), 409–422. https://doi.org/10.1080/15546128.2017.1407980

English, B., Tickle, A., & dasNair, R. (2018). Views and experiences of people with intellectual disabilities regarding intimate relationships: A qualitative metasynthesis. *Sexuality and Disability*, *36*(2), 149–173. https://doi.org/10.1007/s11195-017-9502-z

Friedman, C., & Owen, A. L. (2017). Sexual health in the community: Services for people with intellectual and developmental disabilities. *Disability and Health Journal*, *10*(3), 387–393. https://doi.org/10.1016/j.dhjo.2017.02.008

Gomez, M. T. (2012). The S words: Sexuality, sensuality, sexual expression and people with intellectual disability. *Sexuality and Disability*, *30*(2), 237–245. https://doi.org/10.1007/s11195-011-9250-4

Gougeon, N. A. (2009). Sexuality education for students with intellectual disabilities, a critical pedagogical approach: Outing the ignored curriculum. *Sex Education*, *9*(3), 277–291. https://doi.org/10.1080/14681810903059094

Grieve, A., McLaren, S., Lindsay, W., & Culling, E. (2009). Staff attitudes towards the sexuality of people with learning disabilities: A comparison of different professional groups and residential facilities. *British Journal of Learning Disabilities*, *37*(1), 76–84. https://doi.org/10.1111/j.1468-3156.2008.00528.x

Holmes, L. G., & Himle, M. B. (2014). Brief report: Parent – Child sexuality communication and autism spectrum disorders. *Journal of Autism and Developmental Disorders*, *44*(11), 2964–2970. https://doi.org/10.1007/s10803-014-2146-2

Hott, B. L., Randolph, K. M., & Raymond, L. (2022). *Teaching students with emotional and behavioral disabilities*. Plural Publishing, Inc.

Jones, R. K., & Biddlecom, A. E. (2011). Is the internet filling the sexual health information gap for teens? An exploratory study. *Journal of Health Communication*, 16(2), 112–123. https://doi.org/10.1080/10810730.2010.535112

Kürtüncü, M., & Kurt, A. (2020). Sexual education and development in children with intellectual disability: Mothers' opinions. *Sexuality and Disability*, 38(3), 455–468. https://doi.org/10.1007/s11195-020-09638-z

Löfgren-Mårtenson, L., Sorbring, E., & Molin, M. (2015). "T@ngled Up in Blue": Views of parents and professionals on internet use for sexual purposes among young people with intellectual disabilities. *Sexuality and Disability*, 33(4), 533–544. https://doi.org/10.1007/s11195-015-9415-7

McDaniels, B. W., & Fleming, A. R. (2018). Sexual health education: A missing piece in transition services for youth with intellectual and developmental disabilities. *Journal of Rehabilitation*, 84(3), 28–38.

Montgomery County Pennsylvania. (n.d.-a). *Developmental disabilities supports & services.* www.montcopa.org/1334/Developmental-Disabilities-Supports-Serv

Montgomery County Pennsylvania. (n.d.-b). *Early intervention.* www.montcopa.org/745/Early-Intervention

Pennsylvania Department of Human Services Office of Developmental Programs (ODP). (n.d.). *Everyday lives: Values in action.* www.myodp.org/mod/page/view.php?id=11946

Phasha, T. N., & Runo, M. (2017). Sexuality education in schools for learners with intellectual disabilities in Kenya: Empowerment or disempowerment? *Sexuality and Disability*, 35(3), 353–370. https://doi.org/10.1007/s11195-017-9480-1

Rushbrooke, E., Murray, C. D., & Townsend, S. (2014). What difficulties are experienced by caregivers in relation to the sexuality of people with intellectual disabilities? A qualitative meta-synthesis. *Research in Developmental Disabilities*, 35(4), 871–886. https://doi.org/10.1016/j.ridd.2014.01.012

Sala, G., Hooley, M., Attwood, T., Mesibov, G. B., & Stokes, M. A. (2019). Autism and intellectual disability: A systematic review of sexuality and relationship education. *Sexuality and Disability*, 37(3), 353–382. https://doi.org/10.1007/s11195-019-09577-4

Saul Butler, R., Sorace, D., & Hentz Beach, K. (2018). Institutionalizing sex education in diverse US school districts. *Journal of Adolescent Health*, 62(2), 149–156. https://doi.org/10.1016/j.jadohealth.2017.08.025

Schaefer Whitby, P. J. (2020). Ethical considerations in providing sexuality education to people with autism spectrum disorder: In P. S. Whitby (Ed.), *Advances in early childhood and K-12 education* (pp. 1–15). IGI Global. https://doi.org/10.4018/978-1-7998-2987-4.ch001

Sexuality Information and Education Council of the United States (SIECUS). (2011). *Comprehensive sex education for youth with disabilities: A call to action.* https://siecus.org/wp-content/uploads/2021/03/SIECUS-2021-Youth-with-Disabilities-CTA-1.pdf

Shamrock, O. W., & Ginn, H. G. (2021). Disability and sexuality: Toward a focus on sexuality education in Ghana. *Sexuality and Disability*, 39(4), 629–645. https://doi.org/10.1007/s11195-021-09699-8

Sinclair, J., Unruh, D., Lindstrom, L., & Scanlon, D. (2015). Barriers to sexuality for individuals with intellectual and developmental disabilities: A literature review. *Education and Training in Autism and Developmental Disabilities*, 50(1), 3–16.

Souza, F., Duff, G., & Swait, J. (2021). "Whose plan is it?" understanding how the goal pursuit of consumers and careers influence choices in the Australian disability sector. *Journal of Choice Modelling*, *40*, 100300. https://doi.org/10.1016/j.jocm.2021.100300

Travers, J., Tincani, M., Whitby, P. S., & Boutot, E. A. (2014). Alignment of sexuality education with self determination for people with significant disabilities: A review of research and future directions. *Education and Training in Autism and Developmental Disabilities*, *49*(2), 232–247.

Verrastro, V., Saladino, V., Petruccelli, F., & Eleuteri, S. (2020). Medical and health care professionals' sexuality education: State of the art and recommendations. *International Journal of Environmental Research and Public Health*, *17*(7), 2186. https://doi.org/10.3390/ijerph17072186

Wilson, N. J., & Frawley, P. (2016). Transition staff discuss sex education and support for young men and women with intellectual and developmental disability. *Journal of Intellectual & Developmental Disability*, *41*(3), 209–221. https://doi.org/10.3109/13668250.2016.1162771

Winges-Yanez, N. (2014). Why all the talk about sex? An autoethnography identifying the troubling discourse of sexuality and intellectual disability. *Sexuality and Disability*, *32*(1), 107–116. https://doi.org/10.1007/s11195-013-9331-7

Yektaoğlu, T. (2021). Effectiveness of the self-protection program for students with mental disabilities against sexual abuse. *International Journal of Curriculum and Instruction*, *13*(2), 1478–1492.

# 13
# DISABLED AND/OR CHRONICALLY ILL SURVIVORS OF SEXUAL VIOLENCE AND INTIMATE PARTNER VIOLENCE

*L. B. Klein, Rose C. B. Singh, Jax Kynn, and Kiley J. McLean*

Disabled and/or chronically ill people are more likely to experience sexual and intimate partner violence (SV/IPV) than those without disability and/or chronic illness. Using an intersectional feminist framework, this chapter (1) overviews forms of harm and key terminology, (2) reviews what we know about disability, chronic illness, and SV/IPV, (3) provides considerations for working with disabled and/or chronically ill survivors (DCIS), (4) shares an idea for a relevant classroom activity, and (5) concludes with recommendations and resources.

### Forms of Harm and Terminology

SV/IPV is an umbrella term for multiple forms of interpersonal harm. We use these specific terms, because they are non-legal terms that could encompass a variety of behaviors. Sexual violence (SV) can occur across the life span and includes child sexual abuse, incest, sexual assault, rape, sexual exploitation, and elder abuse (Centers for Disease Control and Prevention, 2016). Beyond this physical and unwanted sexual touching, SV encompasses all forms of sexual harassment. It includes repeatedly asking someone for a date or to have sex as well as threatening someone, providing employment or workplace advancements contingent on sexual acts or sharing sexual photos or messages without consent. It can involve force, but can also involve coercion, manipulation, psychological tactics, or grooming (Jansen, 2016). SV most often occurs in contexts where people know one another such as within intimate partner relationships or among acquaintances and friends (Centers for Disease Control and Prevention, 2016). Even so, SV can be committed by those in helping professions such as medical providers, law enforcement officers, counselors, social work, and teachers.

Intimate partner violence (IPV) refers to violence, abuse, or aggression within a romantic or sexual relationship. An intimate partner can include both current/former spouses and/or dating partners. IPV can be a single act of violence and/or a pattern of abuse, and these acts of violence and abuse can vary in their severity and frequency. IPV is categorized in four main types of abuse: physical, sexual, psychological, and financial (Breiding et al., 2015).

- Physical abuse: a threat, attempt, or act of physical force meant to harm someone (e.g., hitting, kicking)
- Sexual abuse: forcing (or attempting to force) an intimate partner to participate in any kind of sex act when the individual does not or is unable to consent
- Psychological abuse: verbal abuse (e.g., insults and dehumanizing language), emotional manipulation, intimidation, dismissiveness (i.e., gaslighting), excessive jealousy, and other acts used to control and disempower an individual
- Financial abuse: Monitoring spending, controlling the amount of money a partner spends (e.g., giving a partner an "allowance"), impacting a partner's ability to work, taking public assistance checks, or taking money from a partner without permission

For the purposes of this chapter, we will use the term survivor as an umbrella term for people who have experienced one or more forms of SV/IPV. However, people may use a variety of terms (or no terms at all) to describe their experiences of violence, and some people who experience violence do not survive (i.e., people murdered by intimate partners, survivors of sexual violence who die by suicide). We use disabled and/or chronically ill survivors (DCIS) to refer to any people who are disabled and/or chronically ill and have experienced SV/IPV at some point in their lives.

## What We Know About SV/IPV and Disability

### *Prevalence*

Disabled and chronically ill people face both more SV (Amborski et al., 2021; Basile et al., 2016; Martin et al., 2006) and IPV (Breiding & Armour, 2016) than people who are not disabled or chronically ill. Studies vary on estimated rates of SV/IPV for disabled and chronically ill people, and more research is needed to systematically examine rates of SV/IPV by type/s of disability and survivor identities. Indeed, most studies have compared the likelihood of experiencing SV/IPV among cisgender heterosexual women who are disabled and nondisabled (Bowen & Swift, 2019). However, some research indicates higher rates of SV among disabled men (Mitra et al., 2016) than nondisabled men. Samples used to study SV/IPV and disability often lack diversity in or do not measure identities such as race/ethnicity, sexual orientation, and gender. There is also limited information on DCIS who are transitioning from youth to adulthood (Slayter et al., 2018) or who are older adults (Ansello & O'Neill, 2010).

Despite decades of research demonstrating that disabled and chronically ill people have a significantly increased risk of SV/IPV, their voices and experiences are often minimized or invisibilized in conversations about SV/IPV (Deerinwater, 2020; Woody, 2020). This minimization is heightened for survivors who hold multiple minoritized identities (e.g., Black queer disabled survivors). Indeed, as disability justice and liberation activist Lydia X. Z. Brown (2012) has shared:

> The intersectionalities between marginalized communities are not solely that members of one such group may also be members of others but also that the oppressions that affect one marginalized community intersect and overlap with the oppressions that affect others. You cannot operate in silos. You cannot draw attention to a set of issues purportedly belonging to only one marginalized community while ignoring their consequences for other marginalized communities.

Therefore, efforts to support survivors broadly must center DCIS, especially DCIS who face multiple forms of oppression.

Although there are studies showing higher rates of SV/IPV for people indicating learning disabilities (Majeed-Ariss et al., 2020), intellectual disabilities (Byrne, 2018), or who are D/deaf or hard of hearing (Smith & Pick, 2015), many studies combine all disabilities or fail to investigate rates of SV/IPV among people with multiple disabilities or chronic illnesses or who are multiply marginalized. For example, it is evident that disabled trans and nonbinary people (James et al., 2016) and disabled Indigenous women and girls (Gehl & Whittington-Walsh, 2016) are sexually assaulted at higher rates than their cisgender and non-Indigenous counterparts; however, there is limited information available on their experiences. SV by race and disability remain greatly unexamined, but higher prevalence is expected among Indigenous, Black, and Hispanic disabled persons (Stutts, 2022). Furthermore, disability is excluded in SV and IPV reporting practices on college campuses in the United States, despite disabled post-secondary students reporting high rates of SV and IPV (Cramer et al., 2022; National Council on Disability, 2018).

## *Impact*

These unusually high rates of abuse are coupled with increased severity of health, financial, and social consequences, which are further amplified by additional identification with other marginalized identities. For example, in one study, disabled women were found to be more likely to rate their mental health as poor, to have post-traumatic stress order symptoms, or to have difficulty sleeping or going to school than nondisabled women (Coston, 2019). In this study, bisexual disabled women were even more likely to face these consequences than their heterosexual and lesbian counterparts. DCIS are more likely to have depression, self-harm, use alcohol to cope, and experience stress post-assault than nondisabled survivors (Bonomi et al., 2018; Scherer et al., 2016).

Another consequence of SV/IPV is that disabled persons may acquire further impairments or injuries as a result of violence or abuse experienced (Ballan & Freyer, 2021). Furthermore, disability itself can be an outcome of IPV (García-Cuéllar et al., 2022). Traumatic brain injury (TBI), for example, is an underrecognized and underdiagnosed disabling consequence of SV/IPV (Banks, 2007; Manoranjan et al., 2022). Unfortunately, limited SV/IPV service providers and shelter organizations are aware of or prepared to support survivors with this debilitating injury (Haag et al., 2019). Additionally, care providers or caregivers may previously have and/or are currently harming DCIS. In situations like these, DCIS are forced to choose between receiving needed assistance with their daily routines or personal hygiene or limiting abuse toward them (Saxton et al., 2001). Furthermore, caregivers and care providers may retaliate against DCIS who disclose their abuse. This retaliation may include increased abuse during activities that require close physical contact, and often intimate care they provide, such as bathing, toileting, and changing clothes. Providers may also choose to withhold needed mobility aids or medication (Gilson et al., 2001). Increased risk of SV/IPV also adds to the likelihood that DCIS will die prematurely by intimate partner homicide or by suicide.

## Working With Disabled and Chronically Ill Survivors

Ableism is a cause of SV/IPV, and it is also a barrier to disclosing, reporting SV/IPV, and accessing support and services for SV/IPV (Yoshida et al., 2018). DCIS experiences are shaped not only by their disabilities and chronic illnesses but also how sexism, racism, heterosexism, cissexism, classism, xenophobia, and fatphobia shape DCIS lives and affect how service providers and support systems react to their disclosures of harm (Cramer & Plummer, 2009).

The following are key considerations in working with DCIS.

### *Believe and Advocate Alongside DCIS Interacting With Systems*

DCIS face a bias that they lack credibility or perceived capacity to disclose or report and, therefore, may worry they will not be believed when they disclose abuse (Stutts, 2022). Therefore, it is important to tell DCIS that you believe them if they disclose abuse. Disability and chronic illness can decrease the likelihood that DCIS will seek support from healthcare providers or be willing to disclose. For example, pregnant people often disclose abuse to healthcare providers who are assisting with their prenatal care, but partners of DCIS may prevent them from accessing such care or to only permit them to do so while they are in the room (Bradbury-Jones et al., 2015; Cramer et al., 2022). Increasing the points of contact through which DCIS could potentially disclose abuse and receive support could also be a valuable strategy, such as private screenings through disability-related organizations and disability income support providers (Slayter, 2009). Establishing integrated SV/IPV and mental healthcare programs could also help some DCIS access therapeutic support without increasing the number of organizations they need to contact or appointments they need to arrange (Nichols et al., 2018).

SV/IPV, mental health, and other supportive programs should also inventory how accessible they are to DCIS and take steps toward further accessibility. For example, DCIS may not be able to seek help because there are no communication devices or interpreters available; they physically cannot enter a domestic violence shelter without a ramp or are concerned they will not have food they can safely consume; they access transportation through the person who is harming them; they are concerned about leaving a service or emotional support animal; or there is no safe way for them to request accommodations (Browne et al., 2016; Smith & Pick, 2015). Counselors, educators, social workers, and advocates can play vital roles in outreach to organizations to gauge their accessibility for DCIS and work with other providers to ensure accommodations are met.

### Minimize Law Enforcement's Role in Accessing Care

SV/IPV is under-reported (Willot et al., 2020). Many help-seeking systems such as suicide prevention hotlines, orders of protection, and forensic nurse examinations and other post-SV care may directly or indirectly engage law enforcement, a barrier to help for Black and Brown disabled people who are also more likely than white disabled people to be assaulted, arrested without cause, or murdered by police (Lewis, 2017). DCIS who are not citizens of the country in which they are residing may also be afraid to seek support for IPV due to fear of deportation (Cramer et al., 2017). Therefore, confidential resources that do not intersect with law enforcement are crucial to DCIS accessing support.

### Increase Sex and Relationship Skills Education

DCIS, especially intellectually disabled survivors, may lack sex and relationship skill education. Our failure to provide inclusive sexual education are often rooted in pervasive societal myths that disabled people do not, should not, or cannot have sex and/or engage in romantic partnerships (Goulden & Kattari, 2022; Santinele Martino, 2022). This combination of lack of education and infantilization can lead to DCIS who are not able to describe what happened to them or seek help or support (Saxton et al., 2001). Some DCIS may also have difficulty talking about abuse with caregivers or providers who have indicated that they do not believe that disabled and chronically ill people can or should be sexual, or have relationships. Other DCIS may fear that if they were to disclose, they would lose access to their needed care. Education should be provided in stages informed by developmental level and initiated at a young age, including those who are disabled and chronically ill people (Bowen & Swift, 2019). This education should cover topics on providing consent and sexual health, such as use of contraceptives for sexually transmitted infections and pregnancy prevention (Schmidt et al., 2020). Sex and relationship skill education should be provided for all people that discusses disability and chronic illness, and debunks myths that disabled people are more likely to harm or abuse than nondisabled people. Sexual health information should be shared in both virtual and in-person locations frequented by disabled people (Powers et al., 2009).

### Decrease Isolation, Widen Support, and Enhance Communication

SV/IPV is exacerbated by isolation (Owen et al., 2018), and isolation is a common abuse tactic (Mitchell & Raghavan, 2021). DCIS are often reliant on caregivers and socially isolated and abusive partners who have the ability to control their contact with others or prevent opportunities for connection. Caregivers and partners of DCIS often have the ability to deny care or transportation, or even cut off their contact to the internet, communication devices, and other electronics (Brodwin & Siu, 2007; Cramer et al., 2022). Due to the potential for COVID-19 and future pandemics to exacerbate the severity of DCIS symptoms or heighten risk of death (Turk & McDermott, 2020), increasing access to telehealth and virtual meetings as well as proactively discussing mask use, boundaries, and social distancing can be critical to DCIS getting help (Lund et al., 2020). Virtual events should utilize qualified interpreters, and SV/IPV agencies need to hire signing therapists to ensure accessibility for D/deaf and hard-of-hearing survivors (Crowe, 2013). To decrease isolation, providers can help to increase points of contact, widen options for disclosing abuse, provide multiple ways to access resources and support (including virtual options), and widen social opportunities that do not necessitate travel to a specific in-person location (e.g., social media groups, chat platforms).

### Receive Ongoing Training and Feedback

Regardless of someone's role in sexuality or disability education or services, ongoing training specific to the provider's practice setting and populations served is crucial. DCIS cite lack of provider collaboration, misconceptions, lack of provider knowledge, and a need to repeatedly explain cultural factors as reasons they do not seek help (Cramer et al., 2017; McGilloway et al., 2020), so continued education and incorporation of that knowledge into practice, education, and outreach information is an important ongoing process. DCIS should also have opportunities to share feedback on how an organization or educator is doing in service of disabled and chronically ill people and should be compensated for their time for service on advisory boards and consultants (Sins Invalid, 2019).

**Classroom Activity: Searching for SV/IPV Support**

This activity focuses on seeking help as a DCIS. Students could complete this activity during class sessions in small groups, if there is time, or could conduct searches and reflection prior to class to prepare for discussion. Students could also complete this process independently and post what they find as a discussion post or assignment for an asynchronous online course.

*Learning Objectives*

1. Students will identify local organizations that serve SV/IPV survivors.
2. Students will appraise the accessibility of these organizations to DCIS based on website information.
3. Students will summarize barriers and facilitators to accessing help for DCIS.

*Instructor Preparation*

Depending on the scope of the course, decide on what specific form/s of harm you would like to emphasize (e.g., IPV from a caregiver, SV from a medical provider) or types of organizations you would like to include (view the following resource list for examples). The instructor could specify additional characteristics of the DCIS, specify access needs, or delineate a specific step (e.g., access emergency shelter). The following questions may be tailored to meet course objectives and audience but provide a starting point for consideration. Here is a sample prompt for a course targeting students becoming human service professionals:

> *You are searching for organizations in your area that serve SV/IPV survivors and are interested in learning how accessible they will be for DCIS. Conduct an internet search to see if you can find an organization near you that provides crisis intervention, counseling, advocacy, order of protection assistance, emergency shelter, or other services related to SV/IPV. Once you have identified that organization, navigate to their website and reflect on the following.*

## Reflection Worksheet

- What is the name of the organization?
- What is their website URL?
- What is their phone number or other relevant contact information?
- What are your first impressions of the website?
- Is there information relevant to DCIS or that indicates accessibility, potential for accommodations, or training of staff to work with DCIS? If so, what is included?
- Based on reviewing the website, who does the organization seem to serve? What is missing that you would like to know?

## Discussion Questions

- What did it feel like to search for information on this website?
- When you considered who the organization served, who was centered? Who was left out?
- If you could not find the information on the website, what would you do next?
- If you were designing a website for an organization and wanted to indicate that you served DCIS, what content would you include? Are there structural changes that you would make?

If there are SV/IPV-related organizations or providers that serve as models in your area for working with DCIS, make sure to talk about those resources at the end of your discussion and create space to talk about what they do well that could be modeled.

## Conclusion

Through believing DCIS, advocating alongside them within systems, and ensuring that they can access care without law enforcement involvement, educators and care providers can help DCIS exercise self-determination while getting needed support. To prevent both SV/IPV and secondary victimization (i.e., trauma from navigating hostile systems), we can all advocate for increased sexual health and relationship skills education and help curb isolation and create multiple pathways for communication. Preventing and responding to SV/IPV against disabled and chronically ill people will require continued training and venues for feedback that center DCIS voices.

## Recommendations Summary

- Provide training for clinical providers, staff, and educators on SV/IPV and the specific impacts to disabled people and communities.

- Use an intersectional lens to consider the impact of SV/IPV on disabled and chronically ill people.
- Use evidence-based and accessible SV/IPV screening tools and protocols such as CUES (Confidentiality, Universal Education and Empowerment, and Support): Educate Health Providers on How to Respond to Intimate Partner Violence (ipvhealth.org) or IPV-RIA (Risk Identification and Assessment): IPV-RIA-User-Guide-Final.pdf (schliferclinic.com).
- Believe DCIS when they share how they have been harmed, how that harm has affected them, and what kinds of support they might want to access.
- When safety planning with DCIS, incorporate questions about accommodations, accessibility, medical needs, and service animals.
- Locate financial funds and resources, available immediately and without lengthy application processes, to cover any associated costs DCIS encounter.
- Ensure access to communication devices, translators, or aids (such as dolls, drawing materials, or pictures), if applicable.
- Foster partnerships between SV/IPV services organizations, disability rights organizations, and self-advocacy networks.

## Resources

### Connections for Support
- The Deaf Hotline www.thedeafhotline.org/ and (855), 812–1001
- Deaf Abused Women Network www.deafdawn.org/
- National Domestic Violence Hotline www.thehotline.org/ 1–800–799-SAFE (7233)
- National Sexual Assault Hotline About the National Sexual Assault Telephone Hotline | RAINN 1–800–656-HOPE (4673) or via online portal https://online.rainn.org
- Trans Lifeline https://translifeline.org/ and (877), 565–8860
- Hot Peach Pages www.hotpeachpages.net/

### Further Learning
- Abused & Brain Injured (ABI) Toolkit ABI Research Lab
- Centre for Innovation in Campus Mental Health Sexual Violence Response on Campus Toolkit
- DAWN Canada Factsheet: Women with Disabilities and Violence
- End Abuse of People with Disabilities (Vera Institute of Justice) Home – End Abuse of People with Disabilities (endabusepwd.org)
- Guidelines for Providing Rights-Based and Gender-Responsive Services to Address Gender-Based Violence and Sexual and Reproductive Health

and Rights (Women Enabled International). https://womenenabled.org/reports/wei-and-unfpa-guidelines-disability-gbv/ress Gender-Based Violence and Sexual and Reproductive Health and Rights – Women Enabled International
- National Public Radio – Abused and betrayed (special series): www.npr.org/series/575502633/abused-and-betrayed
- Not on the Radar: Sexual Assault of College Students with Disabilities (National Council on Disability) Not on the Radar: Sexual Assault of College Students with Disabilities | NCD.gov
- The Revolution Starts at Home: Confronting Intimate Violence within Activist Communities (Chen, Dulani, and Piepzna-Samarsinha, Editors)
- Rooted in Rights #DisabilityToo: #DisabilityToo – Rooted in Rights
- Training and Resources from the Washington Coalition of Sexual Assault Programs: Disability (wcsap.org)

**References**

Amborski, A. M., Bussieres, E., Vallancourt-Morel, M. P., & Joyal, C. C. (2021). Sexual violence against persons with disabilities: A meta-analysis. *Trauma, Violence, and Abuse.* Advance online publication. https://doi.org/10.1177/1524838021995975

Ansello, E. F., & O'Neill, P. (2010). Abuse, neglect, and exploitation: Considerations in aging with lifelong disabilities. *Journal of Elder Abuse & Neglect, 22*(1–2), 105–130. https://doi.org/10.1080/08946560903436395

Ballan, M. S., & Freyer, M. (2021). Addressing intimate partner violence with female patients with chronic physical disabilities: The role of physical therapists. *Disability and Rehabilitation, 43*(10), 1404–1409. https://doi.org/10.1080/09638288.2019.1664648

Banks, M. E. (2007). Overlooked but critical: Traumatic brain injury as a consequence of interpersonal violence. *Trauma, Violence & Abuse, 8*(3), 290–298. https://doi.org/10.1177%2F1524838007303503

Basile, K. C., Breiding, M. J., & Smith, S. G. (2016). Disability and risk of recent sexual violence in the United States. *American Journal of Public Health, 106*(5), 928–933. https://doi.org/10.2105/AJPH.2015.303004

Bowen, E., & Swift, C. (2019). The prevalence and correlates of partner violence used and experienced by adults with intellectual disabilities: A systematic review and call to action. *Trauma, Violence, and Abuse, 20*(5), 693–705. https://doi.org/10.1177/1524838017728707

Bradbury-Jones, C., Breckenridge, J. P., Devaney, J., Duncan, F., Kroll, T., Lazenbatt, A., & Taylor, J. (2015). Priorities and strategies for improving disabled women's access to maternity services when they are affected by domestic abuse: A multimethod study using concept maps. *BMC Pregnancy and Childbirth, 15*, 350. https://doi.org/10.1186/s12884-015-0786-7

Breiding, M. J., & Armour, B. S. (2016). The association between disability and intimate partner violence in the United States. *Annals of Epidemiology, 25*(6), 455–457. https://doi.org/10.1016/j.annepidem.2015.03.017

Breiding, M. J., Basile, K. C., Smith, S. G., Black, M. C., & Mahendra, R. (2015). *Intimate partner violence surveillance uniform definitions and recommended data elements, Version 2.0.* National Center for Injury Prevention and Control, Centers for Disease Control and Prevention.

Brodwin, M. G., & Siu, F. W. (2007). Domestic violence against women who have disabilities: What educators need to know. *Education, 127*(4), 548–552.

Brown, L. X. Z. (2012). *Sexism, ableism, and rape culture. Autistic Hoya – A blog by Lydia X. Z. Brown about sexism, ableism, and rape culture.* www.autistichoya.com/2012/10/sexism-ableism-and-rape-cu

Browne, A., Agha, A., Demyan, A., & Beatriz, E. (2016). *Examining criminal justice response to and help-seeking patterns of sexual violence survivors with disabilities.* Vera Institute of Justice. www.ojp.gov/pdffiles1/nij/grants/250196.pdf

Byrne, G. (2018). Prevalence and psychological sequelae of sexual abuse among individuals with an intellectual disability: A review of recent literature. *Journal of Intellectual Disabilities, 22*(3), 294–310. https://doi.org/10.1177/1744629517698844

Centers for Disease Control and Prevention, National Center for Injury Prevention and Control. (2016). *Preventing multiple forms of violence: A strategic vision for connecting the dots.* www.cdc.gov/violenceprevention/pdf/strategic_vision.pdf-Dots (cdc.gov)

Coston, B. M. (2019). Disability, sexual orientation, and the mental health outcomes of intimate partner violence: A comparative study of women in the US. *Disability and Health Journal, 12*(2), 164–170. https://doi.org/10.1016/j.dhjo.2018.11.002

Cramer, E. P., Choi, Y. J., & Ross, A. I. (2017). Race, culture & abuse of persons with disabilities. In A. L. Johnson, J. R. Nelson, & E. M. Lund (Eds.), *Religion, disability, and interpersonal violence* (pp. 89–110). Springer.

Cramer, E. P., & Plummer, S. B. (2009). People of color with disabilities: Intersectionality as a framework for analyzing intimate partner violence in social, historical, and political contexts. *Journal of Aggression, Maltreatment, and Trauma, 18*, 162–181. https://doi.org/10.1080/10926777082675635

Cramer, E. P., Plummer, S. B., & Ross, A. I. (2022). Intersectionality and intimate partner violence and abuse: IPV and people with disabilities. In R. Geffner, J. W. White, L. K. Hamberger, A. Rosenbaum, V. Vaughan-Eden, & V. I. Vieth (Eds.), *Handbook of interpersonal violence and abuse across the lifespan.* Springer.

Crowe, T. V. (2013). Intimate partner violence in the deaf community. *Journal of the American Deafness and Rehabilitation Association, 46*(2), 71–85.

Deerinwater, J. (2020). The erasure of Indigenous people in chronic illness. In A. Wong (Ed.), *Disability visibility: First-person stories from the twenty-first century* (pp. 47–52). Vintage Books.

García-Cuéllar, M. M., Pastor-Moreno, G., Ruiz-Pérez, I., & Henares-Montiel, J. (2022). The prevalence of intimate partner violence against women with disabilities: A systematic review of the literature. *Disability and Rehabilitation*, ahead-of-print, 1–8. https://doi.org/10.1080/09638288.2022.2025927

Gehl, L., & Whittington-Walsh, F. (2016). *Indigenous women and girls with disabilities bigger targets of sexual violence.* Rabble.ca. https://rabble.ca/anti-racism/indigenous-women-and-girls-disabilities-bigger-targets-sexual-violence/

Gilson, S. F., Cramer, E. P., & DePoy, E. (2001). Redefining abuse of women with disabilities: A paradox of limitation and expansion. *Affilia, 16*(2), 220–235. https://doi.org/10.1177/08861090122094235

Goulden, A., & Kattari, S. K. (2022). Sexual orientation, sexuality, and the disability community. In E. Slayter & L. Johnson (Eds.), *Social work practice and the disability communities: An intersectional anti-oppressive approach.*

Pressbooks. https://rotel.pressbooks.pub/disabilitysocialwork/chapter/chapter-8-sexual-orientation-and-sexuality/

Haag, H., Sokoloff, S., Macgregor, N., Broekstra, S., Cullen, N., & Colantonio, A. (2019). Battered and brain injured: Assessing knowledge of traumatic brain injury among intimate partner violence service providers. *Journal of Women's Health*, 28(7), 990–996.

James, S. E., Herman, J. L., Rankin, S., Keisling, M., Mottet, L., & Anafi, M. (2016). *The report of the 2015 U.S. Transgender survey*. National Center for Transgender Equality. www.transequality.org/sites/default/files/docs/USTS-Full-Report-FINAL.PDF

Jansen, H. (2016). *Measuring prevalence of violence against women: Key terminology*. Asia and the Pacific Regional Office, United Nations Population Fund. kNOwVAWdata Key Terminology.pdf (unfpa.org)

Lewis, T. A. (2017). Emmett Till and the pervasive erasure of disability in conversations about white supremacy and police violence. *Talila A. Lewis Blog*. www.talilalewis.com/blog/emmett-till-disability-erasurepremacy & Police Violence – TALILA A. LEWIS (talilalewis.com)

Lund, E. M., Forber-Pratt, A. J., Wilson, C., & Mona, L. R. (2020). The COVID-19 pandemic, stress, and trauma in the disability community: A call to action. *Rehabilitation Psychology*, 65(4), 313–322. https://doi.org/10.1037/rep0000368

Majeed-Ariss, R., Rodriguez, P. M., & White, C. (2020). The disproportionately high prevalence of learning disabilities among adults attending Saint Marys Sexual Assault referral centre. *Journal of Applied Research on Intellectual Disabilities*, 35, 595–603. https://doi.org/10.1111/jar.12703

Manoranjan, B, Scott, T., Szasz, O., Bzovsky, S., O'Malley, L., Sprague, S., Perera, G., Bhandari, M., & Turkstra, L. (2022). Prevalence and perception of intimate partner violence-related traumatic brain injury. *Journal of Head Trauma Rehabilitation*, 37(1), 53–61. https://doi.org/10.1097/HTR.0000000000000749

Martin, S. L., Ray, N., Sotres-Alvarez, D., Kupper, L. L., Morocco, K. E., Dickens, P. A., Scandlin, D., & Gizlice, Z. (2006). Physical and sexual assault of women with disabilities. *Violence Against Women*, 12(9), 823–837. https://doi.org/10.1177%2F1077801206292672

McGilloway, C., Smith, D., & Galvin, R. (2020). Barriers faced by adults with intellectual disabilities who experience sexual assault: A systematic review and meta-synthesis. *Journal of Applied Research on Intellectual Disabilities*, 33, 51–66. https://doi.org/10.1111/jar.12445

Mitchell, J. E., & Raghavan, C. (2021). The impact of coercive control on use of specific sexual coercion tactics. *Violence Against Women*, 27(2), 187–206. https://doi.org/10.1177/1077801219884127

Mitra, M., Mouradian, V. E., Fox, M. H., & Pratt, C. (2016). Prevalence and characteristics of sexual violence against men with disabilities. *American Journal of Preventative Medicine*, 50(3), 311–317. https://doi.org/10.1016/j.amepre.2015.07.030

National Council on Disability. (2018). *Not on the radar: Sexual assault of college students with disabilities*. https://ncd.gov

Nichols, E. M., Bonomi, A., Kammes, R., & Miller, E. (2018). Service seeking experiences of college-aged sexual and intimate partner violence victims with a mental health or behavioral disability. *Journal of American College Health*, 66(6), 487–495. https://doi.org/10.1080/07448481.2018.1440572

Owen, M., Hiebert-Murphy, D., & Ristock, J. (2018). Disability, violence, and social change: An introduction. In M. Owen, D. Hiebert-Murphy, & J. Ristock (Eds.),

*Not a new problem: Violence in the lives of disabled women* (pp. 1–14). Fernwood Publishing.

Powers, L. E., Renker, P., Robinson-Whelen, S., Oschwald, M., Hughes, R., Swank, P., & Curry, M. A. (2009). Interpersonal violence and women with disabilities: Analysis of safety promoting behaviors. *Violence Against Women, 15*(9), 1040–1069. https://doi.org/10.1177/1077801209340309

Santinele Martino, A. (2022). Ethically important moments: Researching the intimate lives of adults labeled/with intellectual disabilities. *Qualitative Research*. Advance online publication. https://doi.org/10.1177/14687941221110179

Saxton, M., Curry, M. A., Powers, L. E., Maley, S., Eckels, K., & Gross, J. (2001). "Bring my scooter so I can leave you": A study of disabled women handling abuse by personal assistance providers. *Violence Against Women, 7*(4), 393–417. https://doi.org/10.1177%2F10778010122182523

Scherer, H. L., Snyder, J. A., & Fisher, B. S. (2016). Intimate partner violence victimization among college students with and without disabilities: Prevalence of and relationship to emotional well-being. *Journal of Interpersonal Violence, 31*(1), 49–80. https://doi.org/10.1177/0886260514555126

Schmidt, E. K., Brown, C., & Darragh, A. (2020). Scoping review of sexual health education interventions for adolescents and young adults with intellectual or developmental disabilities. *Sexuality and Disability, 38*, 439–453. https://doi.org/10.1007/s11195-019-09593-4

Sins Invalid. (2019). *Skin, tooth, and bone: The basis of movement is our people: A disability justice primer* (2nd ed.). Sins Invalid.

Slayter, E. (2009). Intimate partner violence against women with disabilities: Implications for disability service system case management practice. *Journal of Aggression, Maltreatment & Trauma, 18*(2), 182–199. https://doi.org/10.1080/10926770802675668

Slayter, E., Lightfoot, E., & Leisey, M. (2018). Intimate partner violence among transitional-aged women with and without disabilities: Implications for social work practice. *Journal of Aggression, Maltreatment & Trauma, 27*(3), 275–290. https://doi.org/10.1080/10926771.2017.1382630

Smith, R. A., & Pick, L. H. (2015). Sexual assault experienced by deaf female undergraduates: Prevalence and characteristics. *Violence and Victims, 30*(6), 948–959. https://doi.org/10.1891/0886-6708.VV-D-14-00057

Stutts, L. A. (2022). Sexual abuse among individuals with disabilities. In R. Geffner, J. W. White, L. K. Hamberger, A. Rosenbaum, V. Vaughan-Eden, & V. I. Vieth (Eds.), *Handbook of interpersonal violence and abuse across the lifespan*. Springer.

Turk, M. A., & McDermott, S. (2020). The COVID-19 pandemic and people with disability. *Disability Health Journal, 13*(3). https://doi.org/10.1016/j.dhjo.2020.100944

Willot, S., Badger, W., & Evans, V. (2020). People with intellectual disability: Underreporting sexual violence. *The Journal of Adult Protection*. https://doi.org/10.1108/JAP-05-2019-0016

Woody, J. (2020). The isolation of being deaf in prison. In A. Wong (Ed.), *Disability visibility: First-person stories from the twenty-first century* (pp. 58–62). Vintage Books.

Yoshida, K. K., Bunch, M., Odette, F., Hardie, S. L., & Willis, H. (2018). Taking action: Gender-based violence, disability, and the social determinants of health. In M. Owen, D. Hiebert-Murphy, & J. Ristock (Eds.), *Not a new problem: Violence in the lives of disabled women* (pp. 172–194). Fernwood Publishing.

# 14
# EXPLORING THE INTERSECTIONS OF SEX WORK AND DISABILITY

What Helping Professionals Should Consider

*Kimberly Fuentes, Adrienne Graf, and Meg Panichelli*

### Introduction

For people with disabilities, sex work is often an accessible form of work within capitalist structures with an ever-diminishing welfare state. However, there is a limited amount of academic scholarship that focuses on sex workers with disabilities, and instead more literature that focuses on sex workers providing services to people with disabilities. In this chapter, we attend to the experiences of sex workers with disabilities across interpersonal, structural, and institutional levels. Increasingly, the grey literature shares these stories, needs, and requests for movement alliance in an attempt to cultivate a more intersectional, accessible, and liberated world.

Disabilities may show up for sex workers in a variety of physical, cognitive, intellectual, and neurological forms before, during, or after trading sex for money. For instance, someone who lives with chronic illnesses, mental health disabilities, pain flares, and or remissions of illness may find traditional work schedules and environments incongruent with their daily needs (Gray, 2022). Trauma at the hands of law enforcement, social service workers, anti-trafficking legislation, dangerous or untrustworthy clients, and vulnerability of risk may all show up in the work lives of sex workers, thereby exacerbating or cultivating disabilities. Supplemental Security Income (SSI) imposes restrictions on the amount of additional money that can be received before benefits for a single person are reduced, which is a maximum of $2,000 for an individual (Altiraifi, 2020). At the same time, the costs of living, including medical bills, housing expenses, transportation, food, and beyond, may far exceed SSI income and that which is allowed on top of it. Therefore, a way of finding underground economy work becomes imperative for people with disabilities and sex work can be a manageable option.

## Disability Justice Framework

As authors of this chapter, we are guided by Sins Invalid, a disability justice-based performance project, and their framework of "10 Principles for Disability Justice." As Snider (2021) so beautifully articulates:

> [D]isability justice is a movement, a mindset, a point of view, and a set of methodologies that prioritizes intersectionality, interdependence, and solidarity in working towards making the world a more just place for neurodivergent, disabled, Mad, and chronically ill people.
> *(Snider, 2021, p. 159)*

One of these principles is recognizing wholeness or the understanding that each individual carries inherent worth with rich life experiences separate from their production value in a capitalist society (Sins Invalid, 2015). As authors, we collectively reside at multiple intersections, inclusive of lived experience within the sex trade as well as chronic illness and disability. As researchers, faculty, and social workers, we are struck with the tension of embodying this principle while also recognizing that much of social work practice rests on the brokerage of state resources for the conceptualized deserving. People with disabilities continuously face discrimination and lower wages in the workforce due to many factors including stigma and perceptions of productivity (Kruse et al., 2018).

## Historical Construction of Deviance

Beginning in early United States (U.S.)-based social welfare policy and social work starting in the late 1800s and continuing still today, a trend has been to punish marginalized groups who did not and do not fit into the "norm." In particular, mental illness has been used as a way of explaining the cause of behaviors that did not circumscribe to white, puritan, chaste, heterosexual, and nondisabled social categories. Casting both disability and sex trade as deviant, disability was used to explain why specifically a woman would step outside of the expected gendered norms by being sexually promiscuous (Blewett, 2014; Hall, 2004; Wahab, 2002).

Middle-class white women social workers, who worked in hopes of re-inscribing social and moral order, targeted supports and services toward preventing the development of risk factors for women at risk of entering prostitution. Social psychologists classified sex workers as

> emotionally sick people who tried to hide their lesbian tendencies by openly engaging in sexual activities with men for money. They were also described to suffer from anxiety, have a poor self-image, have an inability to form lasting relationships, to be lonely, and suffer from depression.
> 
> *(Wahab, 2002, p. 50)*

Similar to the linking of disabilities with sex work, so to was the link drawn between sex work and lesbianism, because both groups defied the heterosexual, chaste, pure, wait-until-marriage-for-sex gender roles that women were assigned. Therefore, the only explanation could be that both groups struggled from mental illnesses including anxiety, poor self-image, an inability to form lasting relationships, to be lonely, and suffer from depression (Duggan, 1993; Faderman, 1978; Hall, 2004; Miller, 2000; Wahab, 2002).

In her influential text, *thinking sex*, Gayle Rubin charted the landscape of conservative, liberal, religious, and feminist-based legal advocacy on sex laws and also engaged with the lived realities of communities and individuals labeled as deviants. Reflective of the institutions invested in the legislation of sodomy were the issues of homosexuality, prostitution, age of consent, sex outside of marriage, kink, and non-monogamy. Intrinsic to such debates, were deeply embedded philosophies of morality, fear, and non-conformity. Binary concepts such as innocence and deviance were pitted against one another depending on the political ideology of activists proposing and defending sex laws. Rubin (1984) addresses the paradox of instituting morality in the following passage:

> Moral panics rarely alleviate any real problem, because they are aimed at chimeras and signifiers. They draw on the pre-existing discursive structure which invents victims in order to justify treating "vices" as crimes. The criminalization of innocuous behaviours such as homosexuality, prostitution, obscenity, or recreational drug use, is rationalized by portraying them as menaces to health and safety, women and children, national security, the family, or civilization itself.
> 
> *(p. 163)*

As Rubin notes, the rationalization of behaviors as "deviant," "immoral," or "vice" by asserting that such behaviors harm the health and safety of the general public, women and children, state security, and the family is ultimately fueled by racism, sexism, classism, ableism, and homophobia. If homosexuality, prostitution, obscenity, or recreational drug use is perceived to be a threat to national citizens, then anyone engaged in sexual behavior falling outside of white, cis, heterosexual, male/female, procreative sex in which a penis was inserted in a vagina, risked the possibility of surveillance and criminalization (Rubin, 1984).

## Constructing the Deserving Versus Undeserving

There have been many systematic strategies used to distinguish the deserving from the undeserving poor, many of which were illuminated during the administrative implementation of the War on Drugs, the War on Poverty, and the Welfare Reform Act of 1996 (Abramovitz, 2017). Although social workers are called to work toward the elimination of poverty, social workers have been complicit in reinforcing such binaries. Sociologist Kari Lerum noted that sex workers are often framed as diseased or sick due to perceived experiences of sexual abuse and drug addiction (1998). Lerum discusses the tendency for helping professionals to assign "sick" status so that sex workers can be seen as *victims in need of help and fixing*.

Furthermore, when substance use is framed as a disease, there is an explanation for why people do bad things, rather than examining the systemic factors that may lead to abuse and drug addiction (Lerum, 1998). This framework of victim or deviant also partially aligns with an individual's willingness to leave "the life." If a sex worker does not want to leave the sex trade, this binary blames them for any harm that comes to them because it's what they chose. At the same time, it fails to acknowledge the benefits that sex workers experience in sex work that are not otherwise provided by the path of admitting victimhood that social service providers offer. For many, the income and financial freedom that sex work provides easily outperform a typical nine-to-five job. Given the reoccurring themes (historically) of labeling sex workers either as victims of social, physical, or mental disease or as deviant, criminal, and sexually promiscuous (and dangerous to society), it is worth going beyond a binary framework to engage with the cultural context, shaping the lives of people in the sex trades.

For instance, public health scholar and ethnographic researcher, Kelly Knight shares that the pregnant people using drugs, living in single-room occupancy hotels, and trading sex for money in her study on pregnancy, addiction, and poverty experienced "the complex relationship between addiction and poverty as addiction was reconstituted from a disabling medical condition (addiction to a disease) to an immoral, malingering set of criminal behaviors (using welfare funds to buy drugs)" (2015, p. 109). The complexity here is similar to what Lerum describes as at one point in time being seen as "sick," but then the same conditions determining "sick status" shifted to criminalized or deviant status. Shifting the status situates a lack of capability onto the individual, thereby further limiting opportunities for systemic change and access to healthcare, stable housing, food, and licit employment options. Similarly, Knight acknowledges that for some people who use drugs, a PTSD diagnosis could be a path "by which advocates and care providers create a space of social recognition, and gain stabilizing economic and housing benefits" (2015, p. 105). Thereby recognizing PTSD as disability, and one that commonly occurs among people who use drugs and trade sex, enables someone to potentially receive benefits that can support their well-being.

Disability as an identity has existed in an ongoing state of flux, lacking a consistent description (Grue, 2016). Similar to the construction of deviance regarding sex work, throughout history, people with physical and intellectual disabilities have been labeled deviant, inferior, and cursed (Munyi, 2012). In the U.S., the rise of institutionalization proliferated in the 1800s. Themes around deserving and productivity were prevalent; many of the early institutions were workhouses. Eugenics was rampant during this time, with many doctors performing forced sterilization and lobotomies (Nielsen, 2013).

As industrialization rose, so did the number of people with disabilities (Meldon, 2017). Disability as a result of dangerous labor conditions gave rise to public conversations about impairment while working, the need for trade unions, and the suffering of laborers as an inevitable part of industry (Turner & Blackie, 2018). Even for those conceptualized as worthy, laborers previously able-bodied who had become disabled at work, there were measures in place to separate the deserving from the undeserving. In England in the mid-19th century, laborers who were found to be negligent at work could lose their disability benefits provided by the trade union. They could additionally be fined if they were discovered drinking alcohol while receiving union benefits (Turner & Blackie, 2018).

Shifting concepts of normality underpin the social construction of disability, similar to the previously explored construction of deviance as it pertains to women suspected to be involved in the sex trade. Baynton (2016) explores the racist framing of intelligence and the use of early eugenics to justify chattel slavery. Similar arguments were used by opponents of women's suffrage, arguing that due to weakness and frailty, women were unable to participate in civic engagement (Baynton, 2016). Trent (1998) further outlines this connection by highlighting the display of disability images at the 1904 World's Fair. The discussions and display of so-called defectives call to mind similar presentations throughout the 19th century of non-European bodies aka "primitives." This popular conception of both non-whiteness and disability as "the Other" had immense implications for public health (sterilization), education, the continued rise of eugenics, and civic discrimination (Trent, 1998).

### *The Current Academic Literature on Sex Work and Disability*

When reviewing the literature, it was evident that researchers view sex workers who provide services to disabled people as the few that deserve validation through their labor. Scholars have framed this acknowledgment as an important way for female sex workers to make strides in their own bodily autonomy for their work (Garofalo Geymonat, 2019). While acknowledging some forms of sex work hold value for the sex worker rights movement overall (Sanders, 2007), we align with critics who ask, who is left behind when we validate only some forms of sex work? Often in these descriptions of sex workers as healers by providing services to clients with disabilities, in the same breath there is an unnecessary contrast with sex workers who wore tight clothes and bright makeup, implied to be their less worthy counterparts (O'Brien, 1990). As small segments of sex workers become "sex surrogates," where does this leave the whores and hookers who have been exempted from the professionalization of sex work? This blatant whorephobia (Tempest, 2019), or the marginalization toward sex workers that stems from a disdain for their existence, creates tension for recognition within the sex worker community. The stratification of labor that happens by valuing some workers over others harms worker solidarity and does little to combat the larger systems of criminalization that affect the collective.

The discourse on sex work and disability is a classic example of ignoring the intersection of two or more identity factors. Academic articles have primarily viewed sex workers as service providers with little acknowledgment that sex workers can be clients with disabilities themselves (Sanders, 2007; Thomsen, 2015). Thomsen explored questions about conditional exemptions for sex buyers if they are disabled. This popular argument rests upon two assumptions: the ableist assumption that disabled people cannot have consensual sex or that they cannot be sexually desirable, and that sex work is bad for society overall unless it can provide a service of value for the aforementioned group (Earp & Moen, 2015). This fails to consider how sex work as a whole deserves to be recognized as real work on the basis of their claim to labor protections regardless of their labor's value to society. Furthermore, sex work is a disability issue.

It is no surprise that traditional underpaying, in-person, eight-hour-day jobs are inaccessible to many people with disabilities. While not directly a response to this, sex work is one mechanism that can address the barriers to finding and keeping a traditional job while averaging a higher hourly rate, which allows its workforce to work less hours for the same amount of pay. Some disabled people may utilize sex work to supplement their income while others who have multiple marginalized identities such as being racialized, transgender, gender diverse, and/or immigrants may only have access to sex work for income (Tastrom, 2019). Sex work advocates have called for greater attention to the institutional oppressions sex workers face that cannot be solved by decriminalization, particularly ableism, to ensure that they can work safely (Lemoon, 2021). A key aspect of this is the integration of narratives by sex workers with disabilities into the discourse of sex work and disability.

## *Voices of Sex Workers With Disabilities*

In efforts to recognize wholeness and intersectionality, we must center on the experiences of disabled sex workers. Through in-depth interviews with sex workers, we can glean the importance of sex work to surviving in a world that is often unkind to people who cannot operate on its levels of productivity (Sins Invalid, 2015). In 2021, 13 in-depth qualitative interviews were held in Los Angeles with sex workers to assess their access to community care and the intersectional factors that may limit community inclusion, such as the whorearchy (Fuentes, 2022). Disability justice asks that we engage in cross-movement solidarity; resisting a one-issue fight not only allows us to honor the entire personhood of individuals but also serves as a reminder that these struggles are interconnected. The interviews were a testament to this, because even though they were not explicitly asked about disability, several workers expressed that sex work allows them to cushion the costs of buying their medication and served as a space of inclusion into the job market. Jenna is a trans sex worker with an autoimmune disease that has drastically changed her access to the formal labor market.

> It got to the point where doing Uber eats and stuff was not even an option. It became like, "I can't keep fucking doing this". I'm going up too many stairs going into too many places is too active. I'm noticeably trans and disabled. When I was job hunting, Warner Brothers was transphobic straight to my face.
> 
> *(Jenna – November 2021)*

Through Jenna's experiences, we see how the convergence of transphobia, ableism, and whorephobia intersect and compound to isolate community members who then have to fight battles on multiple fronts. Jenna highlights a lack of barriers to entry as a draw for sex work. She didn't have to endure discriminatory hiring practices to become a webcam model, and while ableism and transphobia still exist in her clientele, she has the autonomy to reduce the access that those people have to her. Not only was the traditional job market inaccessible to her through hiring practices but also many of the jobs that she was able to attain came with physical barriers that were too taxing on her health. Being able to be a webcam model and content creator gave her the flexibility to harness her skills, give her an income, and allow her rest. Jenna described that she had even chosen to frontload much of her content creation so that it would automatically post every day, meaning that she often had a week where she could just rest knowing that she was still making the money she needed to survive.

In 2022, the Sex Worker Outreach Project Los Angeles (SWOPLA) held focus groups to understand the needs of parents who engaged in sex work. When asked about the value of sex work for their parenting, many several sex working parents mentioned the ways that disability factored into their answers. Here, Bella shares the importance of being able to balance meeting her family's financial needs and her own well-being:

> I have dyslexia dysgraphia. So I have a bunch of neurodivergent issues that only get worse with time and age due to my back and spine and things not communicating properly. I think the disabilities that I identify with have influenced my decision to work as little as possible with as much outcome and reward as possible due to being able to have to keep that up. You have to have that balance between physicality and financial stability.
> 
> *(Bella – June 2022, SWOPLA Parenting focus group)*

Sex workers already employ a principle of disability justice through their practice of anti-capitalist politics. In the U.S., where the norm is a nine-to-five job with limited breaks and vacation time, Bella is able to meet her needs without sacrificing her health. Typically, if her disabilities limit the amount of time she is able to participate as a "productive" member of society, Bella would be systematically punished through a lower quality of life that is reinforced through disability benefits that barely allow her to meet her basic needs. While we should be working toward a culture of interdependence rather than individualism that pressures people to meet all of their needs, it is a huge accomplishment that Bella is able to meet both her needs and that of her family on sex work alone.

### So What?

The principle of collective access asserts that people with disabilities should be able to ask that our needs be met without compromising our integrity. The reality for disabled people is that it can be challenging to receive the government benefits that they are owed. These benefits (i.e., Social Security Disability Insurance in the U.S., Canadian Pension Plan, Erwerbsminderungsrente in Germany, Benefício de Prestação Continuada in Brazil) exhibit strict eligibility criteria that counterintuitively make individuals jump through unnecessary hoops to receive them. The contradictory nature of these benefits is that they often force their beneficiaries to live without significant savings and with a minimal income. The receipt of these benefits further cements their position in poverty. A disabled sex worker shares her story of resistance against these barriers:

> The Government fought me for three and a half years, to get disability, which they finally awarded me. And I still don't give a fuck. I'm working under the table. I create everything to crypto, send it to crypto, send it back to myself through different digital accounts. It never touches the bank account. It's not fucking in any sort of Government eye and as far as I'm concerned, it's what I'm owed because they jerked me around for three and a half years trying to tell me I wasn't disabled. And I had doctors left and right being like this isn't even up for debate.
> 
> *(Jenna – November 2021)*

While Jenna received affirmation from her medical provider, which is not a standard response in itself, the final decision on whether she is worthy of receiving these benefits often falls to impersonal government systems of approval. Jenna's lack of confidence in receiving the aid she is owed is informed by the government's lack of acknowledgment that sex work is work. The invalidation of her labor goes hand in hand with the invalidation of her disability. This practice of finding pathways to hide their income is common among sex workers as a way to avoid getting outed for sex work. When sex workers are misclassified or when their existence is outright criminalized, they are left with no choice but to continue their work in secrecy out of fear of prosecution.

Due to criminalization, sex workers often find themselves at odds with government providers but when critical services are gatekept by social services, sex workers are forced to engage with forces that invalidate them. This practice that Jenna was already employing to hide her sex work involvement serves a dual purpose because she needs the income that sex work provides but her work in itself cannot provide her with disability benefits to pay for her life-saving medication. Current service provision is putting people in the position to choose whether they want to give up benefits that are owed to them or their work that helps to improve their quality of life. This approach to care ironically makes people like Jenna have to jump through extra hoops to access a service that is supposed to be accessible for people with disabilities.

As a group that often lies at the intersection of several system-impacted identities, sex workers are uniquely posited to recognize areas of greatest need for improvement. When asked about what it would mean to be a sex-worker-affirming service provider, Rachel identified that the issue arises when services are not led by those who will be most impacted by them:

> I think like it's easy for administrators and executives of these places [service providers] to be like, 'we just provide the service and then we think

about accessibility'. Like we add-on accessibility to like trans people or Spanish speakers or disabled folk. They don't like to think about how to make a service that is just going to be accessible to begin with.

*(Rachel – October 2021)*

Accessibility should not be an afterthought. Rachel highlights a key concept of disability justice which is that organizations should be doing more than just adding accessibility into their efforts. A sustainable dedication to disability justice consists of changing the systems of power to mend histories of ableism and work toward building with leaders in the disabled community. Disabled people of varying lived experiences should be key contributors to new efforts because they are best positioned to understand how a client will experience your services. Furthermore, we should not be entrusting more control to systems that have a track record of dehumanizing our communities. A key step toward collective access is imagining ways that we can redistribute service provision for people with disabilities to systems that are accessible, caring, and non-carceral.

There are important steps that organizations can take to conduct an internal audit on how aligned they are with the principles of disability justice (Lakshmi Piepzna-Samarasinha, 2018). Protocols around ensuring accessibility of services and events cannot be overlooked, and yet this outer-facing response to people with disabilities is often where most organizations taper off. A deeper look asks that we reflect on not only how many disabled people are hired and valued in leadership positions but also how the organization enmeshes itself with disability organizing and community engagement. However, as the experiences of sex workers with disabilities reveal, often it is the larger system-level policies that gatekeep documentation and prevent access to services, so we must identify the policies that prevent us from truly being a resource rather than another barrier.

Examination of structural vulnerability is essential to understanding how lived experience of disabilities informs participation in the sex trade. Similar to how the construction of deviance explored earlier in this chapter focused on the presumed vulnerability of white women to the ills of prostitution, (Wahab, 2002) disability has been largely understood to be an individual vulnerability. Blewett (2014) argues that disabled people engaged in the sex trade are made vulnerable by punitive, controlling, and ableist laws and policies. Utilizing a framework of necrocapitalism,[1] we contend that a necessary function of capitalism and the state is mass death and disability (Bobby Banerjee, 2008). If then, disability is an inevitable outcome of the colonialist, capitalist state, what incentive does the state have to ameliorate the conditions of disabled people?

Service providers should be working in conjunction with sex-worker-led organizations when possible and ensure that their approach to helping clients does not reproduce stigmatizing messaging that condemns the sex trade. Sex-worker-led organizations have abandoned the tired tropes of "victim" and "deviant" and instead acknowledge sex work as work, in all the legitimacy of any other labor that is deserving of rights and protection (Oselin & Weitzer, 2013).

### Recommendations for Practice

While as authors we recognize that disabled people with experience in the sex trade constitutes a vast and diverse group, we assert the following best practices for social workers, educators, therapists, and other social service providers.

The NASW Code of Ethics offers social workers and other helping professionals ethical guidelines for confronting any bias they may have about working with someone with lived experience in the sex trade. Ethical code 1.05 C and D both point to the constant need for critical self-examination of bias, as well as the professional responsibility of the social worker to obtain education about working with diverse individuals (NASW, 2017).

Social workers should counter assumptions that because they are not working in an organization directly engaging with people in the sex trade, none of their clients are sex workers or have lived experience. There are ways to signal lack of judgment to clients: perhaps there is a local sex worker organizing chapter whose material you have up in your office, a poster that states sex work is work, or material supporting decriminalization of prostitution.

Due to the stigma and fear of criminalization, it may not be safe for your client to disclose sex work affiliation, but as organizers remind us, someone you know is a sex worker, so act accordingly. Most importantly, disability and sex work make up varying pieces of a client's identity and we should not assume that disclosure constitutes an issue needing fixing.

Therapists and counselors should avoid assuming that disclosure of involvement in sex work is the reason the client is in therapy, or that the experience in sex work is traumatic. When a client is disclosing violence or trauma related to sex work, it is essential the therapist remains open and curious instead of rushing to the righting reflex or a desire to "rescue" the client from sex work. What are the systematic barriers the client is facing that diminish their economic options? What discomfort is coming up for you as a provider?

It is also essential practice to evaluate the barriers that your organization or the resources you refer to may cause someone who is engaging in a criminalized profession. Will someone who is disabled and a sex worker be able to access this resource without experiencing ableism and whorephobia? Does the organization require unnecessary verification of employment?

Is the building accessible and within reach of public transit? Likewise, does the provider acknowledge their disabled sex worker community and reflect the community they serve? These are just some considerations that can quickly inform a client's perception of how their personhood might be acknowledged.

Social work education has a responsibility to cover content that contests ideas of "normalcy" in relation to bodies, sex, and sexuality. Within the classroom, educators can rely on intersectional frameworks of oppression to discuss topics about sex, sexuality, and sexual violence. In doing so, educators should engage students in critical thinking at the intersections of race, class, (dis)ability, sex, gender, nation, migration, sexuality, indigeneity, body size, faith, age, and beyond. These interconnected social categories are intrinsic to considering how sex workers with disabilities access medical, social, and legal institutions to ensure their human rights and basic needs are met.

## Case Study for Classroom Activity

Your client is a 29-year-old queer disabled cis woman named Sofia who has been receiving Supplemental Security Income (SSI) due to living with bipolar I disorder and PTSD. Sofia also has fibromyalgia, which is not a covered condition for SSI, but deeply impacts her day-to-day functioning. You work at a community mental health organization that provides case management and therapeutic support. Sofia has been attempting to additionally apply for Social Security Disability Insurance (SSDI) to supplement her monthly income but was recently denied due to mostly absent work history and lack of qualifying work credits. You have been working with Sofia to find a pro bono lawyer to assist in her appeal.

> Sofia has been living in shared housing with 5 roommates; her room is a converted food pantry off the kitchen. She initially liked some of her roommates when she moved in because there were other queer and trans people with disabilities living there, but over time, the roommates have changed and she feels less safe.

Sofia feels trapped in her housing situation. She has been on the waiting list for a Section 8 Voucher and does not currently make enough money to move out. Before receiving SSI, Sofia worked at various strip clubs and "made decent money." However, this work history is not being considered for her SSDI application. Sofia sometimes misses dancing in the clubs, "but mostly I miss the cash and the friendship with some of the dancers." Sofia increasingly struggled with the rigid rules of the clubs (late fees, stage fees, tipping out bouncers, and DJs) and the ongoing abuse from club management. As her fibromyalgia pain symptoms increased, she also found it more difficult to stay for the entire shift, and she would have to pay extra to leave early.

> *Sofia has been struggling with her living situation and recently reconnected with an old friend, Denise, from one of the strip clubs she worked at. Denise has continued working at the club, but is also trading sex for money. Denise asked Sofia if she would like to see a client with her, as a duo, and Sofia agreed. She felt safe with Denise there, and was able to pay her cell phone bill with the money she earned.*

Sofia found that spending an hour with a client is much easier for her chronic pain and mental health than a six-hour shift at the strip club was. She has been continuing to intermittently see clients but is still unable to rent an apartment due to SSI constraints, as she can't have more than $2,000 in saved assets.

> *Sofia is concerned that if she discloses her participation in the sex trade, her cash income will be reported to the social security administration. She is also worried that if other people at the community mental health organization find out, she will be reported to the police.*

### Micro-Considerations

- What are Sofia's presenting and stated needs? What resources does she possess? What resources does she need access to?
- **Documentation:** What are the consequences of charting about Sofia's involvement in the sex trade?
- How might bias be coming up for you as the caseworker? How might it impact your work together?
- What are Sofia's strengths?
- How do Sofia's disabilities affect her day-to-day experience?

### Mezzo-Considerations

- What are the limitations of confidentiality in the organization that you work at?
- As her caseworker, how might you best advocate for Sofia?
- How can you support Sofia's quest for financial access?

### Macro-Considerations

- What is the impact of the criminalization of the sex trade on Sofia? What is the impact of whorephobia and anti-sex work stigma?

- How is Sofia supported by SSI? How is she constrained?
- How does Sofia experience vulnerability due to structural forces? How is she supported by engaging in services at the community mental health agency? How is she hindered?
- What is the impact of ableism, white supremacy, misogyny, heterosexism, cissexism, and other structures of oppression as they intersect with the criminalization of trading sex for money?

## Conclusion

As the authors of this chapter, we see implications for additional research and literature regarding the intersections of disability and participation in the commercial sex trade. We acknowledge that both of these identity markers – *disabled* and *sex worker* – are not static or uniform identities. Definitions of disability are constantly evolving, and disabled people will experience ableism, access, resource acquisition, and stigma in varying degrees depending on their additional social locations. For people involved in the commercial sex trade, there is a spectrum of involvement from legal to criminalized work. Additionally, sex workers themselves will have vastly different experiences with stigma, harm, criminalization, and income generation as a result of their intersecting identities.

## Resources

- Abolition and Disability Justice Collective. https://abolitionanddisabilityjustice.com/
- Disability Justice: An Audit Tool. www.northwesthealth.org/djaudittool
- Sex Worker Outreach Project – Los Angeles. https://swoplosangeles.org/
- The BIPOC Adult Industry Collective. www.bipoc-collective.org/
    - About their founder, Sinnamon Love: https://disabilitycovidchronicles.nyu.edu/filling-in-the-gaps-sinnamon-love-on-disability-and-sex-worker-organizing-in-the-covid-19-pandemic/
- Black Trans Nation. www.blacktransnation.org/

## Note

1 Necrocapitalism, as defined by Banerjee (2006, 2008), is the understanding that capitalism and imperialism rest on continued subjection, violence, and dispossession.

## References

Abramovitz, M. (2017). *Regulating the lives of women: Social welfare policy from colonial times to the present*. Routledge.

Altiraifi, A. (2020, April 7). *A deadly poverty trap: Asset limits in the time of the coronavirus.* www.americanprogress.org/article/deadly-poverty-trap-asset-limits-time-coronavirus/

Banerjee, S. B. (2006). Live and let die: Colonial sovereignties and the death worlds of necrocapitalism. *Borderlands,* 5(1). https://link.gale.com/apps/doc/A169457995/AONE?u=oregon_oweb&sid=googleScholar&xid=6e50b57b

Baynton, D. (2016). Disability and the justification of inequality in American history. In L. Davis (Ed.), *The disability studies reader* (pp. 17–34). Taylor & Francis.

Blewett, L. (2014). The criminalization of sex work: Creating the conditions for disability. In K. Fritsche, J. Monaghan, & E. van der Meulen (Eds.), *Disability injustice: Confronting criminalization in Canada* (pp. 94–115). The University of Chicago Press.

Bobby Banerjee, S. (2008). Necrocapitalism. *Organization Studies,* 29(12), 1541–1563. https://doi.org/10.1177/0170840607096386

Duggan, L. (1993). The trials of Alice Mitchell: Sensationalism, sexology, and the lesbian subject in turn-of-the-century America. *Signs,* 18(4), 791–814.

Earp, B. D., & Moen, O. M. (2015). Paying for sex-only for people with disabilities? *Journal of Medical Ethics,* 42(1), 54–56. https://doi.org/10.1136/medethics-2015-103064

Faderman, L. (1978). The morbidification of love between women by 19th-century sexologists. *Journal of Homosexuality,* 4(1), 73–90.

Fuentes, K. (2022). Sex worker collectives within the whorearchy: Intersectional inquiry with sex workers in Los Angeles, CA. *Affilia.* https://doi.org/10.1177/08861099221103856

Garofalo Geymonat, G. (2019). Disability rights meet sex workers' rights: The making of sexual assistance in Europe. *Sexuality Research and Social Policy,* 16(2), 214–226. https://doi.org/10.1007/s13178-019-0377-x

Gray, C. (2022, July 31). Disabled sex workers don't want to be "rescued". *URevolution.* Retrieved November 8, 2022, from www.urevolution.com/blogs/magazine/disabled-sex-workers-dont-want-to-be-rescued

Grue, J. (2016). The problem with inspiration porn: A tentative definition and a provisional critique. *Disability & Society,* 31(6), 838–849. https://doi.org/10.1080/09687599.2016.1205473

Hall, L. (2004). Hauling down the double standard: Feminism, social purity and sexual science in late nineteenth-century Britain. *Gender & History,* 16(1), 36–56.

Knight, K. (2015). *Addicted. pregnant. poor.* Duke University Press.

Kruse, D., Schur, L., Rogers, S., & Ameri, M. (2018). Why do workers with disabilities earn less? Occupational job requirements and disability discrimination. *British Journal of Industrial Relations,* 56(4), 798–834.

Lakshmi Piepzna-Samarasinha, L. (2018). *Care work: Dreaming disability justice.* Arsenal Pulp Press.

Lemoon, L. (2021, October 29). On SESTA, the COVID-19 pandemic and disability. *SWOP Behind Bars.* www.swopbehindbars.org/post/on-sesta-the-covid-19-pandemic-and-disability

Lerum, K. (1998). 12 Step Feminism makes sex workers sick: How the state and the recovery movement turns radical women into "useless citizens". *Sexuality & Culture,* 2, 7–36. Transaction Publishers.

Meldon, P. (2017, October 31). *Disability history: Early and shifting attitudes of treatment (U.S. National Park Service).* National Park Service. www.nps.gov/articles/disabilityhistoryearlytreatment.htm

Miller, H. L. (2000). Sexologists examine lesbians and prostitutes in the United States, 1840–1940. *NWSA Journal, 12*(3), 67–91.

Munyi, C. W. (2012). Past and present perceptions toward disability: A historical perspective. *Disability Studies Quarterly, 32*(2).

National Association of Social Workers. (2017). *NASW code of ethics*. Retrieved November 18, 2022, from www.socialworkers.org/About/Ethics/Code-of-Ethics/Code-of-Ethics-English

Nielsen, K. E. (2013). *A disability history of the United States (revisioning history)*. Beacon Press.

O'Brien, M. (1990). On seeing a sex surrogate. *The Sun Magazine*. https://thesunmagazine.org/issues/174/on-seeing-a-sex-surrogate

Oselin, S. S., & Weitzer, R. (2013). Organizations working on behalf of prostitutes: An analysis of goals, practices, and strategies. *Sexualities, 16*(3–4), 445–466. https://doi.org/10.1177/1363460713481741

Rubin, G. (1984). Thinking sex: Notes for a radical theory of the politics of sexuality. In Rubin, G., Nardi, P. M., & Schneider, B. E. (Eds.), *Social perspectives in lesbian and gay studies; A reader* (pp. 100–133). Routledge.

Sanders, T. (2007). The politics of sexual citizenship: Commercial sex and disability. *Disability & Society, 22*(5), 439–455. https://doi.org/10.1080/09687590701427479

Sins Invalid. (2015, September 17). 10 principles of disability justice. *Sins Invalid*. Retrieved November 10, 2022, from www.sinsinvalid.org/blog/10-principles-of-disability-justice#:~:text=RECOGNIZING%20WHOLENESS%20People%20have%20inherent,to%20be%20sustained%20long%20term

Snider, S. (2021). Moving toward disability justice: Introduction to "lesbian lives, disabled lives". *Journal of Lesbian Studies, 25*(3), 159–162.

Tastrom. (2019, January 4). *Sex work is a disability issue. So why doesn't the disability community recognize that?* Rooted in Rights. https://rootedinrights.org/sex-work-is-a-disability-issue-so-why-doesnt-the-disability-community-recognize-that/

Tempest, T. (2019). Relationship boundaries, abuse, and internalized whorephobia. *Sexual and Relationship Therapy, 34*(3), 335–338. https://doi.org/10.1080/14681994.2019.1574400

Thomsen, F. K. (2015). Prostitution, disability and prohibition. *Journal of Medical Ethics, 41*(6), 451–459. https://doi.org/10.1136/medethics-2014-102215

Trent, J. W. (1998). Defectives at the world's fair: Constructing disability in 1904. *Remedial and Special Education, 19*(4), 201–211.

Turner, D. M., & Blackie, D. (2018). *Disability in the industrial revolution: Physical impairment in British coalmining, 1780–1880 (disability history)* (1st ed.). Manchester University Press.

Wahab, S. (2002). "For their own good?" Sex work, social control and social workers, a historical Perspective. *Journal of Sociology and Social Welfare, 29*(4), 39–57.

# 15

# RESISTING "TOO YOUNG"

Anti-Adultism in Disability and Sexual Health Justice Advocacy

*syd lio riley*

## Introduction

At the crossroads of ableism and adultism – the ideology that asserts "adults are better than young people, and entitled to act upon [them] without their agreement" – disabled youths face a multitude of sexual and reproductive health and education (SRHE) inequities, often compounded by inaccessible or irrelevant sex education approaches (Bell, 1995, p. 1). This chapter explores recent literature identifying the systems of oppression underlying these inequities and identifies the Youth Advisory Council (YAC) model as one anti-adultist strategy for addressing them. Critical considerations in designing YACs for disabled youth are presented. Health and human service professionals seeking to develop accessible engagement opportunities can learn from these practices, whether in developing a YAC specifically or in developing different opportunities using similar principles.

### Defining "Youth": A Social Model

It is imperative to establish a concordant understanding of what is meant by the word "youth." In this chapter, it refers loosely to individuals between the ages of 13–24, but this definition is incomplete. The YIELD Project aptly describes the challenges in determining a common definition:

> Of course, any definition of "youth" is intrinsically inadequate, as the experience . . . is as varied and diverse as young people themselves. This experience is conditioned by power . . . gender, socioeconomic class, ethnicity, race, sexual orientation, and other shapers of personal identity.

In addition, the process of moving from childhood to adulthood is profoundly influenced by the cultural, social, and political contexts in which people live and grow.

*(Catino et al., 2019)*

Despite the challenges of capturing the varied experiences that characterize "youth" in a single definition, this chapter aims to foreground the experience of navigating adultist structures in its meaning. Just as the Social Model of Disability identifies systemic ableism as a defining characteristic of the experience of "disability," adultism is similarly defining of "youth" (Berne & Milbern, 2017). As such, this chapter is not referring to chronological age *alone* when discussing "youth" but instead to the ontological status of assumed incapacity for autonomy as is culturally denoted by age (Moore, 2020).

As the general age range of 13–24 encompasses varied experiences, some recommendations here may need adjustment; a pre-teen, for example, will likely have different needs than a youth earning a master's degree or working full-time. Additionally, the service professionals reading this chapter may *be* youth themselves. These youths sit at a complex intersection of navigating adultism in the professional world, while also being afforded some adult status by proxy, notably distributed to those with the most access to education and capital.

## Literature Review

### Adultism and Adultcentrism

Despite a large body of research on youth and children, insidious adultist attitudes and social structures have led to few studies acknowledging youth as a socially oppressed group (Bell, 1995). Adultism is a system of oppression characterized by the phenomenon of adulthood's assumed positionality as "the pinnacle of human development" and, in contrast, young people are categorically assumed to be immature and incompetent "human becomings . . . in a state of transition to humanity" (Moore, 2020). Adultism restricts youth's access to political agency, self-determination, and the "goods, services, and privileges of society," reinforced by "institutions, laws, customs, and attitudes" (Bell, 1995; DeJong & Love, 2013; Hall, 2019). Paradigmatically, this "assumption" is often referred to as "adultcentrism" or "adult supremacy" (DeJong & Love, 2015; Florio et al., 2019).

Youths experience adultism differently depending on other systems of oppression they encounter (Bell, 1995). For example, while "Zero Tolerance" policies in schools rest on an adultist belief that young people tend to be dangerous and participate in criminal behavior; they disproportionately harm

Black youths and often trap them in cycles of carceral control (DeJong & Love, 2015; Kilgore, 2015). On the other hand, White youths in the United States (U.S.) are more likely to experience adultism as a proxy for settler colonialism, as child-rearing practices socialize them to accept and re-create their subordination to maintain hegemonic colonial ideologies and structures (DeJong & Love, 2015).

### Youth Sexual Health Inequities

Youths experience multiple inequities related to sexual and reproductive health (SRH). Many youths, especially LGBTQ youths, fear discrimination (United Nations, 2021). For example, in the U.S., many states have introduced or passed legislation barring transgender youth from transitioning or requiring government employees to out LGBTQ youth to their parents (Cole, 2021; MacDonald-Evoy, 2022). Additionally, access barriers such as insufficient funds or lacking reliable transportation prevent youth from receiving this care (National Coalition for Sexual Health, 2013). Finally, actual or perceived legal barriers prevent youth from accessing SRH services. It can be hard to determine confidentiality and parent consent policies for services such as access to safe abortion; STI testing, treatment, and vaccination; support for sexual violence experiences; pregnancy testing and prenatal care; and contraceptives, as these guidelines can vary regionally and even from clinic to clinic (MOASH, 2022, *n.d.*; Morris & Rushwan, 2015).

The SRHE complications youths are likely to face vary based on social, cultural, and economic factors; for example, youths living in countries that have been designated as "low-and middle-income" are more likely to experience an unplanned pregnancy or lack family-planning resources (Morris & Rushwan, 2015). Access to comprehensive sex education also determines youth SRH outcomes. Reach a Hand (*n.d.*), a Ugandan youth organization, connects their abstinence-only education to a high rate of unplanned teenage pregnancies. In a survey of Ugandan youths ages 15–19 who can get pregnant, 25% had given birth or were pregnant at the time of the survey. These early unplanned pregnancies often result in increased risk for complications or halt the pregnant youth's education. Comprehensive sex education for youth, they argue, would work to counteract these risks.

### Disability and Sexual Health

Disabled youths are at an even greater risk of experiencing sexual health inequities, also largely determined by access to sex education. Disabled youths receive less education than their peers on contraceptives, STIs, and screenings for things such as cervical cancer (Kessler et al., 2020). Students in special education, especially young women with intellectual disabilities, are more likely to contract an STI. Finally, disabled youths are exponentially more likely than their peers to experience sexual violence, emphasizing the importance of sex education that includes a variety of knowledge and skills to promote safe, healthy relationships (Shapiro, 2018; Szydlowski, 2016).

Several factors contribute to inequity in disabled youth's sex education. First, many people mistakenly believe that disabled people can't or don't want to engage in sexual activity, leaving them entirely out of SRHE policy and curricula (Szydlowski, 2016; Tasha, 2022). Additionally, abstinence-only education forgoes content on relationships and pleasure; instead, it focuses only on preventing reproduction (Esmail et al., 2010). Eugenicist ideologies debating whether disabled people should be *allowed* to reproduce have been used to justify reproductive violence enacted on disabled populations throughout history, so many assume that sex education is irrelevant to them altogether (Henley, 2017; Holmes, 2021). When the general public does recognize that disabled people have sex, these thoughts and beliefs tend to be heteronormative, phallocentric, and minimize rights and pleasure (Esmail et al., 2010).

Finally, sex education is often hard to access, with many special education classrooms denied participation. Mainstream classrooms often provide instruction that is inaccessible for some disabled students to engage with or understand (Henley, 2017). Lack of access has a disparate impact on students of color, who are more frequently diagnosed with disabilities and are kept out of mainstream classrooms as a result (Holmes, 2021). Often, these diagnoses are rooted in racist stereotypes about behavior and intellect, resulting in segregation of children of color through special education programs and decreased access to necessary health information.

### *Youth Advocacy and Engagement*

Youth advocacy efforts employ many strategies to address SRHE inequities. The YIELD project outlines three levels of agency in SRHE rights efforts, where youth's positionality shifts from "target groups" to "collaborators" to "initiators" as their power increases (Catino et al., 2019). Many adult approaches to youth justice fall within the first two by incorporating youth perspectives, often through consultations (Horgan, 2017). While consultation can be effective in many circumstances, here it often perpetuates adultist structures in which the adult is the decision-maker and the youth is simply an informant who is not given space to advocate for their *own* needs. The YIELD project explains that when youths are core to the development of solutions to the SRHE inequities they face, "all stakeholders do a better job" of implementing solutions (Catino et al., 2019).

Youth organizing (YO) and youth–adult partnerships (Y-APs) are two approaches to youth advocacy that can be explicitly anti-adultist (Hall, 2019). YO develops the sociopolitical and community capacities of youth, giving them the skills to create change within their communities. Y-APs seek to include youth in the processes in which decisions are made about their lives, and youths engage in long-term projects with adults to resolve inequities they face. YO and Y-AP are often done in conjunction with one another. However, YO has the most potential to support youth as *initiators* rather than *collaborators*, as it is often pursued by youth independent of adult influence.

Youth Advisory Councils integrate YO and Y-AP. The terminology used for this kind of programming may vary (e.g., advocacy or justice rather than advisory, and collective or board rather than council). Successful YACs are youth-led, meet regularly, emphasize community-building, provide safe space for youth, and pursue meaningful projects that address the issues they identify (AHI, 2014).

## Building an Anti-Adultist Youth Advisory Council

Organizations seeking to build or improve their youth programs should implement anti-adultist and anti-oppressive practices at all levels. The following pages contain a review of key facilitators to youth engagement. Recommendations are also informed by the author's own experiences with the Michigan Organization on Adolescent Sexual Health (MOASH), where he participated in and evaluated YACs, and co-facilitated MY Access, a YAC advocating for accessible and inclusive SRHE for disabled Michigan youths. The suggestions that follow are not prescriptive, but they should be implemented or discarded as is most beneficial to the youth looking to engage.

At the heart of these recommendations is one central value: disabled youths are individuals who deserve respect, autonomy, and agency. They are experts on their experiences and are not in need of external saviors. Rather than imposing limiting expectations about their capabilities, adult allies and accomplices should offer the support and resources necessary for them to shape their own worlds. If an organization can implement this fundamental value, the rest should intuitively follow.

### *Key Considerations*

#### *Recruitment*

When recruiting disabled youth and/or building an SRHE-focused YAC, consider the best places to advertise your recruitment like schools, health offices, and other youth organizations. Additionally, as social media platforms like TikTok, Instagram, and Twitter may reach a broader youth audience. Peer recruitment from youth already participating in the council may be successful, and beginning with short-term projects builds excitement and investment in the work (AHI, 2014). Meeting youth where they already are will make participation less intimidating, so meeting at a local school or community center might increase comfort and access.

It is important to determine which youth are eligible for your YAC. A YAC might accept anyone who wants to join, or it may have guidelines around the number of youths involved, what ages are included, and what levels of shared identity and affinity are necessary to establish safety and shared understanding. If your council can't accept all youths who apply, the application process should be as accessible as possible so that decisions are not made based on ableist standards. Consider offering some of the following:

- Clear avenues for youth to share their access needs and having an access coordinator to make sure they are met
- Multiple application formats (written, audio, video, verbal, etc.)
- Information sessions or resource guides about the process
- Support in the application process
- Flexible deadlines and interview rescheduling
- Interview all youths who apply so that different communication needs can be met
- Intentionally disregard ableist professional standards around body language, eye contact, non-linear thought processes, speech differences, and communication styles

*Accessibility*

Accessibility considerations for YACs will vary depending on the individual needs represented within the council. For this reason, it is not possible to list every accessibility measure that a council should take; instead, what follows are general considerations to take when making these determinations. First and foremost, it is important that all youths have multiple opportunities to share their access needs rather than assuming what measures will provide access. By asking, facilitators also create a trusting environment where youths can communicate their needs as they change throughout their involvement.

Additionally, many youths face accessibility barriers due to their social and legal standing. When setting accessibility considerations, include these barriers, as well as what facilitators could be provided to counteract them. For example, see the following table:

| Barrier | Facilitator |
| --- | --- |
| • Lack of safe and reliable transportation | • Compensated mileage<br>• Public transportation stipends<br>• Carpooling<br>• Remote meetings |
| • Lack technology and internet access | • Providing laptops/tablets<br>• Tech stipends<br>• Providing office space<br>• Connecting with local library |
| • Busy school/work/extracurricular schedule | • Non-traditional meeting times<br>• Recorded meetings and notes<br>• Multiple ways to meet participation/attendance expectations |
| • Member has to provide childcare for family members | • Childcare stipends<br>• Allowing members to bring those they're caring for to the meeting<br>• Remote meetings; flexible camera and participation policy |
| • Member is experiencing mental health challenges | • Peer or mental health support built in<br>• Access to mental health professionals<br>• Informed consent around mandated reporting<br>• Opportunities for connection and relationship building |

There are also general accessibility considerations facilitators can take. Remote meeting options meet many access needs. Providing meeting materials and agendas in advance can be used to help follow along with conversations and offer clear expectations and structure for what the meeting will look like. YACs should prepare these and other general accessibility considerations, looking to disabled communities and knowledge for guidance.

*Intersectionality*

While this chapter emphasizes the intersection of ableism and adultism, disabled youths are not limited to these experiences. Other experiences of marginalization will impact members' navigation of social justice and advocacy work. For example, adults are more likely to delegitimize the political concerns of racialized youth, so these youths may use different tactics to successfully organize under the gaze of adults (Gordon, 2009; Hall, 2019). It's necessary for organizations to deconstruct on an ongoing basis the practices and policies that allow for oppression to go uncontested. Additionally, multiply marginalized youth should not be expected to carry all of the labor within the group, but their experiences and liberation must be central to ensure liberation for *all* disabled youths.

*Compensation*

When establishing a YAC, it is necessary to prioritize fair compensation of youth members. Compensation has been shown to facilitate successful engagement, whereas a lack of compensation becomes "exploitative at a certain point, especially if [youth] are working alongside compensated adult colleagues" (Catino et al., 2019, p. 26; Peterson et al., 2020). When youth's labor isn't compensated, participation becomes limited to only those who can *afford* to take on unpaid work. Additionally, youth may be working fewer hours at a part-time job to participate in a YAC, and employment discrimination may prevent disabled youths from accessing income elsewhere. Finally, compensating youths will allow them to move toward independence in their own lives. For those experiencing oppression at home, fair compensation offers the material resources necessary to survive.

If youth compensation is not possible due to financial constraints (as compared to a lack of prioritization), consider other forms of compensation. Meetings could provide food (while being aware of food allergies/needs and risk for COVID-19 transmission) or meal stipends. Youth may be able to count their participation as volunteer hours, internships for college credit, or as part of an independent study.

*Youth Leadership, Agency, and Decision-Making*

Prioritize youth leadership opportunities within the YAC. Formal leadership opportunities could include a youth facilitator or coordinator. Informal leadership could occur within meetings and projects. For example, members may manage individual projects within the YAC or take responsibility for a consistent task like note-taking, scheduling meetings, or booking an interpreter. Anti-adultist organizations should also ensure that youths are not siloed into YACs as their only means of participation. Make space for youth elsewhere in the organization by identifying adultist biases and expectations in hiring practices, including what training and support is provided upon being hired. Youth participating in YACs should be doing so, because they are interested in group-based advocacy – not because it's their only option for participation.

Finally, while offering some youth leadership positions may increase organizational equity more broadly, it can replicate top-down power structures in which only those with the highest status make the "important" decisions, also tokenizing the few youths selected for these roles. Some projects may call for identified leaders, but power should generally be distributed among YAC members. One way to mitigate these hierarchies is implementing consensus-based decision-making processes, one of which Dean Spade (2020) explains in *Mutual Aid: Building Solidarity During This Crisis (and the Next)*.

### Mentorship

Youths involved in YACs should be supported in developing peer mentorship and support networks. Peer mentorship arises organically in YAC spaces; in the MY Access YAC, council facilitators and nearly all of the members are disabled youth themselves. Disabled youth identity is at the core of the council's work, and a wide range of experiences within this identity helps members' understanding of disability and advocacy to grow. Members can offer and request advice for the challenges they're experiencing or learn about new access tools that may be useful to them. Additionally, newly disabled or members just beginning to be identified as disabled have the guidance and support of other disabled community members.

Youth members also benefit from positive youth–adult partnerships. One study explains that when mentorship centers around youth–adult partnerships, "mentoring shifts from a[n] . . . approach in which individual youth are the targets of the intervention to a more socially transformative approach" that makes the partnerships more collaborative (Akiva et al., 2017). When reflecting on former youth-engagement participation, individuals share that positive relationships were often more formative and longstanding than the program itself (Body & Hogg, 2019). Collaborative (rather than unidirectional) mentorship increases impactful feelings of safety and belonging.

### Youth Development and Education

Youths should have many opportunities to gain new knowledge and skills around collaboration, advocacy, politics, disability, and sexual and reproductive health, as many may not have previous experience in these areas. Support with logistical elements of the work could include consultations with experienced organizers, regular supervisory check-ins, or shared responsibility and workload. This support should *not* be surveillance or power struggle in disguise, but instead transparent support and flexibility for youths who are learning skills they may be unfamiliar with.

In addition to technical support, youth should have learning opportunities to supplement their participation. There are many formats for successful personal and professional development:

- Groups to explore new topics together through media (books, podcasts, shows, documentaries, etc.)
- Guest speakers or panelists covering various topics

- Skill- and knowledge-sharing sessions devised and led by youth
- Firsthand experiences through YAC projects (e.g., learning about legislation by advocating for a bill or meeting with representatives)

Regardless of method, these opportunities should engage youth about the topics *they* identify as beneficial. These opportunities should initiate dialogue and help the group establish their core values as a collective. Development and educational opportunities should not be pursued to initiate young people into capitalist expectations of professionalism and expertise, but instead to give them the space to learn and reflect on the complexities of advocacy.

## Staff Development and Education

Adultism within youth organizing has been found to limit the success of organizing attempts (Conner et al., 2016). Adult-dominated spaces impose adultist practices and beliefs onto the youth participating, which limits their own opportunity for participation. Youths often internalize the adultism they experience, leading to youth actions that further perpetuate adultism. Therefore, requiring adult staff to participate in ongoing anti-oppressive development and education, with an emphasis on anti-adultism, is necessary to minimize adultist dynamics and outcomes. One of the most successful youth–adult engagement training methods is experiential learning, especially through shadowing and co-facilitating with experienced facilitators (Peterson et al., 2020).

## Navigating YAC Challenges

### Program Evaluation

Frequent opportunities for program evaluation will support a YAC in identifying conflict early on and working to meet all members' needs. Multiple modalities of evaluation opportunities empower youth to share their feelings in ways that feel comfortable to them. Written or verbal surveys, focus groups, anonymous forms, and one-to-one check-ins are all ways youth can offer regular feedback. It may be useful to employ tools designed to measure adult-centric values held by adult programming staff over time to evaluate the efficacy of staff development and education (Florio et al., 2019). Bringing in external evaluation organizations may also be helpful in standardizing and synthesizing feedback to outline explicit next steps and goals for the YAC. When conflict or concerns do arise, they should be prioritized within meetings and goal setting. It may not be necessary to stop all other work while resolving concerns, but concerns should not be set aside for the sake of completing a project. Maintain transparency and youth involvement in all evaluation and resolution processes.

*Limitations of the YAC Model*

Limitations of the YAC model when addressing sexual and reproductive health and education will vary based on culture and political context. In the United States, nonprofit organizations are largely neoliberal, and profit motivations may limit the extent or nature of work completed within YACs – even when those involved have "political commitments and values that resist the . . . non-profit industrial complex" (INCITE!, 2017, p. xix).

Parent/guardian consent requirements for minors may limit who can participate and the security of their participation. Parents/guardians holding different political views around adultism, ableism, and sexual health might prohibit participation. Meetings held remotely may also pose privacy risks for youth not living independently. Disabled youth in residential care may not be able to participate due to a number of barriers. In many regions, public schools are limited in their sex education programming, so YACs may not be able to directly affiliate with public schools or provide YAC-led public events to students. That said, there are some ways to work around this – for example, MY Access hosts all public events with sex education material remotely on weekends so youth in attendance are not considered to be attending for a school event.

Finally, mandated reporting policies might also impose limitations around what topics youth feel comfortable discussing. It is imperative that all youths are made aware of mandated reporting policies and what kinds of disclosures would trigger a report. Mandated reporting can often have dire consequences for youth and frequently harms those it was intended to protect (Lippy et al., 2016). Additionally, as mandated reporting often occurs without youth consent, an anti-adultist response should repair agency in as many ways possible, providing youth with transparency and support throughout the reporting process.

**Classroom Activity**

This activity will bring together some of the considerations outlined earlier within the context of an organization's hiring process. This activity is not designed to have one correct answer. Do not feel the need to "choose" one candidate. Instead, consider the factors at hand and what possibilities could exist outside of what we already know.

*Scenario*

You work for a community-based organization advocating for disabled youth. Your organization decides to hire an advocacy lead for sex education policy, as this issue has received little attention. The advocacy lead would build a YAC to identify specific sex education shortcomings for disabled youth in local schools. They would collectively strategize legislative- and community-based action to resolve these gaps. You receive applications from the three following applicants:

## Applicant 1

Brooke is a 20-year-old rising senior at a top university nearby where she studies sociology. Throughout her schooling, she's developed a robust theoretical understanding of power and oppression. Brooke developed a post-viral syndrome when she was young that causes chronic pain, fatigue, and mobility difficulties, but was never formally diagnosed. Her family did not consider her to be disabled growing up, so she has been exploring this identity since coming to college. She now uses different mobility aids to get around depending on how she feels each day, including a wheelchair, cane, forearm crutches, and sometimes no aid at all. Because Brooke's parents don't accept her disabled identity and she lacks documentation, she navigates her education with no accommodations. She feels that her experiences facing ableism will help her be a strong advocate. She also has a strong grasp on sexual and reproductive health topics due to the education she received from her progressive magnet high school when she was growing up in a neighboring state.

## Applicant 2

Elijah is a 37-year-old Licensed Master's Social Worker with ten years of experience leading an LGBTQ client inclusion initiative at a community mental health clinic. He and his partner recently became the legal guardians of his teenage brother Jonathan, who has an intellectual disability. After spending time with Jonathan and hearing about how teachers treat him, Elijah has been making frequent visits to the school to advocate. His background in social work has proven useful in these conversations, as he can frequently cite policy when arguing for his brother's fair treatment. He always includes Jonathan in deciding when and how to advocate to support his self-determination. These experiences have shifted his interests, and he now hopes to work in youth advocacy. Elijah understands the principles of Disability Justice and frequently attends workshops to engage in ongoing learning about the movement. Elijah feels that his experience caring for his brother and his training as a social worker will inform his advocacy.

## Applicant 3

Quincy is a 19-year-old sophomore attending a "special education" high school. Quincy identifies as Autistic, and this identity was affirmed diagnostically when ze was young. Most of the early responses to Quincy's autism included harmful therapies attempting to suppress hir autistic traits. Quincy's special interest is sexual and reproductive health, because ze thinks it's interesting that sex and relationships are one area where hir allistic (non-autistic) peers are just as likely to use social scripts, misunderstand communication, and gain pleasure from stim-like "repetitive motor movements." Quincy first discovered this interest when searching for online resources, because hir school's sex education is limited. Now, ze frequently educates hir friends at lunch when the teachers aren't listening. Despite never having a job before, Quincy feels that hir interest and perspective as an autistic person can help other youth understand how to navigate these social situations better, regardless of neurotype.

## Discussion

### First reactions:

- When reading the above descriptions, what did you notice about your own reaction to each candidate? Did you make any assumptions or judgments?
- What information mentioned earlier is relevant to the hiring process? Is any information irrelevant?
- How might ableism and adultism arise in this decision? Consider micro- (individual), mezzo- (organizational), and macro- (ideological/institutional) examples.

### Taking action:

- How would you approach this hiring process?
- What level of experience is necessary for this position?
- With what you know about each candidate, what relevant experience do they bring?
  - How did you decide what counts as experience?
  - What examples of experience depended on access to resources? What resources?
  - How did you prioritize between lived experience and learned knowledge?
- With what you know about each candidate, where might they need additional support?
  - In practice, the best way to identify support needs would be asking directly. For this exercise, don't assume what support each candidate *will* need, but instead what they *might* need based on what we know.
  - When thinking about supports, did you consider needs not related to disability or previous work experience?

## Conclusion

Ableism and adultism contribute to negative SRHE inequities among disabled youths. Additionally, many advocacy efforts seeking to support disabled youth reproduce these oppressive structures, ultimately inhibiting themselves in the process. Developing advocacy models that center disabled youth's leadership is one way to combat ableist and adultist practices, but doing so must be supportive of young people who may be new to this work. Understanding the challenges that may arise within the YAC structure can allow for intentional implementation and proactive support. Above all else, disabled youths should be centered and prioritized in this work in ways that are attentive and responsive to the oppression they experience.

**Acknowledgments:** I'd like to share my appreciation for my comrade and peer Devin Goldstein, who helped to conceptualize and outline this chapter, providing feedback along the way. Many thanks to his invaluable support.

## Resources

### Youth, Disability, and Sexuality

Adolescent Health Initiative. *Creating & sustaining a thriving youth advisory council.* https://umhs-adolescenthealth.org/wp-content/uploads/2017/02/manual-for-website.pdf

Advocates for Youth. *Sexual health education for young people with disabilities – research and resources for educators.* www.advocatesforyouth.org/resources/fact-sheets/sexual-health-education-for-young-people-with-disabilities/

Andrew Gurza. "Disability After Dark." Podcast. www.andrewgurza.com/podcast

A. Andrews. "A Quick & Easy Guide to Sex & Disability." docs.google.com/presentation/d/1aNQW_cide3r79qWuKfllDA97sqzE9E_F8q1IeHx16P8/edit?usp=sharing

ETR. *Youth engagement in sexual health programs and services: Findings from the Youth Engagement Network's environmental scan.* https://pages.etr.org/hubfs/YEN/ETR_YEN%20Environmental%20Scan%20Full%20Report_2020.pdf

Jess Tarpey, Andrew Gurza, and Katy Venables. "The Bump'n Book of Love, Lust, and Disability" and getbumpn.com

MOASH MY Access. *MY access toolkit.* Full Youth Toolkit. https://docs.google.com/presentation/d/1aNQW_cide3r79qWuKfllDA97sqzE9E_F8q1IeHx16P8/edit#slide=id.g115ff16794b_0_2063

MOASH MY Access. *MY access toolkit.* Shortened Youth Toolkit. https://docs.google.com/presentation/d/1z3xfS-s0gzwiZFf5gfK0qB1DtJdYNd3RcOpj3Q3sYy4/edit#slide=id.g115ff16794b_0_2063

MOASH MY Access. *MY access provider toolkit.* Full Provider Toolkit. https://docs.google.com/presentation/d/1XL6dsZvWy-MKEMELFpvG7HdidfZK9qS4I1kQc9iFdT8/edit

SIECUS: Sex Ed for Social Change. *Comprehensive sex education for youth with disabilities.* siecus.org/wp-content/uploads/2021/03/SIECUS-2021-Youth-with-Disabilities-CTA-1.pdf

YIELD Project. *Young people advancing sexual and reproductive health: Toward a new normal.* www.summitfdn.org/wp-content/uploads/2018/11/YIELD_full-report_June-2019.pdf

### Anti-Oppressive Organizing Strategies

Dean Spade. *Mutual aid: Building solidarity during this crisis (and the next).*
Inklusion Guide. www.inklusionguide.org
Liberating Structures. www.liberatingstructures.com

### References

Akiva, T., Carey, R. L., Cross, A. Delale-O'Connor, L., & Brown, M. R. (2017). Reasons youth engage in activism programs: Social justice or sanctuary? *Journal of Applied Developmental Psychology, 53*, 20–30. https://doi.org/10.1016/j.appdev.2017.08.005

Bell, J. (1995). *Understanding adultism*. YouthBuild USA.

Berne, P., & Milbern, S. [Barnard Center for Research on Women.] (2017, May 9). *My body doesn't oppress me, society does* [Video]. YouTube. www.youtube.com/watch?v=7r0MiGWQY2g

Body, A., & Hogg, E. (2019). What mattered ten years on? Young people's reflections on their involvement with a charitable youth participation project. *Journal of Youth Studies, 22*(2), 171–186. https://doi.org/10.1080/13676261.2018.1492101

Catino, J., Battistini, E., & Babchek, A. (2019). *Young people advancing sexual and reproductive health: Toward a new normal*. Youth Investment Engagement and Leadership Development Project; The Summit Foundation. www.summitfdn.org/wp-content/uploads/2018/11/YIELD_full-report_June-2019.pdf

Cole, D. (2021). *Arkansas becomes first state to outlaw gender-affirming treatment for trans youth*. CNN. Retrieved April 2022, from www.cnn.com/2021/04/06/politics/arkansas-transgender-health-care-veto-override/index.html

Conner, J., Ober, C. N., & Brown, A. (2016). The politics of paternalism: Adult and youth perspectives on youth voice in public policy. *Teachers College Record, 118*(8).

DeJong, K., & Love, B. (2013). Ageism and adultism. In M. Adams, W. J. Blumenfeld, R. Castaneda, H. Hackman, M. Peters, & X. Zu'niga (Eds.), *Readings for diversity and social justice* (3rd ed., pp. 470–474). Routledge.

DeJong, K., & Love, B. (2015). Youth oppression as a technology of colonialism: Conceptual frameworks and possibilities for social justice education praxis. *Equity & Excellence in Education, 48*(3), 489–508. https://doi.org/10.1080/10665684.2015.1057086

Esmail, S., Darry, K., Walter, A., & Knupp, H. (2010). Attitudes and perceptions towards disability and sexuality. *Disability and Rehabilitation, 32*(14), 1148–1155. https://doi.org/10.3109/09638280903419277

Florio, E., Caso, L., & Castell, I. (2019). The Adultcentrism Scale in the educational relationship: Instrument development and preliminary validation. *New Ideas in Psychology, 57*. https://doi.org/10.1016/j.newideapsych.2019.100762

Gordon, H. R. (2009). *We fight to win: Inequality and the politics of youth activism*. Rutgers University Press.

Hall, S. F. (2019). A conceptual mapping of three anti-adultist approaches to youth work. *Journal of Youth Studies, 23*(10), 1293–1309.

Henley, A. (2017). *Why sex education for disabled people is so important*. Teen Vogue. www.teenvogue.com/story/disabled-sex-ed

Holmes, L. (2021). *Comprehensive sex education for youth with disabilities*. Sexuality Information and Education Council of the United States (SIECUS): Sex Ed for Social Change. https://siecus.org/wp-content/uploads/2021/03/SIECUS-2021-Youth-with-Disabilities-CTA-1.pdf

Horgan, D. (2017). Consultations with children and young people and their impact on policy in Ireland. *Childhood*, 24(2), 245–259.

INCITE! (2017). *The revolution will not be funded: Beyond the non-profit industrial complex*. Duke University Press.

Kessler, R., Hinkle, T. B., Moyers, A., & Silverberg, B. (2020). Adolescent sexual health. *Primary Care: Clinics in Office Practice*, 47(2), 367–382.

Kilgore, J. (2015). *Understanding mass incarceration: A people's guide to the key civil rights struggle of our time*. The New Press.

Lippy, C., Burk, C., & Hobart, M. (2016). *There's no one I can trust: The impact of mandatory reporting on the help-seeking and wellbeing of domestic violence survivors*. A Report of the National LGBTQ Domestic Violence Capacity Building Learning Center. Seattle, WA. http://static1.squarespace.com/static/566c7f0c2399a3bdabb57553/t/5707e33f7da24f872ca86157/1460134725667/There%27s+No+One+I+Can+Trust-+Mandatory+Reporting.pdf

MacDonald-Evoy, J. (2022). *GOP bill would force teachers to out LGBTQ students to parents*. AZ Mirror. www.azmirror.com/2022/01/26/gop-bill-would-force-teachers-to-out-lgbtq-students-to-parents/

Michigan Organization on Adolescent Sexual Health (MOASH). (n.d.). *Youth rights for sexual health services*. www.moash.org/uploads/1/1/5/8/115876627/shs-youth-right_36398738__1_.pdf

Michigan Organization on Adolescent Sexual Health (MOASH). (2022). *Youth advisory council collective*. MOASH. www.moash.org/yacs.html

Moore, A. (2020). Pathological demand avoidance: What and who are being pathologised and in whose interests? *Global Studies of Childhood*, 10(1), 39–52. https://doi.org/10.1177/2043610619890070

Morris, J. L., & Rushwan, H. (2015). Adolescent sexual and reproductive health: The global challenges. *International Journal of Gynecology & Obstetrics*, 131(S1), S40–S42. https://doi.org/10.1016/j.ijgo.2015.02.006

National Coalition for Sexual Health. (2013). *The sexual health of youth in the United States: An audience profile*. National Coalition for Sexual Health. https://nationalcoalitionforsexualhealth.org/data-research/audience-profiles/document/AdolescentBackgrounder-final.pdf

Peterson, A., Drake, P., Tat, S., Silver, G., Bell, H., & Guinosso, S. (2020). *Youth engagement in sexual health programs and services: Findings from the youth engagement network's environmental scan*. Education, Training, and Research. https://pages.etr.org/hubfs/YEN/ETR_YEN%20Environmental%20Scan%20Full%20Report_2020.pdf

Reach a Hand Uganda. (n.d.). *Inadequacy of SRHR information and its effect on young people in Uganda*. Reach a Hand. https://reachahand.org/wp-content/uploads/2019/11/Inadequency-of-SRH-policies.pdf

Shapiro, J. (2018). *For some with intellectual disabilities, ending abuse starts with sex ed*. NPR. www.npr.org/2018/01/09/572929725/for-some-with-intellectual-disabilities-ending-abuse-starts-with-sex-ed

Spade, D. (2020). *Mutual aid: Building solidarity during this crisis (and the next)*. Verso.

Szydlowski, M. B. (2016). *Sexual health education for young people with disabilities: Research and resources for educators.* Advocates for Youth. www.advocatesforyouth.org/wp-content/uploads/2021/06/FinalSexual-Health-Education-for-Young-People-with-Disabilities-Educators.pdf

Tasha, A. L. (2022). *Bridging the gap between persons with disabilities and sexual reproductive health and rights.* Reach a Hand Uganda. https://reachahand.org/story/bridgin-the-gap-between-persons-with-disabilities-and-sexual-reproductive-health-rights-by-akullu-lynn-tasha/

United Nations. (2021). *Young people need their sexual and reproductive health and rights.* United Nations. www.ohchr.org/en/stories/2021/05/young-people-need-their-sexual-and-reproductive-health-and-rights

YACYAC Project Youth as compiled by the Adolescent Health Initiative. (2014). *Creating & sustaining a thriving youth advisory council.* Adolescent Health Initiative. https://umhs-adolescenthealth.org/wp-content/uploads/2017/02/manual-for-website.pdf

**PART FOUR**

# Across Intersecting Identities

# 16
# RACIALIZATION OF DISABILITY AND SEXUALITY

## A Historical and Contemporary Perspective Within the United States

*Natasha M. Lee-Johnson and Nahime G. Aguirre Mtanous*

This chapter presents an overview of historical and contemporary issues about race, disability, and sexuality. Specifically, we outline an inextricable link between the development of race and disability with implications for sexuality. Drawing upon social construction theory, we demonstrate that disability is contextual and socially constructed relative to citizenship, color, culture, ethnicity, gender, and linguistics. In the United States (U.S.), disability status is established by the dominant white racial group that either directly creates social conditions that induce illness, injuries, and poor functioning or develops standards of normality and exclude those who do not meet such a standard due to being minoritized and marginalized through globalization efforts. We acknowledge that the U.S. is diverse; however, this chapter is limited to five distinct racial or ethnic groups because international identities, such as nationalities and ethnicities, are aggregated into Black, Indigenous, Latine, Asian, and White groups in the U.S. We also discuss on these groups within the context of their international origins.

This practice of racial identity construction is deeply rooted in the United States history of ableism and classism. Goddard, an American psychologist and segregationist, described an assessment test of immigrant intelligence among newly arriving Italians, Poles, Hungarians, Slavs, and Russians in the *Journal of Delinquency* (1917). Immigration fit was assessed using the Binet assessment exam, the I.Q. test of the time. Barring test-takers access to an interpreter, the test did not consider cultural differences, travel fatigue, or language barriers. Unsurprisingly, the results suggested that over 80% of the immigrants were "feeble-minded," "morons," or "imbeciles" – all mental health diagnoses of the time. Based on this biased testing, many immigrants were considered disabled and were barred from citizenship. White Americans

DOI: 10.4324/9781003308331-21

of the time explicitly used early standardized tests to disable, discriminate, and perpetuate social hierarchies. Those immigrants considered fit for citizenship were placed in a social hierarchy below white Americans but above Black, Indigenous, Latine, and Asian groups. However, these immigrants were eventually absorbed into what is commonly labeled as whiteness.

To maintain white purity, white people constructed narratives that situated them in positions of superiority, such as the white pure womanhood myth. However, ideals of white purity required racist counternarratives of Indigenous women (i.e., "squaws"), Latine women (i.e., "hot-blooded"), Black women (i.e., "the Jezebel"), and Asian women (i.e., "Suzy Wong") to validate white women's purity and create an under caste of women (Collins, 2004). In this view, Indigenous, Latine, Black, and Asian women were hypersexual, less deserving of the same regard as white women and responsible for their own victimization.

Maintaining white purity called for genetic profiling and subsequent limitation of "defective" or disabled members of society, otherwise referred to as *eugenics*. The eugenic movement aimed to breed out and sterilize the white poor, white disabled people, and white criminals while preventing interracial relationships and procreation between white and non-white people (Mitchell & Snyder, 2003). The U.S. eugenics movement spread internationally, particularly influencing Germany's forced sterilization program engineered by the Nazi Party. Blending antisemitism with eugenic theory, the Nazi Party systemically murdered as many as 200,000 mentally ill or physically disabled people and six million Jewish people to maintain white purity. Another aim of the eugenics movement was to control population growth and reproduction of Black, Indigenous, Latine, and Asian people through forced sterilization.

Here, we examine the legacies of pathology and oppression across disability, race, and sexuality for Black, Indigenous, Latine, and Asian groups. Although we briefly summarize the history of racial groups in the U.S., we recognize that this is forever changing as there is no definitive story, and history is consistently revisited and rewritten with new insights and perspectives. Furthermore, we maintain that disability and sexuality are inherent to the human condition, and the stigmatization of disability and sexuality is a by-product of colonialism and white supremacy.

## Indigenous and Native People

Indigenous or native people share ancestral ties to the lands and natural resources in the U.S., and they are unique in that their existence pre-dates the concept of race. Through white colonialism, Indigenous peoples have endured epidemics, displacement, and near extinction, and they continue to grapple with racialization (Brown, 2020). While some Indigenous-identifying people are not associated with tribal nations, others might argue that Indigenous means being an enrolled member of a Tribal nation (Brown, 2020). There are numerous Tribal nations where people can only enroll if at least some of their ancestors belonged to their specific tribe. A more controversial "blood quantum" system requires a specific fraction of full-blooded Indigenous ancestors. Blood quantum laws were initially imposed upon the Indigenous tribes by the U.S. government to define, measure, and limit the population of the Indigenous race (Brown, 2020). This effort would ensure that only Indigenous people could access treaty obligations and social benefits (like healthcare and education). Blood quantum and other restrictive systems often disrupt dating, marriage, and procreation, because tribal members are concerned with the enrollment status of their potential families and maximizing genetic diversity among tribes (Bachman, 2019).

As with race, concepts of disability have also been imposed on Indigenous peoples through white colonialism. Before colonization efforts, Indigenous people in North America did not view disability as an identity label or something to be fixed (Ineese-Nash, 2020). Rather, Indigenous people adhere to the philosophy that disability is a part of natural biological and neurological diversity (Soldatic, 2015). The tendency of biomedical identification, wherein biological differences are construed as a limitation or disability, imposes the medical model of disability as a form of colonization. The medical model goes beyond identifying biological differences to pathologizing differences (Oliver, 1983) and places the need for accommodations on the individual. Tribal nations beyond the Western hemisphere have long histories of accommodating biological differences (Ineese-Nash, 2020), which would become known as the social model of disability (Oliver, 1983). For Indigenous people with biological differences, accessibility efforts have long been a community effort (Ineese-Nash, 2020).

Stereotyped as uncivil, white colonists established residential schools and separated Indigenous children from their families from 1869 to 1960. The stated aim of these schools was to "Kill the Indian, Save the Man" by indoctrinating white Christian principals and prohibiting Indigenous cultural rituals and languages (Churchill, 2004). Indigenous scholar, Ward Churchill (2004), conceptualized these practices as having genocidal intent. This stereotype would contribute to eugenic practices like involuntary sterilization under the landmark 1927 case of Buck v. Bell, which upheld a compulsory sterilization law (Soldatic, 2015). The sterilization of Indigenous people through federal program like Indian Health Services had grave implications for the population health, because it reduced the potential for genetic diversity, a known protective factor against disease. Such social disadvantages of colonialism are linked to contemporary violence against Indigenous peoples, substance abuse, as well as physical and mental health issues among Indigenous communities (Bachman, 2019).

## Contemporary Issues Within Indigenous and Native Communities

Contemporarily, Indigenous peoples on reservations exist within federally recognized Tribes and state-recognized Tribes. Federally recognized Tribes are independent political entities with their governmental structures and have "nation-to-nation" relationships with the U.S. government. They are eligible for economic benefits, including education, housing, and healthcare. However, state-recognized tribes are those recognized only through individual states and can exercise tribe-to-state relationships. Federally recognized Tribes are often state-recognized tribes, but state-recognized Tribes are not inherently federal-recognized Tribes. These distinctions are important because the government's efforts to suppress Tribal sovereignty are linked with mental, physical, and sexual health disparities among Indigenous peoples (National Association of Social Workers, 2009).

Health and human service professionals working with Tribal communities should understand that Tribal populations may not be identified with prescribed labels associated with race, disabilities, gender, and sexuality. Indigenous people may identify with a range of racialized identities, including "Native," "Tribal Citizen," "First Peoples," "Alaska Native," "American Indian," and "Native American." For professionals who use racial labels like "Native American" or "American Indian," this can create challenges with accuracy of data collection. For example, at least one study suggests that Indigenous mortality rates are underreported due to racial misclassification on death certifications (Arias et al., 2016). Similarly, Indigenous people may not be identified as disabled, given it is language of colonizers, potentially underestimating the representation of disabilities among the community. Indigenous people are more likely to develop a social identity with their respective Tribal backgrounds than with disability (Shakespeare, 1996). Finally, health and human service professionals can work to decolonize processes that limit gender expression to binary constructs (i.e., man and woman or boy and girl). Indigenous people who are identified as *Two-Spirit* perform their gender and sexuality outside of the false woman-man binary. Two-spirited people fulfill a unique role in their communities, as their gender and sexuality presentation plays a role in spiritual guidance for other Indigenous folks from their Nation (Wilson, 1996). Due to its cultural, spiritual, and historical context, Two-Spirit is a term used exclusively by Indigenous peoples. The tradition of Two-Spirit is a type of nonbinary gender and sexual expression; however, it exists outside the colonial definitions of gender and sexuality.

> **Case Study 1.0:** This case has adapted the story "The Erasure of Indigenous People in Chronic Illness" by Jen Deerinwater from the book *Disability Visibility: First-Person Stories From the Twenty-First Century*, edited by Disability Advocate, Alice Wong.
>
> Jen Deerinwater is an Indigenous person with multiple disabilities and a member of the Cherokee Nation of Oklahoma. Jen recalls instances where she is forced to identify as "American Indian," "Native American," or "Other" to access services, but Jen simply identifies as a member of the Cherokee Nation of Oklahoma. Jen also resents the structural inequities related to healthcare on the reservation. Jen describes that Indian Health Service (IHS), a U.S. federally funded health clinic, is often the only healthcare that Native people can access. These clinics cannot provide abortion services due to federal funding laws (except in cases of rape, incest, and life-threatening emergencies), despite 84% of Native women being abused and 50% being raped. In fact, Jen suggests that IHS is rarely staffed with sexual assault nurse examiners and the facility is rarely stocked with rape kits.
>
> **Case Question 1.1:** What tension does Jen describe between needing health services and accessing Indian Health Services?
>
> **Case Question 1.2:** What tension does Jen describe between being forced to choose a racial label and accessing services?
>
> **Case Question 1.3:** As a health and human service professional, how can you improve organizational practices so that Jen is not forced to choose a racial identity?

## Latin(o/a/x/e) People

We refer to Latin American descendants living in the U.S. as *Latine* rather than *Hispanic*. *Hispanic* refers to Spanish-speaking communities that descend from Spanish colonial rule. While *Hispanic* includes people from Spain and excludes those from Brazil, Latin(o/a/x/e) is reserved for those from Latin America, including people from Brazil but not Spain. Etymologically, for peoples throughout Latin America, the use of *Hispanic* word indicates a current ownership of Spain. In observation of the social and legal independence of the peoples within the Latin American region, we will use Latin(o/a/x/e) to refer to the portion of people who have experienced colonization from the Iberian empires. Furthermore, disabled Spanish-speaking Latines focus on using-*e* for inclusive language, as it aids in communication with people with various types of disabilities (Slemp, 2020). For example, disabled people whose primary mode of communication is through high-tech devices can communicate nonbinary gender and sexuality identities with-*e*. Using-*x* will force the device to mispronounce or spell the intended word in Spanish. The suffix-*e* is also seen as more accessible for all modes of Spanish communication as-*e* is already a suffix used in nongendered words in Spanish. Finally, the suffix-*e* is socially preferred to-*x* among disabled folks, as-*x* may serve as a social indicator of advanced education that was historically inaccessible to disabled Latines (Salinas, 2020). Dictating the gendered role of words to identify disabled Latines aligns the region with global disability justice efforts.

Latin America is a multicontinental region that has experienced colonial exploitation. The territorial and economic control by Iberian empires that united the regions also sought to create homogeneity in the social movement of the Latin American peoples (Yun-Casalilla, 2022). The Kingdom of New Spain exerted control over the Indigenous people of Latin America by implementing a caste system (Dikötter, 1998). The Spanish caste system dictated the social mobility of colonized people depending on the color of their skin and their ties to the Spanish Peninsula. The accessibility of employment, wealth-generating ventures, and educational opportunities were all dictated based on an individual's ancestry. Implementing the caste system for the Indigenous populations also came with strict social norms, including the forced religious conversion of a whole continent to Catholicism. Alongside the Spanish racial classifications, Indigenous peoples of Latin America were indoctrinated using religious and sexual codes to create further control over the population by gendering community jobs that were communal duties before colonization (García-Del Moral, 2022). For example, child-rearing duties shifted from community work to individual work for women. The strict binaries during colonial rule dictate what can be done by whom due to their blood quantum and gender.

Though independence from Iberian rule over most of Latin America occurred during the beginning of the 19th century, the effects of colonization are still felt today. One such example of the transcendent nature of colonial rule includes the development of *machismo* [legally codified toxic masculinity] ideologies and the subsequent effect of *femicidio* [femicide] throughout Latin America (García-Del Moral, 2016; García-Del Moral & Neumann, 2019). However, disabled Latines are cast away as people who cannot engage in sexuality nor perform sexual expression (García-Del Moral & Neumann, 2019). Disabled Latines have often been discouraged from engaging in explicit sexual expression due to fear of the sexual reproduction of more disabled people, which has historically led to sexual suppression and forced sterilization (Dikötter, 1998). The disempowerment of disabled Latines is linked to their ability to produce economic value, which itself has long been tied to colorism stemming from the Spanish Caste System implemented during colonization.

## Contemporary Issues Within Latine Communities

Disabled Latines have worked to decolonize their sexual expression and access to education through a focus on language accessibility. Nonbinary disabled Latines in the U.S. can receive accommodations and services to support their lives and health; however, government programs like Medicaid or Social Security impose gender binaries that make these programs inaccessible (Diehl et al., 2017). There are not enough gender-affirming support services for LGBTQ+ disabled Latines (Bailey et al., 1999). They often must make do with multiple imperfect solutions to receive adequate accommodations, especially from providers that assume that Latine culture is a monolith in which all people speak the same language in the same way (Skillern & Carter, 2021; Suarez-Balcazar et al., 2021). In 2019, 36.3% of Latines in the United States had Medicaid or public health insurance coverage, causing many disabled Latines and their families to seek public support to receive appropriate accommodations. Some examples include informal and unstructured job training, community mental health clinics, paying out of pocket for translation services, and living in an unsupportive environment (Suarez-Balcazar et al., 2021).

For people that communicate nonverbally, different modes of sign language, like Creole, Spanish, and Pidgin, are popular modes of communication for Latines Sordos [Deaf Latines]. Modes of translation between sign languages originating from Latin America are not standardized in the United States (Jones et al., 1997). While many organizations require health and human service professionals to be certified in non-English language or use language translators to complete their social work practice, family members of disabled people who are most familiar (often children) with their specific use of nonverbal communication are key translators.

---

**Case Study 2.0:** This case is an adaptation of Angelica's Narrative in Latina Sexuality: De(re)constructing Gender and Cultural Expectations in Midlife by Yvette G. Flores.

Angelica is a middle-age Mexican immigrant who was referred to a mental health professional by her medical doctor for "nerves." Angelica shared that she was a virgin when she married her husband 28 years ago, and she had never experienced an orgasm throughout their time together, though she wanted to experience an orgasm. After confiding in her sister who is more acculturated to the U.S., she was encouraged to purchase a vibrator. Angelica admitted that she tried it and experienced pleasure from the vibrator; however, she also felt guilty, because she believed that she should not touch herself "down there" and that sexual pleasure should only occur with her husband. Throughout therapeutic sessions, Angelica explored how her cultural upbringing and lack of communication within her family about sexual health potentially influenced her relationship with her own body.

**Case Question 2.1:** How does Angelica's culture and "nerves" influence her sex life?

**Case Question 2.2:** What attitudes regarding sexuality does Angelica share?

**Case Question 2.3:** How can the mental health professional support Angelica in obtaining more sexual satisfaction within her marriage?

## African American and Black Peoples

It is no surprise that Africa, a continent with 54 countries, has a wide range of cultural perspectives on disability and sexuality, including a mix of assumptions, misconceptions, and beliefs – spiritual, natural, or supernatural. However, much of what is known about African concepts of disability and sexuality has been disseminated through public health data. Although public health data has an essential role in health equity for African people, the hyper-focus on disease and health disparities pathologies the complex nature of the disability. In addition, the tendency to impose U.S. cultural values of sexuality can erase and paternalize values of African peoples. For example, a prominent ideological debate centers on the practice of female circumcision and the protection of African women and girls from what is perceived as "female genital mutilation." However, ethnographers like Dellenborg (2004) and Leonard (2000) find that such practices are deeply tied to regional differences that involve increasing sexual pleasure within marriage, gaining "magical" knowledge and wisdom, and pursuing social inclusion, among other aesthetic reasons. In the U.S., we must contend that female circumcision can be the practice of female agency that is otherwise empowering within some African cultures in Senegal (Dellenborg, 2004) and Chad (Leonard, 2000). We must also reconcile that much of what the U.S. understands about African views on disability and sexuality has been informed through the lens of global colonialism and anti-Black dominance from white people.

The trans-Atlantic slave trade, or the transfer of West Africans by predominately European slave traders to North America beginning in 1619, resulted in a racial caste system (Alexander, 2012) predicated on ableism. Having colonized Indigenous land, white landowners required physical labor from enslaved Africans to cultivate and maintain it. Enslaved people faced disabling conditions on ships as they were packed and chained into tight, suffocating spaces while exposed to extreme weather, inadequate food and water, limited sanitation, and sexual abuse from captors (Nielsen, 2012).

Labeled as inferior and unintelligent, enslaved African people and their descendants [henceforth "Black people"] had little understanding of the English language or customs. Slaveholders and apologists for slavery used Africans' supposed mental and physical inferiority to legitimize and justify slavery (Nielsen, 2012). African and Black people were consequently sold, objectified, and exploited for their physical and sexual labor productivity. Enslaved women were most vulnerable to sexual abuse. With no right or protection to refute sexual advances, it was possible to be raped by either the white slaveholders or enslaved men. In addition to physical labor, enslaved women were forced into pregnancy and birth. Forced childbirth frequently resulted in disabilities like prolapsed uteruses or vesicovaginal fistula (Nielsen, 2012), limiting mobility and increasing the risk of infection and death. Women who gave birth to children with significant disabilities experienced greater discrimination as their reproductive worth was questioned (Nielsen, 2012). To circumvent the demands of slavery, enslaved people would pretend to be disabled, such as faking cognition issues, pregnancies, or sickness, to obtain a lighter workload or avoid punishment, a practice colloquially called *shuckin' and jivin'*. Though dangerous if discovered, employing the disabled persona sometimes served as a protective factor.

After chattel slavery was abolished in the U.S., anti-Black racism progressed to legalized segregation under the Plessy v. Ferguson doctrine, the mass incarceration, entrenching patterns of social and economic disadvantage in Black communities. Black advocacy groups like the Black Panther Party created mutual aid programs to provide education, food, housing, and medical care, especially to disabled and older adults (Schalk, 2022). The Civil Rights Movement of the 1950s and 1960s contributed to the overturning of Plessy v. Ferguson and established precedent for equal rights for Black people and many other disadvantaged groups (e.g., disabled, LGBTQ+). The height of the civil rights era brought new challenges for reproductive rights as the involuntary sterilization rate rose for Black women (Stern, 2020), likely related to the white fears of desegregation and integration.

## Contemporary Issues Within Black Communities

Black women with disabilities remain less likely to report sexual violence (Barlow, 2020) and utilize sexual violence services (Schalk, 2020). This phenomenon mirrors historic exclusions of Black women from femininity and womanhood (Collins, 2004) and disability (Bailey & Mobley, 2019) discourse. The "strong-Black woman" caricature, a racist trope prescribed to Black women where they are thought to have uniquely high pain tolerance and the innate ability to conquer difficult obstacles, is often internalized within Black communities (Collins, 2004; Miles, 2019). This trope is used to justify physical exploitation that advances the economic labor needs of White supremacy. It is thought that Black women have internalized this trope to cope with economic and social conditions underscored by white supremacy (Geyton et al., 2022), but one counternarrative suggests that Black women have reclaimed this trope as an act of resistance (Davis, 2015). While it is evident that Black women invoke the strong Black woman trope for empowerment, the trope disallows Black women from having disabilities (Bailey & Mobley, 2019).

In tandem with this trope, a Black communal teaching urges Black children to be "twice as good [as white people] to get half as much." This teaching is designed to protect Black children against racism (Bailey & Mobley, 2019) through the virtue of hard work. Through these socialization practices, Black people subsequently learn that they are valued for their strength and excellence, leaving little from identity-based disability, increasing difficulties with discussing trauma, health disparities, and disabilities. Health and human service professionals should be mindful of how they discuss disability, as Black clients may be less likely to relate to such experiences.

Health and human service professions have been linked with a long history of exploiting and mistreating Black people, which is connected to modern mistrust of health and human service establishments. Notably, the field of obstetrics and gynecology is in part built on a history of medical experimentation of Black women. Known as the father of modern gynecology, James Marion Sims purchased three enslaved women (Lucy, Betsy, and Anarcha), to perform over 30 surgical experiments each without anesthesia to develop a surgical treatment for vesicovaginal fistulas, a tearing between the bladder and the wall of the vagina (Washington, 2006). Mirroring this legacy of exploitation, John's Hopkins Hospital harvested cells from Henrietta Lacks, young mother who sought treatment for cervical cancer, without consent. Researchers discovered that her cells were the first and only human cells that could reproduce rather than die (Skloot, 2010). These "HeLa" cells were widely distributed and are still used to study treatment on the growth of cancer cells (Skloot, 2010). These examples coupled with the Tuskeegee Study, where researchers did not inform Black men of their positive syphilis status and rather studied the symptomology of the virus despite having available treatment (Washington, 2006), all relates to hesitancy in help-seeking behaviors that would otherwise improve sexual health.

**Case-Study Activity 3.0:** This case is an adaptation of "When You Are Waiting to Be Healed" by June Eric-Udorie from the book *Disability Visibility: First-Person Stories From the Twenty-First Century*, edited by disability advocate Alice Wong.

June Eric Udorie is a Black English woman born with congenital idiopathic nystagmus, characterized by involuntary and repetitive eye movement, which causes vision impairment. Although June's condition was rarely mentioned in her household, June prayed to be healed from it, because it significantly impacted her social life. However, by age 15, a doctor recommended that June register as partially sighted. She recalls:

I was stunned. The implication – the idea that I could have a disability – was so momentous that I didn't say anything for a while. I was learning to navigate the world as a young Black woman, and I did not feel that I had the right to claim a disability . . . claiming that label felt like lauding myself with an unnecessary burden.

June informed her mother that the doctor recommended registering as partially sighted, but the call went silent, and her mother hung up, never to mention it again. Some years later, June describes embracing herself as a "disabled Black girl" with a visual disability, and no longer waiting to be healed.

**Case Question 4.1:** Was there tension between June's disabled body and racial and gender identity? If so, what was it?
**Case Question 4.2:** How do you think the lack of communication around June's disability might have impacted her willingness to discuss sex and sexuality with her mother?
**Case Question 4.3:** As a health and human service professional, how might you support June in receiving accommodation? In supporting her family unit?

## Asian and Asian American Peoples

Asian American people are often regarded as a homogenous group; however, the term is representative of people who emigrate (and their descendants) to the U.S. from Asia, a continent with 48 countries that can be divided into five regions: Central Asia, East Asia, South Asia, Southeast Asia, and Western Asia. These regions are highly diverse, with high proportions of people who practice Islam, Buddhist, Judaism, Christianity, and Hinduism among other religious and spiritual practices, which all influence sociocultural perspectives of disability and sexuality. Though Asian Americans are diverse, the monolithic perspective is of Asian Americans centers East Asian cultures (e.g., China, Japan, North Korea, and South Korea).

The centering of East Asian people can be traced to early Chinese immigrants, who were among the first Asian people documented to emigrate to the United States in 1847. In pursuit of work, the Chinese immigrants endured violence from white Americans who feared that the Chinese would disrupt white Americans' values, democracy, and economic progress, a set of fear-based beliefs known as "The Yellow Peril." The Yellow Peril was a racist and ableist ideology that hinged, because Chinese immigrants were defective, having many physical and mental disabilities and sexual immorality. Chinese people were considered "unfit" to integrate into white civility (Shim, 1998), and many were involuntarily sterilized (Reilly, 1987). Yellow Peril ideology shaped immigration law, building toward the Chinese Exclusion Act of 1882 – restricting Chinese immigration to the United States – and set a precedent that outlawed Chinese immigration by 1902. It was not until the dawning of the Civil Rights Movement in 1943 that Chinese and American-born descendants retained the right to citizenship. The term "Asian American" can be traced to the Civil Rights Movement, as it was used to build coalitions between racially marginalized people to build coalitions that advanced racial equality.

### Contemporary Issues Within Asian and Asian American Peoples

Asian Americans, particularly those of East Asian descent, are situated in a peculiar racial context, as they face seemingly *positive*, yet still harmful racist stereotypes called the "model minority myth." The model minority myth is a set of Americanized expectations placed upon most Asian people; they are presumed intelligent, wealthy, hard-working, self-reliant, spiritually enlightened, and obedient. Although frequently referred to as *positive*, the myth contributes to the invisibility of disabled Asian people and creates barriers to accessing accommodations, mental health resources, and social services (Cheng et al., 2017). It is estimated that one in ten Asian Americans lives with disabilities (Courtney-Long et al., 2017), but this conservative estimate likely linked to the model minority myth's potential to foster underdiagnosis among Asian Americans.

Further "*positive*" racist stereotypes do not preclude Asian American people from white violence, as demonstrated throughout the COVID-19 pandemic. With the COVID-19 virus originating in Wuhan, China, there was a widespread misbelief in the U.S. that Asian people were the primary cause of the virus and spread, invoking yellow peril ideology, physical violence, and xenophobia toward Asian Americans. While the model minority myth primarily centers East Asia, Asian people from Central and Western Asia – two regions often referred to as "the Middle East" with high proportions of Muslims who have darker skin – are negatively racialized in the U.S. These Asian groups are portrayed as violent religious radicals, whereby they are violent, hypersexual predators, and the women are oppressed, sexually abused, and enslaved by men within the Islamic religion. These racist caricatures were, in part, spread through American media following the September 11, 2001, terrorist attack that was reported as being orchestrated by Islamic extremist groups – despite the peaceful nature of Islam. Given such racist stereotypes of descendants of Central and Western Asian, Asian Americans may be less likely to seek help, especially for issues related to mental, physical, and sexual abuse.

Furthermore, the model minority expectations placed on Asian American families can be internalized, contributing to disability stigmas and fostering feelings of fear, shame, or dismissal from professionals or family members. Therefore, disabled Asian Americans may need support in their daily activities at school and work but have difficulty accessing resources. Many Asian Americans live in multi-lingual and multi-generational households where disability language, such as mental health diagnoses and other diseases, render non-translatable. Thus, it is likely that the prevalence of disabled people is under-identified among Asian American communities, contributing to disparities in accessing economic, educational, and healthcare resources.

Finally, model minority stereotypes also apply within sexual contexts for Asian Americans. Public perceptions of cisgender Asian women as docile and subservient sexual partners were actively created during the 20th century to foster the idea these women were sexually exploitative economic commodities (Chan, 1988). During the American occupation of the Philippines, Japan, and China, these stereotypes were encouraged as a means of colonization efforts, in that U.S. soldiers could partake in sexual encounters with Asian women as stress relief without worry of backlash due to their "naturally subservient" nature. Such perceptions of Asian women abroad continue to affect the social roles available for sexually active Asian Americans today. Stereotypes insinuating that Asian men have smaller penises actively lower the pool of available sexual partners for this population (Chan, 1988). Asian women fighting against stereotypes of sexual subservience experience higher rates of psychological distress (Chan, 1988).

**Case-Study Activity 4.0:** This case is an adaptation of "If You Can't Fast, Give" by Maysoon Zayid from the book *Disability Visibility: First-Person Stories From the Twenty-First Century*, edited by disability advocate Alice Wong.

Maysoon Zayid, an Asian American woman of Palestinian descent, was born with cerebral palsy and raised as a Muslim. One component of the Islamic religion is Ramadan, a month-long fast where no food or beverages are consumed between sunrise and sunset. This is an important time for those of fate, because it allows Muslims to focus on their faith and ultimately become closer to God. As a person with cerebral palsy, Maysoon was technically exempt from fasting, but during her school years, she chose to fast despite the potential harm to her body because she dedicated herself to her religion. Maysoon recalled the difficulty of fasting at school in the United States. She describes how her school teachers would fear for her life, convinced that her Muslim parents were forcing their disabled child to engage in fasting.

**Case Question 4.1:** What tension did Maysoon describe between her disabled body and her Muslim fate?

**Case Question 4.2:** How did Maysoon view her fasting as opposed to her school-teachers? How can the concept of bodily autonomy be applied to this situation?

**Case Question 4.3:** What do you think of Maysoon's decision to fast as a person with cerebral palsy? How might health and human service agencies promote self-determination while promoting safety?

## Conclusion

Although distinct racial and ethnic groups, this chapter presents four commonalities across Indigenous, Latine, Black, and Asian American experiences. One, disability and race have been co-constructed by the white dominant group to discern the worthy from the unworthy, the desirable from the undesirable, and the fit from the unfit. This phenomenon can be traced through policy initiatives implication in the United States ranging from restriction of citizenship to over-incarceration and policing. Two, racial groups have had to contend with the threat of eugenics and sterilization to establish reproductive control and to reduce the unworthy, undesirables, and unfit from the population. This manifested through Indigenous boarding schools, Anti-Black chattel slavery, the Spanish Caste System, and Yellow Peril ideologies. Three, racially marginalized groups often identify more with their race than with disability identity-language. It can be difficult for many marginalized groups such as Indigenous, Latine, Black, and Asian communities to discuss disability and health disparities due to linguistic translation or the need to overcome racist and ableist stereotypes placed on the group. Four, all racially marginalized groups experience some degree of hyper-sexualization or fetishization that is placed upon them by white dominant groups. This is specifically true for women and non-cisgender individuals, making them more vulnerable to sexual violence and abuse.

## Resources

### Books

Care Work: Dreaming Disability Justice by Leah Lakshmi Piepzna-Samarasinha
Bodyminds Reimagined: (Dis)ability, Race, and Gender in Black Women's Speculative Fiction by Sami Schalk
The Kiss Quotient by Helen Hoang (Romance novel featuring autistic Asian character)
A Quick & Easy Guide to Sex & Disability by A. Andrews
Year of the Tiger: An Activist's Life by Alice Wong

### Organizations

The Century Foundation: Bridging Reproductive Justice and Disability Justice (www.youtube.com/watch?v=BSZ65Heqg-0)
Sins Invalid: An Unshamed Claim to Beauty in the Face of Invisibility www.sinsinvalid.org

## References

Alexander, M. (2012). *The new Jim Crow: Mass incarceration in the age of colorblindness. (LSU Library (Main Collection) HV9950.A437 2012; Revised edition/with a new foreword by Cornel West.).* New Press; Louisiana State University. http://libezp.lib.lsu.edu/login?url=https://search.ebscohost.com/login.aspx?direct=true&db=cat00252a&AN=lalu.4592318&site=eds-live&scope=site&profile=eds-main

Arias, E., Heron, M., & Hakers, J. (2016). The validity of race and Hispanic-origin reporting on death certificates in the United States: An update. *National Center for Health Statistics, Vital Health Statistics, 2*(172), 29.

Bachman, J. S. (Ed.). (2019). *Cultural genocide: Law, politics, and global manifestations.* Routledge.

Bailey, D. B., Skinner, D., Rodriguez, P., Gut, D., & Correa, V. (1999). Awareness, use, and satisfaction with services for Latino parents of young children with disabilities. *Exceptional Children, 65*(3), 367–381. https://doi.org/10.1177/001440299906500307

Bailey, M., & Mobley, I. A. (2019). Work in the intersections: A black feminist disability framework. *Gender & Society, 33*(1), 19–40. https://doi.org/10.1177/0891243218801523

Barlow, J. N. (2020). *Black women, the forgotten survivors of sexual assault.* American Psychological Association. www.apa.org/pi/about/newsletter/2020/02/black-women-sexual-assault

Brown, H. E. (2020). Who is an Indian child? Institutional context, tribal sovereignty, and race-making in fragmented states. *American Sociological Review, 85*(5), 776–805. https://doi.org/10.1177/0003122420944165

Chan, C. S. (1988). Asian-American women: Psychological responses to sexual exploitation and cultural stereotypes. *Women & Therapy, 6*(4), 33–38.

Cheng, A. W., Chang, J., O'Brien, J., Budgazad, M. S., & Tsai, J. (2017). Model minority stereotype: Influence on perceived mental health needs of Asian Americans. *Journal of Immigrant and Minority Health, 19*(3), 572–581. https://doi.org/10.1007/s10903-016-0440-0

Churchill, W. (2004). *Kill the Indian, save the man: The genocidal impact of American Indian residential schools. (LSU library (main collection) E97.C57 2004).* City Lights; Louisiana State University. http://libezp.lib.lsu.edu/login?url=https:// search.ebscohost.com/login.aspx?direct=true&db=cat00252a&AN=lalu.219086 4&site=eds-live&scope=site&profile=eds-main

Collins, P. H. (2004). *Black sexual politics: African Americans, gender, and the new racism.* Routledge.

Courtney-Long, E. A., Romano, S. D., Carroll, D. D., & Fox, M. H. (2017). Socioeconomic factors at the intersection of race and ethnicity influencing health risks for people with disabilities. *Journal of Racial and Ethnic Health Disparities, 4*(2), 213–222. https://doi.org/10.1007/s40615-016-0220-5

Davis, S. M. (2015). The "strong black woman collective": A developing theoretical framework for understanding collective communication practices of black women. *Women's Studies in Communication, 38*(1), 20–35. https://doi.org/10.1080/07491409.2014.953714

Dellenborg, L. (2004). A reflection on the cultural meanings of female circumcision. In H. A. Becker (Ed.), *Experiences from fieldwork in Casamance, Southern Senegal.* Nordiska Afrikainstitutet.

Diehl, A., Vieira, D. L., Zaneti, M. M., Fanganiello, A., Sharan, P., Robles, R., & de Jesus Mari, J. (2017). Social stigma, legal and public health barriers faced by the third gender phenomena in Brazil, India and Mexico: Travestis, hijras and muxes. *International Journal of Social Psychiatry, 63*(5), 389–399. https://doi.org/10.1177/0020764017706989

Dikötter, F. (1998). Race culture: Recent perspectives on the history of eugenics. *The American Historical Review, 103*(2), 467–478. https://doi.org/10.1086/ahr/103.2.467

García-Del Moral, P. (2016). Feminicidio: TWAIL in action. *American Journal of International Law, 110,* 31–36. https://doi.org/10.1017/S239877230000235X

García-Del Moral, P., & Neumann, P. (2019). The making and unmaking of Feminicidio/Femicidio laws in Mexico and Nicaragua. *Law & Society Review, 53*(2), 452–486. https://doi.org/10.1111/lasr.12380

García-Del Moral, P. (2022). Indigenous women, multiple violences, and legal activism: Beyond the dichotomy of human rights as "law" and as "ideas for social movements". *Sociology Compass, 16*(6), e12984.

Geyton, T., Johnson, N., & Ross, K. (2022). 'I'm good': Examining the internalization of the strong Black woman archetype. *Journal of Human Behavior in the Social Environment, 32*(1), 1–16. https://doi.org/10.1080/10911359.2020.1844838

Goddard, H. H. (1917). Mental tests and the immigrant. *Journal of Deliquency, 2,* 243–277.

Ineese-Nash, N. (2020). Disability as a colonial construct: The missing discourse of culture in conceptualizations of disabled indigenous children. *Canadian Journal of Disability Studies, 9*(3), Article 3. https://doi.org/10.15353/cjds.v9i3.645

Jones, B. E., Clark, G. M., & Soltz, D. F. (1997). Characteristics and practices of sign language interpreters in inclusive education programs. *Exceptional Children, 63*(2), 257–268. https://doi.org/10.1177/001440299706300209

Leonard, L. (2000). "We did it for pleasure only": Hearing alternative tales of female circumcision. *Qualitative Inquiry, 6*(2), 212–228. https://doi.org/10.1177/107780040000600203

Miles, A. L. (2019). "Strong black women": African American women with disabilities, intersecting identities, and inequality. *Gender & Society, 33*(1), 41–63. https://doi.org/10.1177/0891243218814820

Mitchell, D., & Snyder, S. (2003). The Eugenic Atlantic: Race, disability, and the making of an international Eugenic science, 1800–1945. *Disability & Society, 18*(7), 843–864. https://doi.org/10.1080/0968759032000127281

National Association of Social Workers. (2009). *Sovereignty and the health of Indigenous peoples* (pp. 333–337). Social Work Speaks. www.socialworkers.org/assets/secured/documents/da/da2010/referred/Sovereignty.pdf

Nielsen, K. E. (2012). *A disability history of the United States* (vol. 2). Beacon Press.

Oliver, M. (1983). Conclusions: Some professional and organisational aspects of social work with disabled people. In M. Oliver (Ed.), *Social work with disabled people* (pp. 118–137). Macmillan Education UK. https://doi.org/10.1007/978-1-349-86058-6_8

Reilly, P. R. (1987). Involuntary sterilization in the United States: A surgical solution. *The Quarterly Review of Biology, 62*(2), 153–170. https://doi.org/10.1086/415404

Salinas, C. (2020). The complexity of the "x" in Latinx: How Latinx/a/o students relate to, identify with, and understand the term Latinx. *Journal of Hispanic Higher Education, 19*(2), 149–168. https://doi.org/10.1177/1538192719900382

Schalk, S. (2020). Contextualizing black disability and the culture of dissemblance. *Symposium: Race and the Inner Lives of Black Women in the Middle West, 6*.

Schalk, S. (2022). *Black disability politics*. Duke University Press.

Shakespeare, T. (1996). Exploring the divide: Illness and disability. In C. Barnes & G. Mercer (Eds.), *Disability, identity and difference* (pp. 94–113). The Disability Press.

Shim, D. (1998). From yellow peril through model minority to renewed yellow peril. *Journal of Communication Inquiry, 22*(4), 385–409.

Skillern, S., & Carter, E. W. (2021). La Transición: Parent perspectives on transition for Latino youth with intellectual and developmental disabilities. *Journal of Research in Special Educational Needs, 21*(4), 323–333. https://doi.org/10.1111/1471-3802.12530

Skloot, R. (2010). *The immortal life of Henrietta Lacks. (LSU library (main collection) RC265.6.L24 S55 2010)*. Crown Publishers; Louisiana State University. http://libezp.lib.lsu.edu/login?url=https://search.ebscohost.com/login.aspx?direct=true&db=cat00252a&AN=lalu.3686710&site=eds-live&scope=site&profile=eds-main

Slemp, K. (2020). Latin@s or latinxs? *Innovation in Spanish gender inclusive oral expression* (p. 15). Proceedings of the 2020 Annual Conference of the Canadian Linguistic Association. University of Toronto.

Soldatic, K. (2015). Postcolonial reproductions: Disability, indigeneity and the formation of the white masculine settler state of Australia. *Social Identities, 21*(1), 53–68. https://doi.org/10.1080/13504630.2014.995352

Stern, A. (2020). *Forced sterilization policies in the US targeted minorities and those with disabilities – and lasted into the 21st century*. University of Michigan. https://ihpi.umich.edu/news/forced-sterilization-policies-us-targeted-minorities-and-those-disabilities-and-lasted-21st

Suarez-Balcazar, Y., Early, A., Miranda, D. E., Marquez, H., Maldonado, A., & Garcia-Ramirez, M. (2021). Community-engaged asset mapping with Latinx immigrant families of youth with disabilities. *American Journal of Community Psychology, 70*(1–2), 89–101. https://doi.org/10.1002/ajcp.12578

Washington, H. A. (2006). *Medical Apartheid: The dark history of medical experimentation on Black Americans from colonial times to the present*. Doubleday Books.

Wilson, A. (1996). How we find ourselves: Identity development and two spirit people. *Harvard Educational Review*, 66(2), 303–318.

Yun-Casalilla, B. (2022). Early modern Iberian empires, global history and the history of early globalization. *Journal of Global History*, 17(3), 539–561.

# 17
# NAVIGATING DISABILITY AND SEXUALITY IN OLD AGE

*Jess Francis and Hillary K. Hecht*

## Introduction

While everyone ages over time, not everyone is afforded the opportunity to grow into older adulthood (age 65+). This chapter takes a life course perspective on older adults experiencing disabilities and sexuality as they age. It is the intention of this chapter to disrupt stigmatization of older adults as frail, feeble, depressed, infirm, or asexual. We aim to highlight that while most older adults will live healthily and independently throughout their lives, lesbian, gay, bisexual, queer, transgender, and gender-expansive older adults are significantly more likely to be contending with multiple chronic illnesses and/or disabilities that can impede their ability to age comfortably. We identify ways in which these older adults perform acts of resilience, self-care, and mutual-aid as well as focus on what practitioners and providers can do to serve this community.

## *Language*

We will be referring to a complex and overlapping group of people who share some, but not all, of their identities. In the United States, the term "older adults" typically refers to people aged 65 and older and is used as a threshold to designate social and financial services (Healthy People 2020, 2022). In Nigeria and Indonesia, people aged 60 years and older are considered older adults (Basrowi et al., 2021; Salami & Okunade, 2020). The age at which "older adulthood" starts may be earlier or later along domains of clinical, internal, individual effects of aging within a body, familial and social relationships, or financial retirement thresholds.

*Physical Health*

Physical disabilities can inform people in their mobility, in their activities of daily living, and in the way they interact with other people (Liu et al., 2014; Robb, 2003). In this chapter, we acknowledge a wide range of chronic conditions, disabilities, mobility challenges, injuries, and illnesses that limit our physical health. As we age, many physical changes are expected (like macular degeneration or losing tactile ability). Changes may also be unexpected, happen at different times, or in a different order than we expect. When physical changes do occur, they take effort to adapt to (Jin & Roumell, 2021), and can interrupt how people understand their evolving identities, or the way that their aging affects them (Molton & Yorkston, 2017). Some of these physical health challenges may be congenital disabilities that people have experienced their whole lives, and some are acquired at any age. Evolving physical health needs may impact the role we play in relationships, and how interdependence necessarily functions in our social lives.

> Think about an older adult who you know. How did their physical health change throughout their life? How did they think about their physical health or their physical goals differently as they got older?

*Cognitive Health*

Cognitive and brain health encompass all the functional aspects of mental facilities commonly associated with aging, including dementias. As aging occurs, changes to memory, speed of recall, and other organizing and executive functioning changes occur, but might be hard to recognize in oneself or older adults in your life (Yellowitz, 2005). When seeing patients infrequently or for a short duration of time, it can be difficult to observe changes in cognitive health. Measured scales offer additional, albeit incomplete, information about cognitive and intellectual capacity changes. Cognitive health changes among people with disabilities may take a different trajectory as they age than do the cognitive health changes among nondisabled people. Acquiring new coping strategies for changing cognitive health introduces challenges to recognize, acknowledge, and learn effective responses to evolving cognitive health needs (Meléndez et al., 2018; Baril & Silverman, 2022).

*Mental Health*

Mental health encompasses emotional health, including emotional reactions to life events. Mental health might influence our social identities, and be responsive to how other people treat us because of our social identities

(Hoy-Ellis et al., 2016). Mental health ebbs and flows as we age, get older, or our social circles change.

In current older adults' lifetimes, social perspectives have evolved on experiencing mental health challenges, seeking support, and treatment options available. For example, talking about depression may have been taboo when older adults were coming of age; depression is now, however, commonly discussed among young people (Collins et al., 2014). While young people today might feel comfortable acknowledging their needs and seeking care, older adults may have a range of reactions to the expanded availability of services. Comparably, there may be age discrimination when seeking care in some cultures, creating unique barriers for older adults (Hoy-Ellis et al., 2016). Specialists in geriatrics and gerontology may focus directly on mental health support for older adults, including care for dementias.

### Sexual Orientation

When working with people who are older adults in the 2020s, practitioners can consider the ideas, norms, and language, including cultural-specific attitudes about sexual orientation during older adults' lifespans. Around the world, laws and policies regarding people with marginalized sexual orientations and genders have changed drastically in the past century, and continue to evolve slowly (Farquhar, 2021). While progress has made the world safer and more inviting for people with marginalized sexual orientations, there are responsive backlashes in some places to further disenfranchise people with expansive sexual orientation identities (Farquhar, 2021). Asking clients what language and concepts they use to describe themselves, their communities, and their partner(s) affirms clients' lived experiences.

### Genders

Comparable to how social understanding around orientations have evolved, often quite radically in older adults' lives, so too has the understanding of, labeling of, social and political safety of people with expansive gender identities. Options for safely conceptualizing, exploring, and presenting gender may open safer opportunities today for older adults who came of age in times when it was less safe to do so (Puckett et al., 2022). Clients may have explored or desired to explore their gender in different ways throughout their lives and may continue to evoke their curiosity into their futures.

### Intersecting Social Identities

Older adults have diverse racialized identities, gendered identities and expressions, socioeconomic statuses, and many other fixed and time-variant identities that they have lived (Robinson-Wood & Weber, 2016). Keeping in mind how these social identities may have been perceived throughout a person's lifespan, where in the world they have lived, and the current social context will support providers in acknowledging the aspect of a client's identities that are most salient to them and relevant to their receipt of care and services.

*Stigma Over Time*

Names and labels for many social identities have evolved in the past 60 years, since current older adults were young and coming of age (Emlet, 2016; Puckett et al., 2022). They may have grown up in a time and place where their ideas about identity, the words that they called themselves, and what they called others are words that are perceived very differently today (Puckett et al., 2022). As safety and stigma have evolved, providers can check in and mirror the language that each client uses to build rapport. While socially, language and stigma have changed, clinical and research labels have also evolved.

> Where in your professional life do you notice that your healthcare or service discipline is offering more progressive, affirming language than is the norm in your culture? Where do you notice that you could update language you use in your practice to be less stigmatizing to older adults?

**Review of Literature**

*Socio-Political-Historical Context of LGBTQ2S+ Older Adults*

Considering the lifespan and time period in which current older adults have come of age can give us context for the life experiences that inform their perspectives and worldviews. People who were born in 1955 turned 65 years old in the year 2020, and will be among the younger cohort of older adults in this decade. This generation grew up in the late 1960s and 1970s and witnessed the rapid evolution of global commerce, social rights movements, and technological innovation during their early adulthoods. In the 1980s and 1990s, HIV and AIDS epidemic harmed queer, and multiply marginalized communities globally, while eroding trust in government and healthcare institutions (HIV.gov, 2021). In the 1990s and 2000s, on many continents, civil rights and safety for sexual and gender minorities have expanded rapidly, though in some places, rights have also been restricted and constrained. Since the 2010s, the prevalence of discussing mental health and de-pathologizing LGBTQ2S+ identities has changed clinical and legal contexts for how queer, disabled older adults can access services and resources (Baars, 2019; Beall, 2018; Garrison-Diehn et al., 2022). LGBTQ2S+ people throughout this time period have had considerable safety concerns, social discrimination to housing, employment, education, and healthcare resources, and limited legal access to parenting, marriage, and partner recognition (Cusack et al., 2022; Begun & Kattari, 2016; Gates & Viggiani, 2014; Knochel & Seelman, 2020; Miller et al., 2020; Rowan & Beyer, 2017; Scherrer & Fedor, 2015; Streeter et al., 2020).

Every individual older adult has had a personal experience with each of the aforementioned global events, in addition to their community experiences. As the world today is increasingly safer for LGBTQ2S+ people than 50 years ago, current older adults may have been harmed or disabled by treatment of LGBTQ2S+ people throughout their lifetime. The word "queer" has been a violent slur that has since been reclaimed by some groups of people and current young generations (Morris et al., 2022). Given the pervasive violence using "queer" during their lifetimes, older adults have not universally reclaimed this term (Johnston, 2016). In this chapter, we use a familiar non-comprehensive acronym LGBTQ2S+ to refer to older adults of all marginalized sexual orientations and expansive gender identities.

*Aging and LGBTQS+ Bodies*

LGBTQ2S+ older adults experience unique health disparities compared to older adults in the general mainstream. Compared to their heterosexual counterparts, LGBTQ2S+ older adults are twice as likely to live alone and four times as likely to not have children, (SAGE, 2022). This creates more need for formal caregiving services as informal care from a partner, family member, or child is not guaranteed. This puts them at significantly greater risk for social disconnectedness and loneliness (Fredriksen-Goldsen et al., 2013). Although both social disconnectedness and loneliness are both dimensions of social isolation, loneliness (subjective isolation) and social disconnectedness (objective isolation) have distinct impacts on physical and mental health (Cornwell & Waite, 2009). Furthermore, LGBTQ2S+ elders are more likely to have experienced victimization and discrimination based on gender and sexual identities across their life spans (Fredriksen-Goldsen et al., 2011; Hillman, 2012, 2017). The accumulation of minority stress and societal stigmatization may contribute to both depression and cognitive decline. Exposure to discrimination and chronic stress leaves older adults at distinct risk for developing neurodegenerative health decline such as Alzheimer's disease and related dementias as well as other chronic illnesses and disabilities (Fredriksen-Goldsen et al., 2013). This risk is compounded by the fact that LGBTQ2S+ older adults have been shown to be far less likely to seek out formal healthcare, and more likely to have been denied care by a physician or experience a delay in diagnosis, than heterosexual older adults (Knochel & Seelman, 2020).

These older adults are at increased risk for being discriminated against and denied admittance to assisted living facilities which can exacerbate chronic illness and disability due to lack of adequate and consistent care (SAGE, 2022). For these reasons, LGBTQ2S+ adults are often overlooked and less well served in the healthcare domain. Despite the unique challenges faced by these older adults, this group is known to be resilient and creative in their ability to create community and care for each other and themselves (Fredriksen-Goldsen et al., 2011).

### *Navigating Disability and Sexuality During Aging*

Disability has been conceptualized as a "process of continuous adaptation to changes across the lifespan" (Harley, 2016, p. 622). While disability is grounded in physiological and neurological capacities, it is also a social construct that varies across time and place in relation to a particular culture's normative ideals (Hirschmann, 2013). Similar to the aging process overall, disability can limit autonomy, mobility, and quality of life if adequate supports, assistance, and care are not available. It is estimated that 50% of LGBTQ2S+ older adults experience some form of chronic illness and/or co-occurring disability (Fredriksen-Goldsen et al., 2013). One potential hurdle faced by these adults living with a disability is the need to seek out in-home care and modifications in order to age in place – meaning stay in their homes throughout the aging process. This may be of particular interest to LGBTQ2S+ adults as institutions and facilities have historically enacted discriminatory policies and procedures targeted at the queer community. In the absence of traditional support structures to provide informal care, many LGBTQ2S+ older adults will have to turn to outside care facilities. This presents a paradox for many, as lesbian, gay, bisexual, and transgender individuals have aged with a deep distrust of the healthcare systems and institutions that is based in lived and intergenerational trauma including neglect, abuse, and forced institutionalization (Bloemen et al., 2019). Furthermore, there is a well-documented lack of culturally sensitive and affirming service options for transgender older adults compounding their resistance to seek formal care (Porter et al., 2016).

It is also important to note here that not all LGBTQ2S+ older adults entered into old age with their disabilities and/or chronic illnesses. In fact, some aged into their disability and/or chronic illness. On the other hand, not all LGBTQ2S+ older individuals with a disability and/or chronic illness identified with their sexual orientation throughout their younger years; some came to the realization relatively later in life. These transitions into different identities, especially marginalized identities, may have an impact on an individuals' mental health overall as they process and reconcile their new self-concept (Hirschmann, 2013). Each of these individuals may have also to carry the stress related to a society and healthcare system that can be ageist, ableist, homophobic, and transphobic.

It is not the intention of this section to conflate disability, queerness, or old age with disadvantage or deficit, but rather acknowledge the disproportionate health burden faced by these individuals. Despite disability and marginalization, LGBTQ2S+ older adults with disabilities are creative and resilient and have adopted various practices to adapt and care for themselves and one another.

## *Technology Use as Resilience*

Queer older adults are turning to social technology use (i.e., text, email, social media) to connect with one another as well as gain access important information to aid in their aging process. Social technology use has been shown to bridge both social and physical distance and connect older adults with invaluable social and instrumental support (Cotten et al., 2013). Currently, older adults are the second fastest growing group on Facebook, since starting the COVID-19 pandemic, we have seen a major upsurge in social technology use overall (Faverio, 2022). For older adults living alone in particular, social technology use may be some of their only connection with others on a daily basis (Francis, 2022).

Historically, queer individuals have been more technologically savvy than their peers due in part to the appeal of anonymity, privacy, and safety that social technologies can provide (Devito et al., 2019). For LGBTQ2S+ older adults in particular, social technology use has been utilized to access peer support, gather health information, and even plan for end of life (Mock et al., 2020). Since the COVID-19 pandemic, social technology use is instrumental in easing loneliness and promoting access to telehealth (Faverio, 2022). This was especially important for those living alone and with mobility and intellectual disabilities. There is still much that can be done to improve the design of social technology interfaces for individuals with hearing and vision disabilities (Gell et al., 2015).

Beyond social technology use, assistive and smart technology use is also becoming a more feasible option for many older adults with disabilities to modify their living environments and promote their abilities, including stability bars and railings, voice-activated technologies, and remote- or phone-operated devices. These technologies can be costly however, and for most, would need to be covered by insurance which may pose difficulty for those at low-income levels, especially older lesbians who have been consistently listed among the poorest of the poor (Emlet, 2016). Beyond economic barriers, access to technology and technology training have traditionally been a problem for older adults of all backgrounds. Older adults are consistently among the most digitally divided individuals in our society and the divide grows for those of color, lower income, lower education, and living with disabilities (Wu et al., 2015). One positive impact of the COVID-19 pandemic has been the increase in technology use, access, and education for older adults across the board. Although there is still much work to be done to bridge the digital divide and promote digital literacy for all, we are hopefully on an upward trajectory.

### Sexual Activity in Older Adults

Older adults regularly engage in sexual intimacy and sexual activities (Kolodziejczak et al., 2019). Healthy sexual relationships among older adults have been studied from medical and social, relational contexts (DeLamater & Koepsel, 2015). Tailored sexual education for older adults can highlight harm reduction practices regarding sexually transmitted infection (STI) transmission, negotiating consent, dispelling stereotypes, navigating physical and mental changes, and intimate relationships (Morgan, 2021). Changes in libido, lubrication, and enjoyment in sex can all make for new and evolving facets of sexual life to navigate (Lindau et al., 2007), especially when older adults may be encountering new partners for the first time in their adult lives. While older adults maintain vitality and sexuality as they age, they navigate their community's norms and taboos in how open they are discussing sex with their peers, partners, and with clinicians.

## Information for Providers and Practitioners

### Queering Gerontology (Sandberg & King, 2022)

When we discuss the idea of "queering," we are using the term in its broadest sense to incorporate the experiences, wisdom, and information of individuals whose identities, bodies, sexuality, and brains function, operate, and exist outside of the mainstream. The study of aging, or *gerontology*, consists of a multidisciplinary and multidimensional understanding of the physical, mental, and social aspects of aging (Sandberg & King, 2022). The intention of research in this area is to better inform policies and practices at the societal and governmental levels that will promote healthy aging overall. These policies can impact access to healthcare, accessible accommodations, assisted living facilities, employment opportunities, and more. Although the aim has been to improve circumstances for all older adults, our services and policies targeted to the aging population have historically been narrow in scope, much to the exclusion and detriment of individuals who do not neatly fit into the white, upper-class, nondisabled, cisheteronormative box. Here, we offer some suggestions for practitioners and providers working with LGBTQ2S+ older adults with disabilities. In order to provide the most relevant and comprehensive services we encourage you to focus on your AIM – *Accessibility, Inclusivity, and Mattering*.

## Accessibility

It is important to take a moment and inventory all of the services, information, and resources you are providing. Think about how those services are delivered and/or accessed by others. Then, ask yourself the following:

- When you designed and developed these services, who did you picture in your minds' eye as the user/client/patient? Is this an accurate representation of all of your clients? Are there clients who are not currently patronizing your services that would want to, or could come to your services if they were more accessible?
- Have you ever updated, added, or removed any services based on your client's needs?
- What has changed in society, law, and/or technology since designing your services?
- Are processes in place to offer guidance on how to navigate virtual healthcare portals for clients with less familiarity with or access to smart technologies?
  - Are multiple modalities (i.e., telephone, large print) for communication with providers offered?
- Can your clients:
  - Travel to your services, get into, and navigate the space where services are being provided?
  - Read text, hear service providers, and/or understand instructions or information provided?
    - What assistive technology may be helpful to promote ability and effectively modify the environment?

## Inclusivity

Inclusivity encompasses providing opportunities for equitable access to resources and benefits for all people. When considering inclusive healthcare practice, consider the following questions:

- Do clinical intake forms inquire about multiple identities across the gender, sexuality, and disability spectrum?
- Does the electronic health record store and display relevant identities and allow providers to update identity categories in the record as they change

over time? Does it allow for noting that older adults may still be sexually active?
- Does the physical space (i.e., decor, signage, attire) welcome diverse identities?
- Do promotional materials include images that reflect a diverse population in which clients see themselves represented, including in romantic and sexual ways?
- Do services expand the definition of *caregiver, support people, emergency contact*, and *surrogate* to include chosen family (i.e., family members that are not biologically or legally related, partners)?
- Is information provided in multiple languages and/or are interpreters available?
- Are ongoing opportunities to provide anonymous feedback about inclusive practice offered?
- Is an organizational plan for reviewing and responding to feedback in place?
- Have you and your staff completed relevant trainings for working with people of all sexual orientations and genders, with older adults, and people with disabilities? Are your staff comfortable with the idea of older adults being sexual beings?
- Have you implemented the requisite and relevant accessibility accommodations listed earlier and are they advertised and readily available for individuals who may be in need?

### *Mattering*

Your client has a whole lifetime's worth of lived experience, and their age, disability, sexual behaviors, and gender identity are only part of their story. We as people, regardless of our personal characteristics and situations, need to feel as though we matter – that we are the object of attention, importance, and that others rely on us (Rosenberg & McCullough, 1981). We need to feel as though we are heard and understood. This may be especially so for individuals who have been systematically marginalized throughout their lifetime or even those who have aged into a stage of their lives where they feel less powerful and capable. How can you convey to your clients that they matter not only to you but also to society as a whole? Consider:

- Are you actively listening to your client? Have you considered the socio-historical and environmental circumstances that may be uniquely impacting this individual beyond aging?
- Are you communicating with your client in a way that affirms and validates their dignity, perspective, and concerns?
- Are you offering spaces for your client to share their thoughts, feelings, and concerns around romance and sexuality? Do you have sexuality-focused activities and/or resources to provide?

- If you are not someone who is identified as an LGBTQ2S individual, individual with a disability, or older individual, have you taken the time to update yourself on the latest terminology, statistics, and practices related to each of these designations?
- Are you answering questions completely and providing relevant information and educational resources to your client to better equip them for the future? Are you able to talk about sex with them without having an ageist bias?
- Do you have an established practice or mechanism in place for periodically reaching out to your client throughout the year to indicate your interest in their comprehensive well-being?
- Have you established yourself in the community as a provider who specializes in care for older adults, who may have disabilities, and/or who may identify as LGBTQ2S Have you reached out to invite those individuals to seek your services?

**Classroom Activity**

We can support older adults in learning about the changes happening to and around them, and model conversations ourselves of how we are adapting to the changes in our own lives. We can make plans of how we will manage acquired disabilities over time, and what resources we will reach out to when we need support with changes.

Consider a job you would like to have in the next five years, and how you will interact with clients in that role. Complete this exercise as if you are working in that job:

1. Write down some scripts you will use to ask an older adult client or patient about their evolving sexuality.
   1. How are these questions relevant to the services or care you provide?
   2. When will these questions not be relevant to the services or care you provide, and should not be asked?
   3. How will you ask about evolving sexuality, sexual orientation, and safe, pleasurable sex in older adulthood?
2. Trade scripts with a friend, classmate, or colleague. Offer edits to each other of where you can remove assumptions from your language, and practice using affirming open language instead.
3. Read out these scripts loud to each other. How comfortable are you asking these questions? Is your tone helping you to build rapport with older adults?
4. Find at least two resources that you can share with your client when they respond to your questions. If your client mentions or asks for something that you are not ready to offer, what will be your process for finding and obtaining that resource?

## Conclusion

Older adults living with disabilities depend on their practitioners and providers not only for their required care but also for creating a safe environment for vulnerable moments and conversations. As providers are experiencing overwhelming caseloads, low wages, and a lack of qualified assistance, it is important to know that there are resources available to support your Accessibility, Inclusivity, and Mattering (A.I.M.). These resources include trainings, virtual workshops, assistive technology, and educational materials. Celebrating the resilience and value of older adults allows us to provide better care for aging cohorts.

## Resources

### For Your Entertainment

Gallop, J. (2018). *Sexuality, disability, and aging: Queer temporalities of the phallus*. Duke University Press.

Kauffman, M., & Morris, H. J. (Producers). (2015). *Grace and Frankie* [TV series]. Netflix.

### For Your Education

AARP Sex & Intimacy Website: www.aarp.org/home-family/sex-intimacy/.

Kattari, S. K., Lavery, A., & Hasche, L. (2017). Applying a social model of disability across the life span. *Journal of Human Behavior in the Social Environment, 27*(8), 865–880.

National Institute on Aging. (2022, April 18). *Sexuality and intimacy in older adults*. National Institutes of Health. Retrieved 2022 from www.nia.nih.gov/health/sexuality-and-intimacy-older-adults

SAGE Advocacy & Services for LGBTQ+ Elders Website: www.sageusa.org/.

## References

Baars, G. (2019). Queer cases unmake gendered law, or, fucking law's gendering function. *The Australian Feminist Law Journal, 45*(1), 15–62. https://doi.org/10.1080/13200968.2019.1667777

Baril, A., & Silverman, M. (2022). Forgotten lives: Trans older adults living with dementia at the intersection of cisgenderism, ableism/cogniticism and ageism. *Sexualities, 25*(1–2), 117–131. https://doi.org/10.1177/1363460719876835

Basrowi, R. W., Rahayu, E. M., Khoe, L. C., Wasito, E., & Sundjaya, T. (2021). The road to healthy ageing: What has Indonesia achieved so far? *Nutrients, 13*(10), 3441. https://doi.org/10.3390/nu13103441

Beall, D. R. (2018). *"Do I even remember the list": Identity, place, and legal consciousness of marriage among LGBTQ individuals* (Order No. 10843717). GenderWatch; ProQuest Central; ProQuest Dissertations & Theses Global;

Sociological Abstracts. (2128070303). http://libproxy.lib.unc.edu/login?url=www.proquest.com/dissertations-theses/do-i-even-remember-list-identity-place-legal/docview/2128070303/se-2

Begun, S., & Kattari, S. K. (2016). Conforming for survival: Associations between transgender visual conformity/passing and homelessness experiences. *Journal of Gay & Lesbian Social Services, 28*(1), 54–66. https://doi.org/10.1080/10538720.2016.1125821

Bloemen, E. M., Rosen, T., LoFaso, V. M., Lasky, A., Church, S., Hall, P., Weber, T., & Clark, S. (2019). Lesbian, gay, bisexual, and transgender older adults' experiences with elder abuse and neglect. *Journal of the American Geriatrics Society, 67*(11), 2338–2345. https://doi.org/10.1111/jgs.16101

Collins, R. L., Roth, E., Cerully, J. L., & Wong, E. C. (2014). Beliefs related to mental illness stigma among California young adults. *Rand Health Quarterly, 4*(3).

Cornwell, E. Y., & Waite, L. J. (2009). Social disconnectedness, perceived isolation, and health among older adults. *Journal of Health and Social Behavior, 50*(1), 31–48.

Cotten, S. R., Anderson, W. A., & McCullough, B. M. (2013). Impact of internet use on loneliness and contact with others among older adults: Cross-sectional analysis. *Journal of Medical Internet Research, 15*(2), e2306.

Cusack, M., Montgomery, A. E., & Byrne, T. (2022). Examining the intersection of housing instability and violence among LGBTQ adults. *Journal of Homosexuality*, 1–12. https://doi.org/10.1080/00918369.2022.2085936

DeLamater, J., & Koepsel, E. (2015). Relationships and sexual expression in later life: A biopsychosocial perspective. *Sexual and Relationship Therapy, 30*(1), 37–59. https://doi.org/10.1080/14681994.2014.939506

Devito, M. A., Walker, A. M., Birnholtz, J., Ringland, K., Macapagal, K., Kraus, A., Munson, S., Liang, C., & Saksono, H. (2019, November). *Social technologies for digital wellbeing among marginalized communities*. Conference Companion Publication of the 2019 on Computer Supported Cooperative Work and Social Computing, pp. 449–454.

Emlet, C. (2016). Social, economic, and health disparities among LGBTQ older adults. *Generations, 40*, 16–22.

Farquhar, M. (2021). Structural violence in the queer community: A comparative analysis of international human rights protections for LGBTIQ+ People. *Inquiries Journal, 13*(12).

Faverio, M. (2022). *Share of those 65 and older who are tech users has grown in the past decade*. Pew Research Center. Retrieved January 13, 2022, from www.pewresearch.org/fact-tank/2022/01/13/share-of-those-65-and-older-who-are-tech-users-has-grown-in-the-past-decade/

Francis, J. (2022). Elder orphans on Facebook: Implications for mattering and social isolation. *Computers in Human Behavior, 127*, 107023.

Fredriksen-Goldsen, K. I., Kim, H. J., Barkan, S. E., Muraco, A., & Hoy-Ellis, C. P. (2013). Health disparities among lesbian, gay, and bisexual older adults: Results from a population-based study. *American Journal of Public Health, 103*(10), 1802–1809. https://doi.org/10.2105/AJPH.2012.301110

Fredriksen-Goldsen, K. I., Kim, H. J., Emlet, C. A., Muraco, A., Erosheva, E. A., Hoy-Ellis, C. P., Goldsen, J., & Petry, H. (2011). *The aging and health report*. Institute for Multigenerational Health.

Garrison-Diehn, C., Rummel, C., Au, Y. H., & Scherer, K. (2022). Attitudes toward older adults and aging: A foundational geropsychology knowledge competency. *Clinical Psychology: Science and Practice, 29*(1), 4–15. https://doi.org/10.1037/cps0000043

Gates, T. G., & Viggiani, P. A. (2014). Understanding lesbian, gay, and bisexual worker stigmatization: A review of the literature. *International Journal of Sociology and Social Policy, 34*(50), 359–374. https://doi.org/10.1108/IJSSP-07-2013-0077

Gell, N. M., Rosenberg, D. E., Demiris, G., LaCroix, A. Z., & Patel, K. V. (2015). Patterns of technology use among older adults with and without disabilities. *The Gerontologist, 55*(3), 412–421.

Harley, D. A. (2016). Disabilities and chronic illness among LGBT elders: Responses of medicine, public health, rehabilitation, and social work. In Harley, D. A., & Teaster, P. B. (Eds.), *Handbook of LGBT elders: An interdisciplinary approach to principles, practices, and policies* (pp. 619–635).

Healthy People 2020. (2022, February 6). *Older adults.* www.healthypeople.gov/2020/topics-objectives/topic/older-adults

Hillman, J. L. (2012). *Sexuality and aging: Clinical perspectives.* Springer.

Hillman, J. L. (2017). The sexuality and sexual health of LGBT elders. *Annual Review of Gerontology and Geriatrics, 37*(1), 13–26.

Hirschmann, N. J. (2013). Queer/fear: Disability, sexuality, and the other. *Journal of Medical Humanities, 34,* 139–147.

HIV.gov. (2021, June 17). *A timeline of HIV and AIDS.* www.hiv.gov/hiv-basics/overview/history/hiv-and-aids-timeline

Hoy-Ellis, C. P., Ator, M., Kerr, C., & Milford, J. (2016). Innovative approaches address aging and mental health needs in LGBTQ communities. *Generations, 40*(2), 56–62.

Jin, B., & Roumell, E. A. (2021). "Getting used to it, but still unwelcome": A grounded theory study of physical identity development In later life. *International Journal of Environmental Research and Public Health, 18*(18), 9557. https://doi.org/10.3390/ijerph18189557

Johnston, T. R. (2016). LGBT aging and elder abuse. In *Affirmation, care ethics, and LGBT identity.* Palgrave Macmillan. https://doi.org/10.1057/978-1-137-59304-7_5

Knochel, K. A., & Seelman, K. L. (2020). Understanding and working with transgender/nonbinary older adults. In S. K. Kattari, M. K. Kinney, L. Kattari, & N. E. Walls (Eds.), *Social work and health care practice with transgender and Nonbinary individuals and communities: Voices for equity, inclusion, and resilience* (pp. 120–133). Routledge.

Kolodziejczak, K., Rosada, A., Drewelies, J., Düzel, S., Eibich, P., Tegeler, C., Wagner, G. G., Beier, K. M., Ram, N., Demuth, I., Steinhagen-Thiessen, E., & Gerstorf, D. (2019). Sexual activity, sexual thoughts, and intimacy among older adults: Links with physical health and psychosocial resources for successful aging. *Psychology and Aging, 34*(3), 389. http://dx.doi.org/10.1037/pag0000347

Lindau, S. T., Schumm, L. P., Laumann, E. O., Levinson, W., O'Muircheartaigh, C. A., & Waite, L. J. (2007). A study of sexuality and health among older adults in the United States. *New England Journal of Medicine, 357*(8), 762–774. https://doi.org/10.1056/NEJMoa067423

Liu, C. J., Shiroy, D. M., Jones, L. Y., & Clark, D. O. (2014). Systematic review of functional training on muscle strength, physical functioning, and activities of daily living in older adults. *European Review of Aging and Physical Activity*, 11(2), 95–106. https://doi.org/10.1007/s11556-014-0141-1

Meléndez, J. C., Satorres, E., Redondo, R., Escudero, J., & Pitarque, A. (2018). Well-being, resilience, and coping: Are there differences between healthy older adults, adults with mild cognitive impairment, and adults with Alzheimer-type dementia? *Archives of Gerontology and Geriatrics*, 77, 38–43. https://doi.org/10.1016/j.archger.2018.04.004

Miller, S. J., Mayo, C., & Lugg, C. A. (2020). Sex and gender in transition in US schools: Ways forward. In *Trans youth in education* (pp. 25–39). Routledge. https://doi.org/10.1080/14681811.2017.1415204

Mock, S. E., Walker, E. P., Humble, Á. M., de Vries, B., Gutman, G., Gahagan, J., Chamberland, L., Aubert, P., & Fast, J. (2020). The role of information and communication technology in end-of-life planning among a sample of Canadian LGBT older adults. *Journal of Applied Gerontology*, 39(5), 536–544.

Molton, I. R., & Yorkston, K. M. (2017). Growing older with a physical disability: A special application of the successful aging paradigm. *The Journals of Gerontology: Series B*, 72(2), 290–299. https://doi.org/10.1093/geronb/gbw122

Morgan, S. (2021). *Designing a sexual education curriculum to mitigate the spread of STIs and STDs in older adults* (Master dissertation). California State University, Northridge. https://scholarworks.calstate.edu/downloads/h702qc46s

Morris, K., Greteman, A. J., & Weststrate, N. M. (2022). Embracing queer heartache: Lessons from LGBTQ+ intergenerational dialogues. *International Journal of Qualitative Studies in Education*, 1–15. https://doi.org/10.1080/09518398.2022.2035459

Porter, K. E., Brennan-Ing, M., Chang, S. C., Dickey, L. M., Singh, A. A., Bower, K. L., & Witten, T. M. (2016). Providing competent and affirming services for transgender and gender nonconforming older adults. *Clinical Gerontologist*, 39(5), 366–388. https://doi.org/10.1080/07317115.2016.1203383.

Puckett, J. A., Tornello, S., Mustanski, B., & Newcomb, M. E. (2022). Gender variations, generational effects, and mental health of transgender people in relation to timing and status of gender identity milestones. *Psychology of Sexual Orientation and Gender Diversity*, 9(2), 165.

Robb, C. (2003). *The association of functional disability, personality, social support and subjective well-being in older adult couples* (Order No. 3080006). ProQuest Dissertations & Theses Global. (288004366). http://libproxy.lib.unc.edu/login?url=www.proquest.com/dissertations-theses/association-functional-disability-personality/docview/288004366/se-2

Robinson-Wood, T., & Weber, A. (2016). Deconstructing multiple oppressions among LGBT older adults. In *Handbook of LGBT elders* (pp. 65–81). Springer.

Rosenberg, M., & McCullough, B. C. (1981). *Mattering: Inferred significance and mental health among adolescents*. Research in Community & Mental Health.

Rowan, N. L., & Beyer, K. (2017). Exploring the health needs of aging LGBT adults in the cape fear region of North Carolina. *Journal of Gerontological Social Work*, 60(6–7), 569–586. https://doi.org/10.1080/01634372.2017.1336146

SAGE. (2022, June 17). *Old and bold*. Sage. Retrieved June 30, 2022, from www.sageusa.org/get-involved/take-action/old-and-bold/

Salami, K. K., & Okunade, O. O. (2020). Adults and social supports for older parents in Peri-Urban Ibadan, Nigeria. *Journal of Caring Sciences*, 9(2), 65–72. https://doi.org/10.34172/JCS.2020.010

Sandberg, L. J., & King, A. (2022). Queering gerontology. In *Encyclopedia of gerontology and population aging* (pp. 4108–4114). Springer International Publishing.

Scherrer, K. S., & Fedor, J. P. (2015). Family issues for LGBT older adults. In N. A. Orel & C. A. Fruhauf (Eds.), *The lives of LGBT older adults: Understanding challenges and resilience* (pp. 171–192). American Psychological Association. https://doi.org/10.1037/14436-008

Streeter, C., Braedley, S., Jansen, I., & Krajcik, M. (2020). *"It's got to be about safety": Public services that work for LGBTQ2+ older adults and LGBTQ2+ workers in Canada.* https://cupe.ca/sites/cupe/files/public_services_for_lgbtq2_older_adults_6.0.pdf

Wu, Y. H., Damnée, S., Kervhervé, H., Ware, C., & Rigaud, A. S. (2015). Bridging the digital divide in older adults: A study from an initiative to inform older adults about new technologies. *Clinical Interventions in Aging, 10*, 193.

Yellowitz, J. A. (2005). Cognitive function, aging, and ethical decisions: Recognizing change. *Dental Clinics, 49*(2), 389–410. https://doi.org/10.1016/j.cden.2004.10.010

# 18

# TRANS ENOUGH, QUEER ENOUGH, AND DISABLED ENOUGH

Exploring Issues of Gatekeeping and Legitimacy of Trans, Queer, and Disabled Identities Through Sexuality

*Al Wauldron, Flyn Alexander, and Shanna Katz Kattari*

## Introduction

Queer, transgender, and nonbinary individuals living with disabilities contend with various forms of gatekeeping both medically and socially, and far too often, disabled individuals are asked to prioritize one aspect of their identity over the other when seeking healthcare (Iantaffi, 2010). While transgender and disabled individuals face harmful social messaging regarding their sexualities, queer and transgender disabled activists have explored the use of sexuality as a way to counter the gatekeeping narratives and marginalization they consistently face. Black, queer, disabled activist Dr. D'Arcee Charington Neal explains, "We put the lens of sexuality front and center because [some] believe that is what binds us together, when I think it's more of [our] non-normativity and how we are a very powerful, very large outlier of human society" (Chilukuri, 2022, para. 2).

This chapter explores the non-normative and powerful intersections of disability, transgender identity, and sexuality through centering the voices of queer disabled activists who use sexuality to counter gatekeeping models. The authors are three transgender, nonbinary individuals living with invisible disabilities. We are inspired by our own unique experiences living at these intersections while seeking to challenge the ways gatekeeping models reinforce normative ways of conceptualizing disability, gender identity, and sexuality. While limited academic research addresses these particular intersections, this chapter highlights what practitioners can learn from disabled, queer, trans, and nonbinary activists in treating this client population equitably and compassionately.

## Definitions

*Transgender* is defined as "people whose gender identity differs from social and cultural assumptions connected to the gender associated with their sex assigned at birth, inclusive of nonbinary, gender diverse, and gender non-conforming individuals" (Kattari et al., 2020). This is an umbrella term also including, but not limited to, people who are identified as genderfluid, transfeminine, transmasculine, genderqueer, and others. It should be noted that some nonbinary, genderfluid, or gender non-conforming individuals may choose *not* to consider themselves under the transgender umbrella for a variety of reasons. That said, they are included under the umbrella with the intention to best encompass the breadth of experiences of all who share the difficulty of navigating a world that mainly upholds and centers cisgender identities. It should also be noted that not all transgender people choose to undergo medical transition. Non-operative transgender people are equally as valid in their identities as those who do choose medical, physical transition.

This chapter does not specifically address intersex people and their overlapping experiences in health disparities, disability, medical gatekeeping, cisgenderism, and marginalization (Rosenwohl-Mack et al., 2020). Additionally, similar to gender-diverse individuals who choose not to include themselves under the umbrella label of transgender, many intersex people are not identified as transgender, while others do (InterACT, n.d.). Although the intersex community's experiences not directly addressed here, the chapter offers basic underlying principles and guidelines that healthcare providers can adapt in order to better care for intersex people.

## What We Know?

### Overlaps in Transgender and Disabled Experiences

Globally, disabled individuals are at a higher risk than nondisabled people of experiencing discrimination, marginalization, and inequities in a variety of settings, including healthcare (Ali et al., 2013; Hackett et al., 2020; Krahn et al., 2015). This is a similar experience to those who are on the transgender spectrum (James et al., 2016; Reisner et al., 2016). At these intersections, some studies estimate that in the United States (U.S.), nearly 40% of transgender people report being disabled, as compared to about 25% of the general adult population (Okoro et al., 2018; James et al., 2016).

While there is emerging research regarding the overlaps in transgender and disabled people's experiences, significant gaps in the literature remain where both identities are addressed as a co-occurrence. Furthermore, most literature lumps transgender experiences into the overall experience of the LGBTQ+ community, especially in regard to sexuality. To address extant research gaps and attempt to begin filling them, as well as to uplift the existing knowledge base and voices of those historically excluded from institutional academic research, we include both academic and non-academic literature from authors within queer, transgender, and/or disabled communities. It is of particular importance to center the experiences of those living at the intersections of multiple oppressions, as we seek to apply an anti-oppressive, anti-colonial, and anti-racist lens to our analysis.

## Disability and Diagnostic Paradigms Within Western Medicine

### Gatekeeping of Disabled Identities

Within Westernized medical systems and clinical settings, disabilities are most often defined and conceptualized by a set of standardized experiences or "symptoms" that have been developed through systems of categorization and medical academic research. Mental disabilities are standardized through the Diagnostic and Statistical Manual of Mental Disorders, 5th Edition, Text-Revision (DSM-5-TR) (American Psychiatric Association, 2022), which requires individuals to demonstrate a certain number of qualifying symptoms to receive a clinical diagnosis. While diagnostic systems aim to create a helpful working definition to guide treatment and support, these systems can be confining and even stigmatizing when attempting to encompass the full spectrum of experiences for disabled individuals. As disability activist Simon Brisenden (1986) concisely expressed this, stating:

> [T]he reality of the matter is that under the guise of objective scientific enquiry a particular image of disabled people is being fostered in the minds of the audience, and it is an image full of negative implications which are in themselves disabling.
>
> *(p. 175)*

Through static definitions of disabilities, the medical model depersonalizes disabled people's experiences and overlooks their complex individual lived realities, including their resilience and strengths. In terms of mental disabilities, the DSM-5-TR (2022) frames diagnoses to be "disorders" in which the majority of symptoms taken into consideration must be negatively impacting an individual in order for the diagnosis to be administered. While typical Western medical paradigms create an environment that centralizes challenges and disparities of those with disabilities, research has historically failed to recognize a neutral and even positive, strength-based perspective by which disabilities can offer unique positive traits and assets (Sedgwick et al., 2019). An international study that attempted to capture ADHD from a strength-based perspective was able to identify positive symptoms, such as high energy, empathy, creativity, and the ability to hyperfocus (Mahdi et al., 2017). When we examine disabilities solely from a deficit-based perspective, we lose the ability to fully capture the nuance and complexity of the diversity of disability (Kattari et al., 2017).

### Gatekeeping of Transgender Identities

The theme of distress-based diagnostic qualification within Westernized medical paradigms is similarly true for transgender individuals. The World Professional Association for Transgender Health (WPATH) is widely regarded in medical, psychological, legal, and social work spaces as a central voice in outlining who qualifies for gender affirmation care. WPATH's *Standards of Care and Ethical Guidelines, 7th Edition* (2013) is a manual on providing transgender-related care (WPATH, n.d.). Under WPATH's guidance, transgender people of all ages are required to complete psychological assessments to receive consent by professionals for accessing gender-affirming care such as puberty blockers, hormone replacement therapy, and gender-affirming surgeries (WPATH, 2012). The system in which the consent of healthcare professionals and/or related parties (e.g., insurance companies, governmental regulatory bodies) is required for an individual to receive a diagnosis or access to treatment is also known as medical gatekeeping (Pellegrino, 1986).

Similar to conceptualizing disabled identities, academic literature has largely failed to study and recognize being transgender outside of a deficit-based framework. While the extant research addresses the disparities, hardship, and discrimination faced by the community (as this research is necessary to build insight on the marginalization of transgender people), further research is needed to conceptualize the strengths and assets many feel from holding a transgender identity. One qualitative study (Riggle et al., 2011) found that 90% of participants disclosed what they considered to be positive aspects of being transgender; the themes shared between participants included "congruency of self, enhanced interpersonal relationships, personal growth and resiliency, increased empathy, a unique perspective on both sexes, being beyond the sex binary, increased activism, and connection to the GLBTQ communities" (p. 150). Future literature owes transgender communities a more critically examined perspective that steps away from the deficit-based framework in an effort to capture the entire spectrum of transgender experiences.

### Gatekeeping the Intersections of Trans and Disabled Identities

The conditional nature of accessing gender-affirming treatment in relation to disability can often create a "Catch-22" scenario that convolutes a transgender person's ability to receive the care they desire. The strain of existing as a transgender person – regardless of transition status or history – in a society that actively marginalizes them is associated with experiencing disabling conditions such as hypertension, depression, and anxiety (James et al., 2016). In turn, these symptoms may create a barrier to accessing gender-affirming care, as WPATH standards require additional mental health concerns to be "reasonably well controlled" by the individual (WPATH, 2012), even if the symptoms are directly related to existing in a cisnormative society, and access to treatment would actually decrease distress symptoms of adjacent mental health concerns. Conversely, individuals also must express "persistent, well-documented gender dysphoria" during life prior to transition care in order to demonstrate treatment is "medically necessary" (Coleman et al., 2012, p. 34). Overall, professionals in power assume the role of gatekeeper to grant or withhold services if distress is either too intense *or* too minimal for the individual to be assessed as "appropriate" for treatment.

A recent Pennsylvania court ruling adds additional complications when conceptualizing transgender and disabled conditions in a legal sense. In 2017, a transgender woman sued her workplace after facing intense workplace harassment and subsequent termination from her employment, citing federal laws Title VII (which set protections from sex discrimination) and the Americans with Disabilities Act (which aims to prohibit discrimination against disabled people in workplaces, public accommodations, and other spaces (U.S. Department of Labor, n.d.). While the court rejected the notion that being transgender is a disability, they concluded that the condition of *gender dysphoria* can be interpreted as a disabling condition given its classification in the Diagnostic and Statistical Manual of Mental Disorders, 5th edition (American Psychiatric Association, 2013). This ruling opens challenging questions as to how interweaving systems of institutional medical and social power construct the difficult reality of transgender and disabled experiences.

Gatekeeping and deficit-based models of care can impact transgender disabled people in an intersectional model. When seeking gender-affirming care, many transgender people are harassed, declined care, or mistreated by healthcare practitioners; this risk of harm increases for disabled transgender people (Kattari et al., 2021). Practitioner lack of competency in transgender care can also result in refusal of treatment (Irwig, 2016) or a de-prioritization of transgender-affirming care based on other conditions an individual might be coping with.

### *Sexuality, Sexual Health, and Gatekeeping*

Transgender people living with disabilities face even greater barriers to accessing affirming sexual healthcare and information (Ballan et al., 2011; Jones et al., 2016). As transgender disabled people are socialized and contained by cisnormative, ableist systems, they are forced to interact the limited scope of these systems to receive the care they need. The deficit-model can create insecurity and uncertainty in trans disabled people. Trans and disabled communities have long been dissatisfied by the gatekeeping models especially in regard to sexuality and sex. To break away from the shame-based deficit model, trans and disability activists empower each other, share information, and work together to deconstruct the oppressive internalization of the shame-based deficit model.

### Intersectional Marginalized Identities and Access to Care

Transgender disabled people already face many obstacles when seeking care related to their identities and sexual health. These difficulties can be compounded even further if one falls within other marginalized groups. Black, Indigenous, and other people of color (BIPOC) already have less access to care and are less believed by medical professionals regarding their experiences (Budhwani & De, 2019; Kattari et al., 2016). Additionally, most racial/ethnic groups of trans racialized people experience higher rates of violence compared to their white trans counterparts (Messinger et al., 2021). This violence can contribute to the development of disabling conditions, such as PTSD, anxiety, and depression. It should also be noted that transgender people who have immigrated countries experience higher rates of violence and decreased access to competent healthcare (Castro et al., 2021). Class background also has massive implications for transgender disabled people in accessing and receiving necessary care, particularly in countries with privatized health insurance, or where quality of healthcare is based on ability to pay out of pocket. This is particularly an issue for trans disabled people, who live at the intersection of employment discrimination and un/underemployment that is prevalent at high levels for both identities.

*Sexual Identities and Disability:* Many transgender and disabled people identify as lesbian, gay, bisexual, queer, or another non-heterosexual identity. In a U.S. study, 21% of respondents identified as queer, 18% pansexual, 16% gay or lesbian, 14% bisexual, and 10% as asexual, with 15% identified as heterosexual (James et al., 2016). Considering that nearly 40% were also identified as having a disability, a significant number of transgender disabled people have a sexual identity other than heterosexual. A recent Australian study had similar findings, noting that of their all-transgender sample, 21.2% were queer, 20.5% were fluid in their sexuality, 17.9% were homosexual, 19.2% were bisexual, 7.9% were asexual, and 5.8% were heterosexual (Holt et al., 2023). The existing marginalization of diverse sexual identities adds another difficult layer of access for transgender and disabled people.

*Hyper/Desexualization:* Socially, transgender (and cisgender) women of color face stigma of sexual objectification (Flores et al., 2018), while disabled people also tend to face either pervasive desexualization or oversexualization and fetishizing by nondisabled society (Cohen-Rottenberg, 2012). Trans and nonbinary people receive less education on sexual health that is applicable to their identities and unique sexual health needs (Roosevelt & Ellis, 2020). This is similarly true for disabled people; disabled individuals are less likely to have access to sexual health education that is accessible and inclusive (Frawley & O'Shea, 2020).

Queer and trans BIPOC (QTPOC) activists and community organizers have been working to address these disparities within their communities by developing and centering a framework for accessibility. Researcher and community organizer Matthew Chin reflected on the ways QTPOC organizers create their own counterpublic and "reconfiguring dominant modes of beginning which queer and trans of color community organizers attempt to achieve through their accessibility practices," (Chin, 2018, p. 8). In their work with QTPOC community arts organizers, Chin observed that, "Within a broader context where QTPOC are subject to in various forms of violence, the construction of their own publics operates as a means through which they structure their own belonging in otherwise hostile environments" (p. 9).

Where access to care is limited or obstructed by normative hierarchies, turning to look at the work of community activists most impacted by these limits and obstructions offers unique insights and possible solutions to addressing these experiences both individually and collectively. Chin argues that a process-oriented approach to accessibility is not perfect but reflects the imperfectness of our diverse, intersectional communities and constitutes "a continual open-ended process" that grows and evolves with the community.

Digital spaces such as social media and other aspects of the internet offer unique counterpublics for transgender disabled communities to engage in conversations about sexuality, gender identity, and disability that often go beyond hegemonic discourse. These spaces can often be empowering for transgender and disabled communities as they connect with each other and create shared community in a digital space, which can be more accessible and a great conduit for educating each other as well as reaching a larger audience that may not be disabled and/or transgender. These digital spaces and archives provide a wealth of information for healthcare practitioners to learn directly from transgender and/or disabled community members doing the work on the front lines to deconstruct the systems and ideologies oppressing them.

In her master's thesis, Claudia Garcia Mendoza analyzes one such digital space known as Disabled Twitter with a specific focus on sexuality. She argues that both a neoliberal lens and a queer lens are necessary for this analysis as both are important conduits for social change, "the former is a demand for inclusion, and the latter a conceptualization outside categorizations" (Mendoza, 2020, p. 102). She argues that sexuality and disability have both economic and political dimensions within a neoliberal society. Queer and disabled activism offers critical counternarratives that challenge neoliberal hegemonic norms of productivity as well as cisnormativity and ableism.

One example of this form of digital activism is Andrew Gurza (@andrewgurza1). Andrew is a queer, nonbinary, disabled activist who uses various digital platforms to connect, educate, and share their experiences. They have amassed a large following across their Twitter, TikTok, and Instagram platforms (nearly 25,000 Instagram followers as of this writing). They collaborate with queer, trans, and disabled activists, organizers, writers, sex workers, and more well as host their own podcast, *Disability After Dark*, where they interview disabled, queer, and transgender activists and artist to discuss various intersecting topics related to disability and sexuality. One notable focus of Gurza's work is destigmatizing disabled bodies as well as queer and disabled sexuality including sex work as a form of accessibility.

Pleasure as the measure of freedom, as conceptualized by adrienne maree brown in her book *Pleasure Activism*, challenges the politics of reduction through the reclamation of pleasure, recognizing it as part of the wholeness of our bodies, encouraging a connection to self and nature, and validating our bodies as one with the natural world. This ties into Sonya Renee Taylor's book the *Body Is Not an Apology* wherein she asserts that no bodies are bad bodies and that trans and disabled bodies are one specific location where this truth is actualized.

How queer, trans, and disabled activists are using these concepts to empower themselves in a world not built for them that actively holds them back and often controls their every move including their sexuality. It's impossible for us to talk about affirming trans disabled bodies, supporting these individuals in their sexuality, and discussing intersectionality without centering Black feminist work being done at the community level.

**Best Practices**

Crip theory argues that the "abnormal" arises out of contrast to the definitions of "normality" which are constructed by those in institutionalized power structures (McRuer, 2006). We must move away from what we consider to be "normal" and toward truly embracing our clients in their whole authentic selves. All transgender people hold unique experiences and challenges regarding their decisions on how, when, and why they transition; while some transgender folks may experience more joy and euphoria from transitioning, others may feel the same amount of affirmation in choosing to keep their bodies as they are. Similar to how disabilities manifest differently for everyone, transgender identities are fluid, unique, and not reducible to a single set of experiences.

*Challenging the Deficit-Based Gatekeeping Model*

Reflection upon one's own held beliefs and assumptions is a core principle when caring for and working with disabled transgender people. Before dismissing a disabled person's questions about gender-affirming transition care or enhancing their sexual health, practitioners should engage with individuals in a good-faith, open, and collaborative manner to listen to and address individuals' concerns. For example, when a person in a wheelchair consults with healthcare professionals regarding receiving hormone replacement therapy, practitioners should avoid minimizing concerns under the assumption that gender identity or sexual health should be deprioritized based on disability status. Similarly, intellectually and developmentally disabled people should not be barred from accessible, comprehensive education and care in their sexual health and gender identity. Through the approach of practitioners actively taking a stance of engagement with trans disabled individuals' concerns, we can combat the pervasive issue of gatekeeping that fails to adequately serve and validate transgender disabled peoples' needs and identities.

Trans and disabled people should be free to choose labels that they genuinely feel best fit their life experiences. As practitioners, we must be ready to be nimble around language, as it is constantly fluid and shifting. When we can make space for our clients, especially those who are trans and disabled, to explore who they are, and support them in showing up as their full authentic selves, we disrupt systems of harm.

Moreover, it is time for a true reckoning when it comes to supporting the sexuality, the body/mind/spirit connection, and the wholeness of the individuals and communities with whom we practice. Simply reforming existing structures that exist within harmful systems is not enough. Chin sums this up well by stating:

> Rather than attempting to transform existing human service organizations or establishing new programs to combat mechanisms of social exclusion (or in addition to these efforts), social workers can support the work of minority community initiatives in their bid to establish new modes of belonging. By directing attention away from social work agencies and prioritizing the existing efforts of disadvantaged communities, social workers adopt an empowerment-oriented, strengths-based approach by taking a supportive (as opposed to leadership) role in social change efforts and locating the driver of this change within the communities most affected.
>
> *(2018, p. 19)*

### Case Study – Gray's Story

*Content Note: This case study contains mentions of self-harm and suicidal ideation.*

This study is adapted for this chapter from an article in *Disability and Sexuality*. For more on Gray's story, see Cain and Velasco (2021).

Gray is nonbinary and autistic, and assigned female at birth (AFAB). Gray transitioned using hormone replacement therapy (HRT) at age 30, after being identified as nonbinary and genderqueer in early adulthood. They then "detransitioned," meaning, for Gray specifically, they stopped HRT and self-identifying as a transgender man. They are no longer identified with the term "detransition" and are now identified as nonbinary, have had gender-affirming top surgery, and are not on HRT. However, they are considering going back on testosterone. Gray never felt comfortable being AFAB, but also considered their struggle with gender identity as part of their ASD.

We chose to use Gray's story in part to highlight the academic work being done to lift up and center queer, nonbinary, disabled voices, and diverse experiences. More of this kind of research needs to be done to help practitioners and academics better understand the diverse communities we serve.

## *Disability*

Gray was born 3 months premature and blind in one eye. The first 18 months of Gray's life were spent in an incubator with little physical touch. Gray's speech was delayed and Gray were completely nonverbal until two-and-a-half years old. Gray was diagnosed with ASD at age eight and continued to struggle with verbalization, communication, and social skills throughout elementary school. Gray had difficulty verbalizing the self-experiences of the world with family and struggled to make friends in school.

> *I have a lot of social chameleoning because of the fact that I'm autistic, so I tend to follow the group. . . . I would say that a lot of trans people have that problem too.*
>
> (pg. 368)

Gray struggled with gender as a concept and they attribute this to their ASD. They speculate that feeling left out of traditional social norms, like masculine and feminine coding, led them, and potentially other transgender people with ASD, to consider transitioning. They stress that, for them, there is a deep connection between their identity as a person with ASD and with a nonbinary identity.

> *You don't have to transition. You don't have to do anything. You can just be you. . . . I think what's really important is figuring out what is best for you. For autistic people, that's really hard because a lot of us spend our lives being told that we're burns on society for existing.*
>
> (p. 369)

## Gender Identity

Gray chose to do a low dose of testosterone when undergoing HRT and saw what they described as small changes. Two years after beginning HRT, Gray decided to "detransition" based on two factors: *(1) the aforementioned medical issues and (2) falling in with "militant radical feminists" who were "trans exclusionary."* Gray describes their frustration with their medical issues resulting from *"nothing really happening"* in regard to physical changes. Then, after moving outside of the United States, Gray explained:

> It was really colored by how terrible my entire medical issues were because my [testosterone] dose was too low and then it was too high. They didn't know how to give shots. It was a nightmare. You would think nurses would know how to give shots but they don't and it really made it miserable.

Not seeing the types of changes that they saw in other transgender men, Gray began to disidentify with transgender men. The second factor came from Gray's experience with online trans exclusionary radical feminist (TERF) communities, another form of gatekeeping that is social rather than embedded in the medical model.

> *I think that a lot of people especially just need to be informed about the fact that for some people, getting health care as a trans person and as a non-binary person is hard, and can lead to people detransitioning and whatnot. Not that detransitioning is bad. . . . Identity changes. If there's one thing that people take away from this it's that identity is fluid and can change. I know mine has, even in the last couple of months and that's okay.*

A year later, Gray moves away from identifying with the "detransitioning" as a label. Gray is now considering going back on testosterone at some point in their life and identifies as trans masculine and nonbinary.

## Sexual Orientation

Gray knew from age 8 that they were *"definitely a lesbian"* due to an attraction to a close friend. By age 14, they were an out lesbian, dating girls online. From Gray's perspective, their lesbian sexuality influenced their decision to detransition. The social gatekeeping that they received from their TERF lesbian community influenced feelings of being left out or pushed out of the community for being a *"man"* once on testosterone, alienating them from a community they had been part of since a teen. Their longtime girlfriend broke up with them over their decision to start testosterone, and this played a significant role in their later decision to stop hormones and identify as nonbinary.

### Mental Health

Gray struggled with self-injury and suicidal ideation throughout high school. They went to therapy from age 15 to 17, after their friends shared concerns over their tendency to self-injure through cutting. Gray's friends and family expressed concern that Gray would take their own life. Gray shared that their compounding struggles with gender identity, sexuality, ASD, and their mental health symptoms also impacted their ability to do well in school. They believed they were smart and could do well, but felt they did not receive encouragement from their family or teachers and administrators. Gray eventually pursued education through a local community college later in life even as they continue to struggle with managing their mental health. At 26 years old, they said their mental health struggles impacted their interpersonal relationships.

### Barriers to Accessing Care

Gray faced various social and medical barriers to accessing the care they needed that they attributed to their feelings of distress. When seeking HRT and gender-affirming surgery, they found that their insurance would not cover the cost because they weighed over the 200-pound weight limit required by their provider. This delayed their access to care and caused their mental health to suffer. Gray also expressed that *"not passing"* after being denied access to gender-affirming care contributed to their distress.

> *I know guys that are skinny that didn't have top surgery and they pass fine, but. . . . If you're perceived as male but you're not binding and you walk into a men's changing room, danger! It's just rough. . . . Prioritizing health care while managing dysphoria is hard.*
>
> (p. 370)

Gray's experience highlights the dangerous possible outcomes that can be easily overlooked by practitioners following insurance guidelines. This medical gatekeeping not only delayed Gray's medical transition, it also contributed to Gray's continued struggles with mental health and had an impact on their romantic relationships and friendships. When Gray was able to start HRT, their doctors lacked the knowledge and training to support their care which resulted in further physical and mental health issues. These experiences with the medical system coupled with the social isolation they experienced from their online lesbian community and their long-term relationship ending contributed to Gray considering detransition. While they eventually felt detransition wasn't right for them, Gray experienced considerable stress that exacerbated their existing mental health issues alongside the physical symptoms they experienced while undergoing HRT.

### Reflection and Discussion Questions

1. What forms of gatekeeping do you see in Gray's story? How do these different forms of gatekeeping interact with each other?
2. What are some ways that Gray was able to manage their distress in spite of the barriers they faced?
3. Where do you see the medical model of disability in Gray's story? Where do you see the social model?
4. How is Grey's sexuality influenced (or not) by their gender? By their disabilities? What about the other direction?
5. What are ways that you could support Gray in your practice? What resources might you share with them?

## Conclusion

Queer, trans, and disabled sexualities are liberatory practices of radical joy and pleasure. Adapting this framework, practitioners can provide better support to queer and trans clients with disabilities, while challenging stigma and oppressive constructs. We should look to those with lived experiences, especially the most marginalized, to learn from their lived experiences, to find joy in their creations (whether art, poetry, or digital counternarratives), and share these with our clients to help them feel affirmed and empowered to explore their own paths.

## Resources

Autistic Self Advocacy Network & National Partnership for Women and Families. (2021). *Access, autonomy, and dignity: Comprehensive sexuality education for people with disabilities.* www.nationalpartnership.org/our-work/resources/healthcare/repro/repro-disability-sexed.pdf

Brown, A. M. (2019). *Pleasure activism: The politics of feeling good.* AK Press.

Erickson-Schroth, L. (2014). *Trans bodies, trans selves: A resource for the transgender community.* Oxford University Press.

Fielding, L. (2021). *Trans sex: Clinical approaches to trans sexualities and erotic embodiments.* Routledge.

Jamar, E. (2021, August 3). Why discovering your trans identity as a disabled person can be so confusing. *Autostraddle.* www.autostraddle.com/why-discovering-your-trans-identity-as-a-disabled-person-can-be-so-confusing/

Kay Ulanday Barrett – Award-winning trans, disabled poet: www.kaybarrett.net/

Taylor, S. R. (2021). *The body is not an apology: The power of radical self-love*. Berrett-Koehler Publishers.

TransHub (Australia): transhub.org.au

## References

Ali, A., Scior, K., Ratti, V., Strydom, A., King, M., & Hassiotis, A. (2013). Discrimination and other barriers to accessing health care: Perspectives of patients with mild and moderate intellectual disability and their carers. *PloS One, 8*(8), e70855.

American Psychiatric Association. (2013) *Diagnostic and statistical manual of mental disorders* (5th ed). American Psychiatric Association.

American Psychiatric Association. (2022). Neurodevelopmental disorders. In *Diagnostic and statistical manual of mental disorders* (5th ed., text revision). American Psychiatric Association.

Ballan, M. S., Romanelli, M., & Harper IV, J. N. (2011). The social model: A lens for counseling transgender individuals with disabilities. *Journal of Gay & Lesbian Mental Health, 15*(3), 260–280. http://doi.org/10.1080/19359705.2011.582073

Brisenden, S. (1986). Independent living and the medical model of disability. *Disability, Handicap & Society, 1*(2), 173–178.

Budhwani, H., & De, P. (2019). Perceived stigma in health care settings and the physical and mental health of people of color in the United States. *Health Equity, 3*(1), 73–80. http://doi.org/10.1089/heq.2018.0079

Cain, L. K., & Velasco, J. C. (2021). Stranded at the intersection of gender, sexuality, and autism: Gray's story. *Disability & Society, 36*(3), 358–375.

Castro, V. A., King, W. M., Augustaitis, L., Saylor, K., & Gamarel, K. E. (2021). A scoping review of health outcomes among transgender migrants. *Transgender Health*. http://doi.org/10.1089/trgh.2021.0011

Chilukuri, S. (2022, July). *7 Queer and trans creators with disabilities fighting for an accessible world*. www.them.us/story/queer-trans-creators-disabilities

Chin, M. (2018). Making queer and trans of color counterpublics: Disability, accessibility, and the politics of inclusion. *Affilia, 33*(1), 8–23.

Cohen-Rottenberg, R. (2012). *Caught inside a paradox: How cultural representations perpetuate disability stigma*. Disability and Representation: Changing the Cultural Conversation. www.disabilityandrepresentation.com/caught-inside-a-paradox-how-cultural-representations-perpetuate-disability-stigma/

Coleman, E., Bockting, W., Botzer, M., Cohen-Kettenis, P., DeCuypere, G., Feldman, J., Fraser, L., Green, J., Knudson, G., Meyer, W. J., Monstrey, S., Adler, R. K., Brown, G. R., Devor, A. H., Ehrbar, R., Ettner, R., Eyler, E., Garofalo, R., Karasic, D. H., . . . Zucker, K. (2012). Standards of care for the health of transsexual, transgender, and gender-nonconforming people, version 7. *International Journal of Transgenderism, 13*(4), 165–232. https://doi.org/10.1080/15532739.2011.700873

Flores, M. J., Watson, L. B., Allen, L. R., Ford, M., Serpe, C. R., Choo, P. Y., & Farrell, M. (2018). Transgender people of color's experiences of sexual objectification: Locating sexual objectification within a matrix of domination. *Journal of Counseling Psychology, 65*(3), 308–323.

Frawley, P., & O'Shea, A. (2020). "Nothing about us without us": Sex education by and for people with intellectual disability in Australia. *Sex Education, 20*(4), 413–424. http://doi.org/10.1080/14681811.2019.1668759

Hackett, R. A., Steptoe, A., Lang, R. P., & Jackson, S. E. (2020). Disability discrimination and well being in the United Kingdom: A prospective cohort study. *BMJ Open*, *10*(3), e035714.

Holt, M., Broady, T., Callander, D., Pony, M., Duck-Chong, L., Cook, T., & Rosenberg, S. (2023). Sexual experience, relationships, and factors associated with sexual and romantic satisfaction in the first Australian trans & gender diverse sexual health survey. *International Journal of Transgender Health*. http://doi.org/10.1080/26895269.2021.2016540

Iantaffi, A. A. (2010). Disability and polyamory: Exploring the edges of interdependence, gender and queer issues in non-monogamous relationships. In M. Barker & D. Langdridge (Eds.), *Understanding non-monogamies* (pp. 172–178). Routledge.

Irwig, M. S. (2016). Transgender care by endocrinologists in the United States. *Endocrine Practice: Official Journal of the American College of Endocrinology and the American Association of Clinical Endocrinologists*, *22*(7), 832–836. https://doi.org/10.4158/EP151185.OR

InterACT. (n.d). *Advocates for Intersex Youth*. https://interactadvocates.org/

James, S. E., Herman, J. L., Rankin, S., Keisling, M., Mottet, L., & Anafi, M. (2016). *The report of the 2015 U.S. transgender survey*. https://transequality.org/sites/default/files/docs/usts/USTS-Full-Report-Dec17.pdf

Jones, T., Smith, E., Ward, R., Dixon, J., Hillier, L., & Mitchell, A. (2016). School experiences of transgender and gender diverse students in Australia. *Sex Education*, *16*(2), 156–171. http://doi.org/10.1080/14681811.2015.1080678

Kattari, S. K., Bakko, M., Langenderfer-Magruder, L., & Holloway, B. T. (2021). Transgender and nonbinary experiences of victimization in health care. *Journal of Interpersonal Violence*, *36*(23–24), NP13054–NP13076. https://doi.org/10.1177/0886260520905091

Kattari, S. K., Kinney, M. K., Kattari, L., & Walls, N. E. (2020). Introduction to social work and health care with transgender and nonbinary individuals and communities. In S. K. Kattari., N. E. Walls, L. Kattari, & M. K. Kinney (Eds.), *Social work and health care with transgender and non-binary individuals and communities*. Routledge. https://doi.org/10.4324/9780429443176

Kattari, S. K., Lavery, A., & Hasche, L. (2017). Applying a social model of disability across the life span. *Journal of Human Behavior in the Social Environment*, *27*(8), 865–880. https://doi.org/10.1080/10911359.2017.1344175

Kattari, S. K., Whitfield, D. L., DeChants, J., & Alvarez, A. R. G. (2016). *Barriers to health faced by transgender and non-binary Black and minority ethnic people*. Race Equity Foundation. https://raceequalityfoundation.org.uk/health-care/barriers-to-health-faced-by-transgender-and-non-binary-black-and-minority-ethnic-people/

Krahn, G. L., Walker, D. K., & Correa-De-Araujo, R. (2015). Persons with disabilities as an unrecognized health disparity population. *American Journal of Public Health*, *105*(S2), S198–S206. https://doi.org/10.2105/AJPH.2014.302182

Mahdi, S., Viljoen, M., Massuti, R., Selb, M., Almodayfer, O., Karande, S., de Vries, P. J., Rohde, L., & Bölte, S. (2017). An international qualitative study of ability and disability in ADHD using the WHO-ICF framework. *European Child & Adolescent Psychiatry*, *26*(10), 1219–1231. https://doi.org/10.1007/s00787-017-0983-1

McRuer, R. (2006). *Crip theory: Cultural signs of queerness and disability*. NYU Press.

Mendoza, C. G. (2020). *Counterpublics, abled sex, and crip discourses on Twitter: A discourse analysis of conversations of sexuality and disability* (Doctoral dissertation). Old Dominion University. https://www.proquest.com/openview/8db139288 63a4ab9b9624e013464dd96/1?pq-origsite=gscholar&cbl=51922&diss=y

Messinger, A. M., Guadalupe-Diaz, X. L., & Kurdyla, V. (2021). Transgender Polyvictimization in the US transgender survey. *Journal of Interpersonal Violence.* https://doi.org/10.1177/08862605211039250

Okoro, C. A., Hollis, N. D., Cyrus, A. C., & Griffin-Blake, S. (2018). Prevalence of disabilities and health care access by disability status and type among adults – United States, 2016. *MMWR: Morbidity and Mortality Weekly Report, 67*(32), 882–887. https://doi.org/10.15585/mmwr.mm6732a3

Pellegrino, E. D. (1986). Rationing health care: The ethics of medical gatekeeping. *Journal of Contemporary Health Law & Policy, 2*(1), 23–45. https://scholarship.law.edu/cgi/viewcontent.cgi?article=1604&context=jchlp

Reisner, S. L., Poteat, T., Keatley, J., Cabral, M., Mothopeng, T., Dunham, E., Holland, C. E., Max, R., & Baral, S. D. (2016). Global health burden and needs of transgender populations: A review. *Lancet (London, England), 388*(10042), 412–436. https://doi.org/10.1016/S0140-6736(16)00684-X

Riggle, E. D., Rostosky, S. S., McCants, L. E., & Pascale-Hague, D. (2011). The positive aspects of a transgender self-identification. *Psychology & Sexuality, 2*(2), 147–158.

Roosevelt, L., & Ellis, S. A. (2020). Best practices in sexual and reproductive health care for transgender and nonbinary people. In S. K. Kattari, M. K. Kinney, L. Kattari, & N. E. Walls (Eds.), *Social work and health care practice with transgender and nonbinary individuals and communities* (pp. 57–75). Routledge.

Rosenwohl-Mack, A., Tamar-Mattis, S., Baratz, A. B., Dalke, K. B., Ittelson, A., Zieselman, K., & Flatt, J. D. (2020). A national study on the physical and mental health of intersex adults in the US. *PLoS One, 15*(10), e0240088. https://doi.org/10.1371/journal.pone.0240088

Rowen, T. S., Stein, S., & Tepper, M. (2015). Sexual health care for people with physical disabilities. *The Journal of Sexual Medicine, 12*(3), 584–589. https://doi-org.proxy.lib.umich.edu/10.1111/jsm.12810

Sedgwick, J. A., Merwood, A., & Asherson, P. (2019). The positive aspects of attention deficit hyperactivity disorder: A qualitative investigation of successful adults with ADHD. *ADHD Attention Deficit Hyperactivity Disorder, 11*(1), 241–253. https://doi.org/10.1007/s12402-018-0277-6

U.S. Department of Labor. (n.d.). *Americans with Disabilities Act.* www.dol.gov/general/topic/disability/ada

World Professional Association for Transgender Health. (2012). *Standards of care for the health of transsexual, transgender, and gender nonconforming people* [7th Version]. https://www.wpath.org/publications/soc

World Professional Association for Transgender Health. (n.d.). *Mission and vision.* www.wpath.org/about/mission-and-vision

# 19

# WE'LL MAKE OUR OWN SPACE

Making LGBTQ+ Spaces Accessible

*Jax Kynn, Hannah Boyke, and Brendon T. Holloway*

### Introduction

Accessibility for disabled individuals and inclusivity of queer and trans people are intimately linked social issues. Both bring attention to often overlapping non-normalized identities, highlighting people on the margins of our nondisabled, heteronormative, cisgender, White supremacist, and capitalist society. Historically, queer and trans disabled people of color people have been crucial leaders in disability justice work, consistently advocating that valuing and celebrating disabled people are necessary for liberation (Berne, 2015; Clare, 2009; Piepzna-Samarasinha, 2020). Furthermore, there are between three million and five million disabled people within the wider LGBTQ+ community, and approximately 40% of trans people were identified as disabled (Movement Advancement Project [MAP], 2019). Queer and trans individuals are more likely to be identified as disabled than heterosexual and cisgender people in the United States (MAP, 2019), yet the intersection of disability and LGBTQ+ is often overlooked. In disability-focused spaces, queerness is pushed to the margins; in LGBTQ+ spaces, disability is often ignored and accessibility is unaddressed or is solely an afterthought when designing LGBTQ+ spaces and events. As a result, many spaces ignore the unique needs and experiences of queer and trans disabled folks.

In this chapter, we explore the accessibility for and inclusion of disabled individuals within LGBTQ+ spaces. We are guided by three questions:

1. What does it mean to make a space that is accessible for disabled individuals and inclusive for members of the LGBTQ+ community?

2. What would it look like to have truly accessible spaces across LGBTQ+ identities?
3. Why is this so important?

We begin by defining accessibility, inclusion, ableism, heterosexism, and cissexism. Then we introduce the frameworks of queer crip theory and disability justice as they relate to accessibility and inclusion. Finally, we offer recommendations for developing accessible LGBTQ+ spaces, and conclude with resources that can assist practitioners, organizers, and scholars in developing inclusive and accessible physical and virtual spaces.

## Accessibility and Inclusion

Accessibility seeks to make spaces that every person can reach, enter, and utilize. There is a diversity of disabilities, impairments, and illnesses present among those in both the general population and the LGBTQ+ community, so there are a range of accessibility accommodations that may be required to meet these diverse access needs. Accessibility can mean offering pay-as-you-can options for products or services for disabled folks (Cubacub, 2020; Kafer, 2013), designing spaces that are useable for everyone (Hamraie, 2013; Mace, 1985), expressing solidarity and love (Piepzna-Samarasinha, 2018), and "being able to be and exist in your full self, as you are, without having to change or adapt to the world around you" (A. Hillyard quoted in Jones, 2021). These definitions highlight the infinite ways to actualize accessibility and demonstrate that accessibility goes beyond the accommodations outlined by laws. To make accommodations is not a value-neutral choice; making intentional decisions to create or modify a digital of physical space for anyone to use recognizes the value of disabled folks (Hamraie, 2013; Harrison & Kopit, 2020; Kafer, 2013). Anyone can find solutions that increase accessibility. When we ignore recommendations or react defensively to accessibility requests, we make spaces inaccessible (Radical Access Mapping Project, 2014). Accessibility requires flexibility, creativity, and critical reflections on priorities and decision-making processes (Kafer, 2013; Smith, 2020).

When designing a space or event, it is important to consider stairs, doorways, language, lighting, visual and non-visual formats, transportation, cost, and many other factors that impact individuals' ability to fully participate in a space or event (Harrison & Kopit, 2020; Sins Invalid, 2019; Smith, 2020). Spaces should also be assessed for how inclusive they are. Disabled queer and trans individuals often have their access needs ignored in LGBTQ+ spaces. To truly and fully include LGBTQ+ disabled people within wider community, everyone must be able to access those spaces (Blyth, 2010; Conover & Israel, 2019; Chapman, n.d.; Formby, 2017; Shakespeare, 1998; Toft, 2020). Creating such spaces can mean ensuring that mobility aid users and service dog users can navigate the space, including ASL interpreters or closed captions, designing quiet spaces, and including disabled queer and trans individuals in marketing and publicity materials (Blyth, 2010; Brownworth, 2019; Ishak, 2021). Ignoring access erases and excludes disabled queer and trans folks in LGBTQ+ spaces and the queer and trans community (Blyth, 2010; Toft, 2020). Accessibility is especially relevant when planning Pride events, which have often left many disabled queer and trans people unable to participate (Brownworth 2019; Coi & Hernández-Morales, 2022; Ishak, 2021; Jones, 2021; Vargas, 2019).

Inclusivity is often brought up in relation to the LGBTQ+ community, specifically in reference to inclusive language. In general, such considerations might focus on language that is affirming of gender expansive identities or represents all sexualities and gender identities encompassed under the LGBTQ+ umbrella. Inclusivity is closely related to accessibility. However, rather than focusing on whether someone is *able* to use a space, inclusivity creates a space that anyone would *want* to use (Young, 2019). An inclusive and accessible LGBTQ+ space would mean that any queer or trans person would feel safe and comfortable regardless of their bodymind and could easily utilize and navigate a space.

## Understanding Why Accessibility Is Important for Queer and Trans Spaces

### Ableism, Heterosexism, and Cissexism

As a cultural phenomenon, ableism reflects the beliefs and practices that assume that abled-bodies and abled-minds reflect what is "normal" (Goldbach et al., 2021; Kafer, 2013; McRuer, 2006; Thomson, 1997). Ableism assumes that having a body and mind without an impairment is valuable and desirable and that only abled people can contribute to society (Atkins & Marston, 1999; McRuer, 2006; Wendell, 1989). In effect, ableism normalizes beliefs and practices that ignore and devalue disabled individuals' needs and experiences. As a structural phenomenon, ableism emerges through the interaction of economic, environmental, political, legal, and social oppression, which "render a person with impairment *disabled* [emphasis original]" (Shakespeare, 2014, p. 23). Ableist structures work in tandem with ableist cultural norms to normalize and systematize the disabled people as nonnormal, undesirable, and trivial.

### Heterosexism and Cissexism

Like ableism, heterosexism assumes that heterosexuality is the "natural" sexual orientation, while other sexual orientations and anything related to them are unnatural, deviant, and deplorable (Atkins & Marston, 1999; McRuer, 2006). Cissexism is interconnected with heterosexism. Cissexism (along with the concepts of cisgenderism and gender binarism) describes cultural and social systems that assume that there are *only* two genders and they are immutable (Ansara & Berger, 2021). Within cissexist cultures and social structures, it is abnormal to identify with a gender outside of the binary – as neither a man nor a woman or both a woman and a man. Often, these cissexist beliefs also assume that gender is determined by genitalia and chromosomes: anyone with a penis is a man (with XY chromosomes), and anyone with breasts and vulva must be a woman (with XX chromosomes). Cissexism also assumes that individuals can only be identified with the gender that they were assigned with at birth. If anyone has ambiguous genitalia or chromosomal variations, they may only be identified as one of the two gender options.

### Queer Crip Theory

Queer crip theory challenges notions of assimilating into cisgender, heterosexual, and abled "normality," which often reinforces the shame and deviance culturally and structurally ascribed onto queer, trans, and disabled people (Sandahl, 2003). Intersectionality (Collins, 2000; Crenshaw, 1991) is central to queer crip theory, which recognizes the multiple oppressions that queer, trans, and disabled people of color experience (Harriet Tubman Collective, 2020; Schalk, 2022; Withers et al., 2019). Expanding on queer theory's critique of heterosexism, cissexism, and compulsory heterosexuality, queer crip theory interrogates the role of intersectionality de-stabilizing the hegemonic markers of heterosexual, cisgender, and abled bodies (Sandahl, 2003; Kafer, 2013; Kafer & Kim, 2017). Compulsory heterosexuality refers to the institutional arrangements that reinforce heterosexuality as the natural and normal option (Rich, 1980).

Queer crip theory conceptualizes compulsory heterosexuality as intertwined with compulsory able-bodiedness and able-mindedness (McRuer, 2006). Compulsory able-bodiedness manifests through the culture and structure that assumes that abled-bodies and abled-minds are the "default" option (Campbell, 2001; Hirschmann, 2013; Rees, 2021). Compulsory able-bodiedness is linked with accessibility, for spaces, environments, and institutions are "fundamentally structured in ways that limit access for people with disabilities . . . constructing a world that always and everywhere privileges very narrow (and ever-narrowing) conceptions of ability" (McRuer, 2006, p. 151). Compulsory able-bodiedness emerges when disability is treated as deviant– solely as something to be minimized, to get rid of, or to be cured from (Clare, 2017; Cooper, 2022; Greer, 2019). Here, disability is not a source of pride but a marker of exclusion. However, queer crip theory challenges compulsory ableism and centers queer and trans disabled people's experiences, recognizing the fluidity of disability, gender, and sexual orientation.

Compulsory heterosexuality is inseparable from compulsory able-bodiedness and able-mindedness (Greer, 2019; McRuer, 2006). Historically, queer and trans people, disabled people, and queer and trans disabled people have received similar treatment within society: medicalization, objectification, institutionalization, isolation, denial of rights, and violence (Clare, 2009; Schalk, 2022). These factors have worked to erase and exclude queer and trans disabled people from nondisabled, non-trans, and non-queer spaces. The development of accessible and inclusive spaces departs from this history, as these spaces challenge isolation and the environment that disables people with impairments (Shakespeare, 2014). Even more, at this intersection is the assumption that disabled people are "genderless, asexual undesirables" (Clare, 2009, p. 130). Queer and trans disabled people's exclusion from LGBTQ+ spaces reinforces the intersection of compulsory able-bodiedness and compulsory heterosexuality while discriminating on multiple levels.

## *Disability Justice*

As an activist movement and theoretical framework, disability justice is intractable from queerness. Brought together by shared principles of intersectionality, anti-capitalism, collective liberation, and recognition of a whole person, Patty Berne, Mia Mingus, and Stacey Milbern started the Disability Justice Collective in 2005 (Berne, 2015). Berne, Mingus, and Milbern – all disabled, queer women of color – developed Disability Justice Collective to forge coalitions that challenged ableism within their respective activist communities. Shortly after the group's development, it was joined by additional disabled queer scholars and activists including Eli Clare, Sebastian Margaret, Leroy Moore, and Leah Lakshmi Piepzna-Samarasinha (Berne, 2015). Disability justice, as a concept, grew from the Collective's work, and this concept offers a framework for understanding and challenging the intersections of accessibility and inclusion (Berne et al., 2018). Importantly, however, the theoretical grounding for disability justice can be found in scholarship and activism that arose during the late 20th century. The Disability Justice Collective continued the work of disabled queer and trans activist scholars including Gloria Anzaldúa, Audre Lorde, Eli Clare, Aurora Levins Morales, and Connie Panzarino.

Disability justice centers the experiences of disabled, queer and trans, people of color through its principles, activism, scholarship, and leadership (Sins Invalid, 2019). A key underpinning of disability justice is that it recognizes that everyone has "strengths and needs that must be met" and values the diversity of all human bodies and minds (Sins Invalid, 2019, p. 19). Challenging a deficit-focused framing of disability, disability justice conceptualizes all individuals as "powerful, not despite the complexities of our bodies, but because of them" (Sins Invalid, 2019, p. 19). The core tenants of disability justice – including intersectionality, leadership of the most impacted, recognizing wholeness, interdependence, collective access, and collective liberation – are integral to developing accessible and inclusive spaces.

*Disability Justice Versus Disability Rights*

As frameworks for action and scholarship, disability justice is distinct from a disability rights framework, which focuses on establishing legal rights and protections – such as the Americans with Disabilities Act (ADA) – for disabled people. Disability justice activists argue that disability rights organizing has overwhelmingly privileged the voices and experiences of White, wealthy, cis-het men (Sins Invalid, 2019). Such situations can reinforce ableist, heterosexist, cissexist, racialized, and classist structures that vest the authority of inclusion in those who already have power (Berne, 2015; Sins Invalid, 2019; Tink et al., 2020).

Disability justice argues that legislation alone fails to address the root cause of the oppression and violence that disabled people experience: ableism (Sins Invalid, 2019). Ableism reifies disabled people's exclusion regardless of a space's compliance with ADA minimum requirements. The culture of compulsory able-bodiedness can lead to disabled people feeling ashamed for needing accessibility accommodations (Abrams & Abes, 2021; Kattari et al., 2020). As a result, some disabled individuals may refrain from asking for accommodations out of fear that they will be perceived as a burden, incapable of living up to ableist standards of productivity, or denied the accommodations because they haven't established sufficient proof of suffering (Abrams & Abes, 2021; Kattari et al., 2020). Ableism normalizes a situation in which disabled people might deny or downplay their needs as a strategy to avoid the shame, stigma, guilt, and negative consequences of demanding that their access needs be met.

*Disability Justice and Accessibility*

Within disability justice, accessibility means more than simply adhering to legal mandates about a space's physical environment; to do this is the *bare minimum*. Accessibility requires careful consideration of ableism's role in excluding disabled people even in spaces that meet ADA requirements. When access challenges ableism, embraces intersectionality, and honors disabled people, "access shifts from being silencing to freeing; from being isolating to connecting; from hidden and invisible to visible; from burdensome to valuable; from a resentful obligation to an opportunity; from shameful to powerful" (Mingus, 2017). Through these shifts, access can act as a form of liberation (Mingus, 2017).

*Accessibility as Love*

Leah Lakshmi Piepzna-Samarasinha (2018) conceptualizes accessibility as a radical act of love:

> I think that crip solidarity, and solidarity between crips and non(yet)-crips is a powerful act of love and I-got-your-back . . . when we reach for each other and make the most access possible, it is a radical act of love.
> *(Piepzna-Samarasinha, 2018, pp. 46–47)*

Ensuring that all people can access a space also means seeing value, strength, and vitality in the diversity of bodyminds. Accommodating diverse access needs also means confronting ableist, capitalist, and racialized norms that inform which bodies, minds, and abilities are valued. Rather than just a checklist or guidelines about the physical or digital environment, accessibility is also a recognition that disabled people are needed and wanted by the LGBTQ+ community:

> [W]ithout changing their internal worlds that see disabled people as sad and stupid, or refus[ing] to see those of us already in their lives, they can have all the [American Sign Language] interpreters and ramps in the world, and we won't come where we're not loved, needed, and understood as leaders, not just people they must begrudgingly provide services for.
> *(Piepzna-Samarasinha, 2018, p. 76)*

Accessibility is not an administrative burden carried out as an afterthought solely to avoid legal or social backlash; accessibility is an expression of solidarity. Framing accessibility as a radical act of love allows us to transform access and leverage it for empowerment.

**Making Spaces Accessible**

Like all people, queer and trans individuals need inclusive spaces where they are safe and experience a sense of belonging. Spaces that are not accessible automatically exclude queer and trans disabled people. All physical and virtual spaces must be created with disabled people in mind and with accessibility as a forethought, not an afterthought. Everyone has access needs, which can be talked about without shame (Sins Invalid, 2019). For example, some people are naturally cold, meaning they may prefer a space where a heater is available, while some people rely exclusively on public transit, so they can only access meetings near a public transit stop. It is important to consider and honor the various access needs that people may have.

In the words of Audre Lorde (1997), a Black disabled lesbian poet, "We were never meant to survive." While Lorde wrote this in response to police violence, racialized hate, and anti-Black racism, many disabled activists share Lorde's sentiment. As stated earlier in this chapter, meeting people's access needs is the bare minimum. An accessible space means having an environment that is set up from the beginning to be accessible to all (Sins Invalid, 2019). As academics or service providers, if we are not thinking about how to make a space accessible, we must consider who we may be excluding and how this exclusion contributes to the marginalization of disabled people.

## Physical Spaces

When we think about how to make physical spaces more accessible, we often think of making sure there are no stairs required to enter a space or that wheelchairs can fit through doorways. While these are necessary to consider, making a physical space accessible goes much further than this; it also starts at the beginning of the planning process.

### Starting at the Planning Process

As noted by Sins Invalid (2019), "access [to] information is as important as information about the cost of tickets." Descriptions of the physical spaces that include accessibility and inclusivity information should be available online (Rydstedt & Lachowsky, 2020). All outreach materials and websites should state what access needs have been addressed (e.g., ASL interpretation is included; our space is wheelchair accessible). Outreach materials should provide information about anti-oppressive and anti-ableist policies and training staff receive across all identity groups, rather than just disability (Harrison & Kopit, 2020). There should be designated accessibility and inclusivity coordinators to ensure that these things are accomplished, and the coordinators' contact information should be available on all outreach materials for those who have questions or need other accommodations.

It is crucial to ask what access needs must be met for people to show up (and encouraging folks whose access needs are already met to simply state that their needs have been met). Provide information about any gaps in access, and update the accessibility information on the website regularly. For example, health-service nonprofit organizations can ask people to indicate their accessibility needs on intake forms or when they schedule an appointment. Websites can explicitly encourage people to write or call about specific accessibility concerns and link to anonymous feedback surveys. These options can promote accountability and recognize that individuals' access needs aren't always fixed. It should be noted that if these, it is necessary to try to meet these access needs and follow-up with individuals who have complaints or whose access needs cannot be immediately met. If not, this is performative, and performative accessibility reinforces ableism by devaluating disabled people's needs and experiences.

### Ensuring Restrooms Are Accessible (and Safe)

An additional accessibility consideration in physical spaces are restrooms. At some point, every person who shows up in your space will likely need to use the restroom. For individuals with mobility impairments, restrooms are often inaccessible due to their architectural design (e.g., a wheelchair user and a wheelchair may not fit simultaneously). If the restroom in your space is inaccessible, look at nearby places to identify where an accessible restroom is located. Of course, it should be within a reasonable distance to accommodate the person. Indicate the location of the accessible restroom on the website and with signs inside the building. Disabled people with chemical injuries or sensitivities may become ill or have an allergic reaction to scented soaps and cleaning products. Stocking restrooms with unscented soaps and using chemical-free cleaning products can avoid causing harm. For disabled trans people, restrooms may feel unsafe given the violent anti-trans restroom legislation that has arisen in recent years. Designating and labeling accessible restrooms as "All Gender" or "Gender Neutral" can provide a safe space for trans individuals. To implement an even more progressive policy, we recommend following the lead of the Royal Ontario Museum in Toronto, Canada, which converted gendered multi-stall restrooms into several individual stalls each with a toilet and a sink, allowing multiple people to use the same space yet have privacy (Jones, 2016).

### Accessibility Is (Non-Fluorescently) Lit

Certain types of lighting can trigger some disabilities such as seizure disorders or migraines. The use of strobe lights or flash photography can be overwhelming and even trigger a seizure. It is important to refrain from using this lighting or warn individuals ahead of time about the lighting. In many healthcare settings, fluorescent lighting is used which may also trigger specific reactions. The widespread use of fluorescent lighting can make daily activities inaccessible:

> Avoiding long-tube fluorescent lights means I can't catch public transport at night, or trains that go through tunnels, or go to supermarkets or convenience stores. It means checking ahead whenever I visit any new place,

for every meeting, every show, every venue, every hotel, every airport, every restaurant, every bar, every café, every social engagement, every home, every chore.

*(Anatolitis, 2019)*

Lighting concerns may also come up in academic settings, particularly in the classroom. Most classrooms have fluorescent overhead lights, making the classroom a potentially inaccessible space for some disabled students and educators. We recommend advocating for non-fluorescent lighting with your department's administration. If the department fails to address the lighting concerns, we recommend inquiring about a classroom space with ample natural lighting, so there is no need to use overhead lighting. However, this is a temporary fix, as future students and educators may be impacted by the overhead lighting in the future.

*Seating Options*

An additional accessibility consideration for in-person spaces is seating options. First, it is essential to ensure that the seating options are wheelchair and walker accessible. This includes making sure a wheelchair or walker can fit within the space, but it also means that a wheelchair or walker user can navigate the space in its entirety. In the classroom, desks and chairs should be spaced out enough so that a walker or wheelchair can fit in between them. In health and human service and private office settings, there should be sufficient space for wheelchair or walker users from the moment they enter the lobby. If there is insufficient space, consider rearranging seating to make the space accessible.

Additionally, we recommend prioritizing the comfort of the chairs offered in the space to accommodate individuals with chronic pain and/or illness. People with chronic back pain may experience a pain flare in chairs with hard backs and no cushions. People with chronic neck pain may need a chair with neck support. Thus, we recommend having a variety of chairs to accommodate disabled people with chronic pain. It may take time to switch, so we recommend adding one accessible, comfortable chair at a time if immediate accommodations are unavailable. Often, LGBTQ+ events have no seating or little seating available – consider ensuring that your gala, happy hour, coalition meeting, speed dating event, town hall, and Pride contingent have options for sitting and resting to allow for the full participation of everyone.

Finally, we also recommend having seating options that accommodate fat or larger bodies. Many chairs are designed for thinner bodies. This is especially true in classrooms and waiting rooms, which often only have narrow seats and arms. By not offering seating options that fit fat bodies, fat people are further marginalized in physical spaces. For disabled fat people, this can bring up internalized feelings of fatphobia, trigger pain flares, or other disability-related symptoms and can result in feeling a lack of belonging in the space. Seating options should make the physical space accessible for both disabled people and fat disabled people, too.

*Making Your Physical Space Accessible Checklist*

Although the checklist should not be the end of accessibility, it is an important place to begin. The following items should be a starting point and not treated as an exhaustive list.

- Outreach and/or public-facing materials state which accessibility needs have been addressed;
- You have asked the person(s) about their accessibility needs;
- Restrooms in the space are accessible;
- Restrooms in the space are trans-inclusive;
- No fluorescent lights or strobe effects in the space;
- Seating options accommodate all bodies.

**Accessible Virtual and Digital Spaces**

The COVID-19 pandemic changed how all people across the world gather, connect with one another, and attend events. However, disabled communities have used virtual spaces for years and have advocated for more digital options to promote accessibility. Still, widespread virtual spaces, like most things, did not become widely accessible or acceptable until nondisabled people endorsed them. Prior to the pandemic, phrases like "pre-existing condition" and "risk group" were typically reserved for describing disabled people (Pieri, 2022). With the COVID-19 pandemic, these phrases found mainstream usage (Pieri, 2022). Media representations of "risk" and "pre-existing conditions" often ignored the structural factors that heightened the risks that disabled and chronically ill people experience (Pieri, 2022). As a result, the adoption of such language reinstates the pervasiveness of able-bodiedness being "normal" while simultaneously invisibilizing the experiences of disabled people in the pandemic. Notwithstanding its problematic undertones, increased widespread use of virtual spaces has made events and activities more accessible for disabled people.

*Virtual Platforms and Online Spaces*

Amidst the COVID-19 pandemic, virtual platforms, including Zoom, Discord, Skype, Teams, and Slack, allowed people to hold work meetings, attend and teach classes, gather with friends and family, play video games, and host workshops and events. Perhaps more than anything, online spaces allowed people to connect with one another and find community and validation during a grave time. Disabled communities have consistently advocated for accessible virtual options and events, so we want to offer recommendations to maximize accessibility in virtual spaces.

*Indefinite virtual spaces.* Always offer a virtual option, even at primarily in-person events, class sessions, and appointments. Although many nondisabled people are ready to be exclusively in-person, it is important to check your privilege and recognize that in-person only options will exclude some people, notably disabled and chronically ill people. For educators, we recognize that a hybrid classroom can be difficult to navigate, having some students in in-person classroom and others in the virtual classroom. If this is difficult to balance, we recommend offering an online option for students who need it with the caveat that students who are online may not be able to participate in any in-class discussions or in-class activities. However, we do recommend going beyond this and attempting to find ways to include online students in in-class activities. For example, if more than one student is online, a breakout room can be created to allow the online students to participate in an activity together. Yes, this may create additional labor for educators, but it demonstrates that accessibility is infused within all aspects of your classroom.

For human and health service professionals, we recommend advocating for the option to see clients virtually for the foreseeable future. Not only does this provide disabled people with the option to see someone virtually, but it can also support queer and trans people who may not feel comfortable or safe in a particular office space. Healthcare settings, specifically, can be unsupportive and even harmful spaces for trans people. Trans people experience discrimination (James et al., 2016), victimization (Kattari et al., 2021), and even abuse in these settings (James et al., 2016). These experiences include interacting with office staff, healthcare personnel, and filling out documentation, such as intake forms (Roller et al., 2015; Turban et al., 2017). Thus, offering a virtual space can create an accessible *and* inclusive environment for disabled queer and trans people.

*Making virtual spaces accessible.* In virtual spaces, it is important to think about accessibility on the front end. As discussed earlier, we recommend sharing what has been done to make the space accessible, as well as asking people what they need. A good starting point is to make sure that the person has access to the digital platform you are using. This includes making sure the person has access to the internet. Once that is established, there are a range of accessibility considerations for website design and virtual meetings.

Accessibility should be centered in website design and the content curated on the website and any social media. Content with insufficient color-contrast and hard to read font types are inaccessible. Ensure that all information on your website can be read with a screen reader and navigated with a keyboard. We recommend adding image descriptions (can be abbreviated to ID) below any photo that is on your website and providing alternative text descriptions for the image when developing the webpage. For example, if there is a photo of a provider on your website, an image description may look like:

*ID: [Provider's name] wearing a floral button up while smiling at the camera.*

It's important to manually add alternative text descriptions to any photos posted on social media as well; Facebook and Twitter alternative text descriptions are notoriously vague and often prohibit engagement from blind and vision impaired individuals who may rely on screen readers. If you have forms on your website that need to be downloaded to complete, make sure the documents are accessible for screen readers. There are many resources available online and in the resources section of this chapter for developing and evaluating accessible online and virtual content. Additionally, there are tools, such as the Wave Web Accessibility Evaluation Tool, that can evaluate the extent to which a website meets accessibility standards.

For video conferencing and virtual meetings, ensure that the platform offers closed captioning. Closed captioning displays the audio portion of the call in the form of text, providing deaf, hard-of-hearing, and those with sensory processing disorders a visual to what is being shared rather than being forced to rely on hearing/verbal processing. Additionally, real-time ASL interpretations can be used to increase accessibility, and the interpreter should be pinned as a presenter. Make transcripts and plain language summaries available for individuals to view after the meeting.

**Conclusion**

Accessibility is an expression of solidarity, love, and validation for *everyone*. We must design spaces that are safe for queer and trans people, as well as accessible for individuals with all types of disabilities, impairments, and other access needs. A checklist of access considerations is the starting point for cultivating accessibility, but to make spaces usable and desirable for all, it is crucial to regularly ask individuals utilizing any space if they have unmet access needs. Queer crip theory and disability justice demonstrate that accessibility can be liberatory and empowering, especially for queer and trans disabled folks. Inclusivity for queer and trans people is intimately linked to accessibility for disabled individuals. Keeping access in the forefront can counter compulsory ableism and compulsory cisheterosexism. We must listen to disabled queer and trans people, and ensure that they are able to not only access LGBTQ+ spaces but also feel actively welcomed in them.

## Case Study

Charlotte (they/them), a nonbinary Black nondisabled person, Gabriele (he/him), an Afro-Latinx nondisabled transman, and Quinn (they/them) a nonbinary White nondisabled person, are co-leaders of the Queer Quant Collective (QQC). QQC is an emerging collective that connects queer and trans scholars whose research aims to promote inclusive and intersectional approaches to quantitative data collection and analysis. Charlotte, Gabriele, and Quinn are putting on a regional conference, and they are currently in the planning phase. Last month, Quinn received an email from a member of QQC asking them to include image descriptions on the QQC website because the website was not compatible with the member's screen reader. After that, Quinn started to learn more about accessibility in website design and hopes to integrate accessibility into the conference. Charlotte and Gabriele are excited to help Quinn make the conference as accessible as possible.

### Before Reading On, Reflect on the Following Questions

- What can Quinn, Charlotte, and Gabriele do to plan a meeting that is inclusive and accessible?
- What barriers might emerge when trying to host an inclusive and accessible meeting?

The three co-leaders split responsibilities for conference planning. Charlotte is responsible for an online option for attending the conference. All conference events will be live streamed. Attendees who join online will be able to engage in the Q&A part of presentations by typing questions into the chat online, and there will be a moderator who will monitor the chat during each session.

Quinn is responsible for the physical space of the venue. They booked a small hall at their university, which has five classrooms and a larger central space. The classrooms will be used for presentations, and the central space will be used between presentations and as a reception hall. They made sure that the rooms had dimmable lights and ample natural light and that the tables in the room could be moved to ensure that the space is wheelchair and walker accessible. Although the hall lacks gender neutral restrooms, Quinn spoke to hall manager and was able to label the restrooms as all gender restrooms for the event

Gabriele is designing flyers for the event. He plans to include a map of the conference site that indicates the location of restrooms, pet relief sites, entrances and exits, and elevators. He also will provide a link that attendees can use to indicate their access needs. The flyers state which access needs have been addressed in the physical space and promote the online option of the event. Gabriele also developed an online form that participants can fill out during the conference if their accessibility needs change or if they have feedback regarding any aspect of accessibility of the conference.

## Reflection Questions

- How did the planning process try to address the attendees' potential access needs in the development of outreach materials, a digital event, and an in-person event?
- If you were planning this meeting, how would your plan differ?
  - How would you integrate the Disability Justice Framework into the planning, execution, and review of this event?
- How did inclusivity and accessibility overlap in the planning process?
- What barriers might emerge when trying to host an inclusive and accessible meeting?

## Resources

### Further Reading on Accessibility and Inclusivity

Respectability. (2022). *LGBTQ+ people with disabilities*. www.respectability.org/resources/lgbtq/
This has a list of books, articles, and queer disabled people.

Disability Visibility Project. (n.d.). *ADA 30 In Color*. https://disabilityvisibilityproject.com/ada30/
Essays from disabled BIPOC writers about disability and accessibility since the passage of the Americans with Disabilities Act.

### Resources and Guidelines for Accessible Events

Sins Invalid. (2020, June 8). *Access suggestions for public events*. www.sinsinvalid.org/news-1/2020/6/8/access-suggestions-for-public-events?rq=access
A comprehensive list of accessibility and inclusivity recommendations rooted in disability justice.

Rooted in Rights. (2021). *#Accessthat*. https://rootedinrights.org/accessthat/
Landing page for a range of resources offering guidance on developing accessible materials including transcriptions, videos, documents, and meetings.

### Examples of Accessibility Information on Websites

NOLOSE. (2015). *2015 conference accessibility*. https://web.archive.org/web/20220713184948/http://nolose.org/2015conf/2015-conference-accessibility/
Example of accessibility information provided on a website. The webpage is archived to preserve content.

Convergence. (2022). *Accessibility and inclusion.* https://web.archive.org/web/20220713185030/www.convergence-con.org/at-the-con/services/accessibility/
Example of accessibility information for an event displayed on a website. The webpage is archived to preserve content.

### Resources and Guidelines for Developing Online/Virtual Content

W3C Web Accessibility Initiative. (2022). *Making the web accessible: Strategies, standards, and supporting resources to help you make the web more accessible to people with disabilities.* www.w3.org/WAI/
Resource for developing and evaluating accessible websites.

WebAIM. (2022). *Contrast checker.* https://webaim.org/resources/contrastchecker/
A tool that evaluates the contrast between two colors.

United States General the Services Administration. (2022, March). *Content creation-create accessible meetings.* www.section508.gov/create/accessible-meetings/
Guide for creating accessible virtual meetings.

United States General Services Administration. (n.d.). *Create accessible digital products.* www.section508.gov/create/
Landing page that has resources for developing accessible web and print materials, including documents, pdfs, and videos.

## References

Abrams, E. J., & Abes, E. S. (2021). "It's finding peace in my body": Crip theory to understand authenticity for a queer, disabled college student. *Journal of College Student Development, 62*(3), 261–275. https://doi.org/10.1353/csd.2021.0021

Anatolitis, E. (2019, July 1). Fluorescent light and the brain: A note on Esther's disability. *Esther Anatolitis.* https://estheranatolitis.net/2019/07/01/fluorescent-light-and-the-brain/

Ansara, Y. G., & Berger, I. (2021). Cisgenderism. In A. E. Goldberg & G. Beemyn (Eds.), *The Sage encyclopedia of trans studies* (pp. 119–121). Sage.

Atkins, D., & Marston, C. (1999). Creating accessible queer community: Intersections and fractures with dis/ability praxis. *Journal of Gay, Lesbian, and Bisexual Identity, 4*(1), 3–21.

Berne, P. (2015, June 10). Disability justice-A working draft. *Sins Invalid.* www.sinsinvalid.org/blog/disability-justice-a-working-draft-by-patty-berne

Berne, P., Morales, A. L., Langstaff, D., & Sins Invalid. (2018). Ten principles of disability justice. *WSQ: Women's Studies Quarterly, 46*(1), 227–230. https://doi.org/10.1353/wsq.2018.0003

Blyth, C. (2010). Members only: The use of gay space(s) by gay disabled men. In R. Shuttleworth & T. Sanders (Eds.), *Sex and disability: Politics, identity and access* (pp. 41–58). The Disability Press.

Brownworth, V. A. (2019, July 3). LGBTQ disability and Pride: The case for inclusion. *Philadelphia Gay News.* https://epgn.com/2019/07/03/lgbtq-disability-and-pride-the-case-for-inclusion/

Campbell, F. K. (2001). Inciting legal fictions: Disability's date with ontology and the ableist body of the law. *Griffith Law Review, 10*, 42–62.

Chapman, C. (n.d.). *Accessible design vs. inclusive design*. Toptal. www.toptal.com/designers/ui/inclusive-design-infographic

Clare, E. (2009). *Exile and pride: Disability, queerness, and liberation* (2nd ed.). Duke University Press.

Clare, E. (2017). *Brilliant imperfection: Grappling with cure*. Duke University Press.

Coi, G., & Hernández-Morales, H. (2022, June 16). Disability right activists fight for access to cities' Pride events. *POLITICO*. www.politico.eu/article/disability-rights-activist-lgbtq-pride-parade-events-accessibility-cities-epoa/

Collins, P. H. (2000). *Black feminist thought*. Routledge.

Conover, K. J., & Israel, T. (2019). Microaggression and social support among sexual minorities with physical disabilities. *Rehabilitation Psychology*, 64(2), 167–178. http://dx.doi.org/10.1037/rep0000250

Cooper, N. (2022). The experiences of a disabled dominatrix. *Disabled Studies Quarterly*, 42(2). https://doi.org/10.18061/dsq.v42i2.9127

Crenshaw, K. (1991). Mapping the margins: Intersectionality, identity politics, and violence against women of color. *Stanford Law Review*, 43(6), 1241–1299. https://doi.org/10.2307/1229039

Cubacub, S. (2020). Radical visibility: A disabled queer clothing reform movement manifesto. In A. Wong (Ed.), *Disability visibility: First-person stories from the twenty-first century* (pp. 91–100). Vintage Books.

Formby, E. (2017). How should we 'care' for LGBT+ students within higher education? *Pastoral Care in Education*, 35(3), 203–220. https://doi.org/10.1080/02643944.2017.1363811

Goldbach, C., Knutson, D., & Kler, S. (2021). Heterosexism. In A. E. Goldberg & G. Beemyn (Eds.), *The Sage encyclopedia of trans studies* (pp. 379–383). Sage.

Greer, S. (2019). *Queer exceptions: Solo performance in neoliberal times*. Manchester University Press.

Hamraie, A. (2013). Designing collective access: A feminist disability theory of Universal Design. *Disability Quarterly*, 33(4). https://doi.org/10.18061/dsq.v33i4.3871

Harriet Tubman Collective. (2020). Disability solidarity: Completing the "vision for Black lives". In A. Wong (Ed.), *Disability visibility: First-person stories from the twenty-first century* (pp. 236–242). Vintage Books.

Harrison, E. A., & Kopit, A. G. (2020). Accessibility at the bisexual health summit: Reflections and lessons for improving event accessibility. *Journal of Bisexuality*, 20(3), 273–295. https://doi.org/10.1080/15299716.2020.1774834

Hirschmann, N. J. (2013). Queer/fear: Disability, sexuality, and the other. *Journal of Medical Humanities*, 34(2), 139–147.

Ishak, R. (2021, June 9). A lack of accessibility in queer spaces rushes community pride. *Hello Giggles*. https://hellogiggles.com/disabled-people-pride-events-lgbtq/

James, S., Herman, J., Rankin, S., Keisling, M., Mottet, L., & Anafi, M. A. (2016). *The report of the 2015 US transgender survey*. The National Center for Transgender Equality. https://transequality.org/sites/default/files/docs/usts/USTS-Full-Report-Dec17.pdf

Jones, S. (2016, May 25). Gender-neutral washrooms at the Royal Ontario Museum reflect changing times. *CBC*. www.cbc.ca/news/entertainment/rom-gender-neutral-washrooms-1.3589399

Jones, Z. C. (2021, June 29). Disability activists push for more inclusive Pride celebrations. *CBS News*. www.cbsnews.com/news/disability-activists-push-for-more-inclusive-pride-celebrations/.

Kafer, A. (2013). *Feminist, queer, crip*. Indiana University Press.
Kafer, A., & Kim, E. (2017). Disability and the edges of intersectionality. In C. Barker & S. Murray (Eds.), *Literature and disability* (pp. 123–138). Cambridge University Press.
Kattari, S. K., Bakko, M., Langenderfer-Magruder, L., & Holloway, B. T. (2021). Transgender and nonbinary experiences of victimization in health care. *Journal of Interpersonal Violence, 36*(23–24), NP13054-NP13076.
Kattari, S. K., Ingarfield, L., Hanna, M., McQueen, J., & Ross, K. (2020). Uncovering issues of ableism in social work education: A disability needs assessment. *Social Work Education, 39*(5), 599–616. https://doi.org/10.1080/02615479.2019.1699526
Lorde, A. (1997). *The collected poems of Audre Lorde*. W.W. Norton & Company, Inc.
Mace, R. (1985). Universal design: Barrier-free environments for everyone. *Designer's West, 33*(1), 147–152.
McRuer, R. (2006). *Crip theory: Cultural signs of queerness and disability*. New York University Press.
Mingus, M. (2017, April 12). Access intimacy, interdependence, and disability justice. *Leaving Evidence*. https://leavingevidence.wordpress.com/2017/04/12/access-intimacy-interdependence-and-disability-justice/
Movement Advancement Project. (2019, July). *LGBT people with disabilities*. www.lgbtmap.org/lgbt-people-disabilities
Piepzna-Samarasinha, L. L. (2018). *Care work: Dreaming disability justice*. Arsenal Pulp Press.
Piepzna-Samarasinha, L. L. (2020). Still dreaming wild disability justice dreams at the end of the world. In A. Wong (Ed.), *Disability visibility: First-person stories from the twenty-first century* (pp. 250–261). Vintage Books.
Pieri, M. (2022). When vulnerability got mainstream: Reading the pandemic through disability and illness. *European Journal of Women's Studies*, 1–11. https://doi.org/10.1177/13505068221090424
Radical Access Mapping Project. (2014, September 20). *(Accessibility feature) + (defensiveness) = inaccessible*. https://radicalaccessiblecommunities.wordpress.com/2014/09/20/accessibility-feature-defensiveness-inaccessible/
Rees, Y. (2021). Thinking capitalism from the bedroom: The politics of location and the uses of (feminist, queer, crip) theory. *Labour History: A Journal of Labour and Social History, 121*(1), 9–31. www.muse.jhu.edu/article/837599.
Rich, A. C. (1980). Compulsory heterosexuality and lesbian existence. *Signs: Journal of Women in Culture and Society, 5*(4), 631–660. https://doi.org/10.1086%2F493756
Roller, C. G., Sedlak, C., & Draucker, C. B. (2015). Navigating the system: How transgender individuals engage in health care services. *Journal of Nursing Scholarship, 47*(5), 417–424.
Rydstedt, D., & Lachowsky, N. (2020). Sex research conferences as heterotopias: A queer crip theory perspective on universal design. *The Canadian Journal of Human Sexuality, 29*(2), 197–204. https://doi.org/10.3138/cjhs.2020-0010
Sandahl, C. (2003). Queering the crip or cropping the queer? Intersections of queer and crip identities in solo autobiographical performance. *GLQ, 9*(1), 25–56. https://doi.org/10.1215/10642684-9-1-2-25
Schalk, S. (2022). *Black disability politics*. Duke University Press.
Shakespeare, T. (1998). Choices and rights: Eugenics, genetics and disability equality. *Disability and Society, 13*(5), 665-682. https://doi.org/10.1080/09687599826452

Shakespeare, T. (2014). Deepening disability justice: Beyond the level playing field. *Tikkun, 29*(4), 22–24. https://doi.org/10.1215/08879982-2810026

Sins Invalid. (2019). *Skin, tooth, and bone – The basis of movement is our people: A disability justice primer* (2nd ed.). Dancers' Group.

Smith, S. E. (2020). The beauty of space created for and by disabled people. In A. Wong (Ed.), *Disability visibility: First-person stories from the twenty-first century* (pp. 272–275). Vintage Books.

Thomson, R. (1997). *Extraordinary bodies: Figuring physical disability in American culture and literature.* Columbia University Press.

Tink, L. N., Peers, D., Nykiforuk, C. I. J., & Kingsley, B. C. (2020). "Vulnerable," "at-risk," "disadvantaged": How a framework for recreation in Canada 2015: Pathways to wellbeing reinscribes exclusion. *Leisure/Loisir, 44*(2), 151–174. https://doi.org/10.1080/14927713.2020.1760122

Toft, A. (2020). Identity management and community belonging: The coming out careers of young disabled LGBT+ persons. *Sexuality & Culture, 24,* 1893–1912. https://doi-org/10.1007/s12119-020-09726-4

Turban, J., Ferraiolo, T., Martin, A., & Olezeski, C. (2017). Ten things transgender and gender nonconforming youth want their doctors to know. *Journal of the American Academy of Child & Adolescent Psychiatry, 56*(4), 275–277. https://doi.org/10.1016/j.jaac.2016.12.015.

Vargas, Y. (2019, July 19). Inclusion of disabled people in the LGBTQ+ community is about more than accessibility. *Rooted in Rights.* https://rootedinrights.org/inclusion-of-disabled-people-in-the-lgbtq-community-is-about-more-than-accessibility/

Wendell, S. (1989). Toward a feminist theory of disability. *Hypatia, 4*(2), 104–124.

Withers, A. J., Ben-Moshe, L., Brown, L. X. Z., Erickson, L., Gorman, R. D. S., Lewis, T. A., McLeod, L., & Mingus, M. (2019). Radical disability politics. In R. Kinna & U. Gordon (Eds.), *Routledge handbook of radical politics* (pp. 178–193). Routledge.

Young, L. (2019, August 28). Understanding the key differences between accessible design and inclusive design. *UX Collective.* https://uxdesign.cc/understanding-the-key-differences-between-accessible-design-and-inclusive-design-25b91cb31a22

# 20
# SEXUAL WELL-BEING AMONG YOUNG DISABLED PEOPLE

*Ami Goulden*

## Introduction

Sexual well-being is a positive state of being that embodies dimensions of relationships, agency over one's sexuality, a sense of self-worth and self-esteem, personal security, attachment to others, and self-determination (Roy et al., 2018). Sexual well-being is especially important for young people due to its association with healthy human development (WHO, 2006), life satisfaction (Kriofske Mainella & Smedema, 2021), psychological well-being (Taleporos & McCabe, 2002), and sexual and reproductive rights (Areskoug-Josefsson et al., 2019; Lee et al., 2018). Sexual and reproductive rights are fundamental to the philosophical foundation of health and human service professionals because of their overall goals to improve the health status of populations, advocate effectively for social justice, and respond to global realities (Alzate, 2009; Areskoug-Josefsson et al., 2019). Achieving sexual and reproductive rights involves accessing timely and suitable services and education related to sexual and reproductive healthcare (Alzate, 2009).

Disabled young people, in particular, face various barriers related to their sexual well-being and reproductive rights. They are disproportionately affected by the myriad of social and structural factors that limit access to sexual and reproductive health services and education. Petchesky (2000) identifies several broadly defined factors that limit access to sexual and reproductive health services and education, such as government policy and laws, insufficient investment in healthcare services, inadequate health insurance coverage, and lack of enabling conditions to make individual choices.

DOI: 10.4324/9781003308331-25

In addition, professionals' feelings of unpreparedness, discomfort with discussing topics related to sexual health and well-being, and a limited scope of practice can negatively impact access to the support disabled young people require.

Human service and health professionals conduct comprehensive assessments and interventions by adopting the person-in-environment context to consider various dimensions of people's lives and well-being (e.g., social, familial, temporal, spiritual, economic, physical) (Berzoff & Drisko, 2015; De la Porte, 2016; Dossey & Keegan, 2009; Pyles et al., 2021). The International Federation of Social Workers (IFSW) promotes a holistic view of well-being in the profession (International Federation of Social Workers, 2018), urging social workers to adopt person-centered approaches to explore diverse dimensions of well-being, including sexual well-being. Yet many health and human service professionals are not including dimensions of sexual health and well-being within their scope of practice (Kattari & Turner, 2017). Studies suggest that social workers refrain from including sexual well-being within their practice approaches for various reasons (Goulden, 2021), including societal stigma (East & Orchard, 2014); ableist misconceptions that disabled youth are asexual (Eskay, 1991); lack of time and funding (Rueda et al., 2014); perceived taboos about the subject (Secor-Turner et al., 2017); personal attitudes and motivations (Van der Stege et al., 2016); and minimal attention focused on disability and sexuality in social work education (Ballan, 2008).

This chapter provides a brief overview of sexual well-being among young disabled people, offers best practices for health and human service professionals to support young people with their sexual well-being, and suggests a critical reflection learning activity for instructors to engage with their students. This chapter uses both person-first and identity-first languages when referring to disability. Disability language is continuously evolving, and there is a lack of agreement in the disability community about affirming language (Kattari et al., 2020). Person-first language positions the person before a description of their identity (i.e., people with disabilities) and identity-first language positions the person's identity as central (i.e., disabled people) (Withers, 2012). This chapter alternates between person-first language and identity-first language to reflect the language used by young disabled people, recognizing that disabled people have different perspectives on affirming language (APA, 2022). Moreover, disability is not reduced to specific categories or impairments in this chapter. Hence, disability includes developmental and physical impairments, neurodiversity, chronic illness, chronic pain, and mental illness, among others. Disability is conceptualized as a social identity and a continuum of human variation with a unique voice and complex experience (Rocco, 2005).

## What We Know About Sexual Well-Being, Young People, and Disability

### *What Is Sexual Well-Being?*

The World Health Organization (WHO) defines sexual health as a state of physical, emotional, mental, and social well-being (WHO, 2006). The interrelated nature of the physical, mental, and social dimensions of sexual health supports the notion of sexual well-being (WHO, 2006). Healthy sexual development is closely related to an individual's feeling of living with a positive state of sexual well-being. A person's sexual development transpires over a lifetime but is strongly associated with experiences during adolescence and the period of transition to adulthood (WHO, 2006). Sexual development perceived as "healthy" is subjective and determined within the context of the individual, family, community, society, and culture over time (WHO, 2006). The concept of sexual well-being encompasses dimensions of relationships, the degree of control and agency over one's sexuality, a sense of self-worth and self-esteem, pleasure, desire, personal security, attachment to others, self-determination, and respect for self and others (Powers & Faden, 2006; WHO, 2006). Sexual well-being represents an embodying approach that moves beyond the focus of disease, dysfunction, and illness to represent a positive state of being (Diener, 1994; Roy et al., 2018).

The concept of sexual well-being became prominent in research literature in the early 2000s and is increasingly used to define aspects of sexuality and sexual health issues (Taylor & Davis, 2007). However, sexual well-being is seldom used in affiliation with youth, with some exceptions. Fortenberry's (2016) frequently cited editorial in the *Journal of Adolescent Health* depicts sexual well-being as expanding the traditional concept of sexual health to include dimensions of personal security, attachment to others, appropriate functioning, self-determination, and respect for self and others. Similar to Fortenberry's definition of sexual well-being, additional scholars have defined sexual well-being as a combination of sexuality and sexual health in youth-related research. In Harden's (2014) article advocating for a sex-positive framework in youth-focused research, sexual well-being is broadly defined as a multidimensional construct that incorporates sexual self-efficacy and self-esteem, feelings of sexual pleasure and satisfaction, and freedom from pain and negative affect regarding sexuality. In addition, sexual well-being has been defined as a combination of mutual consent, safe sex, and personal sexual self-acceptance (Espinosa-Hernández et al., 2017), as well as satisfaction with sexual relationships and functioning, sexual awareness, sexual self-esteem, and body image esteem (Muise et al., 2010). Finally, Mastro and Zimmer-Gembeck's (2015) quantitative study measured sexual well-being with reference to partnered behavior, including safe-sex behavioral competence, sexual assertiveness, and emotional reactions. In the examples above, sexual well-being was defined using disparate aspects of sexuality and sexual health. The diversified operationalization of sexual well-being suggests its meaning is loosely related to aspects of sexual health but largely context-specific for researchers and participants.

### *Sexual Well-Being and Disability*

There is a dearth of literature exploring how disabled people conceptualize and define sexual well-being. Sexuality and relationships for disabled people had little attention within the early era of the disability movement (circa 1970 to 2000) and in the developing field of disability studies (Shakespeare et al., 1996). Shakespeare (2000) suggests multiple reasons for this neglect. First, issues of accessibility to public spaces and employment opportunities were prioritized in the disability movement, which was somewhat related to the concurrent labor movement. The disability movement's pressure to end poverty and social exclusion for disabled people overshadowed disabled people's sexual health and reproductive rights. Second, sexuality for disabled people had historically been a matter of distress, exclusion, and self-doubt, so it may have been easier for disabled people to avoid issues around sexual health and relationships than confront them.

Research integrating sexuality and disability predominantly focuses on those areas of distress, exclusion, and self-doubt, which are rightly meaningful experiences to acknowledge and uncover. For instance, disabled people have experienced a reprehensible history of eugenic sterilization in Canada, of which much is unknown. Malacrida's (2006) work describes oral history research she conducted, presenting first-person narratives of the experiences of people with intellectual disabilities who were eugenically sterilized in Canadian institutions. Malacrida explains that many of the memories obtained in the project were highly constrained due to barriers of "protection" by the participants' legal guardians and apprehension among professionals (p. 402). Exploration, recognition, and acknowledgment of events and experiences unique to disabled people regarding their sexual and reproductive rights are necessary. Nonetheless, in consideration of Shakespeare's (2000) suggestions for how to promote discourse and a prioritized agenda for disabled people's sexuality, further attention must be paid to understanding what sexual well-being means to disabled people.

Sally Lee is a social worker and senior lecturer at Bournemouth University in the United Kingdom. Lee (2016) explored the meaning of sexual well-being among physically disabled adults in her dissertation research to inform social work practice in the United Kingdom. She conducted semi-structured interviews with six participants who were physically disabled. Her findings suggest that some participants struggled to define sexual well-being but named things that it was not. The meaning of sexual well-being derived from the participants' narratives wove together the physical, emotional, social, and psychological aspects of sexuality and implied that sexual well-being is complex. Lee combined participants' responses to construct the following definition of sexual well-being:

> Sexual well-being is the experience of – and possibility for – sensual pleasure, where the self is fully present as human body and human emotion. It is the capacity to communicate, give, and receive intense sensual pleasure alerting the self to possibility. The physical structure of the body is irrelevant. Sexual well-being is humanly validating and allows us to acknowledge that all humans have a fundamental need for love and affection.
> *(Lee, 2016, pp. 182–183)*

Lee's definition is a distinctive conceptualization of sexual well-being pertinent to these participants with physical disabilities. First, "the physical structure of the body is irrelevant" suggests that emotional, social, and psychological aspects of sexual well-being override the physical aspects of these individuals (p. 182). Second, the originality of the definition suggests that sexual well-being has a different meaning for everyone. Consequently, assuming and operationalizing sexual well-being to primarily represent physical components of sexuality or negative sexual experiences does not accurately represent disabled people's experiences or contentment with their sexual well-being and sexual development.

### Sexual Well-Being Among Young Disabled People

Disabled people remain largely excluded worldwide from enjoying equal control, access, and choice regarding their sexuality and sexual and reproductive rights (Rohleder et al., 2018). Yet young disabled people are sexual beings and deserve equal rights and opportunities to have control over, choices about, and access to their sexuality, sexual expression, and fulfilling relationships throughout their lives (Shah, 2017). Health and human service professionals need a general understanding of sexual well-being among young disabled people to provide affirming, inclusive, and accessible support. While little is known about how young people conceptualize sexual well-being in their lives, it is clear from first-person narratives (Murray, 2019; Powley, 2017), community presentations (Hunt, 2021; Ramsawakh, 2021), and media representations (Francis, 2021; Lunsky, 2018) that sexuality, sexual development, and sexual well-being are priorities in the lives of young disabled people.

To learn more about young disabled people's understandings of sexual well-being, I conducted a qualitative study from 2021 to 2022 to explore how young people conceptualize and make meaning of sexual well-being in their lives and how those conceptualizations and meanings shift over time (Goulden, under review). I interviewed 24 young people (aged 16 to 24)

Sexual Well-Being Among Young Disabled People  **323**

who self-identified as disabled or living with a disability in Ontario, Canada. The participants represented a diverse group of young disabled people, self-reporting various physical, developmental, and mental disabilities. Examples of self-identified disabilities included developmental disabilities, physical disabilities, neurodiversity, and mental health disabilities. Most participants (88%) identified living with more than one disability and one-third of participants (33%) self-identified with multiple ethnic identities.

In my conversations with young people, we discussed sexual well-being and how disability and other marginalized identities impact understandings and conceptualizations of the term and lived experience. It was clear that young people defined sexual well-being in broadly defined and sex-positive ways, refraining from focusing mainly on physical components of sexuality or negative sexual experiences. However, physical components were important as well. The in-depth phenomenological analysis of the interviews can be found in (Goulden, under review). To illustrate a general overview of young people's meanings of sexual well-being in this chapter, I incorporated terms from our conversations in a word cloud found in Figure 20.1.

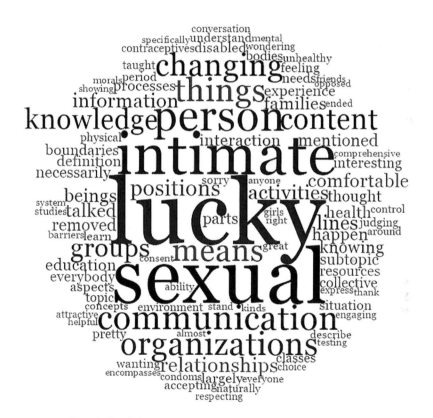

**FIGURE 20.1** Word cloud from conversations

Several terms included in the word cloud may be unsurprising to health and human service professionals. For example, terms such as bodies, contraception, intimate, sexual, and relationships are generally connected to sexual and reproductive health discourses. Several terms in the word cloud that may be surprising relate to categories of prevention and planning, community responsibility, and sex positivity. Along with affirming care, these three categories offer best practice approaches for health and human service professionals supporting young disabled people with their sexual well-being.

**Best Practices**

*Prevention and Planning*

Young disabled people consider access to comprehensive, representative, accessible, and timely information a vital indicator of their sexual well-being and preventing risk-related behaviors and outcomes (Jones et al., 2022). Discussions on comprehensive education and organizations' roles in providing that education surfaced as a priority area. UNESCO (2015) defines comprehensive sexual education as an "age-appropriate, culturally relevant approach to teaching about sexuality and relationships by providing scientifically accurate, realistic, nonjudgmental information." In addition to cultural relevance, comprehensive sexual education must be inclusive of varying identities and representative of the audience it serves.

Many young people felt unrepresented in the sexual and reproductive health education they received and often felt that the information did not pertain to them. For instance, a comprehensive review of the literature published in social science databases from 1995 to 2015 examining the status and effectiveness of sex education curricula for individuals with intellectual disabilities found that formal, individualized, and specific sexual education is lacking (McDaniels & Fleming, 2016). The consequence of non-comprehensive sexual education is that individuals with intellectual disabilities are at a greater risk of sexual abuse, sexually transmitted infections, and misinformation (McDaniels & Fleming, 2016). Moreover, noncomprehensive sexual education hinders young people from achieving sexual well-being. To support prevention in practice settings, health and human service professionals should ensure that all sex educational resources and information provided or referred to young people are comprehensive and representative. For example, sex education for young people with cerebral palsy should be individualized and easily understood (Gray, 2020).

Health and human service professionals should recognize that planning related to sexual well-being can be more burdensome for disabled people than nondisabled people. Researchers and scholars have referred to the additional burdens of financial costs of living with disabilities as the "crip tax" (Dorfman, 2021). Similarly, disabled people experience additional financial costs related to sexual well-being (e.g., equipment, positioning devices). Furthermore, additional service providers are often required to assist disabled people in achieving their sexual well-being. For instance, some disabled people require additional hours from support staff or seek services from professionals with expertise in sex and disability (e.g., clinical sexologist, intimacy coach) (CBC, 2018). To support planning in practice settings, health and human service professionals can support young people in scheduling and attending appointments, making referrals to service providers in the community, and advocating for additional funding that supports sexual well-being.

*Community Responsibility*

In considering expectations and responsibilities related to achieving sexual well-being, young people nuanced how community members and community organizations have roles to play in not just offering comprehensive sexual education but ensuring that young disabled people can achieve their sexual rights and freedom. This perspective contradicts neoliberal discourses, where individuals are compelled to take responsibility for their health, illness trajectories, and personal well-being (Broom et al., 2014). For instance, certain healthcare approaches, such as complementary and alternative medicine, often propagate self-determination and self-responsibility for achieving health and well-being (Broom et al., 2014). Yet well-being is reflected in expressions of individuality and growth, the significance of having close relationships, and a sense of connection with the community (Lam et al., 2020). In fact, ableism and microaggressions in communities are detrimental to the mental health and well-being of disabled people (Kattari, 2020). Given the connection between community and well-being, it is vital for health and human service professionals to consider how factors outside of the individual's immediate contexts impact daily living and sexual well-being.

The bioecological model is a framework that illustrates complex dynamics in different contexts and reflects on various factors that impact human development (Hayes et al., 2017). Contrary to developmental theories, which typically consist of age and stage categories that progress linearly (Mizrahi & Davis, 2008), the bioecological model focuses on the individual's environment and the interaction between the environment and human development. Developmental theories (e.g., Freud, Erikson) can perpetuate ableist norms and expectations, as many disabled people's trajectories do not represent age and stage approaches to human development. Bronfenbrenner was critical of early psychological approaches that were laboratory-based, researched, and practiced with individuals in isolation from their personal contexts and environments (Hayes et al., 2017).

To research and work effectively with people, Bronfenbrenner argued that scholars must recognize their actual environments and systems within which they live and the interact between people and these systems (Bronfenbrenner, 1977). He wrote that "much of developmental psychology is the science of the strange behavior of children in strange situations with strange adults for the briefest possible period of time" (Bronfenbrenner, 1977, p. 513). Bronfenbrenner illustrated individual's contexts by designing different levels of systems that are nested within one another: microsystem (i.e., individual's closest setting such as caregivers), mesosystem (i.e., interactions between components in microsystem), exosystem (i.e., factors external to the individual but that make an impact), macrosystem (i.e., attitudes and ideologies of culture), and chronosystem (i.e., how time impacts human development).

Health and human service professionals can adopt the bioecological model by incorporating questions in their initial and ongoing assessments that explore the contexts outside of young people's individual characteristics and immediate contexts to promote community responsibility. Examples of contexts related to young disabled people's sexual well-being in each system are listed in Table 20.1. Health and human service professionals can develop questionnaires that revolve around these contexts and include them in conversations with young people and colleagues.

### Sex Positivity

While young people were conscientious about the risk factors related to sex and sexual well-being (i.e., had discussions on preventing risks and planning), their conversations stressed the importance of sex positivity. The traditional risk perspective of sexual health is dominant in health and social care literature, education, and practice (Goulden & Kattari, 2022). A traditional risk perspective of sexual health reinforces imbalanced perspectives between

**TABLE 20.1** Bioecological contexts related to sexual well-being

| *Systems* | *Examples* | |
|---|---|---|
| *Microsystem* | Family's reluctance to discuss sex and sexuality | De-sexualization of disabled people by peers |
| *Mesosystem* | Caregivers adopting stigmatizing religious values | Poor relationships between caregivers and service providers |
| *Exosystem* | Abstinence-only education in school | Lack of financial resources to access equipment or nonsubsidized services |
| *Macrosystem* | Ableism, neoliberalism | Homophobia, transphobia |
| *Chronosystem* | Transitions between pediatric and adult healthcare systems | Changes in medication over time |

positive sexuality and sexual health risk factors, emphasizing the latter (Dodd & Tolman, 2017). Counter to the traditional risk perspective is a sex positive practice approach. A sex-positive practice approach embraces sexuality as a human right (Dodd, 2020). This approach also promotes positive discourses about sexuality, aligning with anti-oppressive and strength-based perspectives (Dodd, 2020; Dodd & Tolman, 2017). A sex-positive perspective encourages human agency in sexual decision-making and embraces consensual sexual activity as healthy and something to be enjoyed without stigma or shame. Examples of terms in the word cloud that exemplify sex positivity are choice, consent, intimate, respect, and everybody.

Resources and literature describing how to adopt sex-positive practice approaches are increasing, as more service providers and organizations reject and replace risk-focused approaches (Ali et al., 2020; Dodd, 2020; Laughney, 2022; Nimbi et al., 2021). Adopting sex-positive approaches involves including sexuality and well-being as an integral part of practice, recognizing that sexuality and well-being are interconnected with other dimensions of the self. To promote sex positivity in practice settings, health and human service professionals can incorporate the sexual dimension into the initial assessment and ongoing evaluations, promote young people's self-determination and decision-making, and offer young people confidential opportunities to communicate. Being a sex-positive service provider also involves developing and increasing your own comfort with the topic and engaging in ongoing self-assessments of personal biases and assumptions. Health and human service professionals should unlearn sex-negative messaging and replace it with affirming and nonjudgmental internal dialogue. Ongoing personal reflection and reflexivity are vital to offering affirming and inclusive care, as cognitive and other biases can influence the decision-making of health and human service professionals (Featherston et al., 2020). In addition to critical reflection (Béres & Fook, 2019), promoting, creating, and embedding critically reflective learning and working environments within social care organizations should be a priority (Fook, 2021).

**Classroom Activity**

Experiential classroom activities provide students with opportunities to learn and practice the skills required to support young disabled people with their sexual well-being. As discussed throughout this chapter, service providers who adopt sex-positive practice approaches should assess their comfort level with the topic and engage with critical reflection exercises to evaluate personal biases and assumptions. As an instructor, the comfort level with the topic will also determine the nature and depth of the classroom activities. This section describes a critical reflection exercise meant to engage students. It can be easily adapted based on the comfort level of the instructor and the students.

*Critical Reflection Exercise*

Plan to watch a documentary or film related to sex and disability with your class. Ensure that the documentary or film was created and designed by disabled people. There are many documentaries and first-person accounts available. Some examples include *The Sessions* (Lewis, 2012), *37 Seconds* (Hiraki, 2019), and *Leo and Carol* (Campos & Capella, 2018). *Take Me* (Barbeau-Lavalette & Turpin, 2014), a Canadian short, is particularly applicable for a class of health or human service students, as it centers on a service provider (i.e., a nurse) who is required to assist a young disabled couple in the intimacy room.

Following the documentary, give students time to engage in an individual critical reflection exercise. Fook (2007) suggests several questions to help students begin critically reflecting on specific practice approaches. Examples of critical reflection questions include:

- What was I assuming?
- What beliefs did I have about power (e.g., mine, other people's)?
- What are my most important values, and how do these relate to power?
- As a service provider, how would I influence the situation?
- What preconceptions do I have, and how might these influence what I do or interpret?
- What language/words/patterns have I used? Have I used any binary opposites, and what is the basis for these?
- What perspectives are missing?
- What is the relationship between my beliefs about power and the mainstream or dominant view?
- How has my thinking changed, and what might I do differently now?
- Do I need to change my ideas about myself or the situations in which I work?

There are several ways students can engage in critical reflection following the documentary. For instance, they can work individually to answer the critical reflection questions and then share in small groups or as a larger class. Alternatively, instructors can design an assignment related to this activity, whereby students submit an assignment showcasing their critical reflection process. Examples of assignments include a traditional writing exercise (e.g., short paper) or an arts-based exercise (e.g., poetry, short story, digital story). Regardless of the activity, students should have opportunities to share their reflections with one another, as sharing is an essential part of the learning journey.

## Conclusion

This chapter provided an overview of sexual well-being among young disabled people and suggested three best practices for health and human service professionals to support young people with their sexual well-being: prevention and planning, community responsibility, and sex-positive practice approaches. Health and human service professionals need a general understanding of sexual well-being among young disabled people to provide affirming, inclusive, and accessible support. Being a sex-positive service provider involves developing and increasing personal comfort with the topic and engaging in ongoing self-assessments of personal biases and assumptions. Ongoing personal reflection and reflexivity are vital to practicing affirming and inclusive professional support, as individual attitudes and biases can influence the decision-making of health and human service professionals. As outlined in this chapter, critical reflection activities can assist instructors and students in unlearning sex-negative messaging and ableist norms and stereotypes. Health and human service professionals can promote, create, and embed critically reflective learning and working environments within social care organizations to support young disabled people in their journeys to achieving sexual well-being.

## Resources

### Guides

Comprehensive Sex Education for Youth with Disabilities: https://siecus.org/wp-content/uploads/2021/03/SIECUS-2021-Youth-with-Disabilities-CTA-1.pdf

Conversation Guide for Parents and Caregivers: https://hollandbloorview.ca/sites/default/files/2022-07/HB-Sexuality-ConversationGuide-Accessible.pdf

Kaufman, M., Silverberg, C., & Odette, F. (2007). *Ultimate guide to sex and disability: For all of us who live with disabilities, chronic pain, and illness* (2nd ed.). Cleis Press.

Sentence Starters for Healthcare Providers: https://hollandbloorview.ca/sites/default/files/2022-07/HB-Sexuality-ConversationGuide-Accessible.pdf

What to Say and Words to Use for Parents and Caregivers: https://hollandbloorview.ca/sites/default/files/2022-08/HB-Sexuality_Tip_Sheet-ConversationGuide_for_Parents_and_Caregivers-FNL_FINAL-s.pdf

### Infographic

Disability and Sexuality – More Conversations, More Often: https://hollandbloorview.ca/sites/default/files/2021-03/Disability%20and%20Sexuality%20Infographic.pdf

### Websites

Action Canada for Sexual Health and Rights: www.actioncanadashr.org/
Alberta Health Services – Sexual & Reproductive Health: www.ahs.ca/srh
Centre for Sexuality: www.centreforsexuality.ca/
Disability and Sexuality – Better Health Channel Australia: www.betterhealth.vic.gov.au/health/ServicesAndSupport/disability-and-sexuality

Engender Health: www.engenderhealth.org/
Go Ask Alice – Columbia University (USA): www.goaskalice.com/
Guttmacher Institute (USA): www.guttmacher.org/
Sex Information and Education Council of Canada: www.sieccan.org/
SexandU.ca (Society of Obstetricians and Gynecologists of Canada): www.sexualityandu.ca/
Sexual Education Resources – RespectAbility: www.respectability.org/resources/sexual-education-resources/
Sexual Health Education for Young People with Disabilities – Research and Resources for Educators: www.advocatesforyouth.org/resources/fact-sheets/sexual-health-education-for-young-people-with-disabilities/
Sexual Health Network: www.sexualhealth.com/
Sexuality and Disability – Nest Consulting, New Zealand: www.nestconsulting.nz/parents-teachers-resources/sexuality-disability/
Sexuality Information and Education Network of the United States (SIECUS): www.siecus.org/
SIECCAN (Sex Information and Education Council of Canada): https://sieccan.org/
Teaching Sexual Health Website: www.teachingsexualhealth.ca/
University Center for Excellence in Developmental Disabilities – Sexual Health Resources: www.ohsu.edu/university-center-excellence-development-disability/sexual-health-resources

## References

Ali, S., Keo, B. S., & Chaudhuri, S. (2020). Critically understanding south Asian sexual health: A call for a holistic and sex positive approach. *International Journal of Sexual Health*, 32(3), 177–187. https://doi.org/10.1080/19317611.2020.1768197

Alzate, M. M. (2009). The role of sexual and reproductive rights in social work practice. *Affilia*, 24(2), 108–119. https://doi.org/10.1177/0886109909331695

American Psychological Association (APA). (2022). *Disability*. APA Style. https://apastyle.apa.org/style-grammar-guidelines/bias-free-language/disability

Areskoug-Josefsson, K., Rolander, B., & Bülow, P. (2019). Swedish social work students' attitudes toward addressing sexual health issues in their future profession. *Sexuality and Disability*, 37(2), 161–173. https://doi.org/10.1007/s11195-019-09563-w

Ballan, M. S. (2008). Disability and sexuality within social work education in the USA and Canada: The social model of disability as a lens for practice. *Social Work Education*, 27(2), 194–202. https://doi.org/10.1080/02615470701709675

Barbeau-Lavalette, A., & Turpin, A. (2014). *Take me* [Film]. Prends-moi.

Béres, L., & Fook, J. (2019). *Learning critical reflection: Experiences of the transformative learning process*. Routledge.

Berzoff, J., & Drisko, J. (2015). What clinical social workers need to know: Biopsycho-social knowledge and skills for the twenty first century. *Clinical Social Work Journal*, 43(3), 263–273. https://doi.org/10.1007/s10615-015-0544-3

Bronfenbrenner, U. (1977). The ecology of human development in retrospect and prospect. In H. McGurk (Ed.), *Ecological factors in human development* (pp. 275–286). North Holland.

Broom, A., Meurk, C., Adams, J., & Sibbritt, D. (2014). My health, my responsibility? Complementary medicine and self (health) care. *Journal of Sociology, 50*(4), 515–530. https://doi.org/10.1177/1440783312467098

Campos, A., & Capella, D. (2018). *Leo & Carol* [Film]. Dois Moleques Produções Ltda.

CBC. (2018, March 29). *Medically assisted sex? How "intimacy coaches" offer sexual therapy for people with disabilities*. Out in the Open. https://www.cbc.ca/radio/outintheopen/enablers-1.4579817/medically-assisted-sex-how-intimacy-coaches-offer-sexual-therapy-for-people-with-disabilities-1.4595156

De la Porte, A. (2016). Spirituality and healthcare: Towards holistic people-centred healthcare in South Africa. *HTS Teologiese Studies/Theological Studies, 72*(4), 1–9.

Diener, E. (1994). Assessing subjective well-being: Progress and opportunities. *Social Indicators Research, 31*(2), 103–157. https://doi.org/10.1007/BF01207052

Dodd, S. J. (2020). *Sex-positive social work*. Columbia University Press.

Dodd, S. J., & Tolman, D. (2017). Reviving a positive discourse on sexuality within social work. *Social Work, 62*(3), 227–234. https://doi.org/10.1093/sw/swx016

Dorfman, D. (2021). The everyday struggles of disability law equality. *Jotwell: The Journal of Things We Like (Lots), (6)*, 1–2.

Dossey, B., & Keegan, L. (2009). *Holistic nursing: A handbook for practice*. Jones & Bartlett Learning.

East, L. J., & Orchard, T. R. (2014). Somebody else's job: Experiences of sex education among health professionals, parents and adolescents with physical disabilities in southwestern Ontario. *Sexuality and Disability, 32*(3), 335–350. https://doi.org/10.1007/s11195-013-9289-5

Eskay, C. J. (1991). *Sexuality and sex education among developmentally disabled males residing in California's developmental centers* (303978805) [MSW, California State University, Long Beach]. ProQuest Dissertations & Theses Global.

Espinosa-Hernández, G., Vasilenko, S. A., McPherson, J. L., Gutierrez, E., & Rodriguez, A. (2017). Brief report: The role of three dimensions of sexual well-being in adolescents' life satisfaction. *Journal of Adolescence, 55*, 61–65.

Featherston, R., Downie, L. E., Vogel, A. P., & Galvin, K. L. (2020). Decision making biases in the allied health professions: A systematic scoping review. *PLoS One, 15*(10). https://doi.org/10.1371/journal.pone.0240716

Fook, J. (2007). Reflective practice and critical reflection. In J. Lishman (Ed.), *Handbook for practice learning in social work and social care, second edition: Knowledge and theory* (pp. 363–375). Jessica Kingsley.

Fook, J. (2021). *Practicing critical reflection in social care organisations*. Routledge.

Fortenberry, J. D. (2016). Adolescent sexual well-being in the 21st century. *Journal of Adolescent Health, 58*(1), 1–2. https://doi.org/10.1016/j.jadohealth.2015.10.250

Francis, A. (2021, July 17). Sexual health and disabilities are not mutually exclusive. Youth say it's time doctors and educators stop acting like they are. *Thestar.Com*. www.thestar.com/news/gta/2021/07/17/sexual-health-and-disabilities-are-not-mutually-exclusive-youth-say-its-time-doctors-and-educators-stop-acting-like-they-are.html

Goulden, A. (2021). A critical review of social work interventions and programmes that support disabled youth with their sexual well-being. *Journal of Social Work Practice, 35*(4), 403–417. https://doi.org/10.1080/02650533.2021.1914010

Goulden, A., & Kattari, S. (2022). Sexual orientation and sexuality. In E. Slayter & L. Johnson (Eds.), *Social work practice and the disability community: An intersectional anti-oppressive approach*. Pressbooks. https://disabilitysocialwork.pressbooks.com/chapter/chapter-8-sexual-orientation-and-sexuality/

Gray, S. (2020, July 1). *Talking about sex*. Cerebral Palsy Foundation. https://cpresource.org/topic/womens-health/talking-about-sex

Harden, K. P. (2014). A sex-positive framework for research on adolescent sexuality. *Perspectives on Psychological Science*, 9(5), 455–469. https://doi.org/10.1177/1745691614535934

Hayes, N., O'Toole, L., & Halpenny, A. M. (2017). *Introducing Bronfenbrenner: A guide for practitioners and students in early years education*. Routledge.

Hiraki. (Director). (2019). *37 seconds* [Film]. Knockonwood Hikari Films.

Hunt, R. (Director). (2021, May 11). *Meaningful sexual lives and sexual rights*. www.youtube.com/watch?v=Kb5TljfTk3U

International Federation of Social Workers. (2018). *Global social work statement of ethical principles*. http://ifsw.org/policies/statement-of-ethical-principles/

Jones, C. T., Murphy, E., Lovell, S., Abdel-Halim, N., Varghese, R., Odette, F., & Gurza, A. (2022). "Cripping sex education": A panel discussion for prospective educators. *Canadian Journal of Disability Studies*, 11(2), 101–118. https://doi.org/10.15353/cjds.v11i2.890

Kattari, S. K. (2020). Ableist microaggressions and the mental health of disabled adults. *Community Mental Health Journal*, 56(6), 1170–1179. https://doi.org/10.1007/s10597-020-00615-6

Kattari, S. K., Ingarfield, L., Hanna, M., McQueen, J., & Ross, K. (2020). Uncovering issues of ableism in social work education: A disability needs assessment. *Social Work Education*, 39(5), 599–616. https://doi.org/10.1080/02615479.2019.1699526

Kattari, S. K., & Turner, G. (2017). Examining more inclusive approaches to social work, physical disability, and sexuality. *Journal of Social Work in Disability & Rehabilitation*, 16(1), 38–53. https://doi.org/10.1080/1536710X.2017.1260517

Kriofske Mainella, A. M., & Smedema, S. M. (2021). Sexual health education and life satisfaction for people with congenital neurological disabilities. *Rehabilitation Counseling Bulletin*, 1–12. https://doi.org/10.1177/00343552211031870

Lam, G. Y. H., Holden, E., Fitzpatrick, M., Raffaele Mendez, L., & Berkman, K. (2020). "Different but connected": Participatory action research using photovoice to explore well-being in autistic young adults. *Autism*, 24(5), 1246–1259. https://doi.org/10.1177/1362361319898961

Laughney, C. I. (2022). Advancing sex-positive social work research and practice. *Social Work*. https://doi.org/10.1093/sw/swac036

Lee, S. (2016). *Changing position: An exploration of the meaning of sexual well-being for physically disabled people* (PhD thesis). Bournemouth University, Fern Barrow, Poole, Dorset, BH12 5BB, UK. http://eprints.bournemouth.ac.uk/27374/

Lee, S., Fenge, L.-A., & Collins, B. (2018). Promoting sexual well-being in social work education and practice. *Social Work Education*, 37(3), 315–327. https://doi.org/10.1080/02615479.2017.1401602

Lewis, B. (Director). (2012). *The sessions* [Film]. Fox Searchlight Pictures.

Lunsky, Y. (2018, September 24). Speaking of sex-ed – How about we develop some for students with developmental disabilities? *Opinion | CBC News*. CBC. www.cbc.ca/news/opinion/sex-ed-students-1.4834984

Malacrida, C. (2006). Contested memories: Efforts of the powerful to silence former inmates' histories of life in an institution for "mental defectives". *Disability & Society, 21*(5), 397–410. https://doi.org/10.1080/09687590600785720

Mastro, S., & Zimmer-Gembeck, M. J. (2015). Let's talk openly about sex: Sexual communication, self-esteem and efficacy as correlates of sexual well-being. *European Journal of Developmental Psychology, 12*(5), 579–598. https://doi.org/10.1080/17405629.2015.1054373

McDaniels, B., & Fleming, A. (2016). Sexuality education and intellectual disability: Time to address the challenge. *Sexuality and Disability, 34*(2), 215–225. https://doi.org/10.1007/s11195-016-9427-y

Mizrahi, T., & Davis, L. (Eds.). (2008). *The encyclopedia of social work: 4 volume set*. Oxford University Press.

Muise, A., Preyde, M., Maitland, S. B., & Milhausen, R. R. (2010). Sexual identity and sexual well-being in female heterosexual university students. *Archives of Sexual Behavior, 39*(4), 915–925. https://doi.org/10.1007/s10508-009-9492-8

Murray, A. (2019, January 11). Sex & physical disability. *Coffee & Kink*. https://coffeeandkink.me/2019/01/11/alannah-murray-disability/

Nimbi, F. M., Galizia, R., Rossi, R., Limoncin, E., Ciocca, G., Fontanesi, L., Jannini, E. A., Simonelli, C., & Tambelli, R. (2021). The biopsychosocial model and the sex-positive approach: An integrative perspective for sexology and general health care. *Sexuality Research and Social Policy*. https://doi.org/10.1007/s13178-021-00647-x

Petchesky, R. (2000). Sexual rights: Inventing a concept, mapping an international practice. In R. Parker, R. M. Barbosa, & P. Aggleton (Eds.), *Framing the sexual subject: The politics of gender, sexuality, and power* (pp. 81–103). University of California Press.

Powers, M., & Faden, R. R. (2006). *Social justice: The moral foundations of public health and health policy*. Oxford University Press.

Powley, J. (2017). *Just Jen: Thriving through multiple sclerosis*. Fernwood Publishing.

Pyles, L., Cosgrove, D. T., Gardner, E., Raheim, S., Adam, G. J., Chakravarty, S., & Cooke, C. (2021). "Could we just breathe for 30 seconds?": Social worker experiences of holistic engagement practice training. *Social Work, 66*(4), 285–296. https://doi.org/10.1093/sw/swab031

Ramsawakh, M. (Director). (2021, May 11). *Multiple and converging identities*. www.youtube.com/watch?v=CfVVN25zinM

Rocco, T. (2005, September 17). *From disability studies to critical race theory: Working towards critical disability theory*. Adult Education Research Conference. https://newprairiepress.org/aerc/2005/papers/17

Rohleder, P., Braathen, S. H., Carew, M. T., Braathen, S. H., & Carew, M. T. (2018). *Disability and sexual health: A critical exploration of key issues*. Routledge. https://doi.org/10.4324/9781315648682

Roy, B., Riley, C., Sears, L., & Rula, E. Y. (2018). Collective well-being to improve population health outcomes: An actionable conceptual model and review of the literature. *American Journal of Health Promotion, 32*(8), 1800–1813. https://doi.org/10.1177/0890117118791993

Rueda, H., Linton, K. F., & Williams, L. R. (2014). School social workers' needs in supporting adolescents with disabilities toward dating and sexual health: A qualitative study. *Children & Schools, 36*(2), 79–90. https://doi.org/10.1093/cs/cdu006

Secor-Turner, M., McMorris, B. J., & Scal, P. (2017). Improving the sexual health of young people with mobility impairments: Challenges and recommendations. *Journal of Pediatric Health Care, 31*(5), 578–587.

Shah, S. (2017). "Disabled people are sexual citizens too": Supporting sexual identity, well-being, and safety for disabled young people. *Frontiers in Education, 2*(46), 1–5. https://doi.org/10.3389/feduc.2017.00046

Shakespeare, T. (2000). Disabled sexuality: Toward rights and recognition. *Sexuality and Disability, 18*(3), 159–166. https://doi.org/10.1023/A:1026409613684

Shakespeare, T., Gillespie-Sells, K., & Davies, D. (1996). *The sexual politics of disability*. Cassell.

Taleporos, G., & McCabe, M. P. (2002). The impact of sexual esteem, body esteem, and sexual satisfaction on psychological well-being in people with physical disability. *Sexuality and Disability, 20*(3), 177–183. https://doi.org/10.1023/A:1021493615456

Taylor, B., & Davis, S. (2007). The extended PLISSIT model for addressing the sexual wellbeing of individuals with an acquired disability or chronic illness. *Sexuality and Disability, 25*(3), 135–139. https://doi.org/10.1007/s11195-007-9044-x

United Nations Educational, Scientific and Cultural Organization (UNESCO). (2015). *Comprehensive sexuality education: A global review*. UNESCO.

van der Stege, H. A., Hilberink, S. R., Bakker, E., & van Staa, A. (2016). Using a board game about sexual health with young people with chronic conditions in daily practice: A research into facilitating and impeding factors. *Sexuality and Disability, 34*(3), 349–361. https://doi.org/10.1007/s11195-016-9448-6

Withers, A. J. (2012). *Disability politics and theory*. Fernwood Publishing.

World Health Organization (WHO). (2006). *Defining sexual health: Report of a technical consultation on sexual health*. www.who.int/reproductivehealth/publications/sexual_health/defining_sexual_health.pdf

# 21

# COMPULSORY MONOGAMY IS DISABLING

Connecting Disability Justice and Critical Non-Monogamy

*Laura Yakas and Nicole Ariel Lopez*

### Introduction: A Labor of Love

This chapter is a labor of love. We (its creators) are queer, non-monogamous, neurodivergent "spoonies" (Miserandino, 2003), accomplices in the struggle to love ourselves, love others, love this world, and make love more accessible to all. We were raised in two settler nations, the United States and Aotearoa/New Zealand – white supremacist capitalist cisheteropatriarchies where "compulsory monogamy" is normalized. **Compulsory monogamy** and **mononormativity** are interchangeable terms that describe any culture where (1) monogamy is viewed as the "normal" or "right" way to practice sexuality; (2) this ideal is baked into institutions (like marriage) and laws such that alternative ways of loving, fucking, and family-making become stigmatized and/or prohibited; and (3) monogamy is not only "normal" but also necessary – viewed as the *pinnacle* of relationship types, entitling one to privileges without which one might not be seen as fully adult (Barker & Langdridge, 2010; Hutzler et al., 2016). In settler nations like ours, heterosexual monogamy has become "compulsory" in these ways – forced upon entire populations, smothering sexual diversity (Sheff, 2018; Tallbear, 2021).

There is a lot of natural sexual diversity within any human population – diversity we now understand applies not only to the *who* but also to the *how* of sexuality. In our cultures, it's well established that sexual orientation refers to *who* folks are attracted to. But experts now recognize that sexual orientation can apply not only to the *who* (who we're sexual with) but also to the *how* (how we practice sexuality). For example, some folks experience BDSM/kink as an integral part of their sexual orientation: kink isn't just something they *do*, kink is a part of who they *are* (Sprott & Williams, 2019). For more about kink and disability, see Chapter 22. The same goes for non-monogamy: some experience it as a choice, and others experience it as an identity (Tweedy, 2011). Sadly, in a culture of compulsory heterosexual monogamy, such complex and natural sexual diversity is stigmatized and flattened.

This means **compulsory heterosexual monogamy is a system of oppression**. Something counts as a system of oppression when there are prejudicial ideologies (e.g., ideas like "marriage should be between one man and one woman," or "sex outside of marriage is immoral") *and* structural power imbalances (e.g., laws like "marriage *can* only occur between one man and one woman" and "sex outside of marriage is a *crime*") that result in advantages and disadvantages on the basis of sexuality. When it comes to naming the disadvantages, **polyphobia** and **whorephobia** describe the oppressive consequences (e.g., behaviors, policies) that result from the oppressive ideology of compulsory monogamy. Polyphobia is the oppression of non-monogamy (Sheff, 2017), and whorephobia the oppression of sex work (Simpson, 2022).

If these terms are confusing, here's a clarifying analogy using better-known terms:

- Compulsory monogamy and mononormativity refer to oppressive **ideologies**, ideologies that tell us what a culture views as "right" and "wrong" when it comes to sexuality.
    - As an analogy, consider the related terms "compulsory heterosexuality" (Rich, 1980) and "heteronormativity," which also refer to oppressive ideologies that tell us what a culture views as "right" and "wrong" when it comes to sexuality.
- Polyphobia and whorephobia refer to oppressive **behaviors** and **structures** (i.e., institutions, laws) that result from (and perpetuate) these oppressive ideologies.
    - To continue the analogy, "homophobia" and "queerphobia" describe oppressive behaviors and structures that result from (and perpetuate) the ideology of "compulsory heterosexuality/heteronormativity."

In this chapter, we have two goals. Our first goal is theoretical: to illuminate the connection we see between ableism and mononormativity as systems of oppression. Our argument follows this logic: (1) **all systems of oppression are disabling**; (2) **compulsory monogamy is a system of oppression**; therefore, (3) **compulsory monogamy is disabling**.

Our second goal is to provide evidence for this claim via literature review. There hasn't been much research into the lives of non-monogamous people, but there's enough to convince empiricists that polyphobia is a demonstrable (and disabling) fact. Whether it's stigma in healthcare settings (McCoy et al.,

2015; Vaughan et al., 2019), job discrimination (Tweedy, 2011), child custody issues (Goldfeder & Sheff, 2013), the logistical/legal consequences of not being able to marry one's partners (Goldfeder & Sheff, 2013; Tweedy, 2011), or everyday slut-shaming (Conley et al., 2013; Fleckenstein et al., 2013), life can be *rough* for non-monogamous folks in mononormative cultures. We have felt this roughness firsthand, so we also incorporate autoethnographic data.

We grew up in mononormative cultures where "slut" was an insult, and sexual voracity a sign of sickness or immorality. Non-monogamy was not a valid way of being (except for the cishet man Don Juan vibe), and certainly wasn't (*still* isn't) a legit sexual orientation. Queerness was similarly stigmatized and pathologized. And instead of being valued for our neurodivergence, we were labeled as "disordered" and told our bodyminds were "wrong." In short, we grew up stymied by the intersectionality of **polyphobia, queerphobia**, and **saneism**, a variant of ableism specific to madness/neurodiversity. (For more about sexuality and neurodivergence, see Chapter 4, and for more on madness/saneism and sexuality, see Chapter 7.)

Forgive the bleakness so far and allow us to add that as we grew, we enmeshed ourselves in radical spaces that seek to dismantle these systems of oppression and facilitate loving micro-worlds where folks can heal their wounds and meet their needs – movements like **disability justice**, and **critical non-monogamy**. Here, we found community with shared ethics and shared purpose, we had our identities affirmed, and we learned how to heal/liberate from internalized mononormativity and ableism.

## Part 1: Setting the Theoretical Stage

### *Compulsory Monogamy Is Disabling*

We've been blessed with many opportunities to explore and unpack ableism thanks to our ancestors in the early disability rights and subsequent disability justice movement, and the accompanying discipline of disability studies (naming them all would exceed our word limit! But some include Hedva, 2016/2022; Mingus, 2017; Clare, 2017; Kuppers, 2014; Davis, 2016). Because of our many ancestors, we understand that it's not our bodyminds that limit our ability to live, love, and participate in our culture – it's our culture that creates these limitations. By legitimizing and enabling certain bodyminds as "normal" and "correct," and pathologizing and disabling others as "abnormal" and "wrong," our culture created this violent and inaccessible mess we call ableism.

During Laura's role as an educator (of social work students), she once had a major in-class epiphany and uttered: *"wait. . . aren't ALL systems of oppression ableism?"* The train of thought was: "ableism" names the process whereby a culture "disables" people by pathologizing and stigmatizing their bodyminds and creating systemic barriers to accessing their needs (e.g., employment, housing, community) – so then, aren't *all* systems of oppression "ableist" insofar as they are "disabling" in these ways? In a white supremacist culture, bodyminds of color are pathologized and stigmatized, and there are systemic barriers to BIPOC accessing their needs; in a cisheteropatriarchal culture, women's bodyminds and the bodyminds of LGBTQIA+ folks are pathologized and stigmatized, and there are systemic barriers to accessing their needs. . .! By no means does Laura assert this train of thought was original – Johanna Hedva made a similar point in the powerful essay *Sick Woman Theory* (2016/2022). But it was during this epiphany that the intersectionality of it all really *landed*. "Ableism" names the fact that it is *disabling systems* (like colonialism, cisheteropatriarchy, or mononormativity) that lie beneath many of our collective woes, and more importantly, that it's not our bodyminds that need fixing, but as Johanna Hedva (section 4, para 6) said, *"it's the world that needs the fixing."*

Thus far we've established that all systems of oppression operate in parallel ways, and result in "disabling" conditions. **Systems of oppression are, by their nature, disabling** – and this includes compulsory monogamy. And like other systems of oppression, it's not disabling by mere historical accident. Indigenous scholar Kim Tallbear's work in **critical polyamory** (2019, 2021) asserts that compulsory heterosexual monogamy was strategically used in colonial efforts to subjugate and eradicate Indigenous ways of being. In the Americas, many pre-colonial cultures embraced sexual and gender fluidity (Pruden & Edmo, 2012); this was also true in Aotearoa/New Zealand (Hartendorp, 2019). And among the many cultural genocide tools in their arsenals, colonialists forced heteronormativity, mononormativity, and a gender binary upon Indigenous cultures. Building on the work of queer theorists, Kim Tallbear (2021) therefore refers to compulsory monogamy as **"settler sexuality,"** which she defines as "both heteronormative and homonormative forms of 'love,' 'sex,' and 'marriage' that are produced along with private property holding" (para 8) in settler nations. When we heard her call monogamy "settler sex" in a podcast (2019), we literally *cackled* – way to call a settler spade a settler spade! Kim Tallbear's work reveals how mononormativity is born at the intersections of colonization, white supremacy, and cisheteropatriarchy. And consequently, she sees a solution in **decolonization** – hence the title of the aforementioned podcast: *Decolonizing Sex!* (2019). We love her term **critical polyamory**, because it invites mononormativity (and its resistance) into wider discussions about anti-oppression – similar to how Critical Race Theory inspires us to be *critical* of (and resist) racism, critical polyamory inspires us to be critical of (and resist) mononormativity.

In adrienne maree brown's essay "On Non-Monogamy" in Pleasure Activism (2019), she uses the term **relationship anarchy** to similar effect – coined in 2006 by Andie Nordgren (2012), relationship anarchy describes relationships (sexual, familial, etc.) in which socially constructed expectations, roles, and hierarchies are challenged. Relationship anarchists reject the notion that there's *any* type of relationship at the "pinnacle," and assert that relationship expectations and roles are most ethical when defined collaboratively by those who are *in* that relationship. Critical polyamory and relationship anarchy are valuable overlapping concepts, but the most commonly used term is **ethical (or consensual) non-monogamy**, an "umbrella term that includes any relationship in which all partners agree that each may have romantic and/or sexual relationships with other partners" (Haupert et al., 2017, p. 426). Ethical non-monogamy was popularized in 1997 when the gloriously empowered Dossie Easton and Janet Hardy wrote the first edition of *The Ethical Slut*. In this chapter, we use **critical non-monogamy** in order to keep Kim Tallbear's "critical" at the forefront, and because non-monogamy is more inclusive than polyamory.

Regardless of terminology, the heart of these movements is **justice and healing**. The goal is to (1) shift cultural discourse by affirming and validating the *natural* and *valuable* sexual diversity of our species; (2) support people in healing from the damage inflicted by compulsory heterosexual monogamy (and other systems of oppression); (3) empower folks in developing tools to meet their relational needs (e.g., love, sex, care, belonging) without coercion and violence; and (4) dismantle the unjust institutions, systems, and laws that perpetuate compulsory heterosexual monogamy. In relaying this, we see a clear parallel with the goals of disability justice. Disability justice is also about shifting cultural discourse to affirm and validate natural and valuable bodymind diversity; is also about supporting folks in healing from the damage of intersecting oppressions; is also about empowering folks in developing tools to meet their needs; is also about dismantling unjust systems. Therefore: **we see critical non-monogamy as a way to practice disability justice!**

We have now established that **compulsory monogamy is disabling (and that critical non-monogamy is liberating!)**. To better understand *how* we got here, we now turn to anthropology.

## Anthropological Adventure Into Monogamy!

Baked into the **compulsory monogamy** ideology is the myth that monogamy is *natural* – that humans are *biologically predetermined* or *destined* for monogamy. This is utterly false, but before we go down the rabbit hole, let's define "monogamy" – not "*compulsory* monogamy" the system of oppression (we've already defined that!), not "monogamous *marriage*" the institution (we'll get there soon!), but "monogamy" the *animal mating system*. Mating behavior is complex, so it's difficult for animal behaviorists to agree upon one definition, but Tecot et al. (2016) offer; "a mating and breeding system in which two individuals consistently mate exclusively" (p. 3). Monogamy is when *two* animals mate *exclusively* with *consistency*. Monogamy (thus defined) is one of many biologist-defined animal mating systems. Others (which all fall under non-monogamy) include polygyny (when males have multiple female partners), polyandry (when females have multiple male partners), and polygynandry (when males and females have multiple partners) (Schacht & Kramer, 2019). As a note, please forgive the sex/gender binary language! – we acknowledge that these are imperfect terms created by past scientists (from cisheteronormative cultures) doing their best to explain the astounding diversity in animal mating.

Since 2020, Laura has performed several times a stand-up musical comedy show called *Slut Songs* (Yakas, 2022) – a melodic treatise on critical non-monogamy. In it, she astounds the audience with just how *rare* monogamy is at varying levels of human taxonomy:

- We are **mammals,** and only 3–5% of mammals are monogamous (Díaz-Muñoz & Bales, 2016).
- Within mammals, we are **primates,** and in primates, it's between 15% (Díaz-Muñoz & Bales, 2016) and 30% (Opie, 2019), depending on whether we're talking *sexual* monogamy (an exclusive sexual relationship) or *social* monogamy (shared territory, shared offspring-rearing, but not necessarily an exclusive sexual relationship) (Reichard, 2003).
- Within **primates that live in groups** (like ourselves), it's 0%. "No group-living nonhuman primate is monogamous, and adultery has been documented in every human culture" that has attempted monogamy (Ryan & Jethá, 2010, p. 98)!

She then explains that monogamy was also rare in humans until very recently, and therefore how *surprising* it is, all things considered. She then asks the audience: *so how do we explain it? Why did it evolve? Why is it so pervasive?*

Sidebar: by "evolve," we don't mean by natural selection. **Monogamy in humans is not natural, it's cultural**. It's the result of choices and traditions our ancestors made. We're *not* biologically primed for monogamy. We *are* biologically primed for sex, love, and dyadic attachments (Schacht & Kramer, 2019), but that doesn't assume monogamy. The narrator in *Monogamy Explained* made this point nicely: "love is a feeling; monogamy is a rule" (Posner, 2018, 3.30 min). **We're primed to *feel* love – we invent *rules* that tell us how to.**

And in every show, when asked *"why do we do monogamy?"* someone has shouted:

- *"Because of **inheritance**!"* or *"**capitalism**!"* Yes! This connection between capitalism (private property, intergenerational wealth hoarding, etc.) and mononormativity is obvious not only to scholars like Kim Tallbear but also to Laura's audiences!
- *"Because of **sex negative religions**!"* Yes! "Sex negativity" describes a culture where sex is viewed as inherently dirty or dangerous, especially outside of procreative monogamous marriage (Jorgensen, 2016). And yes, the religions that dominate our cultures are sex negative. Religion *definitely* nudges cultures toward monogamy (Brandon, 2016).
- *"Because of **cisheteropatriarchy**!"* A hundred times, *yes*! Compulsory monogamy was designed by (and to benefit) cisheteronormative folks. Period.

These audiences aren't radical intellectuals, they're everyday people who saw an ad for a show called *Slut Songs* and thought *"Yes, please*!" This brings us hope, for it reminds us that liberating discussions happen in unexpected places! Laura's audiences have missed a few factors though, so let's add more *"why <u>do</u> we do monogamy?"* theories:

- **To avoid sexually transmitted infections (STIs)**. As Chris Ryan said in *Monogamy Explained*, for most of human history, our ancestors lived in small egalitarian foraging groups, and were likely non-monogamous as *"there's no reason to assume that our ancestors shared everything **except** sexual partners"* (Posner, 2018, 6.15 min). Then came the Neolithic Revolution. Circa 12 kya, we started transitioning from small nomadic egalitarian groups into large hierarchical sedentary societies (Blakemore, 2019). With this shift came an increase in infectious diseases (including STIs). Bauch and McElreath (2016) propose that STI avoidance may have driven early societies toward monogamy – a solid theory limited (but not negated) by the fact that we can't assume Neolithic folks understood how STIs spread such that the choice was intentional.
- **To prevent infanticide**. Many non-monogamous primate species have violent patriarchal tendencies like male-inflicted infanticide. In these species, when a new male arrives in a community, they may kill the infants there so that the females/mothers become fertile and receptive to mating again. An evolutionary argument for monogamy is that it prevents this, because monogamous males are (1) motivated to protect their offspring and (2) *not* motivated to kill infants so they can mate with their mothers (Opie, 2019).

- **Because females want male investment.** Old-school theorists argued that monogamy evolved due to "female choice" – a battle of the sexes, whereby males fight to spread their seed (non-monogamy), and females fight for males to commit to them and their offspring (monogamy). In *Monogamy Explained*, Chris Ryan assures us this is nonsense that merely justifies the gender roles and power imbalances of the time (Posner, 2018). One might say this is #ScientificSexism.
- **To prevent the scourge of unpartnered males (#BoysWillBeBoys . . .).** To quote the source:

[I]n suppressing intrasexual competition and reducing the size of the pool of unmarried men, normative monogamy reduces crime rates, including rape, murder, assault, robbery and fraud, as well as decreasing personal abuses. By assuaging the competition for younger brides, normative monogamy decreases (i) the spousal age gap, (ii) fertility, and (iii) gender inequality.

*(Henrich et al., 2012, p. 657)*

This may all be so, but the flawed implication is that non-monogamy is the "problem" (i.e., it makes men rapey and murdery) that has been "solved" by monogamy. But non-monogamy is *not* the problem, the problem is cisheteropatriarchy! The problem is when non-monogamy occurs in a cisheteropatriarchal (i.e., rapey and murdery) context. Yes, many non-monogamous cultures have been cisheteropatriarchal polygynous cultures where men had multiple wives (even child wives) as "property." *Of course* monogamy is an improvement on this. But it's not a fix. If monogamy could fix the problems of cisheteropatriarchy, we'd be first to say *"let's make this compulsory!"* But cisheteropatriarchal violence exists in cultures of compulsory monogamy too. In fact, as we noted earlier, compulsory monogamy has been a tool to *further* cisheteropatriarchy.

We hope this anthropological adventure has dispelled the myth that human monogamy is *natural*, and shown that it's actually a *recent* and *culturally constructed* behavior. In the words of Chris Ryan, who refers to us as "sexual omnivores": "Monogamy is like vegetarianism: you can choose to be a vegetarian, and that can be healthy, it can be ethical . . . but because you've chosen to be a vegetarian, doesn't mean that bacon stops smelling good" (Posner, 2018, 17.30 min).

### Part 2: The Evidence

We've now established at a theoretical level that compulsory monogamy is a disabling system of oppression that flouts our species' natural non-monogamy – but what does this mean at an individual level? How does this impact disabled people? How can critical non-monogamy support disabled people? We'll start by reviewing literature that foregrounds the struggles of non-monogamous folks in mononormative cultures. Then we'll close with a case study highlighting how ableism/saneism and mononormativity can combine to exacerbate these struggles (and how critical non-monogamy can be a balm for that!) and ideas for next steps.

## *From Mononormativity (Ideology) to Polyphobia (Behavior)*

Mononormativity is so entrenched that people often assume monogamous relationships (and monogamous people) are inherently *better* than non-monogamous relationships (and people). This **cognitive bias** is called a "halo effect," and research has shown this halo effect in action. People in monogamous relationships are widely perceived as *better* and *healthier* in multiple measures – even measures as absurd as being more reliable at pet care! (Conley et al., 2013; Hutzler et al., 2016); and people in non-monogamous relationships as untrustworthy, immoral, promiscuous, unsatisfied in their relationships, and as having risky/pathological sexual behavior (Conley et al., 2013; Haupert et al., 2017; Hutzler et al., 2016).

The bias is so entrenched that it's not only research *participants* who reflect it, it's also reproduced by *research/ers*. Many methodologies uncritically buy into mononormativity: for example, the idea that monogamy is a universal sexual desire and experience (Moors, 2018). Many scales, including the Passionate Love Scale, imply monogamy in how they measure "ideal" love and passion (Conley et al., 2017). Most studies don't even offer "multiple committed partners" as a response choice to relationship status!

Because of this biased belief that monogamy (and monogamous people) is superior, **polyphobia** is pervasive. The *Loving More* survey revealed that 25.8% of the 4,062 respondents had been discriminated against solely due to their non-monogamy (Fleckenstein et al., 2013). This discrimination happens at varying levels of society, from interpersonal relationships to healthcare and legal contexts.

## *Healthcare*

In healthcare settings, non-monogamous folks are often perceived as engaging in "higher risk" sexual behavior, despite the fact that consensually non-monogamous folks are more likely to engage in safer-sex practices (like STI testing and sexual health conversations) compared to folks who are adulterous (Hutzler et al., 2016; Conley et al., 2012; Fleckenstein et al., 2013). Within mental health, many clinicians still believe that non-monogamy is the result of pathology – of personality disorder, hypersexuality, sex addiction, or insecure attachment (McCoy et al., 2015). This pathologizing approach is harmful and can lead to inauthenticity insofar as non-monogamous folks may *pretend* to be monogamous to avoid polyphobia (Vaughan et al., 2019).

## *Legal Challenges*

Legal challenges can present in various ways, such as being excluded from the institution of marriage, being excluded from the protection of anti-discrimination laws due to the narrow definition of sexual orientation, and issues like child custody that may follow (Tweedy, 2011; Goldfeder & Sheff, 2013). Marriage is a legal mechanism that ordains and protects monogamy while granting privileges to people who enter into it – such as tax benefits, the right to inherit wealth, the right to enter spaces (like hospitals) restricted to "legal family" (Tweedy, 2011). Since monogamous relationships are the only kind that can enter into marriage, non-monogamous folks are excluded from these privileges. Additionally, non-monogamy isn't legally recognized as a sexual orientation, so polyphobic discrimination isn't illegal in areas like employment, housing or child welfare (Tweedy, 2011; Goldfeder & Sheff, 2013). We know polyamorous folks who've had their polyamory framed as "perversion" in custody proceedings – and without the protection of anti-discrimination law, such injustices can be sanctioned!

Polyphobia runs depressingly deep in our cultures, but we'll close this subsection with hopeful reminders of progress. Coverage of non-monogamy in mainstream media has increased (with increasingly nuanced coverage) in the past two decades (Thomas, 2014). There are organizations fighting for justice (e.g., OPEN/Organization for Polyamory and Ethical Non-monogamy). There are folks striving to de-pathologize non-monogamy, such as clinician Jessica Fern's (2020) book *Polysecure* and activist Clementine Morrigan's (n.d.) work in *Trauma-Informed Polyamory*. And there have been promising legal successes: in 2021, *Three Dads and a Baby* was published by Ian Jenkins, a member of a gay throuple in California who got all three partners' names on their child's birth certificate. Not to mention the fact that Laura can land a show like *Slut Songs* in small-town Aotearoa/New Zealand!

## Laura's Autoethnographic Case Study: Compulsory Monogamy Has Disabled Me

Thus far, part two of our chapter has explored how mononormativity harms/disables non-monogamous folks in general. But the available literature doesn't address the specific intersection of **non-monogamy *and* disability** (yet!) – for example, how disabled non-monogamous folks navigate the intersection of mononormativity *and* ableism. To bridge this, I'm focusing this autoethnographic case study on how mononormativity and ableism (specifically saneism) have disabled me: how they combined to create structural barriers that prevented me from meeting my relational needs, and also how they poisoned me from within, preventing me from understanding or loving myself.

In this violent world, my Mad bodymind is frequently low on "spoons" (Miserandino, 2003). I've always yearned for a life abundant in love, but that was not what my childhood facilitated, and at critical junctures (like college) when folks typically nurture chosen families, I only had the spoons for a basic and lonely survival. I needed others to share their surplus spoons with me. Alas, that glorious and much-needed "access intimacy" that Mia Mingus describes (2017), where spoon-sharing happens interdependently and where no one feels "too needy," eluded me for a long time. Not only because I couldn't even *imagine* it (yet) but also because the world isn't built to facilitate it. **Compulsory monogamy leads to a world of relational resource shortages.** It makes it easier for wealth to be hoarded within nuclear families, and this wealth isn't just economic (money and property), it's also social (love and care). It takes most of the population off the metaphorical "market" (an appropriately capitalistic metaphor!) such that people who *could* be sharing their love and care broadly instead hoard it within their little bubbles. And for me, this relational resource shortage was compounded by saneism, and the fact that many prefer not to date/love/partner with "high maintenance" Madwomen like me – contributing to a debilitating belief that "I'm unlovable." In short: saneism and mononormativity combined to strain and stunt my family bonds, my friendships, and my romantic-sexual development, leaving me *desperate* in unmet relational needs. It's proverbially said that "you must love yourself before others can love you," but for me this was absurd: I only learned to love myself because others showed me how to. The small but mighty chosen family I eventually built, they loved the self-hate out of me.

Until then, I was trapped in the (disabling) "compulsory heterosexual monogamy" story my society had fed me. I fully believed that I needed a husband to complete me, "fix" me, and prove I existed. This limiting belief didn't foster hope. . . . I'm not a simple coherent self, I'm a capricious and volatile human soup of intensity and inconsistent parts, so the prospect of finding *one* person to match *all* of that seemed hopeless. I felt doomed by a cruel cycle: I was "too Mad" to find (or keep) a partner, yet *not* having (or keeping) a partner drove me madder. The loneliness, the hopelessness, the traumatic rejections (lovers who left explicitly *because* I was "too Mad"), led to more madness. And because of internalized mononormativity, I had no idea that critical non-monogamy – a practice generous enough to meet my relational needs – was *possible*. I was prevented from seeing that I was (and had every right to be) a Slut.

It also instilled a deep and disabling shame. My culture had taught me that it was not only immoral but also *sick* to desire anything besides heterosexual monogamy. So mononormativity and saneism again banded together as my sexuality was pathologized, as "hypersexuality" became extra fodder for doctors to label me "bipolar." My beautiful and valid neurodivergence, my beautiful and valid queer sluttery, all reduced to deficit-based diagnostics, and *internalized*. I *believed* I was disordered, wrong, bad, and I *hated* myself for it – a spiritually disabling self-hatred I am still healing from (for more of this story, see my other chapter on Madness and sexuality in Chapter 7).

But to end on a hopeful note: like many ancestors before me, I've found liberation and healing through critical non-monogamy (which as we said earlier, is a kind of disability justice!). I now know *many* Mad, Disabled, "Neuroqueer" (Walker, 2021) spoonies with massive slutty chosen families, surrounded by love, and showing me (and anyone else paying attention) how it's done!

### *Questions to Reflect on After Reading This Case Study*

1. What were your initial reactions to this story?
2. Did you notice any internalized beliefs about non-monogamy and disability coming up? (Remember: we have *all* internalized mononormativity and ableism/saneism – it's inevitable in our culture – so we recommend self-compassion here!)
3. What aspects could you relate to, and what aspects were harder to relate to?
4. How might you support someone on a similar healing journey?

### Ideas for Next Steps

When working with non-monogamous and/or disabled folks, it's important to engage in practices that liberate us from internalized mononormativity and ableism. Reading literature (especially literature produced by disabled/non-monogamous folks!) and engaging in trainings are great strategies. If you are identified as monogamous, it can be helpful to explore what that identity means to you and how mononormativity has influenced your experience (Jordan, 2018). Having authentic and compassionate discussions with peers and loved ones can be helpful too: it's *normal* to have internalized mononormativity and ableism/saneism, but identifying and challenging it within ourselves can *feel* isolating when we do it alone!

Tangible steps to make people feel seen and affirmed are great strategies too. For example, ensuring our spaces – offices, websites, etc. – are accessible, and that we use inclusive and affirming language. You might normalize sharing your pronouns and your relationship to disability (e.g., whether/why you use identity-first or person-first language, whether you're nondisabled, disabled); you might ensure your paperwork has room for folks to self-identify their relationship to disability, and their relationship style (e.g., instead of a menu with options like "married" or "single," leaving it open-ended). You might choose to actively affirm identities that don't usually get affirmed (e.g., hanging a pride flag, wearing an "ableism is trash" T-shirt). Depending on your comfort/safety (regarding transgressing traditional professional norms), we also advocate for self-disclosure of meaningful shared identities. If you and your client are both members of the Disabled community, if you share a queer or non-monogamous identity, sharing about this can deepen your relationship and increase its healing efficacy!

## Conclusion

We hope you enjoyed our labor of love. We loved sharing our thesis that compulsory monogamy is a disabling system of oppression. We loved sharing the research and personal stories that support this (although it also made us sad, because our people have been/are suffering). And we loved sharing ideas for next steps. It's been our pleasure to be a part of your journey to liberate from internalized mononormativity and ableism!

## Resources

Here are some resources (mostly excerpted from our references: go there for full citations and links!) to support your journey:

- OPEN/Organization for Polyamory and Ethical Non-monogamy: https://www.open-love.org
- Kim Tallbear's *Decolonizing Sex*, plus her blog and website: http://www.criticalpolyamorist.com; https://kimtallbear.com
- Johanna Hedva's *Sick Woman Theory*, plus their website: https://johannahedva.com
- Mia Mingus' *Access Intimacy*, plus her blog: https://leavingevidence.wordpress.com
- Clementine Morrigan's *Trauma-Informed Polyamory*
- Easton and Hardy's *The Ethical Slut*
- Jessica Fern's *Polysecure*
- Nick Walker's *Neuroqueer Heresies*, plus her website: https://neuroqueer.com
- *Monogamy: Explained*! Netflix show
- Moor's *Moving past the rose-tinted lens of monogamy: onward with critical self-examination and (sexually) healthy science.*
- Jordan's *"My mind kept creeping back . . . this relationship can't last": Developing self-awareness of monogamous bias*
- For clever comedy: Laura's *Slut Songs!*
- Ryan, C. (2013). *Are we designed to be sexual omnivores?* [Video]. TED. www.ted.com/talks/christopher_ryan_are_we_designed_to_be_sexual_omnivores?language=en

## References

Barker, M., & Langdridge, D. (2010). Whatever happened to non-monogamies? Critical reflections on recent research and theory. *Sexualities*, *13*(6), 748–772.

Bauch, C., & McElreath, R. (2016). Disease dynamics and costly punishment can foster socially imposed monogamy. *Nature Communications*, *7*, 11219. https://doi.org/10.1038/ncomms11219

Blakemore, E. (2019, April 6). Neolithic revolution. *National Geographic*. www.nationalgeographic.com/culture/article/neolithic-agricultural-revolution

Brandon, M. (2016). Monogamy and nonmonogamy: Evolutionary considerations and treatment challenges. *Sexual Medicine Reviews*, *4*(4), 343–352. https://doi.org/10.1016/j.sxmr.2016.05.005

brown, a. m. (2019). On non-monogamy. In brown, a. m. (Ed.), *Pleasure activism: The politics of feeling good* (pp. 409–414). AK Press.

Clare, E. (2017). *Brilliant imperfection: Grappling with cure*. Duke University Press.

Conley, T. D., Matsick, J. L., Moors, A. C., & Ziegler, A. (2017). Investigation of consensually nonmonogamous relationships: Theories, methods, and new directions. *Perspectives on Psychological Science*, *12*(2), 205–232. https://doi.org/10.1177/1745691616667925

Conley, T. D., Moors, A. C., Matsick, J. L., & Ziegler, A. (2013). The fewer the merrier? Assessing stigma surrounding consensually non-monogamous romantic relationships. *Analyses of Social Issues and Public Policy*, *13*(1), 1–30.

Conley, T. D., Moors, A. C., Ziegler, A., & Karathanasis, C. (2012). Unfaithful individuals are less likely to practice safer sex than openly nonmonogamous individuals. *Journal of Sexual Medicine*, *9*, 1559–1565.

Davis, L. J. (Ed.). (2016). *The disability studies reader*. Routledge.

Díaz-Muñoz, S. L., & Bales, K. L. (2016). "Monogamy" in primates: Variability, trends, and synthesis: Introduction to special issue on primate monogamy. *American Journal of Primatology*, *78*(3), 283–287. https://doi.org/10.1002/ajp.22463

Easton, D., & Hardy, J. (1997). *The ethical slut: A practical guide to polyamory, open relationships, and other freedoms in sex and love*. Greenery Press.

Fern, J. (2020). *Polysecure: Attachment, trauma and consensual nonmonogamy*. Thorntree Press LLC.

Fleckenstein, J., Bergstrand, C. R., & Cox, D. W. (2013, June 21). What do polys want? An overview of the 2012 loving more survey. *Loving More Nonprofit*. www.lovingmorenonprofit.org/polyamory-articles/2012-lovingmore-polyamory-survey/

Goldfeder, M., & Sheff, E. (2013). Children of polyamorous families: A first empirical look. *Journal of Law and Social Deviance*, *5*, 150.

Hartendorp, K. (2019, October 23). What do we really know about gender diversity in te ao Māori? *The Spinoff*. https://thespinoff.co.nz/atea/23-10-2019/what-do-we-really-know-about-gender-diversity-in-te-ao-maori

Haupert, M. L., Gesselman, A. N., Moors, A. C., Fisher, H. E., & Garcia, J. R. (2017). Prevalence of experiences with consensual nonmonogamous relationships: Findings from two national samples of single Americans. *Journal of Sex & Marital Therapy*, *43*(5), 424–440. https://doi.org/10.1080/0092623X.2016.1178675

Hedva, J. (2022, March 12). Sick woman theory. *Topical Cream*. www.topicalcream.org/features/sick-woman-theory/ (Original work published 2016).

Henrich, J., Boyd, R., & Richerson, P. J. (2012). The puzzle of monogamous marriage. *Philosophical Transactions of the Royal Society of London. Series B, Biological Sciences*, *367*(1589), 657–669. https://doi.org/10.1098/rstb.2011.0290

Hutzler, K. T., Giuliano, T. A., Herselman, J. R., & Johnson, S. M. (2016). Three's a crowd: Public awareness and (mis)perceptions of polyamory. *Psychology & Sexuality*, 7(2), 69–87. https://doi.org/10.1080/19419899.2015.1004102

Jenkins, I. (2021). *Three dads and a baby: Adventures in modern parenting*. Cleis Press.

Jordan, L. S. (2018). "My mind kept creeping back . . . this relationship can't last": Developing self-awareness of monogamous bias. *Journal of Feminist Family Therapy*, 30(2), 109–127.

Jorgensen, J. (2016, August 12). The sex-negativity mind-set in academe (essay). *Inside Higher Ed*. www.insidehighered.com/advice/2016/08/12/sex-negativity-mind-set-academe-essay

Kuppers, P. (2014). *Studying disability arts and culture: An introduction*. Red Globe Press.

McCoy, M. A., Stinson, M. A., Ross, D. B., & Hjelmstad, L. R. (2015). Who's in our clients' bed? A case illustration of sex therapy with a polyamorous couple. *Journal of Sex & Marital Therapy*, 41(2), 134–144. https://doi.org/10.1080/0092623X.2013.864366

Mingus, M. (2017, April 12). Access intimacy, interdependence, and disability justice. *Leaving Evidence*. https://leavingevidence.wordpress.com/2017/04/12/access-intimacy-interdependence-and-disability-justice/

Miserandino, C. (2003). *The spoon theory. But you don't look sick?* https://butyoudontlooksick.com/articles/written-by-christine/the-spoon-theory/

Moors, A. C. (2018). Moving past the rose-tinted lens of monogamy: Onward with critical self-examination and (sexually) healthy science. *Archives of Sexual Behavior*, 48(1), 57–61. https://doi.org/10.1007/s10508-018-1215-6

Morrigan, C. (n.d.). *Trauma-informed polyamory (workshop)*. www.clementinemorrigan.com/product/trauma-informed-polyamory-workshop

Nordgren, A. (2012). *The short instructional manifesto for relationship anarchy*. The Anarchist Library. https://theanarchistlibrary.org/library/andie-nordgren-the-short-instructional-manifesto-for-relationship-anarchy

Opie, C. (2019). Monogamy and infanticide in complex societies. *Royal Anthropological Institute*, 45, 59–74. https://research-information.bris.ac.uk/ws/portalfiles/portal/190039791/RAI_Chapter5_Opie.pdf

Posner, J (Writer & Director). (2018, May 23). Monogamy (Season 1, Episode 18) [TV series episode]. In E. Klein & C. Mumm (Executive Producers), *Explained*. Vox Media.

Pruden, H., & Edmo, S. (2012, November 1). *Two spirit people: Sex, gender & sexuality in historic and contemporary native America*. National Congress of American Indians. www.ncai.org/policy-research-center/initiatives/Pruden-Edmo_TwoSpiritPeople.pdf

Reichard, U. H. (2003). Monogamy: Past and present. In U. H. Reichard & C. Boesch (Eds.), *Monogamy: Mating strategies and partnerships in birds, humans, and other mammals* (pp. 3–25). Cambridge University Press.

Rich, A. (1980). Compulsory heterosexuality and lesbian existence. *Signs*, 5(4), 631–660. www.jstor.org/stable/3173834

Ryan, C., & Jethá, C. (2010). *Sex at dawn: The prehistoric origins of modern sexuality*. Harper.

Schacht, R., & Kramer, K. L. (2019). Are we monogamous? A review of the evolution of pair-bonding in humans and its contemporary variation cross-culturally. *Frontiers in Ecology and Evolution*, 7. https://doi.org/10.3389/fevo.2019.00230

Sheff, E. (2017, July 14). Polyphobia. *Psychology Today*. www.psychologytoday.com/nz/blog/the-polyamorists-next-door/201707/polyphobia

Sheff, E. (2018, December 2). Against compulsory (non)monogamy. *Psychology Today*. www.psychologytoday.com/nz/blog/the-polyamorists-next-door/201812/against-compulsory-nonmonogamy

Simpson, J. (2022). Whorephobia in higher education: A reflexive account of researching cis women's experiences of stripping while at university. *Higher Education*, 84, 17–31.

Sprott, R. A., & Williams, D. J. (2019). Is BDSM a sexual orientation or serious leisure? *Current Sexual Health Reports*, 11, 75–79. https://doi.org/10.1007/s11930-019-00195-x

Tallbear, K. (2019, March 19). *Decolonizing sex*. All My Relations. www.allmyrelationspodcast.com/post/ep-5-decolonizing-sex

Tallbear, K. (2021, May 22). Yes, your pleasure! Yes, self-love! And don't forget, settler sex is a structure. *Unsettle*. https://kimtallbear.substack.com/p/yes-your-pleasure-yes-self-love-and#details

Tecot, S. R., Singletary, B., & Eadie, E. (2016). Why "monogamy" isn't good enough. *American Journal of Primatology*, 78(3), 1–14.

Thomas, E. (2014, April 9). In mainstream media, polyamory is getting attention. *Bitch Media*. www.bitchmedia.org/post/mainstream-media-has-discovered-polyamorous-relationships

Tweedy, A. E. (2011). Polyamory as a sexual orientation. *University Cincinnati Law Review*, 79(4), 1461–1515. SSRN. http://ssrn.com/acstract=1632653

Vaughan, M. D., Jones, P., Taylor, B. A., & Roush, J. (2019). Healthcare experiences and needs of consensually non-monogamous people: Results from a focus group study. *The Journal of Sexual Medicine*, 16(1), 42–51.

Walker, N. (2021). *Neuroqueer Heresies: Notes on the neurodiversity paradigm, autistic empowerment, and post normal possibilities*. Autonomous Press.

Yakas, L. (2022). *Slut songs* [Playlist]. YouTube. www.youtube.com/playlist?list=PLUrjUAR9YBMnJYnN_apGGJYX6AloqYiwB

# 22
# CARING FOR DISABLED KINKSTERS
## Context and Practical Guidance for Providers

*Maria L. Morrero, Nicole Ariel Lopez, Hillary K. Hecht, Erin E. Dobbins, and Grace Argo*

### Introduction

Social awareness of kink, bondage, domination, submission, and sadomasochism (kink/BDSM) has expanded in recent years due to the popularity of media such as *Secretary* and *Fifty Shades of Gray*. Many kink/BDSM practitioners, however, feel that popular media depictions of kink/BDSM are misleading. Scientific researchers who study issues not depicted in many entertainment media including power dynamics, safety, and consent offer evidence-based understanding of kink/BDSM. Comparably, research on disability and sexuality considers questions about power dynamics, safety, and consent that arise between disabled people and their sexual partners. Research at the intersection of disability and kink/BDSM, however, remains scarce.

Against the idea that disabled people should be asexual, or limit themselves to "vanilla" desires, several disability scholars have characterized participation in kink/BDSM as part of disabled people's fundamental sexual rights (Reynolds, 2007; Tellier, 2017). We affirm these fundamental sexual rights. We begin this chapter by defining kink/BDSM then explore how these topics intersect, discussing kink/BDSM as a pain management tool, as a trauma recovery tool, and as a leisure activity. We also describe experiences neurodivergent kink/BDSM practitioners; consent; and the (dis)empowerment of medical disclosure in play. Finally, we provide kink-aware suggestions and resources for health professionals serving disabled clients. Throughout this chapter, we center disabled kink/BDSM practitioners' needs while also identifying areas for further research.

DOI: 10.4324/9781003308331-27

## Defining Kink/BDSM

BDSM is an umbrella term; this acronym encompasses behaviors categorized within Bondage & Discipline, Domination & Submission, and Sadism & Masochism (Simula, 2019; Tellier, 2017). People may use "kink" interchangeably with BDSM, as will we in this chapter (Simula, 2019). *Bondage* refers to activities that restrict movement which may include use of ropes, handcuffs, and other devices. *Discipline* refers to activities that involve an aspect of punishment, which may be physical or mental. *Domination* and *submission* refer to creating and utilizing differential power dynamics between participants within a BDSM context, or *scene*. *Sadism* and *masochism* involve deriving pleasure from intense sensations, often associated with pain, such as utilizing impact from floggers, paddles, spanking, and other physical activities meant to create intense, controlled physical sensations. People involved in BDSM negotiate all activities, as the culture of BDSM emphasizes communication and consent (Tellier, 2017). *Tops* are players who perform the action of restraining, disciplining, or punishing (*topping*) while *bottoms* are the ones restrained, disciplined, or punished (*bottoming*). Players may *switch* between the role of top and bottom between or within scenes. Although BDSM play can be highly eroticized, it is important to note that people do not always engage with BDSM for the sole purpose of sexual gratification and there are many people who play without genitally oriented sex in mind (Ambler et al., 2016; Turley, 2016).

These broad categories of activities encompass a vast range of actions and individual experiences, so each person will have a unique relationship to their participation in BDSM. Throughout this chapter, we use the term *play* to describe engaging in any kink activity. Before play occurs, participants negotiate and consent to what they expect will happen, define, and discuss risks, safety, and harm reduction, and agree how players will affirm or withdraw consent throughout the scene. Following play, *aftercare* refers to the intentional direct responses to the physical, emotional, mental, and social responses that a scene has had for all participants. Aftercare occurs immediately after play and may extend to regular and agreed upon check-ins during the days or weeks following play, ensuring all participants are comfortably and safely adjusting and healing from the physical, emotional, endorphin, and adrenaline changes that happen after a scene. It may include cuddling, sleep, bathing, skincare, eating and hydrating, telling jokes, watching TV, and conversations reflecting on the play that occurred.

## Kink/BDSM and Disability

Until recently, the mental health profession pathologized kink/BDSM practitioners as sufferers of paraphilic disorders (Glyde, 2015; Simula, 2019;

Tellier, 2017). The treatment of kink/BDSM as symptomatic of mental illness has, unsurprisingly, resulted in a reluctance to engage disability as a category of analysis among kink/BDSM researchers. Tellier (2017), however, observes that studying the intersection of kink/BDSM and disability emphasizes the need for open and ongoing communication in relationships, reveals the interplay of pain and power, and importantly acknowledges that disabled people also have sexual needs and desires. Disability scholars use different models of disability (such as those outlined in this book's introduction) to study how disability is produced, treated, and experienced in various contexts. In this context, researchers can apply different disability models to analyze aspects of disabled kink/BDSM practitioners' experiences. For example, while its emphasis on cure may be troubling, a medical model of disability may be a useful analytic for identifying, measuring, and tracking clinical improvements related to BDSM play. Conversely, while a social model of disability helps to explain how disability is produced by and maintained through social phenomena, it lacks emphasis on disabled people's individual agency, which is crucial in a kink context. Throughout this chapter we approach disability as a capacious category that includes people with all types of disabilities and impairments. We employ different models of disability as suitable and appropriate, using currently available research to suggest best practices and encourage further research on the intersection between disability and kink/BDSM to further support practitioners in better serving their clients.

## Existing Knowledge on Disability and BDSM/Kink

### Kink as a Pain Management Tool

In 2014, at least 10% of the global population, or 60 million people, experienced chronic pain (Jackson et al., 2014). Negative psychological and emotional consequences of chronic pain disrupt independence, interpersonal relationships, and identity (Pitcher et al., 2019; Savvakis, 2019). Disabling pain restricts activity, impeding maintenance of close social connections through shared experience. Caring for someone in pain is an intimate role, often assumed by family or partners, often requiring potentially stressful deviation from previous relationship roles. Communicating about pain is notoriously difficult, further emphasizing the isolating nature of disabling pain. Together, these experiences alter the identity narratives of people in pain (Pitcher et al., 2019). Kink, specifically sensation and pain play, offer an opportunity to reshape these narratives.

In contrast to disabling pain, sensory/pain play is a chosen experience with structured elements agreed upon within the kink/BDSM community. Using this structure, players compose a socially connected sensory/pain narrative. Pre-scene negotiation depends upon mutual understanding of sensation. Players anticipate the type, location, intensity, and duration of sensation during negotiation. Using active communication, players adjust and control sensation throughout a scene. Players must communicate about sensation and anticipate the sensory experience of others (Reynolds, 2007). After a scene, players participate in negotiated caretaking activities (aftercare) to support mutual recovery in caregiver and care recipient roles. Planning, guiding, and recovering from pain/sensation play facilitates cognitive and emotional processing of embodied experience. Sensory and pain play provide valuable tools and opportunities for people experiencing pain to rewrite their physical, social, and cognitive narratives from a position of empowerment and connection (Kattari, 2015; Sheppard, 2019). Continued research is needed to understand how BDSM relates to pain experiences among disabled people.

### Disability and Trauma Play

Trauma play is the practice of intentionally engaging in kink/BDSM activities to "play" with one's past trauma or abuse (Thomas, 2020). Critically, trauma play is defined as "biography based" (Thomas, 2020), that is, drawing upon the *personal* trauma of one or more players. Trauma play does not sexualize subjugation or violence against disempowered and marginalized groups generally, and it may or may not actually involve sex. Following from this reasoning, activities such as rape play (Hammers, 2014), "dark" age play and incest play (Bauer, 2017), humiliation play (Carlström, 2018; Thomas & Williams, 2018), and medical play do not meet the criteria for trauma play unless a person uses them to reenact their own past trauma or abuse.

Some of the benefits of trauma play include a stronger sense of personal agency, confidence, and social belonging; improved mindfulness, assertiveness, and boundary-setting; and the integration of traumatic experiences into one's sense of self, mitigating dissociation and other identity-disrupting effects of trauma (Cascalheira et al., 2021). When trauma play is used in conjunction with trauma support groups, yoga, meditation, and hobbies, it can have profoundly healing effects (Cascalheira et al., 2021). In part, trauma play supports recovery because it allows an individual to share their experience with another person, who simultaneously creates space for and bears witness to their trauma while allowing their partner to safely re-experience and overcome feelings of powerlessness (Hammers, 2019). Negotiation, empathy, and trust are therefore key aspects of trauma play that categorically differentiate reenactment from re-traumatization. In addition to taking pains to describe "reenactment" as a therapeutic activity, scholars have proposed terms such as "rescripting" (Brothers, 1997), "somatic reclamation" (Hammers, 2019), and "therapeutic play" (Easton, 2007) to convey the healing power of trauma play more accurately in trauma recovery.

Little has been written about the relationship between disability and trauma play. Much of the literature on disability and BDSM discusses BDSM as a pain management tool, rather than as a tool for trauma recovery (Reynolds, 2007; Sheppard, 2018, 2019; Tellier, 2017). Conversely, scholars have not used disability as a category of analysis in research on trauma play even though they note that childhood trauma is commonly linked to post-traumatic stress disorders, compromised cognitive functioning, and neurological and musculoskeletal problems in adolescence and adulthood (Cascalheira et al., 2021). Using disability as an analytic in future research on trauma play may help determine whether trauma play contributes to significant clinical improvement in areas of dysfunction. A disability studies framework is important because small scale studies have consistently found that disabled children are significantly more likely than nondisabled children to be abused (Christofferson, 2019; Crosse et al., 1993; Sobsey, 1994; Sullivan & Knutson, 2000). The disabling impacts of trauma must therefore be considered alongside the reality that disabled people are especially vulnerable to abuse. For these reasons, disability is a category that deserves close attention in research on trauma and recovery as well as heightened consideration in clinical practice.

Trauma play is a disability justice issue, because trauma play tends to be stigmatized by both the BDSM community and by mental health practitioners. That stigma often translates to discrimination in healthcare settings and poorer health service outcomes (Sprott & Randall, 2017). Many mental health practitioners misunderstand BDSM as a maladaptive coping mechanism rooted in childhood trauma, while BDSM practitioners sometimes view trauma play as lending credibility to that stereotype (Cascalheira et al., 2021). Significantly, researchers have repeatedly found that BDSM practitioners are no more likely than non-practitioners to have experienced childhood abuse (Brown et al., 2020; Hillier, 2019; Richters et al., 2008; Ten Brink et al., 2021). Moreover, the percentage of BDSM practitioners who engage in trauma play is relatively small, with fewer than one in five practitioners using kink to process trauma (Hughes & Hammack, 2020). Among BDSM practitioners who do engage in trauma play, however, scholars have consistently found that reenacting traumatic memories often functions in a therapeutic manner (Brothers, 1997; Cascalheira et al., 2021; Easton, 2007; Hammers, 2019; Lindemann, 2011; Thomas, 2020).

### *BDSM as Recreation/Leisure*

In addition to therapeutic benefits, reasons that people seek out kink/BDSM includes fun and pleasure (Newmahr, 2010). These experiences may be about spending time with significant others or friends, experiencing desired textures, physical sensations, and positive interactions within one's own body, and in relationship with others' bodies. Sprott and Williams (2019) illustrate how BDSM can belong in the category of "serious leisure," a category that requires continued effort, dedication to honing a craft, and considerations of safety – such as rock climbing or woodworking. Disabled people use BDSM activities to specifically focus on pleasure, particularly accessible, controlled, desired ways to use our bodies, and direct discretion over how our bodies interact with other people. Because kink is so focused on consent and risk management, these encounters can offer pleasurable respite from less accessible, less tailored, and more medicalized contexts that disabled people regularly experience in through the process of seeking care and services.

Particularly when people find a specific community or subculture well suited to meeting their needs, resulting relationships and activities can be a fulfilling part of someone's social life (Jones, 2020). Social hierarchies influence who has the safest access to BDSM play and kink communities, while these communities simultaneously build skills to center the needs and safety of the most marginalized members of their groups, particularly disabled people (Simula, 2019). Coming to BDSM practices for a time-limited experience, or for ongoing community, self-identity, and regular leisure can each allow disabled people to meet play and leisure needs.

Skills of individual tailoring and consideration of bodies involved in play highlight unique strengths kink/BDSM. Disabled people find accommodations in BDSM that may be less familiar to other serious leisure activities' communities. Disabled people and their partners can use combinations of toys, props, outfits, and accessories to participate in desired kink activities safely and comfortably. For example, Andrew Gurza (2022) authors a detailed blog post with tips for people to give and receive oral sex while one partner is using a wheelchair on their Bump!n website, where they sell an accessory for people with mobility constraints to more comfortably access and use a variety of sex toys. Tools with remote controls, long handles, wedges and pillows to prop up body parts, strap on harnesses that affix to a hand, thigh, or arm can give people access to different ways for their bodies and their partners' bodies to interact. The price of specifically designed toys in body safe, easy to clean materials may be a barrier to accessing these helpful and necessary tools.

In addition to price, having clean, safe storage space to keep toys and props easily available may be prioritized or deprioritized depending on someone's housing and accessibility resource situation. Policy can address this access inequality. For example, in Australia, the National Disability Insurance Scheme (NDIS) allows recipients to purchase accessible sex toys that enable independence with support benefits (National Disability Insurance Agency, 2022). Increasingly, sex toys offer new forms of accessibility and create additional opportunities for a wider variety of users to expand their practices safely and pleasurably. Additional research describing leisure benefits of BDSM participation experienced by disabled people is needed. Evidence quantifying benefits of social programs to promote sexual access could aid in the establishment and expansion of other policies.

## BDSM-Based Altered Cognitive States as Reason and Release

Motivations for pursuing kink/BDSM are innumerable, yet the hunt for altered cognitive states, like *subspace* and *topspace*, are ubiquitous across highly localized regional kink scenes and among kinksters. Expect to hear these phrases when providing kink-affirming care to clients. *Topspace* is characterized by a feeling of flow and focus on the present activity and moment; *subspace* is characterized by a feeling of euphoria and deep sense of relaxation (Ambler et al., 2016; Newmahr, 2010). *Topspace*, researchers hypothesize, is an altered state of consciousness that is complex and extremely rewarding (Ambler et al., 2016). *Subspace* has also been hypothesized to arise from "transient hypofrontality" – a phenomenon that occurs in the brain when it diverts energetic resources to other parts of the brain – and is the same mechanism that creates a "runner's high" (Ambler et al., 2016). In other words, kinksters both seek and savor altered cognitive states in BDSM play because both topping and bottoming can result in a profoundly pleasurable physiological response. Disabled people can take either topping or bottoming roles, or opt to switch as well.

Current understandings of altered cognitive states in kink are both physiological and psychological. For example, Klement et al. (2016) measured cortisol and psychological distress levels before, during, and after the *Dance of Souls* – a group ritual where participants applied temporary piercings over their bodies and some danced with weights that were affixed to those temporary piercings. These scholars noted that, although cortisol levels increased during the *Dance of Souls*, psychological stress levels decreased. Put another way, whereas the participants' levels of bodily stress increased, their psychological stress dwindled, resulting in reports of psychological relief. Because disabled people experience unique physical stressors and have divergent cognitive experiences, the altered states of BDSM play can be particularly salient to this population.

### *Neurodivergence*

Neurodivergence refers to a term and activism movement, emerging in the 1990s, that denotes and embraces brains that function outside of the "normal" or "neurotypical" range that most people inhabit (Kapp, 2020; Sickels, 2021). Autistic people have historically been viewed as leading the neurodivergent movement and recognize that the way the autistic brain works is not inherently a deficit, and that change demanded by normative social culture is the source of the challenges autistic people face while navigating the world (Baumer & Frueh, 2021; Kapp, 2020). The neurodivergent movement also includes people who have other kinds of thinking differences, such as obsessive-compulsive disorder, post-traumatic stress disorder, attention-deficit/hyperactivity disorder, traumatic brain injury, dyslexia, Tourette's syndrome, and more (Kapp, 2020). Within neurodivergent communities, neurodiversity is celebrated as a valuable dimension of human difference. To learn more about neurodivergence and sexuality, please read Chapter 4.

Neurodivergent people are as sexually diverse as neurotypical people and engage in sexual activities for many reasons and with varied motivations. BDSM is a tool that neurodivergent people can use to explore their sexualities while honoring their unique needs in an environment that embraces their experience. For example, BDSM play and roles often are pre-determined and structured in a way that creates an explicit script, which may be easier to follow for an autistic person (Sickels, 2021). Since BDSM activities are so diverse, there are opportunities to form special interests or allow those with ADHD to explore multiple areas. BDSM communities can become an affirming place where an autistic person can act on their special interests (Rosqvist & Jackson-Perry, 2020; Sickels, 2021). BDSM play can also allow people to safely explore sensory needs and share a mutual understanding of sensory experiences with their play partner(s) (Jackson-Perry et al., 2020). This mutual understanding can become an outlet for neurodivergent people. BDSM helps bridge mutual understanding of unique needs and wants between parties.

## Negotiating Consent and Disability

Disabled people face denial of autonomy over their sexual and reproductive health. Interpersonally, disabled people experience consent violation more often than their abled peers. Societal consent violations include sterilization and forced contraceptive use (Mapuranga & Musingafi, 2019). Courts often attempt to protect disabled people against sexual violence by describing attributes of disability that render a person unable to communicate sexual dissent or consent (O'Connell, 2019; State v. Fourtin, 2012). Institutions (e.g., nursing homes, care facilities) adopt rules of sexual conduct to protect residents. At times, these rules deny the sexuality of older adults and disabled people (Metzger, 2017). These approaches, rooted in a medical model of disability, focus on individual differences as the source of disability.

Though well intended, these measures perpetuate the myth that disabled people may not be totally free to consent to sex, creating risk for disabled people engaging in BDSM and their partners. For example, a mandatory reporter, predisposed to look for signs of abuse, may not believe a disabled person's self-report of consensual participation in impact play and conclude that bruising is a result of non-consensual physical abuse. A social perspective of disability addresses how context influences disabled peoples' sexual access and autonomy (O'Connell, 2019). Access is a good faith effort to include disabled people in sexual community and autonomy is ability to achieve actualized pleasurable sexual experience (including consent, sexual enjoyment, and sexual and reproductive actualization). A social model of disabled consent aligns closely with frameworks of consent within kink spaces. Kink communities may be particularly well suited to support the sexual access and autonomy of disabled people.

In kink spaces, common frameworks for discussing consent include Freely-Given, Reversible, Informed, Enthusiastic, Specific, Sober (FRIESS) and Risk-Aware Consensual Kink (RACK) frameworks (Gombos, 2022; Planned Parenthood, 2018). Each of these frameworks acknowledges that there are risks involved in kink/BDSM play and ensures that all participants are aware of potential risks and can negotiate harm-reduction measures in advance. Specifically, they ensure that harm reduction plans can be implemented in the moment and empower participants to state their needs, their boundaries, and opt in and out of the risks involved in the scene. These frameworks provide a community context where consent needs of disabled people can be fully met without deviation from the existing social script or community norms. For example, a disabled person who depends on partners or community members to facilitate their sexual experience by ensuring access to communication aids or assisting with physical positioning during a scene can use negotiation to establish their needs before playing (Kattari, 2015). Through negotiation, disabled persons co-create interdependent sexual experiences in which their reliance on others, understood and consented to by all participants, is transformed from dependence (which the medical model would label vulnerability) into a tool for sexual access and autonomy.

O'Connell (2019) argues that sexual autonomy and access are fundamental to disabled consent. Autonomy is an embodied awareness of individual experience (O'Connell, 2019), requiring acknowledgment of social setting where participants must be co-creators, where each person can imagine the embodied experience of the sexual activity, predict how the interaction may go, and influence the outcome of the interaction based on this. Consent is fundamentally required to achieve an actualized pleasurable sexual experience and sexual autonomy. Enthusiastic consent has a similar meaning in the kink community. Both require continuous, uncoerced, eager affirmation of desire to participate for a sexual interaction to continue (Wex Definitions Team, 2022). By focusing on the affirmative aspect of consent, we can generate a more inclusive understanding of what negotiating consent may look like among disabled people. Presently, there is very little research describing the disabled experience of consent, which is crucial to sexual access for disabled people. The BDSM community may be uniquely positioned collaborators because of the culture of consent.

## Best Practices

You are reminded of implicit power dynamics during each interaction with your patients or clients, because your professional calendar is populated with people seeking your expertise, your specialty knowledge, access to potential referrals and medication, and education. Your continued education facilitates practical and innovative care of your clients or patients, especially regarding BDSM practices and patients with disabilities. You can provide positive, affirming care to your patients while supporting their choice to have needs met through play.

Kink-affirming mental healthcare can extend beyond discussing the mechanics of sex, because it is set up to explore complicated, interlocking experiences, preferences, self-concepts, and belief systems. The therapy room is a rich environment for the client to explore both their sexuality and barriers to an enriching sex life. In the mental health field, there has been a more prominent and sustained call for better training regarding kink/BDSM (Sprott & Randall, 2017). Noting and checking your own assumptions and biases about who is interested in kink activities and the types of activities partaken can allow you to focus on the needs and requests of your clients. Fundamental to preventing your assumptions hindering your care of clients is not to impose your beliefs on gender and heterosexuality into your clients' behavior.

In your practice with clients or patients, their relationships and sexual behavior might come up regularly, occasionally, or never at all. Check in with your professional (and personal!) codes of ethics when considering how you work with disabled clients, and how you support your clients in this aspect of their lives and experiences. The more you consider your own biases and lived experiences around these activities, the better you will understand how your perspectives influence your ability to provide care to people with different experiences.

## Classroom Activity

**Work on maintaining neutral reactions:** When providing care and services for disabled clients, you may encounter information that is surprising or displeasing to you. Monitoring your verbal and physical reactions to what you learn about from your clients is an important practice in building and maintaining trust.

1. With a partner or small group in class, take roles of provider and client, and observer(s).
2. Have the learner in the client role talk through specific sex practices for one minute.
   a. This is practice for the "client" to comfortably talk about sex practices too! If you are looking for examples to guide your conversation, use the Internet and your imagination to describe a sex act.

3. The learner in the provider role should acknowledge and respond to the client in an affirming and validating way.
4. Together in the group, reflect on what body language, facial expressions, verbal, and physical reactions came up in this time. Collect reflections from the provider, client, and observer roles. Did your behavior match your intention of delivering affirming feedback? What would you do differently?
5. Repeat again in the same roles for 30 seconds, implementing what you learned from the first practice.
6. Rotate roles through repeating this exercise giving everyone at least two sessions to implement changes and have additional practice.
7. Reflect individually – are there certain practices or descriptions that are harder for you to react to than others? Why is that? What open listening skills do you do well when you are more comfortable? How will you use these skills when you are less comfortable?

**Referring:** Sometimes, you might encounter a client with needs beyond your scope of practice. This is normal in all circumstances; recognizing this and respecting your own boundaries are vital to providing your clients the best care. This exercise will help you refer out to specialists who provide kink-affirming and kink-specific care, when it is appropriate for you to do so.

1. With a partner or small group in class, search for a local provider who specializes in kink-affirming care. Consider providers in a variety of roles (e.g., educator, mental healthcare provider, physical therapist, occupational therapist, physical healthcare provider, sexual surrogate).
2. What can you learn about this provider, about who they support, and how they support their clients? Document three pieces of evidence about this provider's kink-affirming work.
3. Consider how you can assess the provider's capacity to accommodate your clients with disabilities? Document three aspects of how you might know providers are appropriate to refer to for disabled clients.
4. Write a script of how you will offer this provider to your clients or introduce a referral.
5. With your partner or small group, practice offering this referral.

## Conclusion

Throughout this chapter, we've discussed many aspects of kink/BDSM play, including why disabled people practice it and how disabled kink practitioners negotiate accessibility and consent with intimate partners. You should consider how you want to support disabled clients in safely accessing and engaging in kink/BDSM activities, as well as how you can offer non-judgmental support when disabled clients discuss such desires or experiences. By valuing and respecting the experiences our clients share with us, we can destigmatize disabled people's participation in kink/BDSM and promote informed dialogue about the transformative benefits disabled clients may gain from adding this play to their sexual repertoire.

## Resources

**Kat Blaque,** www.youtube.com/watch?v=usgBdw0FjIg
Illustrator, Animator and Public Speaker.
**John Brownstone & Kayla Lords,** https://lovingbdsm.net/
A married D/s couple, sharing thoughts, feelings, and experiences on BDSM.
**Andrew Gurza,** www.andrewgurza.com/
Disability Awareness Consultant and Cripple Content Creator.
**Dr. Lee Phillips,** www.drleephillips.com/post/sex-and-chronic-illness
Psychotherapist.
**Evie Lupine,** www.youtube.com/@EvieLupine/featured
Peer educator on all things related to BDSM, kink and alternative lifestyles.
**Ruby Rousson,** https://arousibility.com/category/articles/bdsm-and-fetish/
I am a queer chronically ill disabled British writer, sex worker, sex educator and founder of Arousibility, Parlour Talk and The Ruby Umbrella.
**Morgan Thorne,** http://msmorganthorne.com/
Sexuality and kink/BDSM educator
**Xan West,** *Being a Disabled Top in Kink Community* https://xanwest.wordpress.com/2015/05/01/being-a-disabled-top-in-kink-community/

## References

Ambler, J. K., Lee, E. M., Klement, K. R., Loewald, T., Comber, E. M., Hanson, S. A., Cutler, B., Cutler, N., & Sagarin, B. J. (2016). Consensual BDSM facilitates role-specific altered states of consciousness: A preliminary study. *Psychology of Consciousness: Theory, Research, and Practice*, 4(1), 75–91. http://dx.doi.org/10.1037/cns0000097

Bauer, R. (2017). Bois and grrrls meet their daddies and mommies on gender playgrounds: Gendered age play in the les-bi-trans-queer BDSM communities. *Sexualities*, 21(1–2), 139–155. https://doi.org/10.1177/1363460716676987

Baumer, N., & Frueh, J. (2021, November 23). *What is neurodiversity?* Harvard Health Publishing. www.health.harvard.edu/blog/what-is-neurodiversity-202111232645

Brothers, D. (1997). The leather princess: Sadomasochism as the rescripting of traumatic scenarios. In A. I. Goldberg (Ed.), *Progress in self psychology: Conversations in self psychology* (pp. 245–268). Routledge.

Brown, A., Barker, E. D., & Rahman, Q. (2020). A systematic scoping review of the prevalence, etiological, psychological, and interpersonal factors associated with BDSM. *Journal of Sex Research*, 57(6), 781–811. https://doi.org/10.1080/00224499.2019.1665619

Carlström, C. (2018). BDSM, interaction rituals and open bodies. *Sexuality & Culture*, 22, 209–219. https://doi.org/10.1007/s12119-017-9461-7

Cascalheira, C. J., Ijebor, E. E., Salkowitz, Y., Hitter, T. L., & Boyce, A. (2021). Curative kink: Survivors of early abuse transform trauma through BDSM. *Sexual and Relationship Therapy*. https://doi.org/10.1080/14681994.2021.1937599

Christofferson, M. N. (2019). Violent crime against children with disabilities: A nationwide prospective birth-cohort study. *Child Abuse and Neglect*, 98, 104150. https://doi.org/10.1016/j.chiabu.2019.104150.

Crosse, S. B., Kaye, E., & Ratmofsky, A. C. (1993). *A report on the maltreatment of children with disabilities. (Contract No: 105–89–1630)*. National Center on Child Abuse and Neglect.

Easton, D. (2007). Shadowplay: S/M journeys to our selves. In D. Langdridge & M. Barker (Eds.), *Safe, sane and consensual: Contemporary perspectives on sadomasochism* (pp. 223–234). Palgrave Macmillan.

Glyde, T. (2015). BDSM: Psychotherapy's grey area. *The Lancet Psychiatry*, 2(3), 211–213.

Gombos, R. (2022, July 7). Kink-aware therapy: Consent & negotiation. *The Affirmative Couch*. https://affirmativecouch.com/kink-aware-therapy-consent-and-negotiation/

Gurza, A. (2022, March 3). Crip tips: How to have great oral sex as a wheelchair user. *Bump'n*. https://getbumpn.com/blogs/bumpn-blog/crip-tips-how-to-have-great-oral-sex-as-a-wheelchair-user

Hammers, C. (2014). Corporeality, sadomasochism and sexual trauma. *Body & Society*, 20(2), 68–90. https://doi.org/10.1177/1357034X13477159

Hammers, C. (2019). Reworking trauma through BDSM. *Signs: Journal of Women in Culture and Society*, 44(2), 491–514. https://doi.org/10.1086/699370

Hillier, K. (2019). *The impact of childhood Trauma and personality on kinkiness in adulthood* (Order No. 13813160). (6597) (Doctoral dissertation). Walden University. ProQuest Dissertations & Theses Global. (2204915839). http://libproxy.lib.unc.edu/login?url=www.proquest.com/dissertations-theses/impact-childhood-trauma-personality-on-kinkiness/docview/2204915839/se-2

Hughes, S. D., & Hammack, P. L. (2020). Narratives of the origins of kinky sexual desire held by users of a kink-oriented social networking website. *The Journal of Sex Research*, 1(12). https://doi.org/10.1080/00224499.2020.1840495

Jackson, T. P., Stabile, V. S., & McQueen, K. A. K. (2014). The global burden of chronic pain. *ASA Newsletter*, 78(6), 24–27. https://pubs.asahq.org/monitor/article-abstract/78/6/24/3059/The-Global-Burden-Of-Chronic-Pain?redirectedFrom=fulltext

Jackson-Perry, D., Rosqvist, H. B., Annable, J. L., & Kourti, M. (2020). Sensory strangers: Travels in normate sensory worlds. In H. B. Rosqvist, N. Chown, & A. Stenning (Eds.), *Neurodiversity studies: A new critical paradigm* (1st ed., pp. 125–140). Routledge. https://doi.org/10.4324/9780429322297-12

Jones, Z. (2020). *Pleasure, community, and marginalization in rope bondage: A qualitative investigation into a BDSM subculture* (Doctoral dissertation). Carleton University.

Kapp, S. K. (2020). *Autistic community and the neurodiversity movement: Stories from the frontline*. Springer Nature. https://library.oapen.org/handle/20.500.12657/23177

Kattari, S. K. (2015). "Getting it": Identity and sexual communication for sexual and gender minorities with physical disabilities. *Sexuality & Culture*, 19(4), 882–899. https://doi.org/10.1007/s12119-015-9298-x

Klement, K. R., Lee, E. M., Ambler, J. K., Hanson, S. A., Comber, E., Wietting, D., Wagner, M. F., Burns, V. R., Cutler, B., Cutler, N., Reid, E., & Sagarin, B. J. (2016).

Extreme rituals in a BDSM context: The physiological and psychological effects of the "dance of souls". *Culture, Health & Sexuality, 19*(4), 453–469. https://doi.org/10.1080/13691058.2016.1234648

Lindemann, D. (2011). BDSM as therapy? *Sexualities, 14*(2), 151–172. https://doi.org/10.1177/1363460711399038

Mapuranga, B., & Musingafi, M. C. (2019). Sex, intimacy and reproductive rights for women with disabilities in Zimbabwe: A snapshot of the views of women with disabilities in Harare. *Journal of Culture, Society, and Development, 51*. https://doi.org/10.7176/JCSD

Metzger, E. (2017). Ethics and intimate sexual activity in long-term care. *AMA Journal of Ethics, 19*(7), 640–648. https://doi.org/10.1001/journalofethics.2017.19.7.ecas1-1707

National Disability Insurance Agency. (2022). *How the NDIS works*. National Disability Insurance Scheme (NDIS). www.ndis.gov.au/

Newmahr, S. (2010). Rethinking kink: Sadomasochism as serious leisure. *Qualitative Sociology, 33*(3), 313–331. https://doi.org/10.1007/s11133-010-9158-9

O'Connell, H. (2019). Cripping consent: Autonomy and access. In J. J. Fischel (Ed.), *Screw consent: A better politics of sexual justice* (pp. 135–171). University of California Press. https://doi.org/10.1525/california/9780520295407.003.0006

Pitcher, M. H., Von Korff, M., Bushnell, M. C., & Porter, L. (2019). Prevalence and profile of high-impact chronic pain in the United States. *The Journal of Pain, 20*(2), 146–160. https://doi.org/10.1016/j.jpain.2018.07.006

Planned Parenthood. (2018, April 3). *Say yes to our consent partnership*. Planned Parenthood. www.plannedparenthood.org/planned-parenthood-pacific-southwest/blog/say-yes-to-our-consent-partnership#:~:text=Planned%20Parenthood%20defines%20consent%20as,influence%20of%20drugs%20or%20alcohol

Reynolds, D. (2007). Disability and BDSM: Bob Flanagan and the case for sexual rights. *Sexuality Research & Social Policy, 4*(1), 40–52. https://doi.org/10.1525/srsp.2007.4.1.40

Richters, J., De Visser, R. O., Rissel, C. E., Grulich, A. E., & Smith, A. M. A. (2008). Demographic and psychosocial features of participants in bondage and discipline, "sadomasochism" or dominance and submission (BDSM): Data from a national survey. *The Journal of Sexual Medicine, 5*(7), 1660–1668. https://doi.org/10.1111/j.1743-6109.2008.00795.x

Rosqvist, H. B., & Jackson-Perry, D. (2020). Not doing it properly? (Re)producing and resisting knowledge through narratives of autistic sexualities. *Sexuality and Disability, 39*(2), 327–344. https://doi.org/10.1007/s11195-020-09624-5

Savvakis, M., & Nikos, K. (2019). Quality of life and chronic pain: Coping practices and experiences of patients with musculoskeletal diseases. *International Journal of Caring Sciences, 12*(3), 1423–1429. www.academia.edu/42114933/Quality_of_Life_and_Chronic_Pain_Coping_Practises_and_Experiences_of_Patients_with_Musculoskeletal_Diseases

Sheppard, E. (2018). Using pain, living with pain. *Feminist Review, 120*, 54–69. https://doi.org/10.1057/s41305-018-0142-7

Sheppard, E. (2019). Chronic pain as fluid, BDSM as control. *Disability Studies Quarterly, 39*(2), n.p. https://doi.org/10.18061/dsq.v39i2.6353

Sickels, L. A. (2021). Spectrums: Autism, sex, gender, and sexuality. In *The Routledge international handbook of social work and sexualities* (pp. 251–268). Routledge.

Simula, B. L. (2019). Pleasure, power, and pain: A review of the literature on the experiences of BDSM participants. *Sociology Compass*, *13*(3), e12668. https://doi.org/10.1111/soc4.12668

Sobsey, D. (1994). *Violence and abuse in the lives of people with disabilities: The end of silent acceptance?* Paul H. Brookes.

Sprott, R. A., & Randall, A. (2017). Health disparities among kinky sex practitioners. *Current Sexual Health Reports*, *9*, 104–108. https://doi.org/10.1007/s11930-017-0113-6

Sprott, R. A., & Williams, D. J. (2019). Is BDSM a sexual orientation or serious leisure? *Current Sexual Health Reports*. https://doi.org/10.1007/s11930-019-00195-x

*State v. Fourtin*, No. 18523. 307 Conn. 186, 52 A.3d 674 Connecticut – Case Law – VLEX 887370846. (2012). https://case-law.vlex.com/vid/state-v-fourtin-no-887370846

Sullivan, P. M., & Knutson, J. F. (2000). Maltreatment and disabilities: A population-based epidemiological study. *Child Abuse and Neglect*, *24*(10), 1257–1273. https://doi.org/10.1016/S0145-2134(00)00190-3

Tellier, S. (2017). Advancing the discourse: Disability and BDSM. *Sexuality and Disability*, *35*, 485–493. https://doi.org/10.1007/s11195-017-9504-x

Ten Brink, S., Coppens, V., Huys, W., & Morrens, M. (2021). The psychology of kink: A survey study into the relationships of trauma and attachment style with BDSM interests. *Sexuality Research and Social Policy*, *18*, 1–12. https://doi.org/10.1007/s13178-020-00438-w.

Thomas, J. N. (2020). BDSM as trauma play: An autoethnographic investigation. *Sexualities*, *23*(5–6), 917–933. https://doi.org/10.1177/1363460719861800

Thomas, J. N., & Williams, D. J. (2018). Fucking with fluids and wet with desire: Power and humiliation using cum, piss, and blood. In D. Holmes, S. J. Murray, & T. Foth (Eds.), *Radical sex between men: Assembling desiring-machines* (pp. 142–150). Routledge.

Turley, E. L. (2016). 'Like nothing I've ever felt before': Understanding consensual BDSM as embodied experience. *Psychology & Sexuality*, *7*(2), 149–162.

Wex Definitions Team. (2022). *Consent*. Legal Information Institute (LII). www.law.cornell.edu/wex/consent

# 23
# WEIGHT STIGMA, DESIRABILITY, AND DISABILITY

*Hillary K. Hecht, Erin N. Harrop, and Ben Lemanski*

## Introduction

Weight stigma refers to the systemic devaluation of people in larger bodies, which results in inequitable distribution of resources and privileges based on body size. Weight stigma results in privileging those in the thinnest, most muscular bodies by devaluing those in the fattest bodies. While weight stigma negatively harms people in all body sizes and shapes, weight stigma is most harmful to people in the largest bodies. Furthermore, this hierarchy of bodies is also racialized, gendered, and ableist, resulting in compounding marginalization for those who are both fat and disabled, in addition to other intersecting identities (Jackson et al., 2015; Schafer & Ferraro, 2011; Strings, 2019; Smith, 2020).

There are many terms used to describe the systematic bias, discrimination, mistreatment, abuse, and violence directed toward higher weight individuals (e.g., fatphobia, fatmisia, anti-fat bias, sizeism, and body size discrimination). For the purposes of this chapter, we use the term "weight stigma" to describe all of these varied experiences, while also acknowledging that this term has been critiqued by activists as being too palatable. We avoid using the terms "overweight" and "obese," as these terms inherently pathologize and medicalize larger bodies (Meadows & Daníelsdóttir, 2016). Rather, we refer to such bodies as "larger" and "higher weight." Additionally, we also use the term "fat" as both a neutral descriptive term, and as a political identity, in line with fat liberation advocates (Meadows & Daníelsdóttir, 2016).

*Accessibility and Inclusion*

Accessibility and inclusion are critically important to both fat and disability advocates. Many modern environments are not designed for fat and/

DOI: 10.4324/9781003308331-28

or disabled bodies, creating systemic barriers to fat and/or disabled people being meaningfully engaged in public/private life. For example, when parking spaces are close together, those in larger bodies and those using mobility devices have difficulty accessing cars. When chairs have immoveable arms, narrow seats, or roll, people in larger bodies or with disabilities may struggle to use the chair safely and comfortably (Lawton et al., 2008; Hu et al., 2017; Molenbroek et al., 2017). When bathroom stalls are narrow or doors open inward, those in larger bodies and/or with mobility concerns may struggle to navigate in and out of toilets, and access cleansing products and menstruation product disposal (Greed, 2010). Airline seats tend to be uniformly narrow. Recent measurements show that the average width of seats is 17.6 inches, excluding many passengers needing more space to comfortably travel (Molenbroek et al., 2017). Accessing safe, supportive, and comfortable seating in educational settings, movie theaters, sporting stadiums, restaurants, transportation, and medical care is challenging for many fat and disabled individuals alike (Brewis et al., 2017; Shanouda, 2021; Stevens, 2018). While fat and disability activists often debate how and to what extent these identities overlap (Herndon, 2021), both fat and disability activists emphasize the importance of designing spaces and resources with body diversity in mind.

To this end, fat activists collaborate with disability activists in demanding universal design (Pritchard, 2014). In fashion, activists request broader size ranges for employment, movement, and celebratory clothing (Alberga et al., 2019; Greenleaf et al., 2020; Mohan, 2021; Peters, 2022). Likewise, activists insist on athletic and recreational equipment for all body sizes, more availability of accessibility devices, furniture (The Wright Stuff, 2022), transportation, (Molenbroek et al., 2017), and healthcare (Phelan et al., 2015), among other tools designed for fat and disabled users (Brewis et al., 2017). It is important that accessible items be widely available, affordable, clearly measured and labeled with user weight limits, and comparably priced to items designed for smaller bodies. When these are not, fat disabled people spend undue money, time, and effort acquiring accessible items; this "Fat Tax" highlights how fat and disabled people face compounding forces of social marginalization and impoverishment.

## Weight Stigma: Past and Present

### *Historical Context of Desirability and Beauty Ideals*

Contrary to modern discourse, fatness has not always been perceived as a negative trait. In some cultures and time periods, fuller, fatter figures were seen as more attractive and viewed as a proxy for wealth (Seid, 1994). In contemporary Mauritania's Moor society, bigger bodies are lauded, and women sometimes strive to make their bodies bigger for social gain (Esposito, 2022;

Tovar, 2018). Similar trends were documented in Northern Africa during the 1500s (Strings, 2019). If a person had visible cellulite, stretchmarks, or body rolls, they were considered healthy, vital, sexually desirable, and admirable; this is in stark contrast to present North American scholars who cite double chins as detracting from facial beauty and warranting surgical intervention (Locker, 1864; Brooke, 1913; Shridharani et al., 2020).

Fatness has a distinctly racialized history, with frequent intersections formed between race, class, and body size (Strings, 2019). Sociologist Sabrina Strings cites that prior to the transatlantic slave trade, European artists "idealized" women's bodies with plump chins, round arms, and full bellies. As a result, white women in the 1520s (much like today) used gendered clothes to accentuate and achieve these aesthetic goals (Strings, 2019). As Europeans consolidated power through global colonialism, they observed and encountered differences between common white European features and those of African descendants. Thus, redefining beauty ideals became a way to distinguish race, gender, and class.

In the 1620s, as the sugar industry began to boom, the term "obesity" was created to describe the growing number of fat, white, wealthy women with ready access to food and alcohol, marking their higher-class standing (Strings, 2019). However, while fatness was admired in women, masculine norms of slenderness implied that fatness in men was both a moral and intellectual failure (Strings, 2019). Later in the 1900s, this thin ideal spread widely across genders, as slender bodies came to distinguish social class, separating the elite from lower classes, "immoral" citizens, and people of non-white racial groups (Strings, 2019).

### *The Moralization of Body Size*

In the 1900s, femininity, body shape and size, skin color, and facial features became essential markers of sexual desirability (Strings, 2019, pp. 76–78). Fatter bodies became moralized and linked to traits of indulgence, gluttony, and laziness (Strings, 2019). Thus people in larger bodies went from being considered desirable, well-resourced citizens to overindulgent, lower-lower class sinners, particularly as the Protestant Church gained traction (Strings, 2019, p. 165). This moralization of fatness has persisted to present day, with fat bodies increasingly linked to unhealthiness, lack of self-control, poverty, and immorality.

Such conceptualizations culminated in the rhetoric of the " '*Obesity*' *Epidemic.*" The "*War on 'Obesity'* " was declared in the late 1900s in response to growing public health concerns about rising body weights in the United States (Bacon, 2010). This Western media campaign focuses on scientific literature highlighting correlations between weight and various disease states, asserting that fat people are destined to die early due to "excess weight" (World

Health Organization, 2020). Rising body weights have also been blamed, in part, for the planet's ecological collapse (Edwards & Roberts, 2009). In response, many governments and healthcare organizations promoted various "solutions" aimed at reducing population body size through dietary restriction and exercise. Many of these interventions have been critiqued for worsening mental health (e.g., eating disorders) and physical health (e.g., weight cycling), while disregarding important issues such as food insecurity, cultural factors, and increased societal stigma (Bacon, 2010; O'Hara & Taylor, 2018; Rich & Evans, 2005).

### The Tenuous Association Between Weight and Health

The body mass index (BMI) measurement has been widely critiqued (Bacon, 2010; Nuttall, 2015; Tomiyama et al., 2016). While BMI has been largely utilized as an individual health indicator in modern medical care, it was initially designed by a mathematician as a way to define the "average (ideal) man" established based on a white European population mean heights and weights (Eknoyan, 2008). Though BMI is a cheap-to-collect and easy-to-calculate biomarker, it has demonstrated poor predictability of individual health (Tomiyama et al., 2016). For example, "grade 1 obesity" is not associated with any increased mortality risk compared to "normal" BMI category participants, and people categorized as "overweight" demonstrate lower mortality risk than those with "normal" weight (Flegal et al., 2013). In the U.S., nearly half of "overweight" individuals, 29% of "obese" individuals, and 16% of "obese grade 2/3" individuals present as metabolically healthy (Tomiyama et al., 2016), with over 30% of "ideal" BMI participants measured as cardio-metabolically unhealthy. The use of this measurement at an individual level inadvertently pathologizes asymptomatic higher weight bodies while missing important symptoms in lower weight bodies. By applying pathologized, category labels to BMI thresholds, we medically "disable" people who people who are in fact not disabled and do not have concerns nor limitations about the size of their bodies.

Despite this scientific evidence, BMI continues to be widely used in healthcare settings, contributing to the further stigmatization of higher weight people. Alongside financial conflicts of interest, the prevalence of "obesity" skyrocketed overnight when BMI thresholds changed arbitrarily in 2000, fueling incentives for pharmaceutical companies to produce, market, and sell new for-profit weight-loss products and services (Bacon, 2010; Moynihan, 2006; Gordon & Hobbes, 2021). Today, BMI measurements are used by health insurance companies to restrict access to care and increase profits; such practices have resulted in many higher weight people being unable to access needed surgeries, including orthopedic surgery, gallbladder removal, fertility care, and gender-affirming surgeries (Zingg et al., 2016; McPhail et al., 2016; Brownstone et al., 2021; Griffin et al., 2021). Sadly, this delay (or refusal) of care to higher weight people often results in heavier individuals living with disabling and painful conditions that could have been treated (e.g., unresolved joint injuries) for years, and at times, the rest of their lives.

In addition to creating barriers to care, weight stigma is associated with many negative health outcomes. Patients who experience weight-based discrimination show increased inflammatory markers (Sutin et al., 2014), risk of dementia (Sutin et al., 2019), and psychological burden (Jackson et al., 2015). Fat shaming, whether by strangers, doctors, family members, or self-inflicted, is associated with increased stress (Major et al., 2018; Tomiyama et al., 2018; Tomiyama, 2014), increased cortisol production (Tomiyama, 2014), and deterred help-seeking (Mensinger et al., 2018; Phelan et al., 2015). As a result of experiencing weight-based microaggressions, patients may delay or avoid important healthcare including sexual health screening and treatment, reproductive care, and care for disabilities and chronic illnesses – each of which may impact one's ability to be safely and pleasurably sexual (Munro, 2017).

While weight stigma manifests externally in various forms of discrimination, it also manifests in self-directed ways, called *"internalized weight stigma."* Internalized weight stigma is the degree to which an individual believes their own body to be unacceptable due to their weight. The degree of weight dissatisfaction was found to be a better predictor of physical and mental health than calculated BMI (Muennig et al., 2008); thus, internalized weight stigma may be a more important driver of health inequities than weight itself. People who report higher levels of internalized weight stigma benefit less from health-based interventions, experience more disordered eating, and are less likely to engage in healthy exercise, independent of body size (Mensinger et al., 2016, 2018, Mensinger & Meadows, 2017; Mensinger, 2021). These findings suggest that teaching people in larger bodies to criticize their bodies (or strive for thinness) may have iatrogenic effects.

### *Opportunities for Size-Affirming Care*

Fat disabled people need tailored care specific to their individual health needs, including primary, preventive, sexual health, orthopedic, cardiac and metabolic, reproductive, mental and emotional care, and additional services. Navigating medical settings which are ill-equipped to care for larger bodies can be disabling.

Providers offering gender-affirming care have been criticized for gatekeeping potentially life-saving procedures (like top surgery), by insisting that fat patients lose weight prior to surgery, despite a lack of evidence to support this practice (Brownstone et al., 2021; King, 2022). When fat disabled patients seek care for joint pain that is limiting their mobility, they often encounter gatekeeping, insurance denials, and providers who focus on weight loss rather than supporting client's mobility goals in seeking safe ways to rehabilitate their joints and gain mobility. Patient advocacy and the availability of correctly sized mobility aids (e.g., crutches, wheelchairs) which are sturdy and intended to support people of higher weights can support people receiving appropriate, goal-oriented care.

Fat disabled people seek care while inhabiting the broadest range of sexualities, genders, and sexual orientations. By respectfully asking about patients' identities, providers can skillfully explore patients' desires for exploratory and pleasurable sex, including solo play and play with partners of all genders, sexual orientations, sizes, and disability statuses. It is recommended that OB/GYN clinics be equipped with exam tables and scanning equipment graded to support patients of higher weights and widths, a wide range of exam gown sizes up to 6xl or larger, extended sizes of blood pressure cuffs to take accurate readings of all patients' vital signs, appropriate size range of gynecological exam tools, and tailored doula and postpartum care, in order to best support all members of the community in accessing and receiving these services (Fonseca-Reyes et al., 2003; James, 2021; Alberga et al., 2019; Tovar, 2020). Comparably, providers should educate higher-weight people on birth control practices, namely awareness that some pharmaceuticals, including Plan B contraceptives, have reduced effectiveness for people who weigh more than 154.32 pounds (Kirley, 2014).

Healthcare providers have been critiqued for touching fat patients less frequently than thin patients (Watson et al., 2008), and using rougher touch, based on the faulty assumption that fatter bodies are less sensitive to pain. People in the biggest bodies have a wide range of pain tolerances, and need caretaking that is respectful of pain reduction. Providers may habitually over-test for or over-prescribe medications for high blood pressure or pre-diabetes care to patients based on body size, in the absence of more meaningful clinical indicators like actual blood pressure or A1C levels (Jones, 2008). Higher rates of surgical interventions for fat birthing people contributes to exacerbated birthing health disparities, particularly for fat people of color (Glazer et al., 2020). Overdiagnosis can increase feelings of illness in the absence of serious disease, leading patients to conclude that sometimes the treatment can be worse than the condition itself (Welch et al., 2011). Providers often have not encountered education about weight-inclusive care, highlighting the role that providers and organizations (through policies and procedures) can play in distinguishing when weight is a relevant factor in treatment (like dosing for anesthesia), when it is not particularly salient (like eligibility for gender-affirming care), and when it is likely to introduce bias or harms (Phelan et al., 2015).

### Desirability Politics, Fatness, and Disability

Desirability politics describe the socio-political contexts that uphold some bodies as worthy of desire, attention, and reward, at the expense of other bodies (Oteju, 2020). Fat disabled people have experienced less access to desirability and sexuality in modern western cultures. The aesthetic of those who are fat and disabled has been devalued; fat disabled bodies have been desexualized, labeled unattractive, and unable to benefit from the privileges of being considered "pretty" (e.g., thin, white, abled, and adhering to gendered norms; Harrison, 2021, pp. 11–13).

Desirability politics are influenced by sexual orientation and gender, and impact who we seek and choose as sexual and romantic partners. Norms within marginalized sexual orientations, such as gay, lesbian, bisexual, and queer groups adopt standards of who is desirable within these communities. Expansive body ideals among lesbian women may promote higher acceptance of body size (Bell et al., 2019). These norms come with their own liabilities, such as pressures toward thinness for the sake of androgyny for those who seek being perceived as less feminine. In Western cultures, gay men may face higher stigma around body size, shape, and muscularity, though there are subcultures of gay men's identities that desire, fetishize, and value larger body types (Calzo et al., 2017). Even when subcultures include broader ranges of beauty ideals regarding body size, people with visible disabilities are often notably absent.

Representation of a diverse range of people in happy, loving, sexually pleasurable relationships in media, on social media, and on dating or porn sites increases visibility for people in the largest bodies to express their sexualities and be desired. Spaces with limited representation of bodies (i.e., which cater to thin, young, white, able-bodied, cisheteronormative aesthetics) can be overtly othering to fat and/or disabled people. Likewise, physical and digital queer spaces that are inaccessible or shaming of diverse bodies can exacerbate social and romantic isolation for those in large and/or disabled bodies. Cultural norms do change over time, vary based on subculture identities (such as racial and cultural demographics), and are experienced based on community member's own lived intersecting identities.

### Fat, Disabled, and Pleasurable Sex

People of all sizes and abilities engage in sexual behaviors to bring themselves and their partner(s) pleasures. Pleasurable sex can include solo or partnered play, short-term or long-term romantic relationships, and casual hookups. In sexual situations, all participants deserve to have their sexual and safety needs met, including positioning, contraceptive use, and respected boundaries (Taylor, 2018; Young, 2022). Engaging in consensual, communicative, curiosity-driven sexual exploration can increase the comfort and pleasure of all involved.

For people who are fat and/or disabled, certain settings (e.g., locations, furniture) or sexual positions may make some sexual experiences uncomfortable or difficult to sustain. Mattresses intentionally designed to support larger bodies prevent bodies from sinking into it during sleep or sex (Big Fig, 2021). Depending on a partner's flexibility, strength, or mobility, some sexual positions may be more challenging to maintain comfortably with partners of different sizes. Tools like wedge pillows, ramps, swings, and positionable furniture can prop bodies into comfortable postures to allow all partners more access to their own and each other's bodies (Liberator, 2022).

Many people utilize toys to experience desired sensations. Some toys are designed without accounting for larger or disabled bodies, have shorter handles requiring more flexibility to reach parts of a person's body, limited lingerie sizing, or shorter straps on dildos that do not account for wearers' stomach. Sex toys with longer handles to extend reach, mindfully or remotely placed buttons and controls, lighter weight toys for less fatigue in holding, straps, slings, and harnesses can each offer support and ease to partners getting into and maintaining the positions they desire, as can non-size specific tools like lubricants. While specialty designed furniture can be prohibitively expensive, using pillows and props that you already have is an entryway to exploring options that feel good.

In all sexual encounters, curious communication and experimentation allow participants to figure out what they like. Feeling comfortable telling your partner(s) what you like, positions and sensations you would like to explore, setting boundaries, asserting what is and is not feeling good, and sharing goals for consensual sexual encounters can introduce additional pleasure for all involved. When aspects of sex don't go as expected or planned, having a lighthearted sense of humor about bodies and attempts to use them can be a way to playfully continue exploring. Abstaining from blaming your own or a partner's body for an experience prevents shame and can get you all back to creative problem-solving for how to try more pleasurable options.

## Integrating Weight-Inclusive Practices

Increasing competent medical, mental, and sexual healthcare requires that providers challenge our existing beliefs and internalized weight stigma through self-reflection, listen to our fat patients, and confront colleagues and organizational policies that perpetuate weight stigma. Professional codes of ethics state that it is ethically impermissible to conduct weight-stigmatizing practices (Ellis-Ordway & Ramseyer Winter, 2022).

*Referring to Fat People*

It is vitally important to be conscientious around our use of language (Meadows & Daníelsdóttir, 2016). We recommend avoiding terms such as "overweight" or "obese" as these have been repeatedly critiqued by fat activists as pathologizing fat bodies and perpetuating stigma (Wann, 1998). We also recommend against using terms like "ideal" or "normal" weight, as these terms imply there is an "ideal" or "normal" to which all bodies should conform. If required to use more medicalized terms, or refer to the BMI due to organizational policies, we recommend using quotes around historically harmful words, adding the caveat, "according to current BMI standards" to highlight the arbitrary and changing nature of BMI categories (Gordon, 2019). When discussing body size with patients, we recommend asking patients how they prefer to describe their body. Asking permission to refer to patients' bodies and body parts, then adopting the terms that patients claim for themselves, returns agency in self-identification. People may identify with some or none of these terms: fat, plus-sized, husky, big bodied, super fat, thick, and so on (Meadows & Daníelsdóttir, 2016). Similar to using identity indicators like pronouns, how a person refers to their body is a highly personal matter. As care and service-providing professionals, it is crucial to use professional judgment and rapport building skills to learn how your fat patients refer to their body size and ability.

*Body Size in Providing Care and Services*

Health At Every Size® (HAES) and other weight-inclusive approaches have become popular for treating fat patients (Bacon, 2010; Tylka et al., 2014). At their core, size-inclusive approaches ask providers to consider, "how would I treat this ailment if seen in a thin person?" considering various ways to decenter weight and recenter health behaviors and outcomes (Tylka et al., 2014). Size-inclusive approaches focus on patients receiving the treatment they need and deserve toward *their* holistic goals (Tylka et al., 2014).

The following brief suggestions are a starting place to implement size-affirming care. First, it is generally suggested that patients are only weighed when medically necessary (e.g., for dosing of certain medications, monitoring water retention). If a weight must be taken, inform the patient why this measure is necessary, request consent, take the measure in a private space, offer patients to orient on the scale so they don't have to observe the output reading, ensure that you make no verbal nor gestural comments about it, and ask whether or not the patient would like to know the measurement. If the patient elects not to know, ensure that their weight is not recorded on any discharge forms nor in fields they might see in their electronic health record. Avoid congratulating weight loss (as this could be the result of an illness, eating disorder, or other negative experience), or providing generic weight loss recommendations. It is also recommended to screen for eating disorders prior to recommending any changes in diet or exercise. Finally, ensure that appropriately sized equipment, clothing, and tools are readily available for all patients in waiting rooms, care, and discharge spaces.

## Classroom Activity: Representation in Media Consumption

This exercise invites you to consider whose voices and perspectives are represented in your personal and professional lives.

Step 1: In 30 seconds, jot down all the spaces where you regularly engage with images (e.g., pictures, memes, videos, films), audio (e.g., podcasts, radio, music, videos, films), and written text (e.g., news, books, magazines, academic writing, Twitter, blogs, short stories, poetry, newsletters).

Step 2: Thinking about some of the content that you've watched, listened to, or read recently, what kind of body sizes are represented? How did the creators note peoples' body sizes? Where and when were physical attributes pointed out? Which attributes were mentioned with positive connotations? Negative connotations? Whose bodies were upheld as the most worthy or attractive? Whose bodies did you find attractive?

Step 3: Choose one of the mediums you have consumed recently. How would you edit it to be more size affirming? Are there alternative sources or creators that you can add to your collection of regular consumption that are by fat creators and center a weight-affirming paradigm?

## Conclusions

Throughout this chapter, we explored the intersections between weight stigma and disability with a critical exploration of how this impacts sexuality and desirability. We invite all readers and practitioners to consider your scope of practice, and incremental updates you can make to contribute to dismantling weight stigma in your spaces.

## Resources

Podcasts:

a. Mercedes, M., Luna, C., Guffey, B., Underwood, J., & Harrison, D. L. (2021). *Unsolicited: Fatties talk back* [Podcast]. https://unsolicitedftb.libsyn.com/
b. Cox, J. A. R. (2017). *Fresh out the cocoon* [Podcast]. https://anchor.fm/fotcpodcast

c. Gordon, A., & Hobbes, M. (2021). *Maintenance phase* [Podcast]. www.maintenancephase.com/
d. Bisbing, Z., & Bloch, L. (2018). *The full bloom project* [Podcast]. www.fullbloomproject.com/podcast
e. Harrison, C. (2013). *Food psych* [Podcast]. https://christyharrison.com/foodpsych
f. Wong, A. (2017). *Disability visibility project* [Podcast]. https://disability-visibilityproject.com/podcast-2/

Books

g. Luna, C. (2022). *Revenge body* (1st. ed., p. 68). Nomadic Press.
h. Tovar, V. (2018). *You have the right to remain fat* (p. 128). The Feminist Press at CUNY.

Professional Organizations

i. Ashline, L. (2022). *Body liberation stock*. https://bodyliberationphotos.com/body-liberation-stock-body-fat-positive-diverse-photos/
j. Association for Size Diversity and Health. (2020). *Committed to size inclusivity in health*. https://asdah.org/
k. Fat Rose. (2020). *Fatties against fascism resist*. https://fatrose.org/
l. National Association to Advance Fat Acceptance. (2020). *Why NAAFA?* https://naafa.org/

**References**

Alberga, A. S., Edache, I. Y., Forhan, M., & Russell-Mayhew, S. (2019). Weight bias and health care utilization: A scoping review. *Primary Health Care Research & Development, 20*, e116. https://doi.org/10.1017/S1463423619000227

Bacon, L. (2010). *Health at every size: The surprising truth about your weight*. BenBella Books, Inc.

Bell, K., Rieger, E., & Hirsch, J. K. (2019). Eating disorder symptoms and proneness in gay men, lesbian women, and transgender and gender non-conforming adults: Comparative levels and a proposed mediational model. *Frontiers in Psychology, 9*, 2692. https://doi.org.10.3389/fpsyg.2018.02692

Big Fig Mattress. (2021). www.bigfigmattress.com/

Brewis, A., Trainer, S., Han, S., & Wutich, A. (2017). Publically misfitting: Extreme weight and the everyday production and reinforcement of felt stigma. *Medical Anthropology Quarterly, 31*(2), 257–276. https://doi.org.10.1111/maq.12309

Brooke, M. E. (1913). The art of beauty. *The Playgoer and Society Illustrated, 8*(43), 26–27.

Brownstone, L. M., DeRieux, J., Kelly, D. A., Sumlin, L. J., & Gaudiani, J. L. (2021). Body mass index requirements for gender-affirming surgeries are not empirically based. *Transgender Health*, 6(3), 121–124. https://doi-org.10.1089/trgh.2020.0068

Calzo, J. P., Blashill, A. J., Brown, T. A., & Argenal, R. L. (2017). Eating disorders and disordered weight and shape control behaviors in sexual minority populations. *Current Psychiatry Reports*, 19(8), 1–10. https://doi.org/10.1007/s11920-017-0801-y

Edwards, P., & Roberts, I. (2009). Population adiposity and climate change. *International Journal of Epidemiology*, 38(4), 1137–1140. https://doi.org/10.1093/ije/dyp172

Eknoyan, G. (2008). Adolphe Quetelet (1796–1874) – The average man and indices of obesity. *Nephrology Dialysis Transplantation*, 23(1), 47–51. https://doi.org/10.1093/ndt/gfm517

Ellis-Ordway, N., & Ramseyer Winter, V. (2022). Weight stigma as a violation of the NASW code of ethics: A call to action. *International Journal of Social Work Values and Ethics*, 19(1), 65–81. https://doi.org/10.55521/10-019-109

Esposito, A. (2022, April 25). Force-feeding and drug abuse: The steep price of beauty in Mauritania. *Harvard International Review*. https://hir.harvard.edu/force-feeding-and-drug-abuse-the-steep-price-of-beauty-in-mauritania/

Flegal, K. M., Kit, B. K., Orpana, H., & Graubard, B. I. (2013). Association of all-cause mortality with overweight and obesity using standard body mass index categories: A systematic review and meta-analysis. *JAMA*, 309(1), 71–82. https://doi.org/10.1001/jama.2012.113905

Fonseca-Reyes, S., de Alba-García, J. G., Parra-Carrillo, J. Z., & Paczka-Zapata, J. A. (2003). Effect of standard cuff on blood pressure readings in patients with obese arms. How frequent are arms of a "large circumference"? *Blood Pressure Monitoring*, 8(3), 101–106. https://doi.org/10.1097/00126097-200306000-00002

Glazer, K. B., Danilack, V. A., Werner, E. F., Field, A. E., & Savitz, D. A. (2020). Elucidating the role of overweight and obesity in racial and ethnic disparities in cesarean delivery risk. *Annals of Epidemiology*, 42, 4–11. https://doi.org/10.1016/j.annepidem.2019.12.012

Gordon, A. (2019, October 18). The bizarre and racist history of the BMI. *Medium*. https://elemental.medium.com/the-bizarre-and-racist-history-of-the-bmi-7d8dc2aa33bb

Gordon, A., & Hobbes, M. (2021, March 8). *The body mass index (No. 23)* [Podcast]. In *Maintenance phase*. https://podcasts.apple.com/us/podcast/the-body-mass-index/id1535408667?i=1000530850955&l=ar

Greed, C. (2010). 6. Creating a nonsexist restroom. In H. Molotch & L. Noren (Eds.), *Toilet: Public restrooms and the politics of sharing* (pp. 117–144). New York University Press. https://doi.org/10.18574/nyu/9780814759646.003.0014

Greenleaf, C., Hauff, C., Klos, L., & Serafin, G. (2020). "Fat people exercise too!": Perceptions and realities of shopping for women's plus-size exercise apparel. *Clothing and Textiles Research Journal*, 38(2), 75–89.

Griffin, S. B., Palmer, M. A., Strodl, E., Lai, R., Burstow, M. J., & Ross, L. J. (2021). Elective surgery in adult patients with excess weight: Can preoperative dietary interventions improve surgical outcomes? A systematic review. *Nutrients*, 13(11), 3775. https://doi.org/10.3390/nu13113775

Harrison, D. (2021). *Belly of the beast: The politics of anti-fatness as anti-blackness*. North Atlantic Books.

Herndon, A. (2021). Fatness and disability: Law, identity, co-constructions, and future directions. In C. Pausé & S. R. Taylor (Eds.), *The Routledge international handbook of fat studies* (1st ed., pp. 88–100). Routledge. https://doi.org/10.4324/9781003049401-13

Hu, L., Tor, O., Zhang, J., Tackett, B., & Yu, X. (2017). Analysis of back forces while sitting down, seated, and rising from a stationary chair in subjects weighing 136–186 kg. In M. Soares, C. Falcão, & T. Ahram (Eds.), *Advances in ergonomics modeling, usability & special populations. Advances in intelligent systems and computing* (Vol. 486, pp. 39–49). Springer. https://doi.org/10.1007/978-3-319-41685-4_4

Jackson, S. E., Beeken, R. J., & Wardle, J. (2015). Obesity, perceived weight discrimination, and psychological well-being in older adults in England. *Obesity, 23*(5), 1105–1111. https://doi.org10.1002/oby.21052

James, C. (2021). *Big fat pregnancy.* www.bigfatpregnancy.com/

Jones, K. L. (2008). Role of obesity in complicating and confusing the diagnosis and treatment of diabetes in children. *Pediatrics, 121*(2), 361–368.

King, J. (2022, November 19). Fat trans people are having their lives put on hold because of devastating medical fatphobia. *Pink News.* www.thepinknews.com/2021/11/19/fat-trans-medical-fatphobia/

Kirley, K. (2014). Patient's weight limits the effectiveness of emergency contraception. *Evidence-Based Practice, 17*(8), 4. https://doi.org/10.1097/01.EBP.0000540706.52438.fa.

Lawton, C., Cook, S., May, A., Clemo, K., & Brown, S. (2008). Postural support strategies of disabled drivers and the effectiveness of postural support aids. *Applied Ergonomics, 39*(1), 47–55. https://doi.org/10.1016/j.apergo.2007.03.005

Liberator. (2022). *Wedge/Ramp combo sex wedge pillow | plus-size sex furniture.* www.liberator.com/wedge-ramp-combo-plus-size.html#custom.sizeguide

Locker, F. (1864). On an old muff. *The Cornhill Magazine, 9*(52), 474–474.

Major, B., Tomiyama, A. J., & Hunger, J. M. (2018). The negative and bidirectional effects of weight stigma on health. In B. Major, J. F. Dovidio, & B. G. Link (Eds.), *The Oxford handbook of stigma, discrimination, and health* (pp. 499–519). Oxford University Press.

McPhail, D., Bombak, A., Ward, P., & Allison, J. (2016). Wombs at risk, wombs as risk: Fat women's experiences of reproductive care. *Fat Studies, 5*(2), 98–115. https://doi.org/10.1080/21604851.2016.1143754

Meadows, A., & Daníelsdóttir, S. (2016). What's in a word? On weight stigma and terminology. *Frontiers in Psychology, 7*, 1527. https://doi.org/10.3389/fpsyg.2016.01527

Mensinger, J. L. (2021). Traumatic stress, body shame, and internalized weight stigma as mediators of change in disordered eating: A single-arm pilot study of the Body Trust® framework. *Eating Disorders*, 1–29. https://doi.org/10.1080/10640266.2021.1985807

Mensinger, J. L., Calogero, R. M., & Tylka, T. L. (2016). Internalized weight stigma moderates eating behavior outcomes in women with high BMI participating in a healthy living program. *Appetite, 102*, 32–43. https://doi.org/10.1016/j.appet.2016.01.033

Mensinger, J. L., & Meadows, A. (2017). Internalized weight stigma mediates and moderates physical activity outcomes during a healthy living program for women with high body mass index. *Psychology of Sport and Exercise, 30*, 64–72. https://doi.org/10.1016/j.psychsport.2017.01.010

Mensinger, J. L., Tylka, T. L., & Calamari, M. E. (2018). Mechanisms underlying weight status and healthcare avoidance in women: A study of weight stigma, body-related shame and guilt, and healthcare stress. *Body Image*, *25*, 139–147. https://doi.org/10.1016/j.bodyim.2018.03.001

Mohan, S. (2021). Fashion doesn't want you to be Fat and neither do prisons. *Fabric of Crime: MA Fashion at The Creative School*, 1–13. https://fabricofcrime.ca/2021/05/04/fashion-doesnt-want-you-to-be-fat/

Molenbroek, J. F. M., Albin, T. J., & Vink, P. (2017). Thirty years of anthropometric changes relevant to the width and depth of transportation seating spaces, present and future. *Applied Ergonomics*, *65*, 130–138. https://doi.org/10.1016/j.apergo.2017.06.003

Moynihan, R. (2006). Obesity task force linked to WHO takes "millions" from drug firms. *BMJ (Clinical Research Edition)*, *332*(7555), 1412. https://doi.org/10.1136/bmj.332.7555.1412-a

Muennig, P., Jia, H., Lee, R., & Lubetkin, E. (2008). I think therefore I am: Perceived ideal weight as a determinant of health. *American Journal of Public Health*, *98*(3), 501–506. https://doi.org/10.2105/AJPH.2007.114769

Munro, L. (2017). Everyday indignities: Using the microaggressions framework to understand weight stigma. *Journal of Law, Medicine & Ethics*, *45*(4), 502–509. https://doi.org/10.1177/1073110517750584

Nuttall, F. Q. (2015). Body mass index: Obesity, BMI, and health: A critical review. *Nutrition Today*, *50*(3), 117. https://doi.org/10.1097/NT.0000000000000092

O'Hara, L., & Taylor, J. (2018). What's wrong with the "war on Obesity"? A narrative review of the weight-centered health paradigm and development of the 3C framework to build critical competency for a paradigm shift. *Sage Open*, *8*(2), 215824401877288. https://doi.org/10.1177/2158244018772888

Oteju, M. (2020, April 27). Desirability politics and why I'm no longer talking about it (for now). *Medium*. https://mhannahoteju.medium.com/desirability-politics-and-why-im-no-longer-talking-about-it-for-now-8f47218aa84f

Peters, L. D. (2022). On fat clothes: Unraveling plus-size design discourse. *Design Issues*, *38*(1), 17–28. https://doi.org/10.1162/desi_a_00667h

Phelan, S. M., Burgess, D. J., Yeazel, M. W., Hellerstedt, W. L., Griffin, J. M., & van Ryn, M. (2015). Impact of weight bias and stigma on quality of care and outcomes for patients with obesity. *Obesity Reviews*, *16*(4), 319–326. https://doi.org/10.1111/obr.12266

Pritchard, E. (2014). Body size and the built environment: Creating an inclusive built environment using universal design. *Geography Compass*, *8*(1), 63–73. https://doi.org/10.1111/gec3.12108

Rich, E., & Evans, J. (2005). "Fat ethics" – The obesity discourse and body politics. *Social Theory & Health*, *3*(4), 341–358. https://doi.org/10.1057/palgrave.sth.8700057

Schafer, M. H., & Ferraro, K. F. (2011). The stigma of obesity: Does perceived weight discrimination affect identity and physical health? *Social Psychology Quarterly*, *74*(1), 76–97. https://doi.org/10.1177/0190272511398197

Seid, R. P. (1994). Too "close to the bone": The historical context for women's obsession with slenderness. In P. Fallon, M. A. Katzman, & S. C. Wooley (Eds.), *Feminist perspectives on eating disorders* (pp. 3–16). Guilford Press.

Shanouda, F. (2021). Medical equipment: The manifestation of anti-fat bias in medicine. In H. Brown & N. Ellis-Ordway (Eds.), *Weight bias in health education: Critical perspectives for pedagogy and practice* (pp. 30–41). Routledge. https://doi.org/10.4324/9781003057000-4

Shridharani, S. M., Baumann, L., Dayan, S. H., Humphrey, S., Breshears, L., & Sangha, S. (2020). Attitudes toward submental fat among adults in the United States. *Dermatologic Surgery*, 46(11), 1384–1387. https://doi.org/10.1097/DSS.0000000000002442

Smith, A. (2020). Heteropatriarchy and the three pillars of white supremacy: Rethinking women of color organizing. In C. McCann, S. Kim, & E. Ergun (Eds.), *Feminist theory reader: Local and global perspectives* (pp. 141–147). Routledge. https://doi.org/10.4324/9781003001201-18

Stevens, C. (2018). Fat on campus: Fat college students and hyper (in) visible stigma. *Sociological Focus*, 51(2), 130–149. https://doi.org/10.1080/00380237.2017.1368839

Strings, S. (2019). *Fearing the black body: The racial origins of fat phobia*. New York University Press. https://doi.org/10.18574/9781479891788

Sutin, A. R., Stephan, Y., Luchetti, M., & Terracciano, A. (2014). Perceived weight discrimination and C-reactive protein. *Obesity*, 22(9), 1959–1961. https://doi.org/10.1002/oby.20789

Sutin, A. R., Stephan, Y., Robinson, E., Daly, M., & Terracciano, A. (2019). Perceived weight discrimination and risk of incident dementia. *International Journal of Obesity*, 43(5), 1130–1134. https://doi.org/10.1038/s41366-018-0211-1

Taylor, S. R. (2018). *The body is not an apology: The power of radical self-love* (1st ed., p. 160). Berrett-Koehler Publishers.

Tomiyama, A. J. (2014). Weight stigma is stressful. A review of evidence for the cyclic obesity/weight-based stigma model. *Appetite*, 82, 8–15. https://doi.org/10.1016/j.appet.2014.06.108

Tomiyama, A. J., Carr, D., Granberg, E. M., Major, B., Robinson, E., Sutin, A. R., & Brewis, A. (2018). How and why weight stigma drives the obesity "epidemic" and harms health. *BMC Medicine*, 16(1), 1–6. https://doi.org/10.1186/s12916-018-1116-5

Tomiyama, A. J., Hunger, J. M., Nguyen-Cuu, J., & Wells, C. (2016). Misclassification of cardiometabolic health when using body mass index categories in NHANES 2005–2012. *International Journal of Obesity*, 40(5), 883–886. https://doi.org/10.1038/ijo.2016.17

Tovar, V. (2018). *You have the right to remain fat* (p. 128). The Feminist Press at CUNY.

Tovar, V. (2020). *The self-love revolution: Radical body positivity for girls of color* (p. 184). New Harbinger Publications.

Tylka, T. L., Annunziato, R. A., Burgard, D., Daníelsdóttir, S., Shuman, E., Davis, C., & Calogero, R. M. (2014). The weight-inclusive versus weight-normative approach to health: Evaluating the evidence for prioritizing well-being over weight loss. *Journal of Obesity*, 2014(983495), 1–18. https://doi.org/10.1155/2014/983495

Wann, M. (1998). *Fat! So? Because you don't have to apologize for your size!* Random House Digital, Inc.

Watson, L., Oberle, K., & Deutscher, D. (2008). Development and psychometric testing of the nurses' attitudes toward obesity and obese patients (NATOOPS) scale. *Research in Nursing & Health*, 31(6), 586–593. https://doi.org/10.1002/nur.20292

Welch, H. G., Schwartz, L. M., & Woloshin, S. (2011). *Overdiagnosed: Making people sick in the pursuit of health*. Beacon Press.

World Health Organization (WHO). (2020, February 21). *Obesity*. www.who.int/health-topics/obesity#tab=tab_1

The Wright Stuff. (2022). *Bariatric turn wedge body positioner: Side lying wedge for users 600 lb*. Activities of Daily Living (ADL) Devices & Equipment. www.thewrightstuff.com/bariatric-turn-wedge-body-positioner.html

Young, V. (2022). *Dating while fat*. https://substack.com/profile/13769689-victoria-nachos

Zingg, M., Miozzari, H. H., Fritschy, D., Hoffmeyer, P., & Lübbeke, A. (2016). Influence of body mass index on revision rates after primary total knee arthroplasty. *International Orthopaedics*, 40(4), 723–729. https://doi.org/10.1007/s00264-015-3031-0

# INDEX

ableism 3, 6; defined 301; madness and 109; mutual aid and 53; SV/IPV and 204; world without, abortion access and 35
abortion rights 32–34
abuse: blindness and acknowledging 132–133; IPV types of 202
accessibility: checklist 309; defined 300–301; disability justice and 304–305; information, access to 306–307; lighting and 307–308; as love 305; for physical spaces 306–309; for queer and trans spaces 301–305; restrooms and 307; seating and 308–309; for virtual/digital spaces 309–311; weight stigma and 366–367; when working with LGBTQ2S+ older adults 275
Accessibility, Inclusivity, and Mattering (A.I.M.) 275–277, 278
acquired immunodeficiency syndrome (AIDS) 55–57
acute mutual aid 49
Addams, Jane 30
adultcentrism 231
adultism 231–232
Africa, sexuality/disability(ies) policies in 19
African American/Black peoples 256–259
aftercare, described 352

aging and LGBTQ2S+ bodies 271–272
Ahsan, Sanah 118
Alim, H. Samy 173
American Association of Intellectual and Developmental Disabilities 82
American Deaf culture 96–97
American Sign Language (ASL) 96–97
American with Disabilities Act 304
Andrews, A. 2
anti-capitalist politic principle 6
Anzaldua, Gloria 303
Applied Behavioral Analysis (ABA) therapy 31
Arani, Alexia 53–54
the Ashely Treatment 16–17
Ashley X case 16–17
Asian/Asian American peoples 259–262
attention-deficit/hyperactivity disorder (ADHD) 68–69
augmentative and alternative communication (AAC) 98
Australia: *National Disability Strategy* 22; sexuality/disability(ies) policies 22
Australian National Disability Insurance Scheme 22
autism 66–68
Autism Speaks 31–32

Barnett, J. P. 67
Baston, Semona 1
Bauch, C. 341

Bauman, H. D. L. 97
Baynton, D. 218
BDSM as recreation/leisure 355–357
Begich, Nick 36
Bell, D. M. 144
Beresford, P. 109
Berne, Patty 303
best practices: for gatekeeping models 290–291; for hearing loss and d/Deaf individuals 101–103; kink/BDSM patients/clients 360; sexuality education for disabled individuals 193–194; to support neurodivergent individuals 71–74; for working in reproductive/disability justice 37–38; for working with IDD people 88–90; young disabled people sexual well-being 324–327
Better Health Channel 86
"big D" Deaf, described 96–97
biopower 112
Black, Indigenous, and other people of color (BIPOC) access to care 288; queer and trans 289–290
Black Panther Party 257
Black peoples *see* African American/Black peoples
Black & Pink (prison letter writing project) 49
Blewett, L. 223
blindness 124–134; abuse and 132–133; class activity 134; described 124; flirting/dating and 129–130; introduction to 124–125; knowns/unknowns concerning 125; parenting and 130–131; partner identities and 128; pregnancy and 130–131; providers and 126; reproduction and 130–131; sex and 126–131; sexual education/health and 128–129; social energy and 133
blind or visually impaired (BVI) persons 125; *see also* blindness
blood quantum system 251
Blume, H. 65
bodies, sexuality and regulation of 14–15
*Body Is Not an Apology* (Taylor) 290
bodymapping 146–147; disability-affirming sex therapy and 165–167

body mass index (BMI) 369–370
bodymind 3
bondage, defined 352
bottoms/bottoming, defined 352
Bri M 50
Brisenden, Simon 285
Bronfenbrenner, U. 325–326
brown, adrienne maree 290, 338–339
Brown, Lydia X. Z. 203
Brown-Lavoie, S. M. 68
*Buck v. Bell* 16, 33, 251
Bump!n (website) 356

Cain, L. K. 291
"Cairo Agenda" 17–18
Calacro, Jessica 34
Canada forced sterilization 16
care-full methodology 170–183; background to 171–174; case studies 178–182; overview of 170–171; roleplay prompts 183–184; strategies for 174–178
caregivers, sexuality education for disabled individuals and 189
caremongering 29
care webs 51–52
case studies/activities: African American/Black peoples 259; Asian/Asian American peoples 261–262; care-full methodology 178–182; compulsory monogamy 344–346; disability-affirming sex therapy 156–157, 167–168; gatekeeping models 291–295; Indigenous/native people 253; intellectual and developmental disabilities 90–92; Latina sexuality 255–256; LGBTQ+ space, disability-focused 312–313; mutual aid 58–59; neurodivergent people 74–76; sex work, disability and 225–227; for working in reproductive/disability justice 38
Center for Parent Information and Resources 86
Centers for Disease Control and Prevention (CDC) 139, 140
Cesaire, Alysha Princess 33, 38
Chamberlin, J. 109
childbirth as disabling 36–37
Chin, Matthew 289, 291

China: One Child Policy 21; sexuality/disability(ies) policies 21
Chinese Exclusion Act of 1882 260
Christofascism 29
chronically ill 3
chronic illness/pain 3–4; bodymapping and 146–147; COVID-19 and 140–141; examples of 139; introduction to 139–142; reflective activity 148–149; sensate focus exercises for 144–147; sexuality and 139–149; spoon theory and 142–144; tools/ideas to aid in sex 147–148; types of 3–4
Chung, Nicole 35
Churchill, Ward 251
Cipriani, Belo Miguel 130
Circles of Sexuality model 7
cisheteronormativity 116
cissexism, defined 302
Clare, Eli 3, 173, 303
Clark, M. D. 99
classroom activities: access-ability, sexuality education for disabled individuals 195–196; blind clients/patients care 134; d/Deaf individuals' sexuality 103; disability/sexuality policies 23; media consumption representation 375; for providing kink-affirming/kink-specific care 360–361; for sexual and reproductive health and education (SRHE) inequities 240–242; for sexual well-being 327–328; sex work, disability and 225–227; for SV/IPV support 207–208; working with older adults 277
Coalition for Women Prisoners 56–57
Coalition to Support Women Prisoners 56–57
cochlear implants (CIs) 97–98
cognitive health, older adults 268
collective access 7
collective liberation 7
Collins, Patricia Hill 172
commitment to cross disability solidarity 7
commitment to cross movement organizing 7
compulsory able-bodiedness 302–303

compulsory monogamy 335–347; case study 344–346; defined 335; as disabling 337–339; healthcare and 343–344; introduction to 335–337; legal challenges 344; monogamy defined 339–340; monogamy terms/beliefs 340–341; monogamy theories 341–342; from mononormativity to polyphobia 343; as system of oppression 336
Concannon, B. 90
consent, disabled people and 358–359
Corinna, Heather 1
countertransference 126
COVID-19 6; accessibility for virtual/digital spaces and 309–311; American women parenting burdens during 34; as chronic illness 140–141; disabled mutual aid and 52–54; LGBTQ2S+ older adults and 270–272; mutual aid and 47, 53–54
Creating Collective Access 52
Crip Fund 52
Critical Design Lab 52
critical polyamory 338
*Critical Youth Research in Education: Methodologies of Praxis and Care* (Alim) 173
Cross Bay Mutual Aid Project 52
cross disability solidarity, commitment to 7
cross movement organizing, commitment to 7

Dailey, Dennis 7
*Dance of Souls* 357
Darwin, Charles 29–30
dating, blind-inclusive 129–130
d/Deaf individuals *see* hearing loss and d/Deaf individuals
d/Deaf sexuality mythconceptions 98–99
Deafax 100
Deaf culture 97
Deaf Gain 97
Deaf/hard-of-hearing 4; *see also* hearing loss and d/Deaf individuals
*Decolonizing Sex!* (Tallbear podcast) 338
Deerinwater, Jen 253

deficit-based gatekeeping model, challenging 290–291
Dellenborg, L. 256
deserving *versus* undeserving sex work 217–218
desexualization 288–290
desirability politics 372
deviance, sex work/disability and 215–217
Diagnostic and Statistical Manual of Mental Disorders, 5th Edition, Text-Revision (DSM-5-TR) (American Psychiatric Association) 285
Dirty Lola 1
disability-affirming sex therapy 155–168; best practices for 158–167; bodymapping and 165–167; case studies 156–157, 167–168; curiosity and 163–164; empowerment and self-acceptance 160–161; exploring/challenging sexual narrative 159–160; introduction to 155–156; literature pertaining to 157–158; loss and grief 161–163; in relation to identity and ability/disability 158–159; self-discloser and 164–165; sexual props/toys and 167
*Disability After Dark* (podcast) 290
disability-focused LGBTQ+ space *see* LGBTQ+ space, disability-focused
disability(ies); *see also* old age, disability/sexuality in; racialization of disability and sexuality: Africa policies concerning 19; Australia policies concerning 22; bodies and 14–15; challenges of 4; China policies concerning 21; classroom activities 23; compulsory monogamy as 337–339; conceptualizing 13–14; definitions of 3–4; eugenics and 16–17; Europe policies concerning 20–21; Ghana policies concerning 20; Hong Kong policies concerning 21–22; intersections of, and policy 15–22; introduction to 1–8; kink/BDSM and 352–353; medical model of 5, 6; in old age 267–278; policy impact on 23; racialization of 249–262; sexual education policy and 17–18; sexual identities and 288; sexuality and 4; sexual well-being and 321–322; social model of 5–6; trauma play and 354–355; types of 3–4; United States policies concerning 18–19

*Disability Inclusion Act* of New South Wales 22
disability justice 303–304; accessibility and 304–305; described 6; *versus* disability rights 304; principles of 6–7
Disability Justice Collective 303
Disability Justice Culture Club 52
disability justice movements 6
Disability Law Center (DLC) 17
disability rights: described 6; *versus* disability justice 304
disabled and/or chronically ill survivors (DCIS) 202; working with, considerations in 204–207
disabled identities, gatekeeping of 285–286
disabled mutual aid 50–54; COVID-19 and 52–54; examples of 51–52; interdependence and 50–51; overview of 50
Disabled Twitter 289
discipline, defined 352
Dolmage, J. 171
domination, defined 352
*Down Girl: The Logic of Misogyny* (Manne) 29
Down syndrome 32–33, 81

Easton, Dossie 339
educators, sexuality education for disabled individuals and 189–190
ElevatUs Training 86
El-Metwally, A. 140
emergency-response care webs 53
epilepsy 68
epistemic oppression 110
Eric-Udorie, June 259
erotica 147
Esmail, S. 90
ethical (or consensual) non-monogamy 339

*Ethical Slut, The* (Easton and Hardy) 339
eugenics 16–17, 29; movement, history of 29–30; white purity and 250
Europe, sexuality/disability(ies) policies in 20–21
Evans, A. 119–120
*Evolution of Beauty, The* (Prum) 114

fat shaming 370
*femicidio* 254
Fern, Jessica 344
Fetal Alcohol Syndrome 81
Fienberg, Leslie 54
Final Solution 30
financial abuse 202
flirting/dating, blind-inclusive 129–130
Fook, J. 328
Fortenberry, J. D. 320
Foucault, Michel 109, 112
Fragile X Syndrome 81
Freely-Given, Reversible, Informed, Enthusiastic, Specific, Sober (FRIESS) 359

Gallo-Silver, L. 144
Galton, Francis 16, 29
gatekeeping models 283–295; best practices for 290–291; case study 291–295; challenging deficit-based 290–291; of disabled identities 285–286; intersections of trans/disabled identities 286–287; introduction to 283; sexuality/sexual health and 287–290; transgender defined 284; transgender/disabled experience overlaps 284–285; of transgender identities 286
gender dysphoria 287
gender euphoria 290
genders, older adults and 269
gerontology: described 274; queering 274–277
Ghana, sexuality/disability(ies) policies in 20
Goldstein, Devin 243
Gorsuch, Kim 33, 38
Grieve, A. 191
Gurza, Andrew 290, 356

Halberstam, J. 173
halo effect 343
Hamraie, Aimi 52
Harden, K. P. 320
hard-of-hearing 4
Hardy, Janet 339
Hartley, Nina 1
Health At Every Size (HAES) 374
hearing loss and d/Deaf individuals 96–104; best practices for 101–103; class activity 103; hearing loss defined 96; introduction to 96–98; mythconceptions of 98–101; sexuality and 96–104
Hedva, Johanna 338
heterosexism, defined 301–302
Hispanic 253
*History of Sexuality: Volume I* (Foucault) 109
HIV/AIDS epidemic 55–57
Hong Kong: Family Planning Association of 21; sexuality/disability(ies) policies 21–22
"How Do Queer, Chronically Ill Creatives View Art-Making?" (Noonan) 179
Human Relations Media 86
Human Sexual Response Cycle 155–156
hypersexualization 288–290
hyposexuality 68

IDD *see* intellectual and developmental disabilities (IDD)
IDD specific sexuality training 85–86
identity-first language 5
ideologies, oppressive 336
inclusivity: defined 301; weight stigma and 366–367; when working with LGBTQ2S+ older adults 275–276
indigenous/native people 250–253
Individuals with Disabilities Education Act (IDEA) 81
infanticide 341
intellectual and developmental disabilities (IDD) 81–92; background about 83–84; best practices for 88–90; case study 90–92; defined 81; Down syndrome and 81; individual rights for 82–83; introduction to 81–82; policy issues 84–85; sexuality and 81–92; sexuality training for 85–86; workshop for

people with disabilities 87–88; workshop for providers 86–87
interdependence principle: described 7; disabled mutual aid and 50–51
International Conference on Population and Development's Programme of Action 17–18
International Federation of Social Workers (IFSW) 319
intersectionality principle 6, 236–237; queer crip theory and 302
intimate partner violence *see* sexual and intimate partner violence (SV/IPV)
IPV *see* sexual and intimate partner violence (SV/IPV)

Jenkins, Ian 344
Job, J. 98–99
Joharchi, H. A. 99
Johnson, Marsha P. 54, 55
Johnson, Virginia 155
*Journal of Adolescent Health* 320
*Journal of Delinquency* (Goddard) 249

Kafati, Lopez 130
Kaposi's Sarcoma 55
Kaufman, Miriam 1, 141–142
Kavanaugh, Brett 36
Keller, Hellen 36–37
Kennedy Krieger Institute 86–87
kink/BDSM 351–362; altered cognitive states in 357–358; BDSM as recreation/leisure 355–357; best practices for, patients/clients 360; consent and 358–359; defining 352; disability and 352–353; introduction to 351; neurodivergence and 357–358; as pain management tool 353–354; patients/clients classroom activity 360–361; practitioners 351–362; trauma play, disability and 354–355
Klement, K. R. 357
Knight, Kelly 217–218
Kramer, Larry 56
Kropotkin, Peter 48

Lacks, Henrietta 258
Latin(o/a/x/e) people 253–256
leadership of those most impacted principle 6

Lee, Sally 321–322
LeFrancois, B. A. 109
*Leo and Carol* (Campos and Capella) 328
Leonard, L. 256
Lerum, Kari 217
LGBTQ2S+ older adults 270–272; aging and bodies of 271–272; navigating disability/sexuality in 272–273; overview of 270–271; technology use and 273–274
LGBTQ+ space, disability-focused 299–313; *see also* accessibility; ableism and 301; accessibility and inclusion to 300–301, 305–306; case study 312–313; cissexism and 302; disability justice and 303–305; heterosexism and 301–302; importance of 301–305; introduction to 299–300; physical space accessibility 306–309; queer crip theory and 302–303; virtual/digital space accessibility 309–311
Liegghio, Maria 110
lighting, accessibility and 307–308
limerance 117
literal declaration 67
"little d" deaf, described 96
long COVID 140
Lorde, Audre 303, 306

*machismo* 254
Mad Justice movement 109
madness 108–120; healing-centered approach to 110–112; introduction to 108; love as madness 117–120; pathologization of 108–113; queerness as natural argument and 113–117; reflection activity 118; saneism and 109–110, 112; sexuality and 108–120; termed 108–109
*Madness: The Invention of an Idea* (Foucault) 109
Mad Pride 3
Malacrida, C. 321
Manne, Kate 29
Margaret, Sebastian 303
Maryland Center for Developmental Disabilities 86–87

masochism, defined 352
Masters, William 155
Mastro, S. 320
Maticka-Tyndale, E. 67
mattering when working with LGBTQ2S+ older adults 276–277
McCain, John 28
McElreath, R. 341
McLaughlin, Katherine 88
McRuer, Robert 2
medical model of disability 5, 6
Melby, T. 144
Mendoza, Claudia Garcia 289
Mental Deficiency Act of 1913 16
mental health, older adults 268–269
mental illness, pathologizing and 109
Michigan Organization on Adolescent Sexual Health (MOASH) 234
Milburn, Stacey 52, 303
Mingus, Mia 50–51, 52, 303, 345
Miserandino, Christine 142
modified sensate focus exercises 145–146
Mollow, Anna 2
Monk, Julia 114, 119
monogamy, defined 339–340
*Monogamy Explained* (Ryan) 342
mononormativity 335, 343
Moore, Leroy 303
Morales, Aurora Levins 303
Morrigan, Clementine 344
Murray, J. J. 97
mutual aid 47–59; *see also* disabled mutual aid; case study example of 58–59; components of 48–49; connecting clients to 58; COVID-19 and 47, 53–54; defining 48–49; described 48; in disabled communities 50–54; forms of 57; intersections of, in queer, trans, and disabled communities 55–57; introduction to 47–48; ongoing *versus* acute 49; in queer and trans communities 54–55; supporting practices for 57–58
*Mutual Aid: Building Solidarity During This Crisis (and the Next)* (Spade) 238
"My Disabled Life Is Worthy" (grassroots online movement) 28
mythconceptions 98–101

National Disability Day of Mourning 34
National Disability Insurance Scheme (NDIS) 356
National Disability Rights Network 17
National Down Syndrome Society 88
National Institute of Deafness and Other Communication Disorders 96
National Library of Medicine 139
natural neurodiversity 109
natural trauma responses 109–110
Neal, D'Arcee Charington 283
Nelson, G. 48
neurodivergence 3; healing-centered approach to 110–112; kink/BDSM and 357–358; natural 109
neurodivergent people 65–76; attention-deficit/hyperactivity disorder and 68–69; autism and 66–68; best practices for supporting 71–74; case study 74–76; challenges related to 70–71; described 65; epilepsy and 68; introduction to 65–66; post-traumatic stress disorder and 69–70; sexuality support of 65–76; traumatic brain injury and 69–70; types of 65
*Neuroqueer Heresies* (Walker) 65–66
nondisabled 125
Nordgren, Andie 339
*No Right to Be Idle: The Invention of Disability, 1840s–1930s* (Rose) 15

The Oakland Power Projects 49
O'Connell, H. 359
Odette, Fran 1, 141–142
old age, disability/sexuality in 267–278; accessibility, practitioners/providers and 275; classroom activity 277; cognitive health 268; genders 269; inclusivity, practitioners/providers and 275–276; introduction to 267; language 267; LGBTQ2S+ older adults 270–272; mattering, practitioners/providers and 276–277; mental health 268–269; navigating 272–273; physical health 268; queering gerontology and 274–277;

sexual activities and 274; sexual orientation 269, social identities 269–270; technology use and 273–274
older adults, described 267
ongoing mutual aid 49
online spaces, accessibility to 309–311
*Other Countries Have Social Safety Nets: The U.S. Has Women* (Petersen) 34

paid supports, sexuality education for disabled individuals and 190–192
painsomnia 1
Palin, Sarah 28, 36
Palin, Trig 28, 36
Panzarino, Connie 303
parenting, blindness and 130–131
parenting burdens, US women and 34–35
partner identities, blindness and 128
Passionate Love Scale 343
pathological pathologizing *vs.* healing-centered pathologizing 113
pathologization: described 108–109; madness and 108–113; as tool for social control 109–110
Peltola, Mary 36
person-first language 5
Petchesky, R. 318
Peterson, Anne Helen 34
physical abuse 202
physical health, older adults 268
Piepzna-Samarasinha, Leah Lakshmi 51, 52, 53, 171, 303, 305
play, described 352
pleasurable sex, weight and 372–373
*Pleasure Activism* (brown) 290, 338–339
*Plessy v. Ferguson* doctrine 257
polyandry, defined 340
polygynandry, defined 340
polygyny, defined 340
polyphobia 336, 343
*Polysecure* (Fern) 344
porn/pornography 1, 68, 100, 147, 159, 189, 372
post-COVID syndrome 140
post-traumatic stress disorder (PTSD) 69–70
Poussaint, Alvin 117–118

*Power Not Pity* (podcast) 50
pregnancy: blindness and 130–131; as disabling 36–37
Prum, Richard 114, 116
psychological abuse 202
public charge 14

queer and trans BIPOC (QTPOC) 289
queer and trans communities, mutual aid in 54–55
queer crip theory 302–303
*Queer Ducks (and Other Animals)* (Schrefer and Zuckerberg) 114–115
queering gerontology 274–277; accessibility 275; described 274–275; inclusivity 275–276; mattering 276–277
queerness as natural argument 113–117; reflection activity 115
*Quick and Easy Guide to Sex & Disability, A* (Andrews) 2

racialization of disability and sexuality 249–262; African American/Black peoples and 256–259; Asian/Asian American peoples and 259–262; indigenous/native people and 250–253; Latin(o/a/x/e) people and 253–256; overview of 249–250
Radical Access Mapping Project (RAMP) 52
Raphael, Ade 50
Reach a Hand 232
recognizing wholeness principle 7
relationship anarchy 338–339
reproduction, blindness and 130–131
reproductive/disability justice, best practices for working in 37–38
reproductive justice movement 28–39; ableism and 35; best practices for in 37–38; COVID-19 parenting burdens and 34–35; eugenics movement and 29–32; false abortion rights assumptions and 32–34; pregnancy and childbirth as disabling 36–37; vulnerability and 28–29
RespectAbility 86
restrooms, accessibility and 307
Richmond, Mary 30
Rio (autistic trans advocate) 55

Risk-Aware Consensual Kink (RACK) 359
Rivera, Sylvia 54–55
Rose, Sarah 15
Rose Marie, Bubbles 54
Rubin, Gayle 216–217
Russo, J. 109
Ryan, Chris 341, 342

sadism, defined 352
Sala, G. 67
saneism 109–110; intersectional examples of 112
Sanger, Margaret 30
Sapolsky, Robert 116
Schrefer, Eliot 114–115
Seagrave, Rita 103
seating options, accessibility and 308–309
self-discloser, therapeutic 164–165
sensate focus exercises 144–147; bodymapping as 146–147; modified 145–146
sensory systems 70
*Sessions, The* (Lewis) 328
settler sexuality 338
sex, blindness and 126–131
*Sex and Disability* (McRuer and Mollow) 2
sex furniture 373
sex negative cultures 113
sex therapy *see* disability-affirming sex therapy
sex toys 148, 167, 373
sexual abuse 202
sexual activities in older adults 274
sexual and intimate partner violence (SV/IPV) 201–209; classroom activity for 207–208; forms of 201–202; impact of 203–204; overview of 201; prevalence of 202–203; recommendations for 208–209; working with survivors of 204–207
sexual and reproductive health and education (SRHE) inequities 230–243; *see also* Youth Advisory Council (YAC); adultism and 231–232; classroom activity for 240–242; disabled youths and 232–233; introduction to 230; youth advisory council considerations 234–240; youth advocacy strategies 233–234; youth defined 230–231
sexual diversity, defined 113
sexual education/health, blindness and 128–129
sexual education policy: disability(ies) and 17–18; impact of 23
sexual health: defined 320; gatekeeping and 287–290
sexual identities, disability and 288
sexuality; *see also individual headings*: Africa policies concerning 19; Australia policies concerning 22; blindness and 124–134; China policies concerning 21; chronic illness/pain and 139–149; classroom activities 23; concepts of 7; education policy 17–22; eugenics and 16–17; Europe policies concerning 20–21; gatekeeping and 287–290; Ghana policies concerning 20; hearing loss and d/Deaf individuals and 96–104; Hong Kong policies concerning 21–22; intellectual/developmental disabilities and 81–92; introduction to 1–8; madness and 108–120; neurodivergent people and 65–76; in old age 267–278; policy impact on 23; racialization of 249–262; regulation of bodies and 14–15; United States policies concerning 18–19
sexuality education for disabled individuals 187–197; access-ability classroom activity 195–196; best practices for 193–194; caregivers and 189; educators and 189–190; facilitators of 188–189; introduction to 187; literature review 187–188; paid supports and 190–192; social informants and 192–193
sexually transmitted infections (STIs) 341
sexual orientation, older adults 269
sexual violence *see* sexual and intimate partner violence (SV/IPV)
sexual violence, defined 113

sexual well-being 318–329; among young disabled people 322–324; best practices 324–327; classroom activities for 327–328; community responsibilities and 325–326; concept of 320; definition of 320–321; disability and 321–322; introduction to 318–319; prevention/planning practices 324–325; sex positivity and 326–327
sex work, disability and 214–227; academic literature on 218–220; case study 225–227; deserving *versus* undeserving 217–218; deviance and 215–217; disability justice framework 215; interviews with sex workers 220–224; introduction to 214–215; recommendations for practice 224–225; Sins Invalid and 215
Sex Worker Outreach Project Los Angeles (SWOPLA) 221
Shakespeare, T. 321
Shapiro, J. 84
Shoah/Holocaust 30
Shuttleworth, R. 14
*Sick Woman Theory* (Hedva) 338
sighted people 125
Silverberg, Cory 1, 141–142
Sims, James Marion 258
Singer, Judy 65
Sins Invalid 215, 306
size-affirming care 370–371
*Slut Songs* (Yakas) 340, 341
Snider, S. 215
social energy, blindness and 133
social identities, older adults 269–270
social informants, sexuality education for disabled individuals and 192–193
social model of disability 5–6
Social Security Disability Insurance (SSDI) 50, 225
Soldati, L. 69
Spade, Dean 48, 238
#SpoonieChat 143
spoon theory 142–144
Sprott, R. A. 356
SRHE *see* sexual and reproductive health and education (SRHE) inequities

*Standards of Care and Ethical Guidelines, 7th Edition* (WPATH) 286
Stanford Blish 18
stimming 70
Stonewall Riots 54
Street Transvestite Action Revolutionaries (STAR) 54–55
Strings, Sabrina 368
strong-Black woman trope 258
submission, defined 352
subspace 357
Supplemental Security Income (SSI), sex work and 214–215
sustainability 7
SV/IPV *see* sexual and intimate partner violence (SV/IPV)
Sweeney, A. 109

*Take Me* (Barbeau-Lavalette & Turpin) 328
Tallbear, Kim 338
Taormino, Tristan 1
Tarnished Spoonies 143
Taylor, Sonya Renee 290
Tecot, S. R. 340
Tellier, S. 353
Tennov, Dorothy 117
Tepper, Mitchell 1, 144
*37 Seconds* (Hiraki) 328
Thomsen, F. K. 219
*Three Dads and a Baby* (Jenkins) 344
Title IX, Education Amendments, 1972 18
topspace 357
tops/topping, defined 352
traditional sexual script 99, 144
trans/disabled identities, gatekeeping intersections of 286–287
transgender, defined 284
transgender identities, gatekeeping of 286
*Trauma-Informed Polyamory* (Morrigan) 344
trauma play: benefits of 354; defined 354; disability and 354–355
traumatic brain injury (TBI) 69–70, 81, 204
treatment, defining 31
Trent, J. W. 218
Turner, George 92
Two-Spirit 252
tyranny of vulnerability 29

*Ultimate Guide to Sex and Disability, The* (Kaufman, Silverberg, and Odette) 1, 141–142, 164
UNESCO 324
United Nations Convention on the Rights of Persons with Disabilities (CRPD) 20
United States: body legislative acts 14–15; sexuality/disability(ies) policies 18–19

Velasco, J. C. 291
Virginia Sterilization Act of 1924 16
virtual platforms, accessibility to 309–311

Walker, Joann 57
Walker, N. 65–66
Washington Protection & Advocacy System 17
Wave Web Accessibility Evaluation Tool 311
weight-inclusive practices 373–375
weight stigma 366–375; accessibility/inclusion and 366–367; body mass index measurement and 369–370; body size, moralization of 368–369; classroom activity 375; described 366; desirability politics and 372; historical context of 367–368; introduction to 366; language use and 374; pleasurable sex and 372–373; providing care and services for 374–375; size-affirming care opportunities 370–371; weight-inclusive practices, integrating 373–375
white purity 250
wholeness, recognizing 7
whorephobia 219, 336
Will, George F. 32
Williams, D. J. 356
Wong, Alice 253
World Health Organization (WHO) 96, 320
World Professional Association for Transgender Health (WPATH) 286, 287

The Yellow Peril 260
YIELD Project 230, 233
young disabled people, sexual well-being among 322–324
youth, defined 230–231
youth-adult partnerships (Y-APs) 234
Youth Advisory Council (YAC) 230, 234–240; accessibility considerations for 235–236; compensation and 237; decision-making processes 237–238; intersectionality and 236–237; limitations of 240; peer mentorship/support networks 238; program evaluation 239; recruiting for 234–235; staff development/education 239; youth development/education 238–239; youth leadership opportunities 237–238
youth organizing (YO) 234

Zayid, Maysoon 261–262
Zimmer-Gembeck, M. J. 320
Zuckerberg, Jules 114–115

Printed in the United States
by Baker & Taylor Publisher Services